THIS BOOK BELONGS TO

Mali Bakes

For my khun yaa, my beautiful grandmother,
whose unwavering support has been
the soul of my journey.

For my mom, who blessed me with
the gift of love for creativity.

For Luke, my love —
Mali Bakes simply would not have
come to life without you!

Make and decorate
the retro cakes of your dreams

Mali Bakes

Patti Chimkire

Smith Street Books

CONTENTS

Batter, butter and beginnings	7
Baking tools	13
Decorating tools	17
Essential ingredients	23

Chapter 1:
All things cake — 28

Chapter 2:
Simple finish cakes — 58

Chapter 3:
Layer cakes — 100

Chapter 4:
Retro decorating 101 — 154

Chapter 5:
Decorating projects — 188

Scaling up recipes for the decorating projects	321
Cutting cakes into party portions	334
Index	336
Acknowledgements	342

MALI BAKES

BATTER, BUTTER AND BEGINNINGS

Mali, the Thai word for jasmine, carries a deep significance in Thailand, where it is the flower of Mother's Day — a symbol of love, gratitude and warmth. I chose the name Mali Bakes as a tribute to my mom, who inspired me to follow my passions and find beauty in the world — in vibrant colours, intricate craftsmanship, and the delicate details that make life extraordinary. For me, Mali is a reflection of the love, creativity and cherished moments I was blessed to share with her.

Mali Bakes started humbly in my little sharehouse kitchen back in 2019. It was a side hustle that quickly turned into a full-time gig. Like so many, I found myself briefly out of work during the COVID pandemic — I was a kitchen chef at the time. Sitting still isn't really my thing, so I got to work immediately. What started as baking cookies for home delivery soon blossomed into a full-blown cake business.

In 2020, my partner Luke and I decided to take a leap of faith. We signed a commercial lease and poured every ounce of energy (and every last penny) into transforming the space into a studio. With Red Bull replacing coffee and determination fuelling our sleepless nights, we renovated the shop ourselves. It was exhausting, exhilarating and wonderfully chaotic — all the ingredients for a dream worth chasing.

Fast forward five years and Mali Bakes is now a thriving cake studio. If someone had told me back then that we'd have a beautiful team, be creating stunning celebration cakes, and even writing a book, I wouldn't have believed them. Yet, here we are!

The heart of this journey has always been the stories our cakes tell. Every order is more than just flour and sugar — it's a reflection of someone's joy, a chapter in their celebration. Couples bring us their love stories to weave into their wedding cakes. Families return, year after year, to mark new milestones — birthdays, anniversaries, the firsts ... and even the remarkable hundredth! These are the moments that remind me why I love what we do.

On weekends, when our studio opens its doors to sell slices of cake, there's a certain magic in the air. The counters are lined with cakes of every kind, bathed in the soft glow of morning light. Customers step in, their eyes lighting up as they take in the possibilities. Some are here for a first taste of their celebration cake; others are indulging in the ritual of a sweet Saturday morning treat, starting their day with a slice of joy.

Cake is our life, and we feel so fortunate to do what we love every single day. Mali Bakes is more than a business; it's a place where love, laughter and buttercream come together to create something truly special. We are endlessly grateful for the moments we get to share with our community and the memories we help bring to life — one cake at a time.

A slice of my life

I never imagined that one day I would call myself a baker. Growing up in Bangkok, in a home where cooking was more of an occasional necessity than a cherished ritual, the thought of crafting cakes or swirling buttercream into delicate roses seemed as distant as snow falling on the tropics. Food is the heartbeat of life in Bangkok, but baking belonged to another world – one I hadn't yet imagined stepping into.

In those early years, I followed a more predictable path. I was a diligent student, pursuing a bachelor's degree in logistics management! But life, like baking, has a way of surprising you. During my third year of studies, I joined an exchange program and moved to Vancouver Island in Canada for a year. It was there, far from home, that my heart began to stir in an entirely different direction.

While others buried themselves in textbooks, I was drawn to markets and cafes, captivated by the stories food could tell. During university breaks, I'd board the ferry to Seattle and wander the vibrant chaos of Pike Place Market, tasting, observing, and soaking in the magic of it all. Food became more than just nourishment – it became an experience, a connection, a kind of artistry I hadn't realised I was hungry for.

When I returned to Bangkok, it became clear that my love for food wasn't fleeting – it was calling me. I packed my bags once again, this time heading to Melbourne and enrolling in culinary school.

In 2016, I arrived in Melbourne with little more than a suitcase and an insatiable curiosity. I worked in bustling kitchens, from waking before dawn to roll doughnuts at Shortstop Coffee & Donuts to joining the rhythm of the team at Proud Mary's cafe kitchen, where I found myself immersed in the constant clatter and hum of a kitchen in full swing. It was in those moments, surrounded by talented chefs and the camaraderie of a shared purpose, that I began to understand what it truly means to be a chef. It's not just about the final dish, though that certainly matters – it's about the process. It's about bringing out the best in each other and in the ingredients. It's about nurturing the people around you, finding joy in the work itself, and sharing knowledge, mistakes and growth along the way.

Yet, even in the adrenaline-fuelled world of the hot kitchen, something felt incomplete. I turned to the executive chef one day and asked if I could bake. His 'yes' opened a door I hadn't known I was waiting for. Soon, I transitioned to the production kitchen, entrusted with baking hundreds of small cakes and biscuits for the wholesale side of the business. It was there, amid the hum of ovens and the scent of warm batter, that my passion began to take shape.

I fell in love with the quiet moments spent with batter and dough – the meditative rhythm of measuring, mixing and watching transformations unfold. Mistakes were inevitable, but each misstep became a lesson, pushing me forward. I immersed myself in learning, devouring books, watching videos, and seeking knowledge from every chef I knew.

When I decided cakes would be my true focus, I didn't have a clear vision of what Mali Bakes would become. I only knew it would be an extension of myself – of my love for flavour, my belief in creating something meaningful, and that a celebration cake should be extraordinary, inside and out. Coming from Bangkok, where flavour and vibrancy reign, I couldn't imagine cakes reduced to a dense mudcake with store-bought fillings. A celebration cake, I felt, should tell a story, reflecting the beauty and significance of the moment it represents.

Soon, decorating became as much a passion as baking itself. The moment I began adding colour to buttercream and held a piping bag in my hand, it felt as though my life spilled out in vivid hues. Bangkok's vibrant energy – the bold colours, intricate architecture and lively streets – all flowed into my work. I immersed myself in vintage Wilton decorating books and eagerly collected as many piping nozzles as I could find. My partner, Luke, often stepped in with lessons on colour theory, teaching me how to create the perfect shade of purple from just pink and blue. During lockdown, while my housemate sat in Zoom meetings in the lounge room, his colleagues would often spot me in the background, piping swirls and roses in the kitchen.

Those early days were messy and magical. Cakes cracked, buttercream slid, and my nights stretched into the early hours as I learned through trial and error. But slowly, through patience and persistence, I began to trust the process – and myself. Baking became my language, my way of expressing creativity, love and joy. It's a language I continue to learn, and I hope you will, too.

BATTER, BUTTER AND BEGINNINGS

About this book

There's something undeniably special about cake. From the moment you gather ingredients at the market to the quiet joy of mixing, folding and baking, cake has a way of turning the ordinary into the extraordinary. And then there's the magic of unveiling it – whether it's at a grand wedding, a birthday celebration, or after a simple dinner with friends. You bring out the cake, cut it, share it and savour every bite.

This book is a love letter to cake – everything I've come to adore and learn over the years. Inside, you'll find recipes inspired by the flavours of my memories and experiences, designed for every skill level and occasion. There are simple, inviting cakes like my Coconut dream cake (page 60) and Cherry chip poppyseed and toasted rye crumble cake (page 65), as well as plenty of impressive bakes like my Pandan and mango sandwich cake (page 74), and an indulgent Vietnamese coffee flan cake (page 86).

If you're seeking a little challenge, you'll discover inspired layer cakes in delightful flavour combinations, as well as intricate retro-style multi-tiered creations to suit decorators of all levels. If decorating isn't your thing, many of these cakes can be finished simply. But if you've ever dreamed of creating your own wedding cake or a striking retro-style birthday cake, this book is filled with techniques and tips to help you succeed.

Decorating is an art that requires time, patience and practice. It's as much a journey as baking itself, and I hope to guide you through it with encouragement and care. If your cake doesn't look exactly like the photo, don't be discouraged. Take notes, learn from the process and try again. Each attempt brings you closer – and with practice, you'll see your skills and confidence flourish.

These pages are a collection of everything I know about cake – lessons shaped by years of perseverance and enriched by the incredible people who have shared this journey with me, especially my current and past team at Mali Bakes.

This book is my offering to you. It's more than just a collection of recipes; it's a celebration of creativity, learning and sharing. It's about understanding the materials, embracing the process, and finding beauty in every step. So, take a breath, roll up your sleeves, and let's bake something extraordinary together.

BATTER, BUTTER AND BEGINNINGS

Baking Tools

Baking, like any craft, begins with the right tools in hand. Having the proper equipment sets the tone, making the process smoother and more enjoyable. You won't need anything extravagant – just the essentials. Many of these tools may already reside in your kitchen, ready to serve their role. Others might call for a trip to a kitchenware store or a moment spent browsing online. I recommend checking hospitality stores or online retailers, where you'll often find durable, professional-grade equipment at better prices and quality.

Baking consumables

Baking paper. Invaluable for so many baking tasks, such as lining cake tins and marking cakes for decorating projects. Go for eco-friendly options whenever you can; if you handle your baking paper carefully, you can roll it up to use again.

Food grade plastic wrap. Essential for keeping cake layers moist during storage.

Cheesecloth (muslin). You'll need this for some of the cakes in Chapter 2. Cheesecloth is also perfect for tasks like hanging yoghurt and ricotta or straining brewed tea.

Aluminium foil. For this book, you'll only need foil to seal roasting trays. If you have an oven-safe plate or roasting tray with a lid, feel free to use that instead.

Measuring tools

Digital kitchen scales. If you don't have a digital kitchen scale yet, now's the time to get one! It's essential for accurate and consistent baking, as measuring by weight is far more precise than by volume – which is why all the ingredients in this book are measured in grams. A digital kitchen scale is also a time-saver and a clean-up hero – goodbye extra dishes! When recipes call for ingredients to be weighed together, simply weigh them in the same bowl, using the 'tare' function to reset the scale to zero after each addition. For dry ingredients that need sifting, place a sieve over a bowl on the scale, zero it out, and weigh as you sift. A compact scale that can weigh up to 5 kg (176.37 oz) is perfect for all of the recipes in this book.

Measuring spoons. I always use measuring spoons for really small ingredient quantities that weigh less than 10 grams (0.35 oz) – so I've also included spoon measures for such ingredients in this book. It gives me peace of mind, especially when measuring important ingredients like leavening agents. The spoon measurements in this book are based on the standard metric system, where 1 tablespoon equals 15 ml (½ fl oz).

Mixing and slicing tools

Bowls. A good set of heatproof kitchen bowls is an absolute must for this book! I highly recommend stainless-steel bowls – they're lightweight, easy to clean and stackable. You'll need at least one large bowl for hand-mixing batters such as chiffon cakes. A few medium-sized and small bowls are just as important for tasks like measuring ingredients, making curd over a double boiler, or pre-colouring buttercream for decorating projects.

Sieve. I prefer using a slightly coarser mesh for sifting dry ingredients and an extra-fine mesh for straining custards or curds. Choose a sieve with a sturdy, long handle that can rest easily over a bowl while you measure or strain.

Spatula. Have at least one stiff, heatproof spatula, about 35 cm (14 in) long, for folding batters. For decorating projects, you will need a few smaller flexible spatulas for mixing colours into buttercream.

Balloon whisk. A medium-sized stainless-steel balloon whisk is perfect for folding dry ingredients into light cakes such the matcha chiffon roll on page 90 or the olive oil ricotta cake on page 142. A smaller whisk is handy for reaching saucepan corners when making custards.

Immersion blender. The immersion blender is easily one of my most-used tools. Whether it's emulsifying melted white chocolate for whipped mascarpone cream or blending gel-based food colouring into buttercream, it gets the job done quickly and efficiently.

Spice grinder or a pestle and mortar. A spice grinder is specifically designed for grinding spices. It has a smaller blade and bowl, allowing even the smallest amounts of spices to be ground effectively and evenly. If you don't have a spice grinder on hand, a pestle and mortar works just as well – you'll just need a little extra arm strength! Simply grind in small batches, pressing and twisting the spices until you achieve the desired texture.

Blender. You will only need this for making the pandan extract for the Pandan and mango sandwich cake (page 74). A small, countertop smoothie blender will also work.

Food processor. Any standard food processor will work for the recipes in this book.

Stand mixer. All of the recipes in this book call for a stand mixer. If you don't already have one, it might feel like a big investment, but a good stand mixer is a faithful companion that will serve you for a very long time. My Kenwood mixers have been going strong for years! KitchenAid is another well-loved option. A hand-held mixer can step in if needed, though it does make things a bit trickier – especially for recipes like Italian meringue buttercream, where having your hands free makes all the difference. Keep in mind that larger stand mixers can struggle with smaller quantities, such as whipping a small amount of egg whites.

Cake leveller. This tool has an adjustable wire or blade, supported by two stable feet that rest on a flat surface. It's designed to glide smoothly through a cake, creating perfectly flat and even layers. For the simple finish cakes in Chapter 2, a long, thin serrated knife will do the job – but if you're tackling layer cakes for decorating projects, I can't recommend a cake leveller enough! It's a bit of an investment, but it guarantees perfectly even, level layers, which means your cake will stack straight.

At Mali Bakes, we use an Agbay leveller, which is designed for commercial use, but it comes with a higher price tag. Wire levellers are a budget-friendly option and work great for most cakes – just keep in mind they can struggle with chocolate chip cakes, and may not be large enough for cakes over 25 cm (10 in). For an affordable blade option, Loyal offers a great alternative.

Always be sure to use your leveller on a flat surface.

Knives. Your trusty, sharp everyday kitchen knife will be your go-to for just about everything in this book. For those perfect, clean cake slices – especially for the simple finish cakes in Chapter 2 – a thin, serrated cake knife is super handy.

Cooking tools

Cake tester or skewer. This essential tool ensures your cakes are perfectly baked. You can use a metal cake tester or a simple wooden toothpick. To check your cake's doneness, simply insert a skewer into the centre of the cake and remove it. If it comes out clean or with just a few crumbs, it's a sign that your cake is ready.

Digital timer. While using your phone as a timer is an option, I find a dedicated digital timer much more convenient – especially if you're baking a cake and cooking other things at the same time. It's always handy to have a couple on hand. A simple, basic model works perfectly – no need for anything fancy.

Digital thermometer. Invest in a good instant-read digital thermometer – it's an essential tool for this book! Whether you're checking ingredient temperatures, doneness for curds or custards, or most importantly, making Italian meringue buttercream, this tool will take out the guesswork and make your life so much easier. Being able to easily and accurately read a sugar syrup temperature is half the battle for success! Opt for a thermometer with a slightly longer probe to keep your hands safely away from the heat. You can also find digital thermometers that clip onto the saucepan for added convenience.

Saucepans. You'll need at least two saucepans: one large and one small, both heavy-bottomed stainless steel. The large saucepan is perfect for tasks that need a double boiler or for cooking jams. The smaller saucepan – ideally 12–15 cm (4¾–6 in) in diameter and 8–10 cm (3¼–4 in) in height – is ideal for cooking sugar syrup and allows the syrup to pool deeply enough for easy and accurate temperature reading with a digital thermometer. Heavy-bottomed stainless-steel saucepans heat evenly, which is absolutely essential when working with custards or sugar. Plus, they're non-reactive, so they won't interfere with the flavours of dairy or acidic ingredients.

Bakeware

Cooling racks. Have at least two cooling racks on hand – non-stick and stainless-steel options both work perfectly fine. I always recommend spraying the rack with a little oil to prevent sticking, just to be safe. Make sure you have enough racks, or a large enough rack, to cool all your cakes at once, especially if you're baking larger cakes for decorating projects.

Silicone baking mat. If you bake often, I can't recommend a silicone baking mat enough – they're such a great reusable alternative to disposable baking paper. In this book, you'll only need it for the Heart of Glass project on page 308, where it's used to create the royal icing and isomalt toppers. (It's also handy for the drop flowers for the Secret Garden project on page 288.)

Roasting tray. You will need a roasting tray for tasks like a water bath for the Vietnamese coffee flan cake (page 86) or for roasting fruit fillings. You don't need anything fancy – just use whatever you have on hand, as long as it's at least 5 cm (2 in) deep. Avoid aluminium trays, as they can affect the flavour of the fruit. Instead, opt for non-reactive options like glass, ceramic, stainless steel, or enameled cast iron.

Cake tins

The tables on the following page list all the tins you will need for this book. For the simple finish cakes in Chapter 2 I've kept the list of essentials as short as possible. For best results, always use the same-sized cake tin that your recipe calls for. Using a different-sized tin can throw the cook time off, or result in a different final height or texture.

You can collect cake tins over time, as you choose to tackle each new baking project. Note that cake tins are generally sold in imperial measurements, so if you're struggling to find the perfect tin in centimetres, it's worth searching for the inch equivalent online or in kitchen supply stores. I've included measurements in centimetres and inches throughout the book.

If you're heading out to buy cake tins, I highly recommend choosing anodized ones. Brands such as Loyal, Mondo and Fat Daddio's make excellent options. They heat up evenly, last for years, and because they're lighter in colour (compared to non-stick options), they reflect heat rather than absorbing it – meaning your cakes will bake more gently and won't brown too quickly around the edges.

One thing that's easy to overlook is the height of your cake tin. Ideally, the tin should be about the same height as the cake will rise to at its tallest point while baking (it'll settle down slightly towards the end of baking). If the tin is too tall, it can block heat from reaching the batter properly, which can leave you with a cake that's a bit denser, drier and paler than you'd like.

Heart-shaped cake tins with a 5 cm (2 in) depth can be a little tricky to find, as they're not as commonly stocked. If you come across a 7.5 cm (3 in) deep tin instead, don't worry – it will work just fine. Just keep in mind that the extra depth might mean your cake needs a little more baking time, so it's a good idea to keep an eye on it as it bakes.

All the cake tins I use here (except for the angel food cake tin) are solid-bottomed. A solid-bottom tin has a fully sealed base, which is perfect for containing runnier batters and helping your cakes bake nice and evenly. You can definitely use a springform or loose-bottom tin if that's what you have on hand – just be sure to wrap the outside with foil to catch any potential batter leaks.

Simple finish cakes (Chapter 2)	
1 × solid bottom round tin, in the following sizes	20 × 7.5 cm (8 × 3 in)
	23 × 5 cm (9 × 2 in)
1 × bundt tin	23 × 9.5 cm (9 × 3¾ in)
1 × loaf (1-pound loaf) tin	22.5 × 12 × 7 cm (8⅞ × 4¾ × 2¾ in)
1 × angel food cake tin	23 × 10 cm (9 × 4 in)
2 × lamington tins (rectangular cake pans)	30 × 20 × 3.5 cm (12 × 8 × 1⅜ in)
1 × sheet pan (jelly roll pan)	38 × 25.5 × 2.5 cm (15 × 10 × 1 in)
3 × round tins with checkerboard divider rings (mine are from Wilton)	23 × 4 cm (9 × 1½ in)

Layer cakes (Chapter 3) and Decorating projects (Chapter 5)	
3 × solid bottom round tins, each in the following sizes	15 × 5 cm (6 × 2 in)
	18 × 5 cm (7 × 2 in)
	23 × 5 cm (9 × 2 in)
	30 × 5 cm (12 × 2 in)
4 × solid bottom round tins	18 × 5 cm (7 × 2 in)
3 × solid bottom heart-shaped tins	20 cm (8 in)
3 × solid bottom square tins, each in the following sizes	15 × 5 cm (6 × 2 in)
	25.5 × 5 cm (10 × 2 in)

Decorating Tools

This is the list of decorating tools you'll need for this book. Keep in mind that everything that goes onto the cake must be food safe. If you're a cake-decorating enthusiast, chances are your kitchen drawers are already overflowing with most of these tools! But if not, no worries – you don't need to buy everything at once. Each project comes with a handy list of what you'll need, so you can pick things up as you go. Specialty cake decorating and online stores are the best places to find these tools.

For frosting

Palette knives

Angled (offset) palette knife. The unsung hero of baking – a tool that no caker should ever be without! This could just as easily sit in the baking tools section as I don't just use my angled palette knife for decorating, and you'll see it make countless appearances throughout this book. I love using one that's around 15 cm (6 in) long.

Straight palette knife. I find it a bit awkward to use an angled palette knife when applying buttercream to the sides of a cake. A straight palette knife is incredibly handy for this task as you can apply buttercream evenly and with more control. Choose one that's about the same height as the cake you're working on. A 15 cm (6 in) knife is just the right size for most projects in this book.

Pointed palette knife. A little tool with big talent! Choose a pointed palette knife that's about 10 cm (4 in) long. It's useful for marking decorations and popping out piping mistakes.

Scrapers

Plain edge scraper. A must-have for smoothing and scraping the sides of your cake. I swear by stainless-steel scrapers – they last longer than acrylic ones and give a cleaner finish. Look for one that isn't too thick; thinner scrapers glide better and give you a sharper, cleaner edge. I love one with a ruler etched on the side – they're so handy for making decorations. My go-to brand is Sprinks. When choosing a scraper, make sure it's just a bit taller than your cake. If it's too tall, it's harder to hold straight and can leave you with a wonky finish. For all the projects in this book, an 18 cm (7 in) scraper is a perfect size. Take care when storing, as any dents will show on your cakes.

Bench scraper. When it comes to smoothing the top of your cake, you can use the same plain scraper as you use for the sides, or even a palette knife, but I find a slightly flexible scraper with a top handle works best. Also called a top scraper, these flexible steel scrapers can be purchased from hardware stores and are fantastic for the job. I prefer one about 18 cm (7 in) wide – it's the perfect size to easily ensure a smooth finish across the top of your cake.

Rake scraper/comb. This is the tool for adding texture! These are usually made of plastic and have ridged teeth on the sides. For this book we use one with finer teeth. Be sure to choose a scraper that's taller than your cake.

For piping

Piping bags. You can't pipe without piping bags – unless you're feeling nostalgic and want to try folding your own from baking paper like they did back in the day! For this book, 46 cm (18 in) non-slip, compostable piping bags will be your best friend. While cotton bags might seem the more eco-friendly choice, they can be a nightmare to clean, especially if your frosting is tinted with food colouring. Compostable bags, however, can be washed and reused many times. I suggest buying piping bags that come in rolls (I love using ones from Loyal). Since you'll need several for each decorating project, buying them in bulk is a much more cost-effective option.

Couplers. Two-piece plastic tools that let you switch piping nozzles without changing the piping bag, couplers come in standard, medium and large sizes, and for this book I recommend having a few of each size. I'll use a coupler even when I don't need to change the nozzle during piping, because once I've finished, the coupler makes it easier to remove the nozzle without tearing the piping bag.

Piping nozzles. Also known as tubes or piping tips, these are the magic wands of cake decorating, turning simple frosting into intricate designs. Each nozzle has a number, which is standardised across brands. I've listed all the nozzles you'll be using in this book opposite.

When selecting nozzles, pay attention to the thickness of the metal – if it's too thick, it can affect your piping control. I'm a big fan of Loyal and Ateco nozzles; they're also slightly longer than most, making them easier to handle and a joy to work with.

Take care when cleaning and storing your nozzles to keep them in perfect condition. The little pointy metal teeth can bend easily, which can affect the details of your piping, so it's worth investing in a proper storage container. To clean your nozzles, soak them in hot, soapy water to loosen any buttercream, then wash them gently by hand. Treat them well and they'll remain your trusty decorating companions for years to come!

Round nozzles
Standard sizes: 2, 3, 4, 5, 10
Medium and large sizes: S/P4, S/P12, S/P14, S/P15

Petal nozzles
Standard sizes: 101, 102, 103, 104, 104W
Medium sizes: 124K, 126K

Star nozzles
Standard sizes: 16, 18, 32
Medium sizes: S/S3, S/S5, S/S7, S/S9, S/S11, S/S13

French star nozzles
Medium and large sizes: S/F5, S/F7, S/F9, S/F11, S/F13, S/F15

Open star nozzles
Medium sizes: 172, 1M

Leaf nozzles
Standard sizes: 70, 75, 352
Medium size: 115

Basketweave nozzles
Standard size: 44
Medium size: 2B

Drop flower nozzles
Standard sizes: 30, 232, 192

For marking decorations

Ruler. Be sure to have one handy, as you'll need one for all the decorating projects in this book.

Wing caliper. Retro cake designs are all about balance and repetition, and a wing caliper is such a handy tool to have! It helps you measure and evenly space your border designs. You can easily find one at a hardware store. Opt for the type with pointed ends on both sides, rather than the ones that require inserting a pen.

Edible marker. A food-safe option for marking dowels or tracing on baking paper.

Cookie cutters. Used to mark and outline neat, uniform piping details such as a perfectly round ring in the centre of a cake, or cute heart-shaped details on the sides.

DECORATING TOOLS

For layer and tiered cakes

Brush or squeeze bottle. For adding soaks to cake layers. If you choose a brush, go for a flat natural-bristle type for even application – avoid silicone brushes as they don't hold syrup well. If using a squeeze bottle, pick one with multiple nozzles or holes to distribute the syrup evenly and prevent over-soaking.

Turntable. A rotating cake stand is an essential tool for assembling, frosting and decorating layer cakes. It allows you to rotate your cake smoothly, making it much easier to work on every side without awkward stretches or constant adjustments. Look for one with a smooth rotation and a sturdy cast-iron base – it will be strong enough to support heavier cakes and is built to last for years.

Non-slip mat. Place one of these between your cake board and turntable to keep everything steady while you frost or pipe onto your cake. It provides a secure grip, ensuring your cake stays in place as you work. Look for a thinner mat to allow the cake board to sit as flat as possible on the turntable. It's also handy for transporting cakes – I always tuck one under the cake box in the car to keep everything stable and prevent any unwanted movement.

Cake board. This is a sturdy, flat base that supports your cake while you assemble, frost and decorate it. For a more sustainable choice, opt for reusable acrylic boards or a stylish platter – just ensure the surface is completely flat. Raised edges can get in the way, making it difficult to smooth the frosting evenly on the sides.

When working on the decorating projects in this book, pay attention to the minimum thickness requirement of the cake board. This ensures the board will be sturdy enough to support the cake's weight without cracking or damaging the decorations. For double-tier cakes, reusable cake boards are often not strong or large enough. In these cases, you'll need a single-use option like Masonite or drum cake boards. If you can't find one thick enough, you can always glue two thinner boards together.

The cake board should match the cake's shape: round boards for round cakes, square boards for square cakes. For heart-shaped cakes, both round and square boards work, so go with what you prefer.

Perforated cake board. This is a thin cardboard board with a pre-drilled centre hole, designed specifically for stacking tiered cakes (page 174). They are available from most cake-decorating stores and are inexpensive. Don't attempt to drill a hole in a board yourself – it can be tricky to achieve a perfectly centred hole, and stray cardboard bits may end up on your cake. For heart-shaped or square cakes, if a perforated board of the right shape and size is not available, simply choose a board that is large enough and cut it to shape using your sharpest scissors.

Cake pillars. Cake pillars are plastic pieces designed to resemble elegant columns that support cake tiers – they are a hallmark of classic retro cake design. The hollow columns are used alongside a separator set to provide stability while creating a beautifully elevated look. They come in different designs and heights and can be found at most cake-decorating stores.

Cake separator set. This is essential for creating elevated cake tiers! The set includes a plastic disc with three cylindrical feet on the bottom, and dowels that can click into the feet. This setup lets you decorate each tier on its own board and transport them separately with ease. When assembling, simply attach the top tier to the disc using double-sided tape to keep it stable. Cake separator sets are easy to find online.

Dowels and dowel cutter. Dowels are support rods used in tiered cake construction to keep the layers stable and prevent sinking. They are typically made of wood or plastic and are inserted into the lower tiers to support the weight of the tiers above. Dowels work alongside cake boards or separator plates to distribute weight evenly. Whenever possible, opt for wooden dowels instead of plastic for a more sustainable choice. Dowels that are about 5 mm (¼ in) thick will be sturdy enough to support the double-tier cakes in this book.

While there are cutters specifically made for cake dowels, cutting pliers or a pipe cutter from a hardware store will work just as well. To achieve a clean and flat cut, score around the marked level before making the cut. These tools are only needed for tiered cake projects.

Other handy decorating tools

Flower nail. This small handheld tool, like a mini turntable, is used for creating delicate buttercream flowers and leaves. They come in all sorts of sizes, but for this book, you'll only need sizes 13 and 14.

Flower wire, florist tape and wire cutter. These are important tools to have in the drawer when adding fresh flowers to cakes. Flower wire makes it easy to secure the flowers to the cake, and gives the stems some extra support so they stay upright and look their best. The higher the gauge number, the thinner the wire. For this book, I recommend sticking with 22 gauge wire.

Florist tape is used for securing the wire and keeping the flower stems from directly touching the cake. Go for the parafilm type – it's waterproof and does a much better job protecting the cake than the paper kind.

DECORATING TOOLS

Essential Ingredients

Here is a list of the ingredients you'll need to get started with your bakes. Most of these are pantry staples, so you might already have them on hand. But if not, use this section to guide you on what to look for when stocking up!

Dairy

Butter. Always choose high-quality unsalted butter for your cakes. The better the butter, the better your bake will be – it's as simple as that. With buttercream, you're essentially whipping butter into your meringue, so the flavour of your butter really matters. Each recipe lists the precise amount of salt required, so always opt for unsalted butter.

Butter quality varies based on fat content, the type of milk it's made from, and the production process. Most supermarket butters in Australia have a fat content of 80–82 per cent, but for baking, I recommend going for at least 82 per cent. Some high-quality butters can contain up to 86 per cent fat, and your cakes will benefit from the extra richness.

For decorating, you should know that butters with a lower fat content (meaning they have a higher water content) can be trickier to work with. The extra water can make buttercream prone to separating, which makes it harder to get smooth, consistent results – and it doesn't hold up as well. So again, choose a butter with a high fat content.

Cultured butter offers a more complex flavour thanks to the fermentation process it has undergone, and it's what we use at Mali Bakes. However, be cautious – some brands can have a cheese-like tanginess that might not work well for cakes or buttercream.

Ultimately, buy the best butter you can afford – the brand with a taste you love. It makes all the difference in your final bake!

Cream. I tend to use thickened cream (called heavy cream or whipping cream in some parts of the world). It contains stabilisers like gum or gelatine, which helps improve its consistency and makes it whip more easily. It typically has a fat content of at least 35 per cent. Pure cream, which contains no thickeners, can be used instead of thickened cream for the recipes in this book, just make sure it has a similar fat content.

Full fat is best! Always use full-fat (full-cream/whole) milk and sour cream in your cakes. Skim or light options will affect the recipe's ratios. Full-fat cream cheese is also essential – I only use Philadelphia.

ESSENTIAL INGREDIENTS

Eggs

Choose the freshest and best-quality eggs your budget allows – and always opt for free-range (not 'cage free') eggs, for obvious reasons. Eggs can vary in size and how they are labelled, so if you want your cakes to rise and shine as they should, weighing your eggs is your best bet, as their ratios can vary even within the same carton of eggs.

In this book, all the ingredients are measured by weight, so the size of your eggs doesn't matter too much. As a general guide, the recipes in this book use large eggs, from a 700 g (24.7 oz) 12-egg carton, with each whole egg (after the shell is removed) weighing around 50 g (1.75 oz). I've included the approximate number of eggs you will need next to each weight measurement.

How to weigh eggs. Crack them one at a time into a bowl and weigh as you go. If you're close to the required weight but need just a small amount more, crack the next egg into a separate bowl, whisk it well, and add only the amount needed. A small variance of around 10 g (0.35 oz) over or under usually won't affect the recipe.

Separating yolks and whites. It's much easier to separate eggs while they are cold, as the yolks are less likely to break. Carefully crack all the eggs into a large bowl, then use your clean hand to gently scoop out the yolks one at a time, letting the whites drip through your fingers. This approach is quicker and more graceful than separating the yolks one at a time as each egg is cracked. If you accidentally drop a piece of shell into the bowl, use another piece of eggshell to scoop it out – the sharp edge slices through the whites more easily than a spoon.

Whipping egg whites. Fresh egg whites give the best volume and stability. Avoid pre-cracked egg whites sold in convenience packs, as the pasteurisation process makes them runnier, less stable, and unable to yield great volume. Fresh egg whites can be frozen for up to 2 months and still perform better than pasteurised egg whites. Just be sure to store them in small portions and thaw them overnight in the fridge as needed.

To bring refrigerated eggs to room temperature. Let them sit in warm water (not hot water) for about 10–15 minutes before using.

Flour

One of the best things about cake is its soft, tender crumb – and the type of flour you use plays a huge role in achieving this. Different flours vary in protein content, which influences gluten development – the network of proteins that give baked goods their structure. For cakes, it's important to stick to flours with a low-to-medium protein content.

The quality of your flour can also make a big difference to your cakes. Though shelf-stable, flour is a product of the earth – and its flavour, texture and character can vary between brands. Higher-quality flour offers a more pleasant and natural flavour, while lower-quality flour may taste bland or slightly starchy. Like everything that goes into your cakes, always buy the best your budget allows.

Bleached flour. Treated with chemicals like chlorine gas or benzoyl peroxide, which strip away the essence of what flour should be, bleached flour should be avoided.

Plain flour. Also known as all-purpose flour, plain flour has a medium protein content of around 10–12 per cent and is the type of flour mostly used in this book.

Cake flour. Has a low protein content of around 7–9 per cent and is ideal for delicate cakes, such as chiffon or sponge cakes, but it isn't as commonly available in Australia and some other parts of the world. To replicate cake flour, many recipes in this book call for cornflour (corn starch) to help lower the overall protein content. If you do have cake flour on hand, you can use it by replacing the combined weight of plain flour and cornflour with cake flour.

Self-raising flour. One thing to avoid at all costs for this book is self-raising flour. With built-in leaveners, it's like a wildcard that throws everything off balance.

Sugar

There can never be a cake without sugar – the soul of sweetness, but it does so much more. Sugar locks in moisture, tenderises the crumb, and creates that irresistible golden, caramelised crust we all adore.

Caster sugar. Also called superfine sugar, caster sugar is finely ground into smaller crystals than granulated sugar. It dissolves quickly and blends smoothly into batters, making it perfect for baking. It's the sugar most commonly used in this book.

Brown sugar. Also called light brown sugar in some parts of the world, brown sugar is made by adding molasses back to white sugar, giving it a rich, slightly caramel note that deepens the overall flavour profile of your cakes. It's naturally moist and tends to clump, so always break it up before use.

Icing sugar. Also known as confectioners' sugar or powdered sugar, icing sugar is white sugar that has been ground into a fine powder. Icing sugar mixture contains a small amount of cornflour (corn starch) to help prevent clumping. You can use pure icing sugar or icing sugar mixture for the recipes in this book, except for Royal icing (page 168), which requires pure icing sugar (cornflour will prevent the icing from drying properly). Always sift icing sugar before using to remove any lumps. If it's clumping too much, a quick blitz in a food processor will do the trick!

Coconut sugar. Made from the sap of coconut palm flower buds, this sugar has a deep, caramel-like flavour with a touch of earthy, savoury warmth and delightful hints of toffee and molasses. It's the star ingredient in my Coconut sugar buttercream on page 136, which is my favourite as it pairs beautifully with so many flavours – you might just want to eat it straight from the bowl!

Fresh and frozen fruits

A lot of my recipes are fruit-forward because I love the brightness that fruit brings to cakes. Always try to use fruit that's in season and, when you can, buy locally – it makes a noticeable difference. There's not much point making the Strawberry and cream olive oil sponge roll (page 82) if strawberries aren't at their best where you are. If this is the case, try swapping in whatever is in season – roasted rhubarb or plums would be just as lovely.

That said, don't underestimate the value of frozen fruit! It's a fantastic option, especially for recipes where the fruit will be cooked, such as jams or roasted fillings. Most frozen fruits are picked and frozen at their peak, preserving their flavour and quality. Locally sourced frozen fruits are ideal. If you can, visit your nearest farmers' market and chat with the berry farmers – they often have frozen fruit tucked away, perfect for off-season baking projects.

ESSENTIAL INGREDIENTS

Oil

Like butter, oil is a fat that helps keep cakes moist, tender and soft. Unlike butter, oil remains liquid at room temperature, adding richness without making the crumb dense. In this book, we use vegetable oil, but any neutral-flavoured oil, such as canola, sunflower or grapeseed oil, works just as well.

Olive oil. The star of the show when it wants to be. Yes, it's pricier and adds its own personality, but in bakes like the olive oil ricotta cake (page 142), it's the leading character. In these moments, don't hold back – choose a high-quality extra virgin olive oil to let its bold, unique flavour shine through.

Leavening agents

Leaveners like baking powder and bicarbonate of soda (baking soda) are essential for helping cakes rise, creating a light and fluffy texture. While they both produce air bubbles, they work differently and can't be used interchangeably.

Bicarbonate of soda. Also called baking soda, bicarb soda is pure sodium bicarbonate, an alkaline ingredient that needs an acidic component – such as lemon juice, sour cream or buttermilk – to activate it. When mixed with an acid, it produces carbon dioxide gas, which lifts the batter and helps the cake rise.

Baking powder. This leavening agent already contains both bicarbonate of soda and a dry acid (like cream of tartar, see opposite), meaning it doesn't require an additional acidic ingredient to work. It's double-acting, releasing gas twice – first when mixed with liquid and again when heated, giving cakes a steady, controlled rise.

Some recipes call for both bicarbonate of soda and baking powder to achieve the best lift and structure. But keep in mind that if your leaveners are old, they lose their effectiveness, leading to a dense, flat cake instead of a beautifully fluffy one. Always check their freshness before baking!

To check freshness. Test baking powder by mixing 1 teaspoon with 80 g (2.82 oz) hot water – if it bubbles vigorously, it's still fresh. For bicarb soda, mix ¼ teaspoon with 2 teaspoons vinegar or lemon juice – if it fizzes immediately, it's good to use.

Replace your baking powder and bicarbonate of soda every 6–12 months after opening, and store them in a cool, dry place to maintain their effectiveness.

Other pantry staples

Salt. This seasoning does more than simply add saltiness – it enhances flavour by interacting with our tastebuds to heighten the perception of other flavours. It brightens other ingredients such as chocolate, vanilla and spices while balancing the sweetness in a cake. Always choose fine sea salt, as it dissolves quickly and evenly in a batter and has a milder saltiness compared to cooking salt. Opting for non-iodised salt is also important to avoid any metallic aftertaste.

Cream of tartar. If a recipe calls for whipping egg whites, you will always need cream of tartar. It increases the acidity, which strengthens the egg-white proteins, helping them trap air better and create more consistent foam.

Chocolate. Like butter, chocolate varies in quality. It's made up of two key components: cocoa solids, which provide the flavour, and cocoa butter (the natural fat from the cocoa bean), which gives chocolate its smoothness and texture. Always use good-quality chocolate made with cocoa butter and avoid compound chocolate, which uses vegetable fats and leaves a waxy mouthfeel. My favourite brand is Callebaut – the chip size is perfect for cakes and melts easily.

For dark chocolate, a bittersweet chocolate 55–60 per cent cocoa solids is ideal for the recipes in this book. For white chocolate, choose one with at least 28 per cent cocoa butter.

Cocoa powder. Always use Dutch-processed cocoa powder for baking. Avoid drinking cocoa, as it contains added sugar and other ingredients, and avoid raw cacao as it behaves differently in baking. Cacao, which is essentially a fruit, is naturally acidic, and the fermentation process adds even more acidity. Dutch-processed cocoa powder goes through an alkalisation process, which neutralises this acidity, reducing bitterness and bringing out deeper, earthier flavours. It also helps the cocoa react better with leavening agents, allowing your cakes to rise properly. Cocoa powder loses its flavour over time, especially once the container is open. Always check the expiry date and store it in a cool, dry place in an airtight container.

Vanilla. When it comes to vanilla, don't skimp – always use high-quality pods, paste or extract, and steer clear of essence (trust me, your cakes will thank you). Good-quality vanilla should have a rich, almost punchy aroma when you sniff it straight from the jar. Yes, it's a bit pricey, but a little goes a long way. I'm a die-hard Heilala fan!

Food colouring

You'll want a good range of food colourings for the decorating projects in this book. But don't panic – you don't need to buy every colour under the sun! On this page you will find an overview of the different colours you will need to follow the projects in this book. You'll find more information about the different types of food colouring, how to use them, and even a guide to mixing your own shades in Chapter 4.

You don't need to strictly follow the colours used in each project. Feel free to get creative – use any colours you love or simply work with the food colourings you already have. As long as you're using the right type of food colouring, you will be able to bring each cake to life in your own unique way!

Gel food colouring

I use Chefmaster or Magic Colours gels.

- Neon Brite Green (Chefmaster)
- Dijon (Magic Colours)
- Red (Chefmaster Christmas Red gives the nicest red)
- Orange (Chefmaster)
- Neon Brite Pink (Chefmaster)
- Egg Yellow (Magic Colours)

Oil-based food colouring

For oil-based food colouring, I use Colour Mill products. If you don't use food colouring often, it's best to buy smaller bottles since the pigment tends to settle over time. Always give the bottle a good shake before using.

- Black
- Cobalt
- Forest
- Hot Pink
- Lime
- Mustard
- Orange
- Purple
- Red
- Sky Blue
- White
- Yellow

Vegetable shortening. This budget-friendly alternative to butter is perfect for practising your piping skills. Available at most cake-decorating stores, it's a solid fat made from vegetable oils and is temperature-stable, meaning it won't melt or harden easily.

Meringue powder. Used in the Stabilised buttercream (page 167) and Royal icing (page 168) recipes, meringue powder is essentially dried egg whites mixed with stabilisers, designed to replace fresh egg whites in products that require stiffness or air-drying. You'll find it in most cake-decorating stores. Meringue powder can lose its freshness over time, so always check the expiry date and buy in small quantities. Avoid substituting it with egg white powder, as it doesn't perform as well.

Isomalt. This sugar substitute is made from sugar alcohol rather than traditional sugar. Regular sugar tends to absorb moisture from the air quickly, causing it to dissolve. Isomalt, however, is more resistant to humidity and less likely to crystallise, making it perfect for cake decorating. You can find isomalt at most cake-decorating stores – opt for the non-coloured crystal variety, as it's the easiest to work with. In this book, you'll only need Isomalt for the Heart of Glass project on page 308.

ESSENTIAL INGREDIENTS

When I started Mali Bakes, it was a big shift from my days in a fast-paced cafe kitchen, where I spent hours tackling menu orders on endless dockets. Baking beautiful cakes was a whole new world, and I quickly learned that it isn't something you can rush or wing, it's a practice of precision, trusting the method, and using your intuition to account for all the little variables along the way. Unlike most other forms of cooking, you can't just toss in a pinch of salt after the fact, or pop something back in the oven to fix it. Baking demands patience and focus – it's a process that invites you to slow down and pay attention.

This chapter offers simple guidance for all things cake, from cake baking to buttercream making – principles and tips you can apply throughout this book to set yourself up for success.

All Things Cake

BRILLIANT BAKING 101

Baking a cake can be a magical experience, but it is also an exacting art and, unfortunately, there are quite a few factors that can get in the way of your beautifully baked cake! Below I've included the key principles I follow religiously, through every step of the process, to help ensure your own creations turn out perfectly every time.

Plan, organise and learn from mistakes

Take the time to read the recipe through a couple of times to ensure you don't miss any important details. Visualise the steps in your mind and gather all the ingredients and tools before you start. Remember to plan for recipe components that may need extra time to chill or set, such as custards and curds. When everything is prepared and you know what to expect, you can enjoy the process without feeling rushed or overwhelmed.

And if things don't go as planned, don't let it discourage you – it's all part of the baking journey. Trust me, we've all been there. Maybe the oven ran a little hot, you measured something slightly off, or life just distracted you for a second. It happens! Think of it as a learning moment – figure out what might have gone sideways, make a note, and give it another go. And hey, even if your finished cake isn't picture-perfect, chances are it's still pretty tasty. Baking isn't all about being perfect; it's about giving yourself the space to learn and the time to try. You've got this!

Measure your ingredients by weight

In all the recipes in this book, all the ingredients – including liquids such as oil, milk and water – are measured by weight, rather than volume, because it's simply the best way to bake! It's faster, easier and way more accurate than measuring ingredients, such as flour, using cups – especially when you're scaling up cake recipes for decorating projects (page 321). Measuring by weight gives you consistent results every time. So if you don't already have them, please invest in a simple set of digital scales to help you on your way. You'll be so glad you did!

For ingredients weighing under 10 grams (0.35 oz), spoon measurements are included for convenience. Eggs are also listed by weight, along with an approximate number of eggs you'll need, but remember that eggs can vary in size. To be extra sure, crack the eggs into a separate bowl and whisk them lightly before weighing.

Precision is everything in baking, so weigh your ingredients carefully and correctly – a small variation of ±10 grams (0.35 oz) is fine for most ingredients, but anything more can throw off the recipe's ratio. To save time, weigh ingredients in the same bowl and use the 'tare' function on your digital scales to reset the scales between

> *'If your cake domes and browns too much, the oven is likely too hot. If it sinks in the middle and looks pale, the oven might be too cool.'*

each addition. For leavening agents such as baking powder or bicarbonate of soda (baking soda), though, I recommend weighing them in a separate bowl. For these particular ingredients, even the slightest difference in weight can have a big impact, and let's be honest – even the best of us can get distracted and forget what we've already added sometimes. This extra step is a great safety net.

Temperature really matters

In baking, temperature is everything – it's the quiet but essential force behind a perfect rise or beautifully whipped cream. Whether it's the temperature of your oven or your ingredients, getting it right makes all the difference between a perfect bake and a disappointing one. Below are a few important things to keep in mind.

Oven temperature

Every recipe in this book uses a convection (fan-forced/fan-assisted) oven. These ovens have a built-in fan that circulates hot air, which ensures a more even heat distribution compared to traditional gas or conventional ovens, which rely solely on static heating elements. This even airflow means you can bake at lower temperatures and achieve more consistent results. If you have a conventional oven, you may need to increase the temperature by 10–20°C (50–68°F).

Keep in mind that every oven is built and performs differently. Here are things I recommend checking beforehand.

Temperature accuracy. Not all ovens have a temperature display, and even when they do, it's not uncommon for them to be slightly inaccurate. An oven thermometer is a simple and affordable tool that takes the guesswork out of baking. Place it inside your oven to check if the actual temperature matches what you've set, so you can adjust it up or down as needed.

A properly baked cake should come out with a flat top and even colour. If your cake domes and browns too much, the oven is likely too hot. If it sinks in the middle and looks pale, the oven might be too cool.

Hot and cool spots. Every oven has hot and cool spots – even the powerful commercial ones we use at Mali Bakes! To get to know your oven better, it's a good idea to do a test bake with something simple and light in colour, like the Buttermilk vanilla cake (page 108). Pay attention to which areas of the oven cause the cake to brown too quickly and which areas leave it undercooked. Once you've identified these spots in your oven, you can adjust your future bakes by placing your cake tins in the most even areas, or rotating them during baking to account for uneven heat distribution.

Ingredient temperature

Getting the temperature of your ingredients just right can make or break your bake. They say baking is a science, and this is one of the reasons why – think of it as setting the stage for your baking success!

When you're whipping up a fluffy cake batter or a silky buttercream, you want the ingredients to emulsify properly – and that starts with using room-temperature ingredients. Softened butter blends seamlessly into meringue when making buttercream and helps trap air when whipped, creating a light and fluffy cake. Eggs and dairy at room temperature incorporate more easily into the batter, helping cakes rise properly.

If your ingredients are too cold, the batter can curdle, leaving you with a coarse-textured cake. On the flip side, if your butter or batter gets too warm, things can get oily or loose, and the cake may turn out dense and greasy.

In this book, all ingredients are assumed to be at room temperature unless a recipe indicates otherwise. Obviously room temperature can vary depending on where you live and the season, but as a general rule, ingredients should be around 20–22°C (68–72°F).

Butter usually needs an hour or two to soften, while eggs, sour cream, buttermilk and milk should sit out of the fridge for 30–60 minutes before you start baking. If you're in a rush, you can submerge the eggs in warm water for 10–15 minutes or warm the dairy ingredients in the microwave in short 5–10 second bursts – just be careful not to overdo it.

Some recipes in this book call for chilled ingredients – such as the whipped mascarpone or yoghurt cream – but this will be clearly specified in each recipe. For these recipe components, it's essential to keep your ingredients cold, ideally between 0–4°C (32–39°F). Even a little warmth can cause the fat to soften too much, making it difficult to hold air and increasing the risk of the cream splitting. To avoid this, chill the cream mixture, mixing bowl and whisk in the fridge for 10–15 minutes before starting.

When whipping egg whites, whether for chiffon cakes or buttercream, using chilled whites at 0–7°C (32–45°F) can be particularly effective. Chilled egg whites are thicker, and their proteins are less relaxed, allowing them to create a more stable foam. While they take slightly longer to whip compared to room-temperature whites, this added stability reduces the risk of overwhipping.

> 'All ingredients are assumed to be at room temperature unless a recipe indicates otherwise.'

Whipping with control

When incorporating air into a mixture, whether it's cream, meringue or whole egg foam, always start your stand mixer at medium speed. This allows air to gently work its way into the mixture, creating smaller, more stable bubbles. Jumping straight to high speed might seem like a time-saver, but it can lead to large, fragile air pockets that are more likely to collapse. High speeds also generate extra friction, adding heat to the mixture. With cream, this added warmth can cause it to destabilise or even split. Starting slow ensures better control.

Stop and scrape. All stand mixers and their attachments are different, and even the best ones can't do all the work for you. Scraping the side and bottom of the bowl, as well as the beating attachment, is one of those small but important steps that makes a big difference. Ingredients like butter and sugar tend to cling to the edge of the bowl, while flour can settle at the bottom, waiting to be forgotten. Taking a moment to pause and scrape ensures everything is evenly mixed, giving your batter the best chance to shine in the oven.

Wonderful ways with batter

There's more than one way to whip up the perfect cake, and each method has its own unique character. Here are the main techniques you will find in this book.

Mix and combine

As simple as it gets, this method is used for oil-based cakes such as our carrot cake (page 68). It's a straightforward process: wet ingredients go in one bowl, dry ingredients in another, and then the dry is gently folded into the wet in three additions.

Reverse creaming

Most of the butter-based cakes in this book use the reverse creaming method – a brilliant technique introduced by Rose Levy Beranbaum, author of *The Cake Bible* (1988). This method offers a clever twist on the traditional way of making cake batter and is excellent for achieving cakes with a fine, even crumb. Instead of creaming the butter and sugar first, the process begins by mixing the dry ingredients – sugar, flour and leavening agent. Softened butter and a small amount of liquid are then added, and the mixture is beaten quickly to incorporate air and develop the cake's structure. The remaining liquid and eggs are added in three parts, with each addition starting at low speed and then increasing to high speed to strengthen the structure, ultimately yielding a batter that is light, smooth and custard-like.

INFUSED SUGAR ROCKS!

A brilliant way to pack flavour into your bakes is to infuse your sugar with edible fragrance. The recipes in this book often call for 'vanilla sugar' or 'lemon sugar', which you can make by simply rubbing sugar with vanilla beans or lemon zest. The sugar absorbs the natural oils, drawing out their aroma, and evenly spreads the flavour throughout the mixture.

Whole egg foam

This method gives the delicate, airy texture of a sponge, combined with the rich, buttery flavour of a classic butter cake. It begins with whole eggs and sugar, whipped together until they reach the magical 'ribbon' stage – a process that traps air to create a light and fluffy foundation. Next, the dry ingredients are gently folded in to preserve the airy structure. Finally, warm melted butter and liquid (generally milk or buttermilk and some type of oil) are added, enriching the batter and helping the cake achieve a beautiful rise in the oven.

This technique is used for the brown sugar cake (page 148), as well as the olive oil ricotta cake (page 142).

Ribbon stage

Folding in meringue

Folding meringue into batter is a delicate and essential step in creating light, airy cakes such as the chiffon and sponge cakes in this book. The key is to gently combine the meringue without deflating the air bubbles that will give the cake its signature fluffy texture. Rather than stirring, use a balloon whisk to scoop, lift and fold the mixture over itself until everything is just combined.

Preparing cake tins

Each type of cake requires its tin to be prepared a little differently to ensure it rises perfectly and releases effortlessly. While each recipe will provide specific instructions, here are the key tips to get you started.

Oil- and butter-based cakes

For these simpler cakes, you only need to line the bottom of the tins. Start by thoroughly coating the bottom and the side of the tins with cooking oil spray, then line the base with baking paper, cut to size.

For heart-shaped or square tins, just trace the shape of the tin onto the baking paper and cut the paper to fit. I also like to give the baking paper a light spray of cooking oil afterwards – it makes releasing the cake much easier, especially for rich, delicate cakes such as the sour cream chocolate cake (page 104).

Chiffon and sponge cakes

To help this type of cake rise properly, it needs to cling to the sides of the tin. If you're using an angel food tin, like the kind used for the Thai tea chiffon cake (page 71), there's no need to line or grease it – just make sure it's squeaky clean and completely grease-free.

For chiffon and sponge cakes baked on a sheet pan (jelly roll pan), a little prep goes a long way. Cut a piece of baking paper to fit the bottom of the pan, give it a good spray with cooking oil spray, then pop it onto the sheet pan. Be sure to keep the sides of the tin free from grease so the cake can rise nice and tall!

Bundt cakes

Preparing a bundt tin properly is the secret to getting a perfectly released cake, with all those beautiful details intact. Grease your bundt tin thoroughly (I prefer using softened butter), making sure to cover every nook and cranny. Then lightly dust it with flour, tilting and tapping the tin to coat it evenly. Shake out the excess flour, then pop the tin in the fridge to let the butter firm up while you prepare the batter. With this extra step, your bundt cake will release beautifully every time!

In the oven

In general, it's best to bake in the centre of your oven, wherever possible. Position your oven rack in the centre of the oven so your cake sits evenly between the heat sources, whether they're at the top, bottom, or both. This helps the cake bake evenly, so the top doesn't burn while the middle stays undercooked. Be sure to leave enough space around the tin for air to circulate freely.

If baking a sheet chiffon cake in a conventional oven, place the oven rack in the lower third of the oven. This keeps the heat gentle and helps the cake rise evenly.

If you're baking multiple cakes at the same time, check if you can comfortably fit all the cake tins on one oven rack, ideally before you turn the oven on. If you can't fit them on one rack, you should arrange two oven racks near the centre of the oven, ensuring there are at least two rack levels of space between them.

When baking multiple cakes at once over two oven racks, offset the tins so they're not directly above or below each other, to ensure proper airflow. It's also a good idea to rotate the tins two-thirds of the way through baking – swap the tin position on the racks from top to bottom and turn the tins around from front to back – to help everything bake evenly.

Avoid opening the oven door during the first two-thirds of baking, as the sudden drop in temperature can cause your cake to collapse. You can safely check or rotate the tins once the cake has set, usually about two-thirds of the way through the baking time. When the cake is nearly done, it will release gas as part of the baking process, causing it to deflate slightly in the tin.

Checking your cake is ready

The baking times provided in the recipes are guidelines, as ovens can vary in temperature and performance. To check if your cake is done, gently press the centre – it should spring back when fully baked. If you're using a skewer, insert it into the centre of the cake to a depth of about 1–1.5 cm (½ in), as this is typically the last bit of batter to cook through properly. The skewer should come out clean, or with a few dry crumbs, but it should not have any wet batter on it.

> 'Avoid opening the oven door during the first two-thirds of baking, as the sudden drop in temperature can cause your cake to collapse.'

For chiffon cakes baked in a sheet pan (jelly roll pan) or an angel food cake tin, checking doneness requires a slightly different approach to preserve the cake's delicate structure. Avoid using a skewer, as piercing the cake can damage its airy texture. Instead, gently press the surface in the centre with your finger – the cake should spring back lightly and leave no indentation. Additionally, observe the edges of the cake; they should begin to pull slightly away from the sides of the tin when the cake is fully baked.

Unmoulding your creation

Unmoulding is the pivotal 'reveal all' moment that can quite literally make – or break – your cake! Allow layer cakes and bundt cakes to cool in the tin for about 10 minutes until they feel just warm. Larger cakes and delicate cakes with fragile crumbs, such as the sour cream chocolate cake (page 104), will need a little bit longer in the tin, say an 5 additional minutes. This brief rest gives the cake some time to set, without sticking to the sides. But don't let the cake overstay its welcome! If left in the tin too long, the trapped steam can make the cake edges soggy and overly soft.

To remove your cake, loosen the sides by carefully running a straight palette knife or butter knife around the inside of the tin, then carefully flip the cake onto a cooling rack, and let it cool completely.

Sponge cakes, which are baked at a high temperature and have a delicate texture, should be removed from their tins immediately after coming out of the oven, to avoid overcooking and minimise shrinkage.

For chiffon cakes baked in a sheet pan, allow them to cool completely in the tin to maintain their delicate structure, then loosen the edges and gently lift or flip the cake out. (If you're making a cake roll, you'll need to use a different method – see below.) Chiffon cakes baked in an angel food cake tin will need to cool upside down in the tin for at least 2–3 hours to preserve their airy, delicate texture.

Resting and cooling

Before you dive into frosting or glazing your cake, make sure it's completely cool. Even the slightest residual heat can turn this step into a nightmare. Not only will your cake be too delicate to handle, but the frosting may also melt or slide off. For butter-based cakes, like the Buttermilk vanilla cake on (page 108), allowing enough resting time also gives the crust a chance to soften slightly, resulting in a better texture overall.

A special note on cake rolls. When it comes to cake rolls, such as sponge or chiffon rolls, the cooling process works a little differently. Rolling a cooled cake can lead to cracks, which is something you want to avoid. Instead, pre-roll the cake while it's still warm, using a clean tea towel to help you gently roll it into shape – then allow it to cool completely in that form. This little trick makes rolling the cake up with fillings so much easier later on!

Storing

Delicate cakes, such as chiffon or sponge cakes, are best served on the day you bake them, or the next day, for the freshest taste and texture. However, if you're baking one of the layer cakes in Chapter 3 – especially if you're then planning on using it in one of the decorating projects in Chapter 5 – you may want to prepare the cake layers in advance. The good news is that all of the layer cakes in Chapter 3 can be wrapped in plastic wrap and stored at room temperature for up to 3 days. The even better news is that these cakes freeze beautifully for up to 1 month when stored properly.

To freeze, make sure the cake layers are fully cooled before wrapping each one individually (and untrimmed) in plastic wrap. Lay them flat in the freezer rather than stacking them, as the weight can press them down and affect their texture.

When it's time to defrost, take the wrapped cake layers out of the freezer and let them thaw in the fridge for at least 6 hours or overnight. Keeping them wrapped prevents condensation from forming directly on the cake. Before assembling, place the cakes on the counter for about 30 minutes to bring them to room temperature. Make sure they are completely thawed before decorating, as excess moisture from thawing can affect the buttercream's texture and finish.

THE BRILLIANCE OF BUTTERCREAM

Buttercream lies at the heart of this book – and the type of buttercream you choose will greatly impact the final look, texture and taste of your cake creation.

Buttercream plays two main roles when it comes to building a great cake. First, it binds the different layers together – but it's so much more than just an adhesive. It also provides structure, keeping your other fillings secure between the layers. When chilled, it sets firmly, adding stability to the cake. Different flavours can also be incorporated into the buttercream to complement and enhance the cake and its other components.

The second purpose of buttercream is decoration. Its versatility makes it an essential material for cake artistry. Colours can be added, and the consistency adjusted – soft for a smooth, flawless base, or medium to stiff for piping detailed designs through a nozzle, allowing endless creative possibilities.

Given how much buttercream is used in different parts of a layer cake, it goes without saying that it must be delicious – not overly sweet, but delicately balanced, with a light, buttery richness. Each bite should be as delightful as it looks, ensuring no one is tempted to scrape any buttercream off!

At Mali Bakes, our buttercream of choice is Italian meringue buttercream (IMBC). This magical buttercream – my best friend! – is light, silky and delicately sweet, melting away on your tongue like a dream. Its subtle sweetness and velvety texture make it ideal for cakes that require ample frosting.

IMBC is wonderfully versatile and incredibly stable – it pipes smoothly, holds its shape beautifully, and works brilliantly as a base for fillings, carrying a wide variety of flavours, making it the perfect companion for layer cakes. In my opinion, it outshines its cousin, Swiss meringue buttercream: IMBC is less labour intensive to prepare than Swiss meringue buttercream, which requires whisking egg whites and sugar over a double boiler, and IMBC is also easier to scale up for larger batches.

The following section covers everything you need to know about Italian meringue buttercream – including troubleshooting tips and advice on adjusting the consistency for different uses.

> 'IMBC is wonderfully versatile and incredibly stable – it pipes smoothly, holds its shape beautifully, and works brilliantly as a base for fillings.'

Understanding Italian meringue buttercream

Whether using your IMBC for frosting and layering the layer cakes in Chapter 3, or decorating the project cakes in Chapter 5, here are some useful tips to help you master the perfect IMBC for all the recipes in this book.

Uses for different IMBC consistencies

Understanding buttercream consistency is key to building and decorating layer cakes, as different tasks will require different consistencies. I recommend referring back to this section whenever you're working on a cake or decorating project, especially when starting out on your decorating journey.

Thin consistency. Thin buttercream has a soft, silky and smooth texture that spreads with ease. It holds just enough shape to coat a cake beautifully, but isn't firm enough for intricate piping or detailed decorations. When scooped with a spatula, it falls back into the bowl in soft peaks rather than holding stiff peaks. Thin buttercream isn't the same as melted buttercream. It should still be pliable and easy to work with, but never runny or soupy. **Ideal for** applying frosting, creating a crumb coat and piping delicate leaves.

Medium consistency. Medium buttercream is the most common type used in this book, and for good reason. It has a smooth, creamy texture that's firm enough to hold its shape, without being too stiff. When you lift it with a spatula, it forms soft peaks that gently fold over instead of standing straight or collapsing. It's more stable than thin buttercream, but still soft enough to spread easily or pipe through nozzles. **Ideal for** spreading between cake layers and piping most borders.

Stiff consistency. Stiff buttercream is thick, firm and holds its shape perfectly. When lifted with a spatula, it forms sharp peaks that stand upright without folding or collapsing. It has a dense texture and is less spreadable than the softer consistencies. Despite its firmness, stiff buttercream should still be smooth and creamy, though it requires more effort to work with. **Ideal for** creating a dam between cake layers to hold fillings securely and for piping elements that need to hold their structure, such as buttercream flowers.

Thin consistency 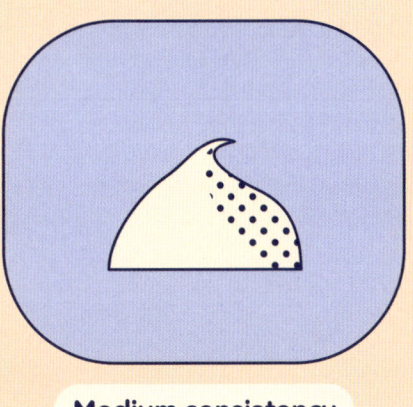 | Medium consistency 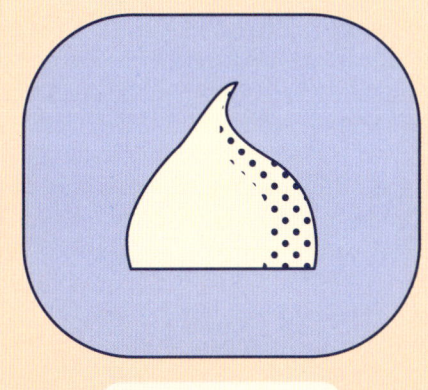 | Stiff consistency

Adjusting your consistency

To thin buttercream. Set up a double boiler by filling a small saucepan with 5 cm (2 in) of water and bringing it to a gentle simmer. Place the buttercream in a heatproof bowl over the water, stirring with a rubber spatula until it reaches the desired consistency. Alternatively, you can use a microwave in 5-second increments, though I find the double boiler method gives you better control.

To firm up buttercream. If you need to firm up buttercream you can simply place it in the fridge until it reaches your preferred consistency. Check it every 30 seconds to 1 minute, depending on the amount of buttercream, and stir it through to prevent the edges from setting hard. This will ensure your buttercream is smooth and lump-free. Alternatively, if you have some extra buttercream in the fridge, simply scoop out small spoonfuls, break them into smaller pieces, add them to the soft buttercream, and whip on high speed until the mixture firms up again. If the buttercream is tinted, be cautious, as adding uncoloured buttercream can alter the shade and make it harder to match.

Air bubbles. When whipped at high speed, air bubbles form in buttercream, which creates a light and airy texture. While this is perfect for fillings, giving them a lovely, light mouthfeel, it's not ideal for decorating. Air bubbles can disrupt the smooth, consistent flow needed for piping and frosting, leaving visible imperfections on the surface of the cake. During piping, these bubbles may cause the buttercream to burst or break mid-flow, making it challenging to achieve clean lines or delicate details (such as drop strings) from a small nozzle. So it's important to ensure your decorating buttercream – whether for frosting or piping – is free of any air bubbles before use.

To remove air bubbles. Whether it's freshly made or made-ahead buttercream, after whipping it on high speed to achieve a light, airy texture, reduce the mixer to the lowest speed and let it run for about 4 minutes. This helps smooth out the buttercream and removes any excess air bubbles. For the best results, make sure the buttercream is at a medium consistency – not too stiff or too soft. You can use the whisk or paddle attachment to do this. Just be careful as prolonged mixing can generate heat and soften the buttercream. If you're only using the buttercream to fill a layer cake in Chapter 3, there's no need to worry about removing the air bubbles!

Re-whipping made-ahead buttercream. If you've prepared the buttercream in advance, it will need a quick re-whip before use. To soften it, microwave the buttercream in 15–30-second bursts, stirring in between, until it just starts to soften, then whip on high speed using a stand mixer for about 30 seconds, until it's light and fluffy again. If you're using it for decorating, don't forget to remove any air bubbles using the above step. (Alternatively, place the buttercream in a heatproof bowl over simmering water, stirring until softened, then whip using the stand mixer.) If the buttercream has been frozen, thaw it overnight in the fridge before softening and re-whipping.

> *'The key is to stay observant. Watch how the ingredients transform.'*

Rescuing over-melted buttercream. If your buttercream has completely melted into a soupy mixture, you may notice the fat and liquid separating. To fix this, you will need to incorporate some cold buttercream into the melted buttercream. Break some cold buttercream into small pieces and mix it into the melted batch, then whip immediately to bring it back together to a smooth, creamy consistency. Avoid placing the melted buttercream in the fridge, as chilling can cause the separated fat to solidify, resulting in a gritty texture that may affect your final decoration.

If you don't have any spare buttercream on hand, unfortunately, there's not much that can be done. To prevent this from happening, always warm up buttercream in small amounts and use short intervals if microwaving to avoid overheating.

Mastering Italian meringue buttercream

Creating the perfect Italian meringue buttercream requires precision and rhythm. Sugar syrup needs to be heated to just the right temperature while egg whites are whipped to soft, airy peaks. The syrup, poured into the beaten egg whites in a steady, deliberate stream, transforms the whites into a glossy meringue. Once cooled, softened butter is vigorously whisked in, creating the smoothest, most luxurious buttercream imaginable.

The key is to stay observant. Watch how the ingredients transform – the egg whites go from loose, frothy bubbles to a finer foam, and finally, to peaks. Similarly, the sugar syrup starts bubbling rapidly, then slows down as the water evaporates and the bubbles become steadier as the temperature rises. Understanding these subtle changes makes the process much easier.

Before you start

Use fresh chilled egg whites. To achieve the lightest, fluffiest buttercream, steer clear of pre-cracked egg whites sold in convenience packs – fresh eggs create the best meringue. The buttercream recipes in this book call for chilled egg whites instead of the traditional room-temperature ones. While chilled egg whites whip more slowly, they create a much more stable meringue and help prevent over-whipping.

Have your butter at room temperature. The butter should be softened to a pliable consistency without becoming greasy or overly soft. The ideal texture is soft and slightly squishy, with a temperature between 20°C and 22°C (68°F and 72°F).

Clean your mixing bowl and saucepan. Both need to be squeaky clean and completely free of grease. Even a tiny bit of grease can stop your meringue from whipping up properly, and a greasy saucepan can cause your sugar syrup to crystallise. I like to play it safe by giving everything a quick wipe with a little vinegar before I start making my buttercream.

Choose a saucepan that is deep enough. You want the syrup to pool deeply so you can get an accurate temperature reading. A saucepan that's 12–15 cm (4¾–6 in) wide and 8–10 cm (3¼–4 in) deep is perfect.

Have a thermometer handy. An instant-read digital thermometer is highly recommended for its quick and accurate readings, making it much easier to use than a traditional sugar thermometer. When measuring the temperature, be sure to hold the thermometer in the centre of the sugar syrup, avoiding contact with the bottom or side of the pan, as these areas will be significantly hotter.

Keep everything close by. Position your stand mixer close to the stovetop so you can quickly and easily pour the sugar syrup into the beaten egg whites as soon as the syrup reaches 115°C (240°F).

Some notes on whisking and egg white stages

The goal is always to add the sugar syrup just as your egg whites reach soft peaks. But if that doesn't quite happen, don't worry – there's no need to throw everything away! As long as the whites aren't over-whipped to the point of separating, or under-whipped with liquid egg still remaining, you can still go ahead.

If the sugar syrup is ready but the egg whites haven't quite reached soft peaks, start pouring in the sugar syrup as slowly as possible, pausing briefly to allow the peaks to develop before gradually increasing the pouring rate. If the whites are nearly at stiff peaks, add the sugar syrup more quickly to ensure it fully incorporates before the whites become over-whipped.

Never stop whisking the whites. Never completely stop the mixer while whisking egg whites, as this will cause the air bubbles to collapse and the proteins to separate, making it nearly impossible to whip everything back up again. Instead, adjust the speed up or down.

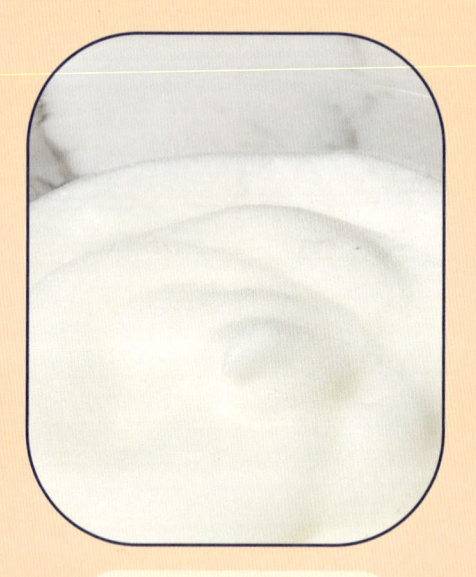

❶ **Foamy whites with small bubbles**

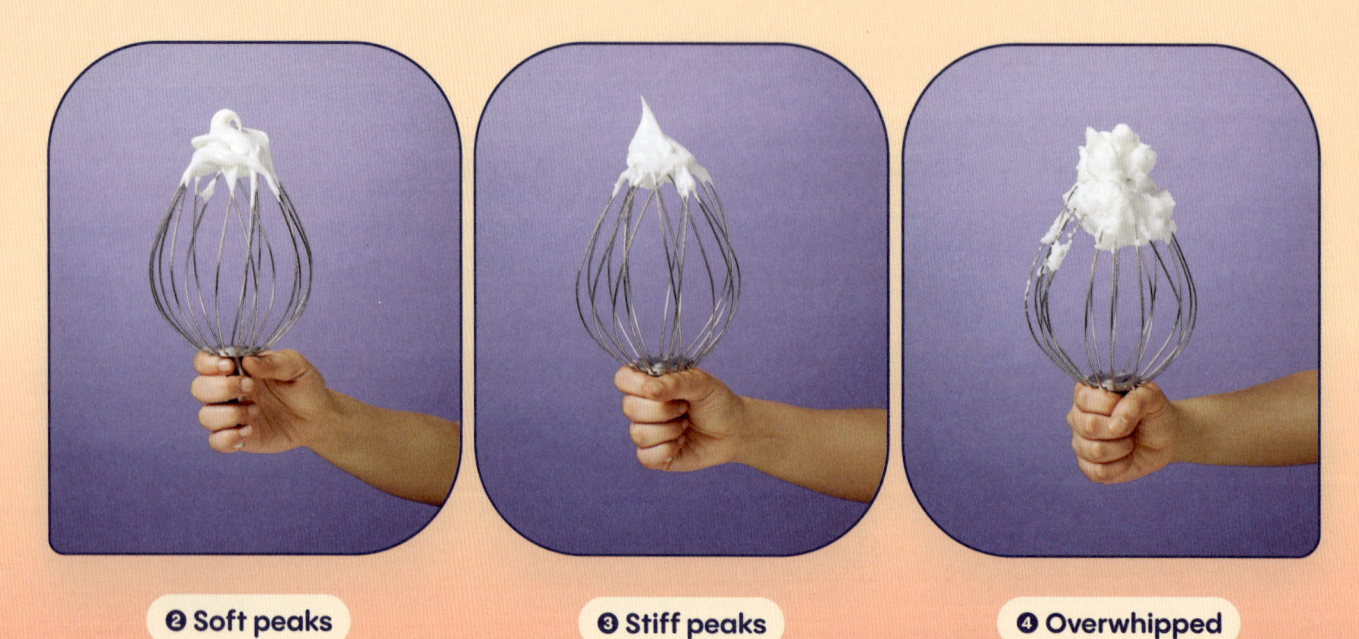

❷ **Soft peaks** ❸ **Stiff peaks** ❹ **Overwhipped**

MALI BAKES

Italian meringue buttercream

Makes: 1250 g (44.09 oz)
Store: Refrigerate for 1 week, or freeze for 3 months

This vanilla-flavoured buttercream recipe is specifically used for the decorating projects in Chapter 5 — but the same basic method is the basis for all the flavoured buttercreams in Chapter 3.

While each decorating project will specify the amount of buttercream you need, I recommend making a full batch rather than halving or dividing the recipe. Any leftover buttercream can be frozen and kept ready for your next creation — it's always handy to have some on standby!

You will need a stand mixer bowl with a capacity of at least 4.7 litres (159 fl oz) to make this quantity of buttercream. It's important to avoid the buttercream rising above the whisk, as this will prevent the meringue from being whipped properly.

250 g (8.82 oz) egg whites, chilled (about 8 eggs)
5 g (1 teaspoon) fine sea salt
4 g (1 teaspoon) cream of tartar
120 g (4.23 oz) water
360 g (12.7 oz) caster (superfine) sugar
650 g (23 oz) unsalted butter, cubed
5 g (1 teaspoon) vanilla extract

Weigh and prep all your ingredients. Things move quickly when making buttercream, so have all your ingredients weighed and ready to go. Place your chilled egg whites in the bowl of a stand mixer, along with the salt and cream of tartar. Place the bowl in the fridge to chill for at least 15 minutes.

Set up your sugar syrup pot. Pour the water into a saucepan, then add the sugar. Gently stir until all the sugar is evenly moistened, making sure there are no dry spots that could cause crystallisation. Use a damp pastry brush to wipe down the side of the saucepan, removing any stray sugar granules. Place the saucepan on the stovetop, ready to heat, and have an instant-read digital thermometer ready.

Start whisking the egg whites. Attach the mixing bowl to the stand mixer and begin whisking the egg whites on medium speed. Whisk until the whites turn foamy with small bubbles forming (see image 1, opposite) this should take about 2–3 minutes. Once the egg whites have reached this stage, begin heating the sugar syrup while keeping the mixer running.

Start warming the sugar syrup. Cook the sugar syrup over medium–high heat until it reaches 115°C (240°F) — keep the thermometer centred in the syrup, avoiding the saucepan's sides or bottom for an accurate temperature reading. The syrup should take about 3–4 minutes to reach the right temperature.

Once the syrup is on the heat, don't stir it — this can cause crystallisation. If you see the sugar cooking unevenly, use the pan handle to gently swirl the saucepan to even things out. At first, the bubbles will be small and fast as the water evaporates; as the syrup cooks, the bubbles will get larger and slow down. When the bubbles start to move evenly across the surface of the saucepan it's a sign the syrup is cooking properly.

Once the syrup reaches 115°C (240°F), immediately remove the saucepan from the heat.

MALI BAKES

Add the sugar syrup to the whipped whites. When the sugar syrup is ready, the egg whites should be at the soft peak stage, with fine, smooth bubbles (see image 2 on page 42). Increase the mixer speed to high, then slowly pour the hot syrup into the meringue, beginning with a thin stream and gradually increasing the flow. Aim to pour the syrup between the side of the bowl and the whisk to prevent splattering. Use a heatproof spatula to scrape any remaining syrup into the egg whites.

Whisk to stiff peaks. Keep whisking the meringue on high speed for another 6–7 minutes as it cools slightly. It should turn glossy and hold stiff peaks (image 3 on page 42). When you touch the side of the bowl, it should feel warm, not hot. The meringue should be about 35°C (95°F), which means it's ready for the butter to go in. Keep whisking if the meringue still feels too warm. If the bowl starts to feel too full, you can turn the speed down slightly – but only after the meringue has reached stiff peaks. If the meringue cools too much, the butter won't blend in and may leave visible flecks. If the meringue is too warm, the mixture will become soupy.

Add the butter. While mixing on high speed, gradually add the softened butter cubes one at a time, ensuring each cube is fully incorporated into the meringue before adding the next (I count to five between additions). Once all the butter is incorporated, continue beating for 3–4 minutes, until the buttercream changes from a pale yellow to a creamy white, and slightly increases in volume. This is where the magic happens – air is whipped into the butter, creating a beautifully light and airy buttercream.

If making IMBC for the layer cakes in Chapter 3

Add any flavours. Once the buttercream is whipped to a silky and airy consistency, it's ready for any buttercream flavourings used in the individual cake recipes in this book. Make sure everything you add is at room temperature so it mixes in easily. If you're using chocolate, melt and stir until smooth and let it cool to room temperature – you don't want to be adding anything with lumps or heat. For caramel, let it cool completely before adding it to the buttercream.

If making IMBC for the decorating projects in Chapter 5

Add the vanilla and remove air bubbles. Add the vanilla and continue mixing on high speed until fully incorporated (about 10 seconds), then reduce the mixer speed to its lowest setting and let it run for at least 4 minutes. This final step smooths out the buttercream, leaving it glossy, shiny and completely free of air bubbles – ideal for decorating. However, be mindful not to leave it mixing for too long, as extended mixing can generate heat, which might soften your buttercream.

> **TIP**
>
> If your mixer is quite full as you're about to add the butter, you can lower the speed to medium as you add one piece of softened butter at a time.
>
> Once all the butter has been added, turn the speed up to high to whip everything together.

Storing IMBC

If you're making buttercream ahead of time, store it in an airtight container – I prefer this over wrapping it in plastic wrap since it's one less single-use item to throw away! IMBC will keep in the fridge for up to 1 week.

For longer storage, you can freeze it right away for up to 3 months. When you're ready to use it, thaw the buttercream in the fridge for at least 8 hours or overnight, then follow the instructions on page 40 for re-whipping made-ahead buttercream. Once defrosted, do not freeze again.

Troubleshooting

If your buttercream appears to be splitting. This is likely because the mixture has cooled down too much. Don't panic – just keep mixing and it will often come back together. If it doesn't, set up a double boiler by bringing water to a simmer in a large saucepan. Place the mixing bowl over the simmering water for about 30 seconds, allowing the buttercream at the bottom to soften slightly. Return the bowl to the stand mixer and whisk on high speed; the mixture should whip back up into a smooth, glossy consistency.

If your buttercream becomes soupy. Briefly chill the buttercream in the fridge to allow it to firm up, then whip again. Alternatively, you can gradually add small pieces of room-temperature butter until the mixture regains its perfect consistency. However, keep in mind that adding extra butter will alter the ratio of the recipe, which might result in the buttercream having a heavier mouthfeel than intended.

ALL THINGS CAKE

BRINGING IT ALL TOGETHER

A great layer cake should never feel monotonous – each bite should bring something new, with different textures and flavours to enjoy. In my opinion, the perfect layer cake consists of at least three layers of cake, with just the right thickness: not too thick, not too thin. Adding a 'soak', either milk- or simple syrup-based, keeps the cake moist and adds an extra layer of flavour. The perfect layer cake should also include at least two delicious fillings – think curds, jams, whipped mascarpone, or even a satisfying crunch from crumbs – and a beautiful buttercream to seamlessly bind all those gorgeous layers and flavours together.

How to assemble a layer cake

The following step-by-step guide will help you build the perfect layer cake. This is the process that you will follow when making any of the layer cake recipes in Chapter 3, or the decorating projects in Chapter 5. For the more elaborate decorating projects that have multiple tiers, turn to pages 174–179 for instructions on stacking tiered cakes.

Set up

Trim the cake. On a flat, level surface, trim the top of each cake layer using a cake leveller set to 2.5 cm (1 in).

Add the soak. Use a pastry brush or squeeze bottle to generously apply your chosen soak to the exposed crumb side of each layer. Be careful not to overdo it – applying too much soak can make the cake soggy.

Let's begin!

Set up the first layer. Place a cake board in the centre of your turntable, with a non-slip mat underneath the board to keep it steady. Using a cake spatula, add a small dollop of buttercream to the centre of the board to act as an adhesive to anchor the cake in place. Position the first cake layer in the centre of the board with the cut side facing up.

(If you are building a layer cake intended to be an upper tier of a tiered design – like some of the decorating projects in Chapter 5 – assemble the layer cake on a perforated cake board set on a temporary cake board. For more on this, see page 175.)

Spread the first layer with buttercream. Add a generous dollop of buttercream and spread it evenly with an angled palette knife, using broad strokes while rotating the turntable. Smooth the surface by holding the palette knife parallel to the cake, with the edge lightly touching. Rotate the turntable with slight speed until the top is smooth and the buttercream is about 5 mm (¼ in) thick.

You'll need

Your chosen layer cakes (completely cooled); soak; fillings and buttercream

Cake leveller

Pastry brush or squeeze bottle

Cake board (perforated if being used as the upper tier of a tiered design)

Turntable and non-slip mat

Spatula

Angled (offset) palette knife

Piping bag

ALL THINGS CAKE 49

Create a dam. Fill a piping bag with buttercream and cut an opening about 2 cm (¾ in) wide at the tip of the bag. Pipe a continuous, unbroken ring of buttercream around the top edge of the cake to create a 'dam' to help contain the filling. Note that it's best to use buttercream with a medium-to-thick consistency for this (see page 39)

Add the filling. Spread the filling evenly within the buttercream dam, taking care not to overfill, to ensure the cake layers remain stable. If your cake includes multiple fillings, start with the softest, such as jam or curd, and sprinkle any crumbs the recipe calls for (such as brown butter crumbs or sesame crumbs) on top. Whipped mascarpone is best piped in small dollops after spreading the jam.

If a jam or fruit filling contains excess liquid, strain it slightly beforehand to prevent the cake becoming soggy, or the filling from spilling excessively when sliced.

Add the next cake layer and leave to set. Place the second cake layer on top, with the cut surface facing up, pressing gently to ensure the cake adheres properly. Quickly check that the layer is level and aligned straight. Use a straight palette knife to smooth out any excess buttercream from the sides of the cake, as the buttercream will firm up when chilled. Refrigerate the cake for about 10 minutes, or freeze for about 5 minutes, to set the layers.

Repeat this process for the remaining layers. Spread a layer of buttercream, pipe a dam, and add the filling for each additional layer.

For the lower layers, always position the exposed crumb side facing up, while the top layer should be placed with the baked surface facing up. This ensures you will have a flat, smooth surface for the top of your cake.

Apply a crumb coating. Once all the cake layers are assembled and set, apply a thin layer of buttercream all over the cake surface to seal in any loose crumbs – this process is called 'crumb coating'. Use the same techniques as described on pages 53–54 for frosting, but apply a much thinner layer here and don't worry too much about perfection. The goal is simply to lock in any loose crumbs. Allow the crumb coat to fully set in the fridge for at least 10 minutes before moving on to frosting your cake.

Next steps

Now you're ready to frost your cake and create a smooth, even finish. The following pages will walk you through all the tips and tricks you'll need to get it just right.

If you're moving on to one of the decorating projects in Chapter 5, use the plain vanilla Italian meringue buttercream recipe on page 43 to frost the cake as each project indicates.

If you prefer to keep it simple and aren't continuing with a project, you can simply use the remaining flavoured buttercream you used to fill the cake to frost and finish it.

How to frost your cakes and create smooth finishes

Every beautiful cake begins with a smooth, flawless base – a blank canvas ready for your decorations. Depending on the shape of the cake you are working with, you might need to use slightly different techniques. Round cakes are the easiest to frost, since the turntable allows you to rotate the cake smoothly, making it simple to get an even finish. But when it comes to heart-shaped, square or rectangular cakes, you'll need a bit more finesse, especially when working around those tricky corners and curves and making sure that the cake is perfectly symmetrical. This section will guide you through the best way to approach each of these shapes.

You'll need

- A crumb-coated cake
- Your chosen buttercream
- Angled (offset) palette knife
- Straight palette knife
- A scraper that is taller than the cake height (stainless steel works best)
- Bench scraper with plastic handle (for top scrapping, optional)
- Heatproof container or jug, taller than the scraper (for holding warm water)
- Turntable and non-slip mat

Set up

Crumb coat your cake (see opposite) and let it set in the fridge. Check the buttercream has set by gently touching it – if no buttercream sticks to your finger, your cake is ready for frosting.

Adjust your buttercream consistency. Make sure your buttercream is smooth, free of bubbles, and has a thin but spreadable consistency. See page 40 for detailed instructions on removing air bubbles and page 39 for adjusting the buttercream consistency.

Set up your tools. Keep your tools in a heatproof container filled with warm water. The warm water helps keep them clean and allows the frosting to glide onto your cake more smoothly, resulting in a better finish. Make sure your scraper is the right height – just slightly taller than your cake for better control (not too tall, and definitely not shorter). Check that your scraper is free of scratches, as any marks can show up on your final finish.

You want to work quickly when frosting your cake, as frosting sets fast on a cold cake from the fridge and may cause a patchy finish.

Centre the cake on the turntable. Your cake should be perfectly centred on the turntable, with a non-slip mat between the cake board and turntable to keep everything steady and secure.

Let's begin!

Now that you're all set up, you're ready to begin frosting your layer cake. The following pages will take you through the steps to frost the common cake shapes you will encounter in this book.

MALI BAKES

To frost a round cake

Start with the top surface. Place two generous dollops of buttercream on the top surface. Use a warm, dry, angled palette knife to spread the buttercream evenly across the top with broad front-and-back strokes while rotating the turntable with your other hand. Once evenly distributed, smooth out the top by holding the palette knife parallel to the cake with the edge closest to you just touching the cake surface and the other side slightly raised. Rotate the turntable with slight speed with your other hand until the top is smooth. Allow the buttercream to extend slightly over the edge.

Frost the sides. Once the top is smooth, begin working on the side using a straight palette knife. Hold the palette knife parallel to the cake, keeping it as straight as possible, and use long, even strokes to spread the buttercream around the side. Add more buttercream as needed.

Smooth the side. Once the side is fully covered, hold a warm, dry scraper parallel to the cake's side, with its bottom edge resting on the cake board. Keep your hand steady and slowly rotate the turntable with your other hand in a smooth motion. This will evenly smooth the buttercream on the side. After a few rotations, carefully lift the scraper away to avoid creating marks or uneven spots.

Fill any gaps. If you see any air bubbles or gaps, use a straight palette knife to add more buttercream as needed. Then, smooth the side again with a warm, dry scraper. Repeat until the cake is perfectly smooth.

If you are not going ahead with any of the decorating projects in Chapter 5, feel free to skip the following two steps and simply finish the cake with beautiful, natural ridges on top!

Smooth out the top edge. To remove excess buttercream on the top, hold the warm, dry scraper horizontally and level with the top surface of the cake. Gently drag the buttercream inward in one confident stroke, working your way around the cake. After each stroke, use the palette knife to scrape off any excess buttercream from the scraper.

Final scrape. If you notice slight dips or unevenness along the top edge, carefully scrape the side again with gentle pressure as a final scrape.

Clean the cake board. Use a damp, clean paper towel wrapped around your finger to wipe any excess buttercream off the cake board.

To frost a heart-shaped cake

Start with the sides. Fill your piping bag with buttercream and cut an opening about 1.5 cm (½ in) wide. Pipe the buttercream evenly around the sides of the cake, working from the bottom to the top while rotating the turntable with your other hand. Focus on creating an even layer of buttercream to establish a symmetrical heart shape, leaving the top uncovered for now. Starting with the sides ensures the heart shape is perfectly symmetrical without over-applying frosting.

Smooth the sides and define the front corner. Once the sides are fully covered, smooth them using a warm, dry scraper. Start at the back centre curve and scrape toward the pointed front of the heart, letting the buttercream extend slightly over. To refine this front corner, guide the buttercream around it with the scraper, then scrape towards the back centre curve again on the opposite side.

Fill the gaps and ensure symmetry. Check if both sides of the heart are symmetrical, adding more buttercream if needed. Fill any areas with air bubbles or gaps and repeat the smoothing step.

Frost the top. Once the sides are perfectly smooth, add a generous dollop of buttercream to the top and follow the same smoothing technique used for a round cake.

Smooth out the top edge. After finishing the top, some excess buttercream may extend over the edges. Use a warm, dry scraper to gently scrape the sides, moving the excess buttercream upwards. Begin again at the back centre curve and scrape towards the pointed front, then from the pointed front back towards the back centre curve again on the opposite side. For the top surface, apply the inward scraping technique used for a round cake to neatly finish the edges. (If you are not going ahead with the decorating projects in Chapter 5, feel free to skip this last step and finish the cake with beautiful, natural ridges on top!)

Final scrape. If you notice slight dips or unevenness along the top edges, carefully scrape the sides again with gentle pressure, working in the same order – back to front and front to back.

To frost a square or rectangular cake

Using a similar technique to a heart-shaped cake, begin by applying an even layer of buttercream to each side of the cake, leaving the top uncovered for now. Smooth each side from one corner to the next, allowing the buttercream to extend slightly over the edges. Carefully guide the buttercream around each corner, smoothing the next side as you go. Repeat for all four sides, ensuring crisp, clean edges and an even coat of frosting on all sides.

Once the sides are neatly frosted, follow the steps outlined for the heart-shaped cake to finish the top and smooth out the top edge.

ALL THINGS CAKE

55

Finishing touches

Once you have perfectly smoothed out your frosting you can decorate the cake however you prefer – perhaps with edible fresh flowers or seasonal fruits for a simple, beautiful finish. You can also follow the instructions for one of the decorating projects in Chapter 5 of this book.

Creating a raked finish

Some cake designs look fantastic with a textured base, which you can easily create using a rake or buttercream comb – a plastic scraper with teeth on one side. Do this immediately after frosting the cake, while the buttercream is still soft.

Hold the rake scraper firmly, positioning the toothed edge parallel to the side of the cake while resting the bottom of the scraper on the cake board. Gently press the scraper against the frosting and follow one of the methods below.

As you work, the scraper will create a continuous pattern around the sides. Keep the scraper steady and at a consistent height to avoid uneven lines. Once finished, carefully lift the scraper away. If you notice any imperfections, lightly go over the pattern again to fix them.

- **Round cake.** Rotate the cake smoothly on the turntable.
- **Heart-shaped cake.** Start from the back curve, move towards the pointed front, then from the pointed front to the back curve on the other side.
- **Square cake or rectangular cakes.** Work on one side at a time.

ALL THINGS CAKE 57

Not every cake needs layers or frills to make an impression. Sometimes, it's the quiet confidence of a perfectly baked sponge, the golden crust of a bundt, or the shine of caramel on an upside-down cake that speaks the loudest.

This chapter is a celebration of cakes in their purest form — they're recipes that don't rely on elaborate decorations, but instead highlight texture, technique and flavour. They offer something a little bit different from what a layer cake does.

Chiffons, sponges, loafs, bundts, cheesecakes, roll cakes — each one plays by its own rules. Some batters want to be handled gently, barely stirred. Others need air whipped in at just the right moment, or a folding technique so specific it almost becomes muscle memory. You start to recognise the signals: the gloss on a meringue at medium peaks; the tension in one that's gone stiff. A chiffon will thank you for restraint, a sponge wants structure and lift. Then there are cakes that rely on calm — like a Japanese cotton cheesecake or Vietnamese coffee flan cake — baked low and slow in a water bath, coaxed into that perfectly-set, custardy texture.

You don't master these cakes by chance. You master them by paying close attention, getting it wrong, and trying again with a little more understanding each time. They ask for care, patience and a light touch — but when they come out right, there's nothing more satisfying.

This section is where these lessons will come together. These are the cakes I return to often — not because they're the simplest (though some are), but because they feel honest. They stand on their own — and that's the beauty of them.

Simple Finish Cakes

Coconut dream cake

MAKES: 1 × 23 cm (9 in) cake
SERVES: 8–10
STORE: at room temperature for up to 3 days

Drømmekage, or Danish dream cake, is adored for its soft, fluffy sponge and irresistible caramelised coconut topping. My version puts a spin on tradition by making it gluten free and pairing it with a tender almond cake base for a subtle nuttiness that complements the coconut beautifully.

ALMOND CAKE
190 g (6.7 oz) unsalted butter, cubed
190 g (6.7 oz) caster (superfine) sugar
260 g (9.17 oz) almond flour
5 g (1 teaspoon) baking powder
2 g (¼ teaspoon) fine sea salt
250 g (8.82 oz) eggs (about 5 eggs)
4 g (1 teaspoon) vanilla extract

COCONUT TOPPING
75 g (2.65 oz) unsalted butter, cubed
75 g (2.65 oz) brown sugar
75 g (2.65 oz) coconut sugar
50 g (1.75 oz) full-cream (whole) milk
2 g (¼ teaspoon) fine sea salt
50 g (1.75 oz) shredded coconut
60 g (2.17 oz) desiccated coconut

Make the cake batter

Preheat your oven and prepare the tin. Preheat the oven to 200°C (400°F) and position an oven rack in the centre of the oven. Thoroughly spray a round 23 cm (9 in) cake tin with cooking oil and line the bottom and side with baking paper.

Cream the butter and sugar. In the bowl of a stand mixer fitted with the paddle attachment, beat the butter and sugar on medium speed for 7 minutes, or until pale and fluffy. Scrape down the side and bottom of the bowl halfway through.

Prepare the dry and wet ingredients. In a small bowl, whisk together the almond flour, baking powder and salt until evenly combined. In another small bowl, lightly whisk the eggs and vanilla extract.

Alternate the wet and dry ingredients. Start by adding one-third of the egg mixture to the butter and beat on medium speed until just combined. Stop the mixer, add one-third of the almond flour mixture, and mix again until just combined. Repeat until all ingredients are incorporated, scraping down the side and bottom of the bowl between each addition.

Bake the cake

Fill the tin and bake. Pour the batter into the cake tin and smooth the top with an angled (offset) palette knife. Bake for 40–45 minutes, until just cooked, rotating the tin after 30 minutes so it cooks evenly. A skewer inserted into the centre should come out with a few damp crumbs.

Combine the coconut topping ingredients. Just before the cake is ready, combine the butter in a saucepan with both sugars, milk and salt. Stir constantly over medium–high heat until the sugar has dissolved, then cook for 1 more minute, until slightly thickened. Stir in both coconuts, ensuring they are evenly coated in the butter mixture.

Add the topping and bake again. When the cake looks set and dry on top, with no glossy patches, it's ready for the topping. Remove the tin from the oven and pour the coconut topping over, smoothing it with an angled (offset) palette knife. Return to the oven and bake for another 10–15 minutes, or until the topping has caramelised.

Remove from the oven. Let the cake cool in the tin for about 1 hour.

Turn out and serve. Place a plate over the cake tin and carefully invert the cake onto it. Remove the baking paper. Place a serving plate on top and flip the cake again so the coconut topping is facing up. Serve warm or at room temperature.

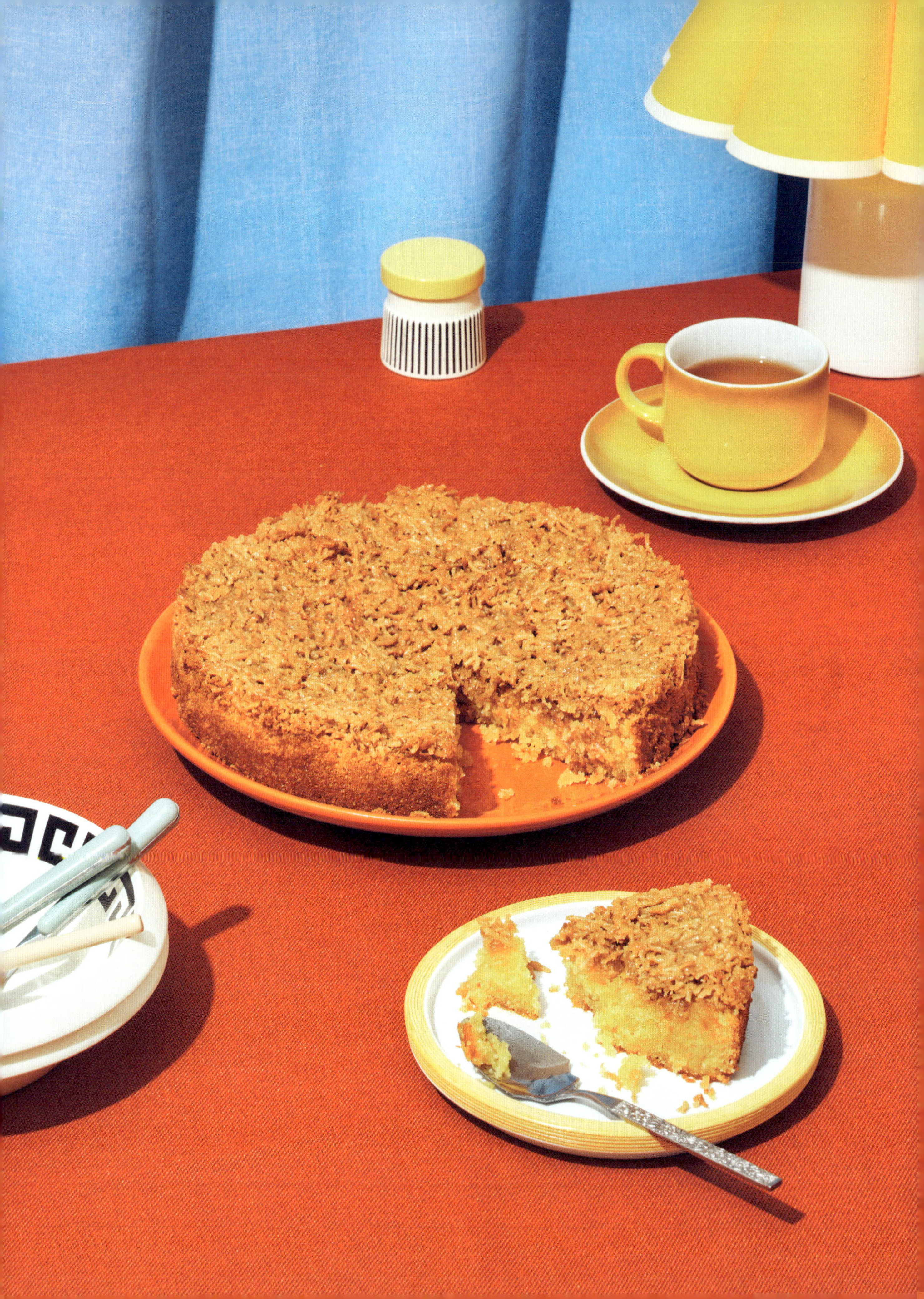

Ginger & black sesame swirl cake

MAKES: 1 × 23 cm (9 in) bundt cake
SERVES: 8–12
STORE: at room temperature for up to 3 days

I've always had a complicated relationship with black sesame in cakes. The flavour can be intense, even overpowering. So, I wondered, what if I paired it with something just as bold? A tender, fragrant ginger cake, marbled with a rich black sesame swirl and finished with a drizzle of ginger glaze. Fresh ginger is the heart of this cake – it brings a subtle yet punchy spice that lingers beautifully. It's the kind of cake I'd happily enjoy for breakfast, lunch and dinner ... and a cheeky midnight snack, too!

BLACK SESAME SWIRL
40 g (1.41 oz) black sesame seeds
20 g (0.7 oz) egg white
20 g (0.7 oz) vegetable oil
30 g (1.06 oz) brown sugar

GINGER CAKE
80 g (2.82 oz) caster (superfine) sugar
60 g (2.17 oz) brown sugar
20 g (0.7 oz) finely grated ginger
200 g (7 oz) plain (all-purpose) flour, plus extra for dusting the tin
40 g (1.41 oz) cornflour (corn starch)
12 g (2½ teaspoons) baking powder
6 g (1 teaspoon) bicarbonate of soda (baking soda)
3 g (½ teaspoon) fine sea salt
100 g (3.5 oz) eggs (about 2 eggs)
200 g (7 oz) buttermilk
150 g (5.3 oz) unsalted butter, cubed, plus extra for greasing the tin

INGREDIENTS LIST CONTINUES →

Get ready to bake

Preheat your oven and prepare the tin. Preheat the oven to 160°C (320°F) and position an oven rack in the centre of the oven. Prepare a 23 cm (9 in) bundt tin by giving the inside a thorough brush with softened butter, making sure to get into all the little crevices. Sprinkle in a handful of flour, then tilt and shake the tin to coat it evenly. Gently tap the tin on the counter to knock out any excess flour. Pop the tin in the fridge until needed – this helps keep the butter nice and firm for an easy cake release later on.

Prepare the black sesame swirl

Toast and grind the sesame seeds. Place a large dry frying pan over medium heat and toast the black sesame seeds, stirring constantly, for 3–4 minutes, until a few seeds start to pop. Remove from the heat. Measure out 30 g (1.06 oz) of the toasted seeds and grind them using a spice grinder or mortar and pestle until they reach a sandy paste consistency. Keep the remaining seeds whole for garnishing the cake.

Add the other ingredients. Transfer the cooled black sesame paste to a bowl. Add the egg white, vegetable oil and brown sugar and whisk together until smooth and well combined. Set aside.

Make the cake

Combine the dry ingredients. In the bowl of a stand mixer, combine the caster sugar, brown sugar and ginger. Using your fingertips, rub the mixture together until the ginger is evenly distributed and the sugar is infused with its aroma. Sift in the flour, cornflour, baking powder, bicarbonate of soda and salt. Using the paddle attachment, mx on low speed for 1 minute, or until everything is evenly combined.

Mix the eggs with a bit of buttermilk. In a bowl, whisk together the eggs and one-third of the buttermilk, then set aside.

Add the butter and buttermilk to the dry ingredients. Add the butter and the remaining buttermilk to the flour mixture. Mix on low speed for about 1 minute, until just evenly moistened. Increase the speed to medium and mix for another minute, until the mixture comes together and becomes slightly paler.

Recipe continues

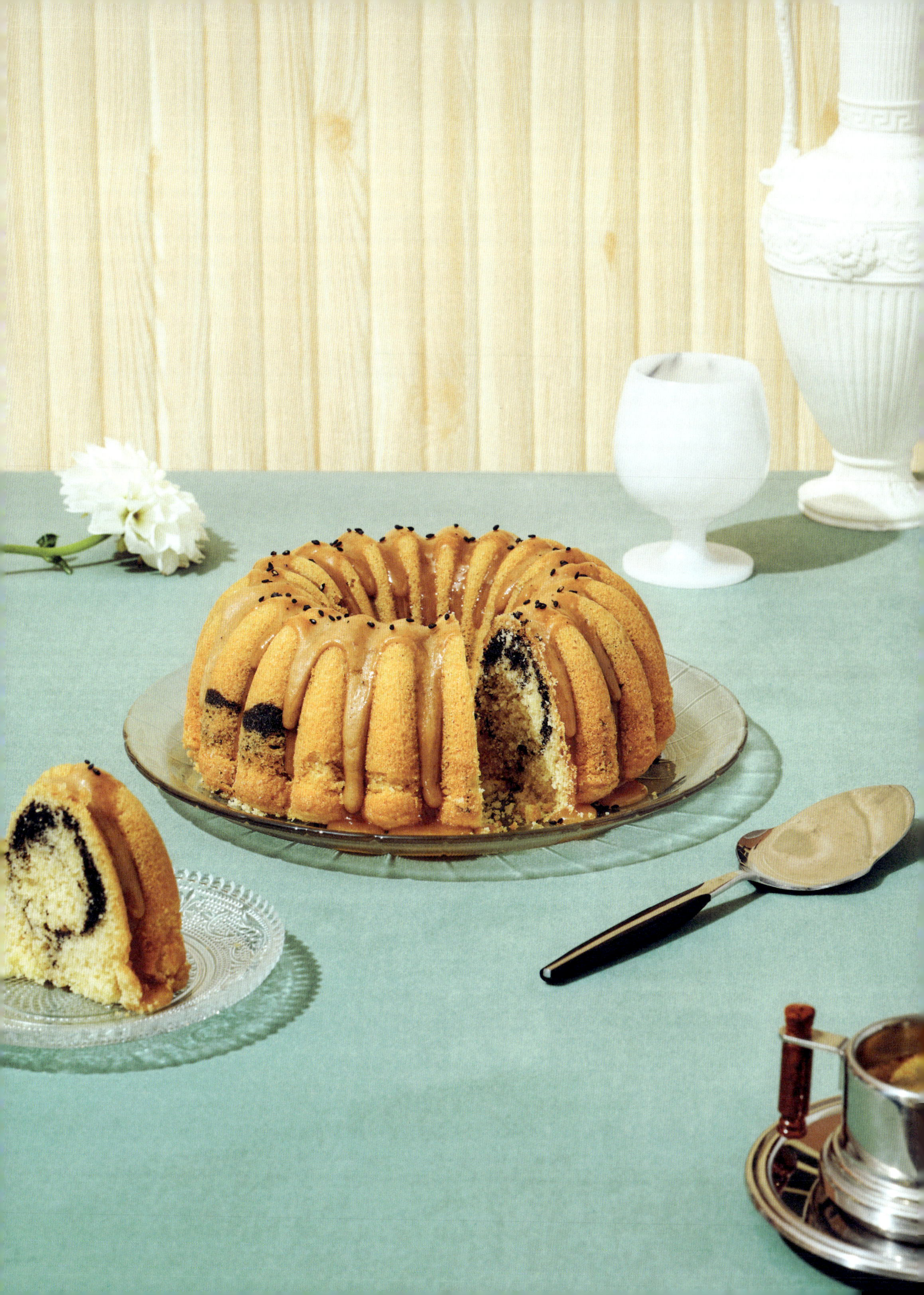

GINGER GLAZE
90 g (3.17 oz) fresh ginger, peeled
60 g (2.17 oz) unsalted butter, cubed
50 g (1.75 oz) brown sugar
2 g (¼ teaspoon) fine sea salt
15 g (0.53 oz) full-cream (whole) milk
80 g (2.82 oz) icing (confectioners') sugar, sifted

Add the remaining wet ingredients. Add the egg mixture in three additions. Start each addition by mixing on low speed, then pour the wet mixture in a thin stream until it begins to combine. Increase the speed to medium–high and mix for about 5 seconds until fully incorporated. After each addition, scrape down the side and bottom of the bowl, as well as the paddle attachment. The batter should be smooth, thick and have a custard-like consistency.

Fill the tin. Pour half the batter, or about 450 g (15.88 oz), into the bundt tin and smooth the surface. Using a teaspoon, spoon half the sesame swirl mixture in small dollops over the batter. Pour over half the remaining batter, covering the dollops, and smooth the surface again. Repeat with the remaining sesame swirl, and finish with a final layer of batter.

Add the swirl. Use a skewer to gently swirl the batter in a circular motion to create a marbled effect. Tap the tin on the counter a few times to release any large air pockets.

Transfer to the oven. Bake for 30–35 minutes, or until a skewer inserted into the centre comes out clean, or the cake springs back when gently pressed in the middle. Rotate the tin from front to back after 25 minutes to ensure even baking.

Let cool, then turn out of the tin. Lightly spray a cooling rack with cooking oil. Let the cake cool in the tin for about 10 minutes, until just warm to the touch. To turn it out, place the rack on top of the tin, then gently flip it over. If the cake doesn't release right away, give the tin a gentle tap on the counter. Once released, leave the cake to cool completely on the rack for at least 2 hours.

Prepare the ginger glaze

Juice the ginger. Grate the peeled ginger and wrap in a piece of cheesecloth (muslin). Squeeze out as much of the juice as possible into a small bowl. You should end up with about 40 g (1.41 oz) juice.

Brown the butter. In a small saucepan, melt the butter over medium heat, then continue cooking for 5–8 minutes, stirring constantly. Once the butter starts to foam, use a heatproof spatula to scrape the bottom of the pan to prevent burning. The butter is ready when it develops a nutty aroma and the milk solids turn golden brown. Remove from the heat and leave to cool slightly for about 10 minutes.

Combine the glaze ingredients. Add the ginger juice, brown sugar, salt and milk to the brown butter and whisk to combine. Place the saucepan back over medium heat and bring to a gentle boil, whisking constantly until the sugar dissolves. Stir in the sifted icing sugar and cook over medium heat for another 4–5 minutes, until the mixture thickens.

Glaze and decorate the cake

Glaze the cake. Place the cooled cake on a serving plate. While the glaze is still warm, pour it over the top of the cake, letting it drip naturally down the sides. Sprinkle the reserved black sesame seeds on top.

Slice and serve. Serve at room temperature, cut into portions.

Cherry chip poppyseed & toasted rye crumble cake

MAKES: 1 × 20 cm (8 in) loaf cake
SERVES: 8–12
STORE: at room temperature for up to 3 days

This cake is a loaf-style take on my all-time favourite cookie recipe by Dorie Greenspan. Instead of the traditional citrus pairing, I love how the poppyseeds complement the rich, nutty depth of chocolate and rye flour. Loaf cakes can sometimes feel a bit one-note, but this one flips the script! It starts with a buttery vanilla base, studded with chocolate chips and poppyseeds, then swirled with a tangy cherry jam and topped with a crunchy toasted rye crumble. A little nostalgia, a little surprise — every bite keeps you coming back for more!

TOASTED RYE CRUMBLE TOPPING
- 20 g (0.7 oz) light rye flour
- 50 g (1.75 oz) unsalted butter, cubed
- 50 g (1.75 oz) plain (all-purpose) flour
- 2 g (¼ teaspoon) fine sea salt
- 50 g (1.75 oz) brown sugar
- 20 g (0.7 oz) caster (superfine) sugar

CHERRY JAM
- 100 g (3.5 oz) frozen pitted sour cherries
- 30 g (1.06 oz) caster (superfine) sugar
- 10 g (2 teaspoons) lemon juice
- 1 g (¼ teaspoon) lemon zest

INGREDIENTS LIST CONTINUES →

Start preparing the toasted crumble topping

Toast the rye flour. In a small saucepan, toast the rye flour over medium–low heat, stirring constantly for about 8 minutes, until it smells nutty and fragrant and turns a shade darker. Transfer to a small bowl and leave to cool completely at room temperature.

Make the cherry jam

Warm the cherries until jammy. In a small saucepan, combine the cherries, sugar, lemon juice and lemon zest. Warm over medium–high heat until the cherries soften and release their juices. Reduce the heat to medium. Using the back of a wooden spoon to break up the cherries as they cook, stir constantly for 10–12 minutes, until the mixture thickens. You should end up with about 75 g (2.65 oz) cherry jam.

Blend and cool. Transfer the jam to a tall container or jug. Blend using an immersion blender, leaving some chunks for texture. Leave in the fridge to cool completely.

Finish the crumble topping

Melt the butter. In a small saucepan, warm the butter over medium heat until just melted. Set aside to cool.

Combine the topping ingredients. Sift the toasted rye flour into a bowl, along with the plain flour and salt. Add the sugars and whisk until evenly combined. Pour in the cooled melted butter. Using your hands, gently massage together until crumbs form, then lightly toss the bowl to ensure even crumbs. Chill the crumbs in the fridge until needed.

Recipe continues

SIMPLE FINISH CAKES

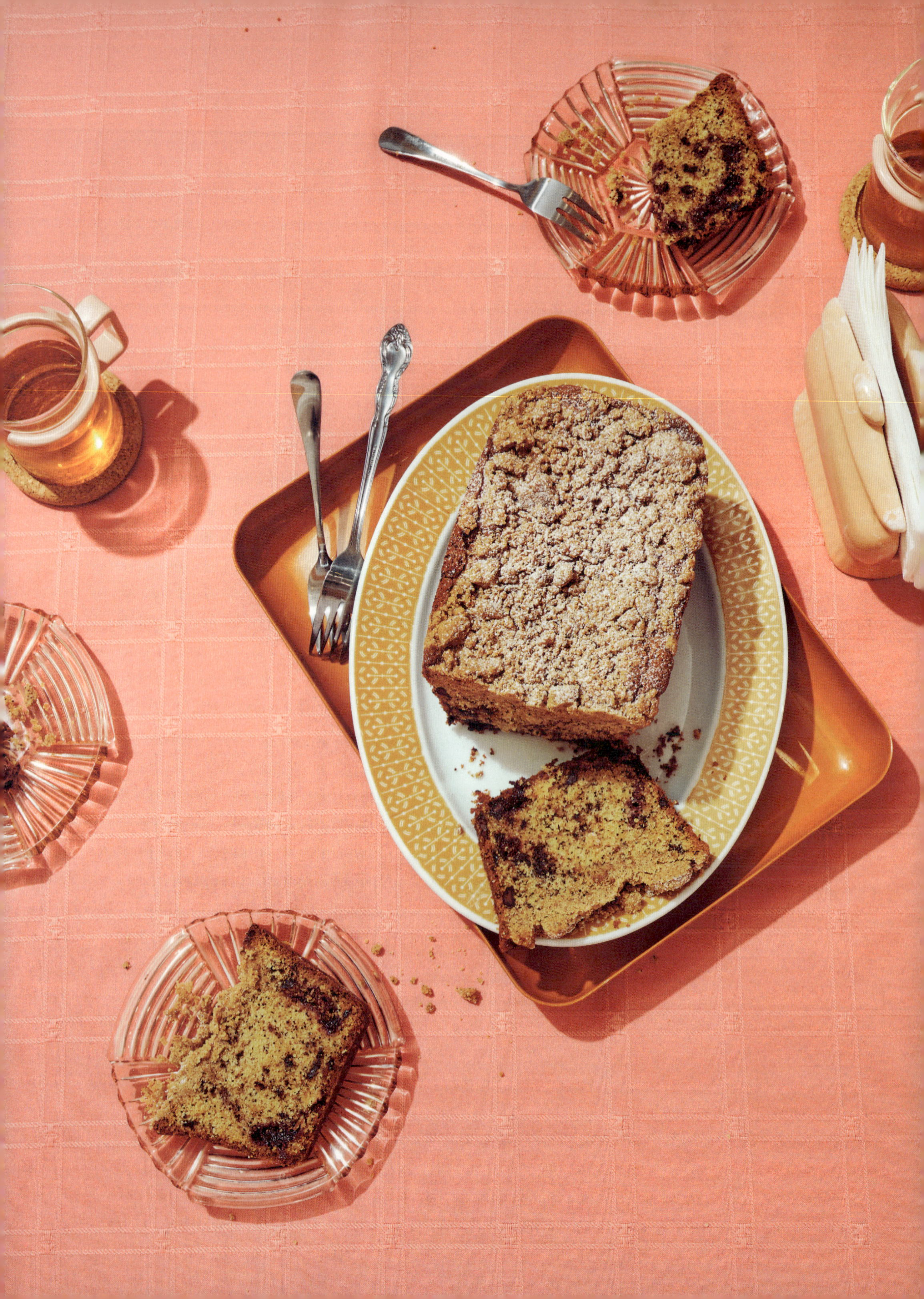

CHOC CHIP POPPYSEED CAKE

100 g (3.5 oz) bittersweet dark chocolate, chopped into 5 mm (¼ in) chunks
200 g (7 oz) plain (all-purpose) flour
10 g (4 teaspoons) poppyseeds
5 g (1 teaspoon) baking powder
2 g (¼ teaspoon) bicarbonate of soda (baking soda)
2 g (¼ teaspoon) fine sea salt
150 g (5.3 oz) caster (superfine) sugar
100 g (3.5 oz) eggs (about 2 eggs)
60 g (2.17 oz) full-cream (whole) milk
20 g (0.7 oz) vegetable oil
4 g (1 teaspoon) vanilla extract
85 g (3 oz) unsalted butter, cubed
90 g (3.17 oz) sour cream

Make the cake batter

Preheat your oven and prepare the tin. Preheat the oven to 160°C (320°F) and position an oven rack in the centre of the oven. Thoroughly spray a 22.5 × 12 cm loaf tin (1-pound loaf pan) with cooking oil. Cut a sheet of baking paper large enough to line the sides and bottom of the tin, leaving about 2 cm (¾ in) overhanging on the long sides. Press the paper into the tin, making sure it fits snugly into the corners and lies flat against the sides.

Dust the chocolate. Toss the chopped chocolate in a bowl with 1 tablespoon of the flour. Set aside.

Combine the dry ingredients. Sift the remaining flour into the bowl of a stand mixer, along with the poppyseeds, baking powder, bicarbonate of soda, salt and sugar. Using the paddle attachment, mix on low speed for about 1 minute, until evenly combined.

Combine the wet ingredients. In a bowl, lightly whisk together the eggs, milk, oil and vanilla. Set aside.

Add the butter and sour cream to the mixer bowl. Add the butter and sour cream to the flour mixture. Mix on low speed for about 1 minute, until just evenly moistened. Increase the speed to medium and mix for another minute, until the mixture comes together and becomes slightly paler.

Add the remaining wet ingredients. Add the egg mixture in three additions. For each addition, start by mixing on low speed then pour the egg mixture in a thin stream until it starts to combine. Increase the speed to medium–high and mix for about 5 seconds, until just incorporated. After each addition, scrape down the side of the bowl and the paddle attachment, to ensure even mixing. The finished batter should be smooth, thick and custard-like in consistency.

Fold in the chocolate. Using a spatula, gently fold the chocolate through the batter until evenly distributed.

Bake the cake

Fill the tin. Spoon half the batter into the loaf tin, or about 400 g (14 oz), and smooth the surface evenly. Using a teaspoon, spoon the cherry jam, in small dollops, over the batter. Pour the remaining batter over the top and smooth the surface again. Use a skewer to gently swirl the batter, creating a lovely jam-swirl pattern.

Add the topping. Sprinkle the toasted rye crumble mixture evenly over the cake, ensuring full coverage.

Transfer to the oven. Bake for about 1 hour 20 minutes, or until a skewer inserted into the centre comes out clean. Rotate the tin front to back after 1 hour to ensure even baking.

Cool briefly, then lift out. Remove the cake from the oven and place the tin on a cooling rack. Let the cake cool in the tin for about 10 minutes, before carefully lifting it out using the overhanging baking paper.

Cool further and serve. Let the cake cool for a further 1 hour before slicing and serving.

SIMPLE FINISH CAKES

Upside-down pineapple & roasted carrot cake

MAKES: 1 × 23 cm (9 in) cake
SERVES: 8–10
STORE: in the fridge for 3 days; serve at room temperature

There are countless carrot cake recipes out there, but I truly hope this one becomes a staple in your repertoire. To me, carrot cake and pineapple are a match made in heaven — a perfect balance of warm spices and tropical sweetness.

This version reimagines the classic carrot cake as an upside-down cake, layered with caramelised pineapple slices and a rich ginger caramel glaze. Though it takes a little extra time, the reward is a cake that's deeply spiced, tender and utterly comforting.

Roast the carrot

ROASTED CARROT PUREE
400 g (14 oz) carrots, peeled and cut into 1 cm (½ in) dice
40 g (1.41 oz) water
20 g (0.7 oz) vegetable oil
1 g (small pinch) fine sea salt

ROASTED PINEAPPLE
½ pineapple peeled and eyes removed
2 g (¼ teaspoon) orange zest (from about 1 large orange)
120 g (4.23 oz) orange juice (from about 1 large orange)
160 g (5.64 oz) brown sugar
120 g (4.23 oz) water

TOASTED GROUND PECANS
65 g (2.3 oz) pecans

INGREDIENTS LIST CONTINUES →

Preheat your oven. Preheat the oven to 200°C (400°F) and position an oven rack in the centre of the oven.

Roast the carrot. Place the diced carrot in a roasting tray with the water, oil and salt, mixing well to coat the carrot evenly. Cover with a sheet of baking paper, then seal the tray tightly with foil. Roast for about 1 hour, or until the carrot is fully tender.

Puree the carrot. While the carrot is still hot, transfer to a food processor and blend until smooth. You should end up with 200 g (7 oz) carrot puree. Leave to cool to room temperature before using.

Reset the oven for the pineapple. Reduce the oven temperature to 160°C (320°F).

Roast the pineapple and toast the pecans

Slice the pineapple. While the carrot is roasting, prepare the pineapple. Lay the pineapple flat on a cutting board and cut it in half lengthwise. Trim the tough centre core from both pieces. Thinly slice into 3 mm (1/10 in) thick pieces. Arrange the pineapple slices in a roasting tray, spacing them out evenly.

Prepare the roasting liquid. In a small saucepan, combine the remaining roasted pineapple ingredients. Warm over medium–high heat until the sugar has dissolved, then pour over the pineapple. Cover with baking paper, then seal the tray tightly with foil.

Roast the pineapple and toast the pecans. Transfer the pineapple to the oven and roast for 25–30 minutes, or until translucent and fully tender. Meanwhile, spread the pecans on a separate tray and toast alongside the pineapple for about 15 minutes, until fragrant and lightly golden, keeping an eye on them to avoid over-toasting.

Remove from the oven, but leave the oven on. Remove both trays from the oven and let the pecans cool to room temperature for about 20 minutes. Keep the oven running at 160°C (320°F).

Recipe continues

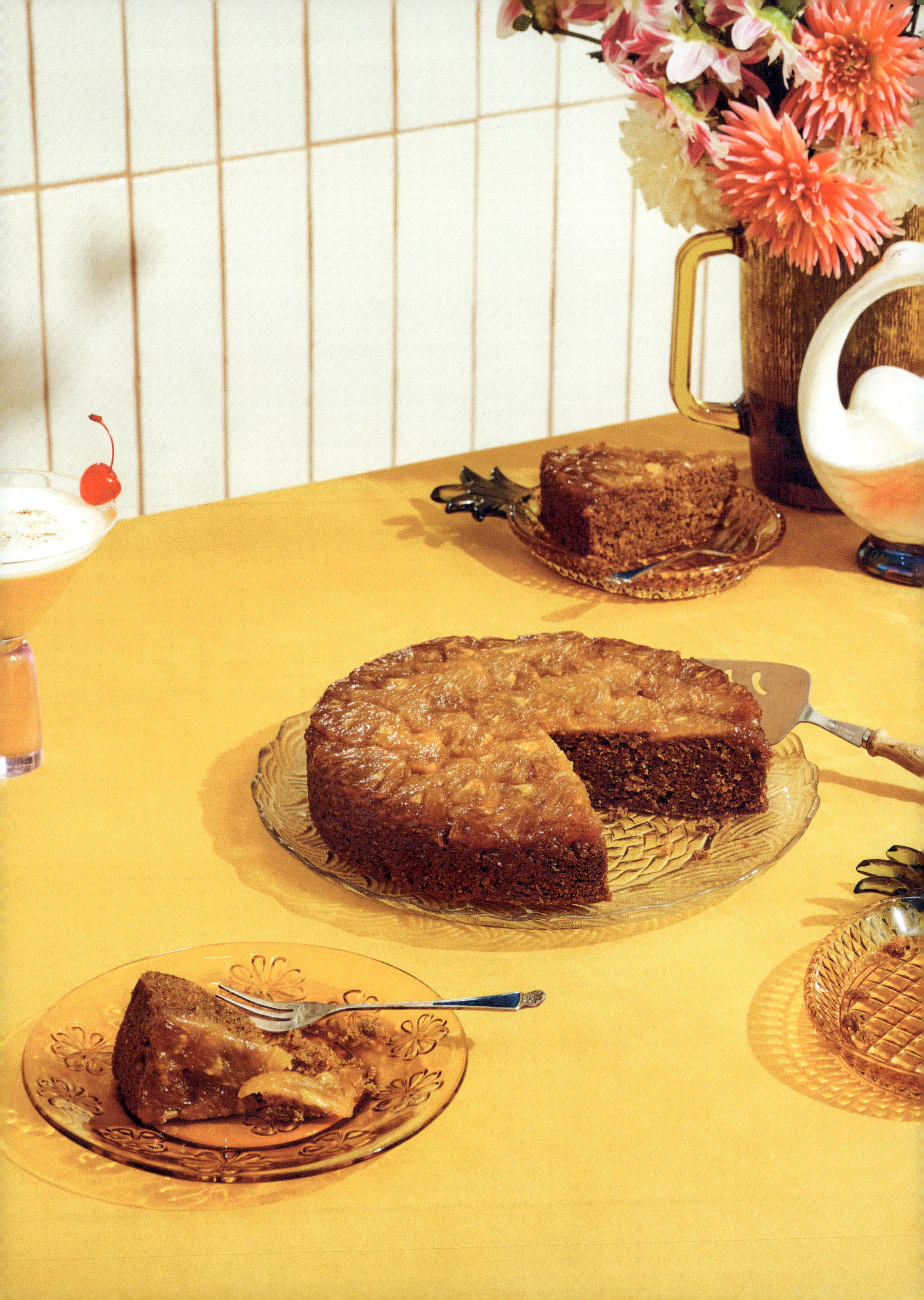

GINGER CARAMEL
reserved pineapple roasting syrup (see previous page)
10 g (0.35 oz) unsalted butter, cubed
2 g (1 teaspoon) finely grated ginger

CARROT CAKE
200 g (7 oz) vegetable oil
65 g (2.3 oz) caster (superfine) sugar
200 g (7 oz) brown sugar
100 g (3.5 oz) eggs (about 2 eggs)
30 g (1.06 oz) sour cream
4 g (2 teaspoons) finely grated ginger
160 g (5.64 oz) plain (all-purpose) flour
6 g (1 teaspoon) bicarbonate of soda (baking soda)
3 g (½ teaspoon) fine sea salt
3 g (1½ teaspoons) ground cinnamon
2 g (1 teaspoon) ground allspice
2 g (1 teaspoon) ground cardamom
200 g (7 oz) roasted carrot puree (see previous page)
ground toasted pecans (see previous page)

Make the ginger caramel

Warm the pineapple roasting syrup. Carefully remove the pineapple slices from the roasting tray and set aside to cool to room temperature. Pour the roasting liquid into a small saucepan and bring to the boil over medium–high heat. Let it cook for about 10 minutes, until it reduces by half and turns lightly golden.

Meanwhile, prepare your cake tin. While the roasting liquid is reducing, thoroughly spray a round 23 cm (9 in) cake tin with cooking oil and line the bottom with baking paper.

Finish the caramel and pour it into the tin. Remove the pineapple syrup from the heat and whisk in the butter and ginger. Pour the ginger caramel into your cake tin, tilting the tin to ensure the bottom is evenly coated. Place the tin in the fridge until needed.

Blitz the toasted pecans

Grind to fine crumbs. Place the cooled pecans in a food processor and blitz until finely ground. Be careful not to overprocess, or the nuts will release their oils and turn into a paste. Set aside.

Make the cake batter

Prepare the wet and dry ingredients. In the bowl of a stand mixer, combine the oil, sugars, eggs, sour cream and grated ginger. Using the whisk attachment, mix on medium–high speed until well combined. In a separate bowl, sift the flour, bicarbonate of soda, salt and ground spices.

Mix the dry ingredients into the wet. Gradually add the dry ingredients to the wet mixture in three additions. Mix on medium–low speed for 5 seconds after each addition, until just combined. Scrape down the side of the bowl, ensuring no visible lumps of dry flour remain after each addition.

Add the carrot and pecan. Add the carrot puree and ground pecans to the batter and mix on high speed for a few seconds until fully incorporated.

Bake the cake

Arrange the pineapple in the tin. Take the cooled pineapple slices and arrange them in the cake tin, starting from one side and working in a neat row. Overlap the slices slightly, ensuring there are no gaps between them. Position each slice so that the peeled edge of the pineapple is being overlapped, as this will be the visible side once the cake is turned out of the tin.

Fill the tin and bake. Pour the cake batter over the pineapple slices and bake at 160°C (320°F) for 50–55 minutes, or until a cake tester inserted into the centre comes out clean, or the cake springs back when gently pressed in the middle. Rotate the tin front to back after 40 minutes for even baking.

Let cool, turn out and serve. Remove the cake tin from the oven and leave it on a cooling rack for 10 minutes. Use a straight palette knife to loosen the edges, then carefully flip the cake onto a serving plate. Serve warm or at room temperature.

Thai tea chiffon cake

MAKES: 1 × 23 cm (9 in) cake
SERVES: 10–20
STORE: at room temperature for up to 2 days; add the Thai tea cream frosting just before serving

There's something deeply comforting about Thai tea — its bold aroma, gentle warmth, and the way its spiced notes linger long after the last sip. Brewed from black tea leaves infused with cardamom, tamarind pod and star anise, then swirled with sweetened condensed milk, it captures the essence of bustling Bangkok. This chiffon cake is a tribute to that beloved drink. Light as air and delicately infused with Thai tea, the cake is soft, fragrant and full of warmth. A final swirl of whipped cream — steeped in Thai tea — ties all these elements together, mirroring the tea's creamy sweetness.

Thai tea is easy to find in most Asian grocers. My go-to brand is Cha Tra Mue, and I highly recommend their loose-leaf version for the richest flavour.

Infuse the Thai tea cream

Warm the cream and tea leaves. In a saucepan, heat the cream with the tea leaves over medium heat until the cream just starts to simmer. As soon as bubbles form around the edge, remove from the heat — you don't want the cream to boil. Leave the tea to steep in the warm cream for about 10 minutes.

THAI TEA CREAM FROSTING
400 g (14 oz) cream (about 35% fat), chilled
15 g (1½ tablespoons) loose-leaf Thai tea
80 g (2.82 oz) sweetened condensed milk

Strain and let chill. Strain the steeped cream into a small bowl, discarding the tea leaves. (A basket tea infuser works brilliantly for catching all the tiny bits!) You should have about 300 g (10.58 oz) cream left. Press a piece of plastic wrap directly onto the surface of the cream to prevent a skin forming. Pop the bowl into the fridge to cool until you are ready to serve the cake.

Make the cake batter

THAI TEA CHIFFON CAKE
25 g (2½ tablespoons) loose-leaf Thai tea
200 g (7 oz) boiling water
270 g (9.52 oz) egg whites (from about 9 eggs)
5 g (1¼ teaspoons) cream of tartar
250 g (8.82 oz) caster (superfine) sugar
200 g (7 oz) plain (all-purpose) flour
40 g (1.41 oz) cornflour (corn starch)
15 g (0.53 oz) baking powder
3 g (½ teaspoon) fine sea salt
120 g (4.23 oz) egg yolks (from about 6 eggs)
120 g (4.23 oz) vegetable oil

Preheat your oven and prepare the tin. Preheat the oven to 150°C (300°F) and position an oven rack in the centre of the oven. Clean and dry a 23 cm (9 in) angel food cake tin, but do not grease it.

Brew the tea. Place 15 g (1½ tablespoons) of the tea leaves in a tea infuser and set it in a heatproof bowl. Pour the boiling water over the tea leaves, then place the bowl in the fridge and leave to steep for about 20 minutes, until completely cool. Remove the tea infuser with the leaves; you should have around 160 g (5.64 oz) brewed tea left.

Make the tea powder. Grind the remaining 10 g (1 tablespoon) tea leaves into a fine powder using a spice grinder or a mortar and pestle. Set aside.

Chill the egg whites. Place the egg whites in the bowl of a stand mixer with the cream of tartar and half the sugar. Using a cupped hand, firmly stir the egg whites against the side of the bowl until the sugar is fully dissolved — there should be no graininess when you rub a bit between your fingers. This 'dump-in' method simplifies the meringue preparation. Once the sugar is completely dissolved, chill the bowl in the fridge for about 20 minutes, or in the freezer for about 10 minutes.

Recipe continues

SIMPLE FINISH CAKES

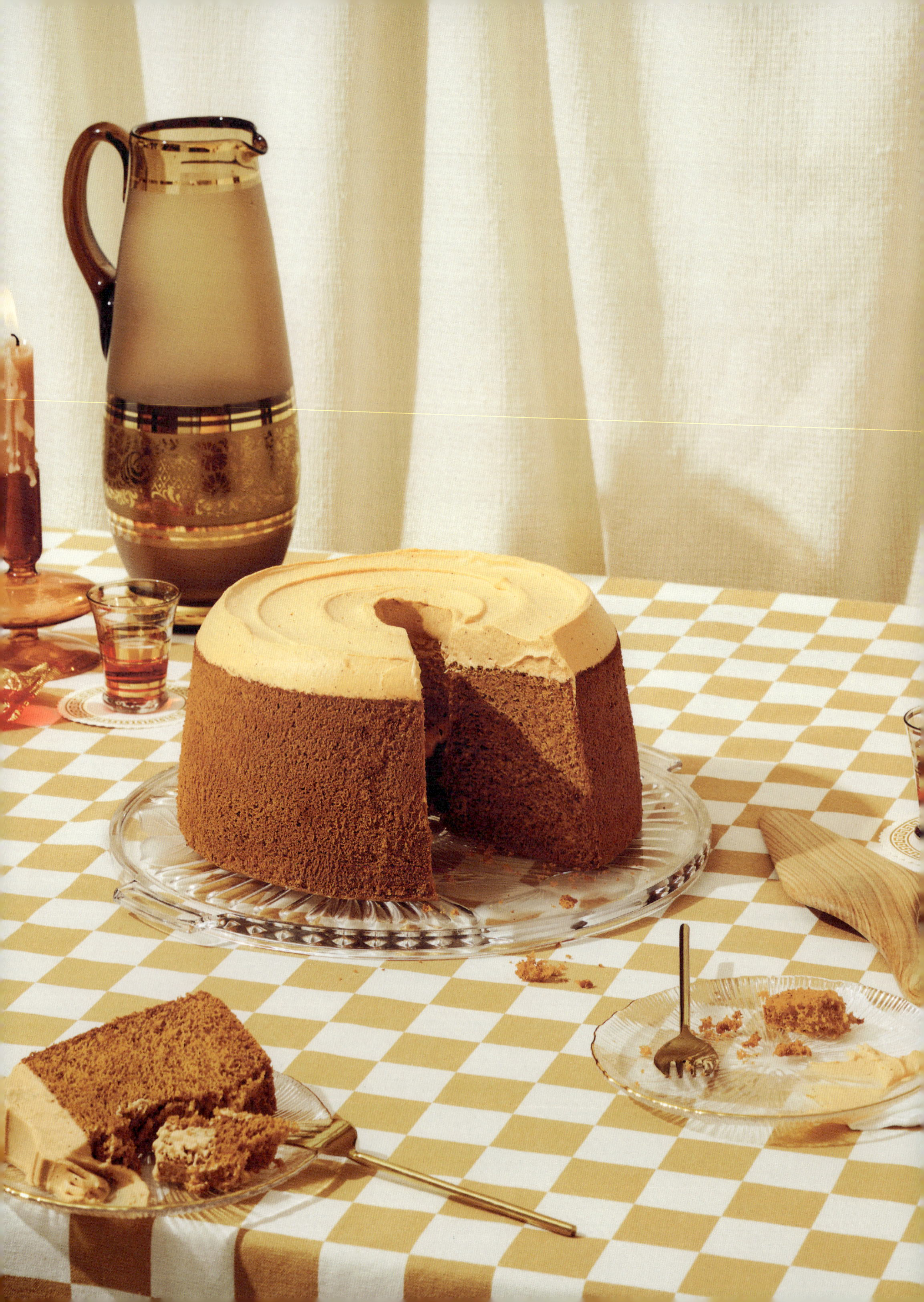

Combine the dry ingredients. In a small bowl, combine the flour, cornflour, baking powder and salt. Set aside with a sieve ready.

Whip the meringue. Attach the chilled bowl of egg white mixture to the stand mixer. Start whipping on low speed, then gradually increase the speed to medium. Whip for about 2 minutes, then increase the speed to medium–high and whip for another 2–3 minutes, or until medium peaks form. The key is to gradually increase the speed – this helps create a stable meringue with fine and even bubbles.

Mix the wet ingredients. While the meringue is whipping, place the remaining caster sugar and egg yolks in a large bowl. Whisk immediately and vigorously using a hand whisk until the mixture turns pale and the sugar has fully dissolved – be careful not to let the sugar sit in the yolks too long, as this can cause them to harden. Add the oil, tea powder and brewed tea, and whisk until fully incorporated.

Whisk the dry ingredients into the wet. Sift the dry ingredients into the egg-yolk mixture in three additions. Whisk until the batter is just combined after each addition, ensuring no lumps of flour remain.

Fold in the meringue. Gently fold one-third of the meringue into the batter using a spatula. Once combined, add the remaining meringue and fold until just incorporated, with no white streaks visible. Take care not to deflate the mixture – use smooth, confident motions, scooping from the bottom and folding over the surface while rotating the bowl with your other hand.

Bake the cake

Fill the tin and bake. Pour the batter into the cake tin, spreading it out evenly. Gently tap the tin on the counter a few times to pop any air pockets. Wipe away any batter from the top of the tin and around the centre tube – this will stop those bits burning in the oven. Bake for 55–60 minutes, until the top is golden and the cake starts to pull away slightly from the sides and centre tube.

Cool, release and finish the cake

Cool for several hours. Remove the cake from the oven and immediately invert the tin. Let the cake cool completely in the tin for 2–3 hours – this helps maintain its airy structure. If your tin doesn't have built-in feet, place the centre tube over the neck of a sturdy bottle (like a wine bottle) to keep it elevated while it cools.

Release and invert. To release the cake once completely cooled, lay the tin on its side and carefully run a long thin knife around the inner edge, then lift the cake out along with the removable base. Run the knife between the cake and the base to free it. Carefully flip the cake upside down onto a serving plate.

Finish the Thai-tea frosting. Just before serving, combine the chilled tea-infused cream and condensed milk in the bowl of a stand mixer. Using the whisk attachment, whip on medium speed for 1–2 minutes, until medium peaks form.

Frost the cake. Spoon the whipped tea cream evenly over the cake, then smooth it over the top using an angled (offset) palette knife.

Slice and serve. Slice the cake and serve immediately.

SIMPLE FINISH CAKES

Pandan & mango sandwich cake

MAKES: 1 × 30 cm (12 in) two-layer cake
SERVES: 6–12
STORE: best eaten immediately but keeps in the fridge for 1 day

Light yet luscious, and sandwiched with salted coconut-infused cream and sun-kissed mango, this cloud-like pandan chiffon cake is made for long, lazy afternoons, where laughter drifts through the air and plates are left empty in no time.

Pandan, coconut and mango are a classic trinity in Thailand. Their flavours take me back to childhood summers at my grandparents' farm, where pandan bushes sprawled wild and mango trees hung heavy with golden fruit. For the best flavour, make your pandan extract from scratch – the difference is night and day compared to bottled essence. You'll find pandan leaves tucked away in the freezer section at most Asian grocers.

TOASTED COCONUT CREAM
60 g (2.17 oz) flaked or desiccated coconut
600 g (21.16 oz) cream (about 35% fat)
4 g (¾ teaspoon) fine sea salt
20 g (0.7 oz) icing (confectioners') sugar

PANDAN CHIFFON CAKE
240 g (8.47 oz) egg whites (from about 8 eggs)
4 g (1 teaspoon) cream of tartar
200 g (7 oz) caster (superfine) sugar
70 g (2.47 oz) fresh or frozen pandan leaves, sliced into 5 mm (¼ in) wide strips
140 g (4.94 oz) water
6 g (2 teaspoons) full-cream (whole) milk powder
150 g (5.3 oz) plain (all-purpose) flour
30 g (1.06 oz) cornflour (corn starch)
5 g (1 teaspoon) baking powder
3 g (½ teaspoon) fine sea salt
160 g (5.64 oz) egg yolks (from about 8 eggs)
120 g (4.23 oz) vegetable oil
5 drops of green food colouring (lime green recommended)

INGREDIENTS LIST CONTINUES →

Prepare the toasted coconut cream

Toast the coconut. In a saucepan, toast the coconut over medium–low heat, stirring constantly, until fragrant and golden. Remove from the heat and leave to cool for about 5 minutes.

Infuse and chill the cream. Add the cream and salt to the saucepan, place over medium heat and bring to a gentle simmer. As soon as bubbles form around the edge, remove from the heat – you don't want the cream to boil. Pour the mixture into a small bowl and press a piece of plastic wrap directly onto the surface of the cream to prevent a skin forming. Leave to steep and chill in the fridge for at least 1 hour while you prepare the cake.

Make the cake batter

Preheat your oven and prepare the tins. Preheat the oven to 140°C (275°F) and position an oven rack in the centre of the oven. Cut two sheets of baking paper to fit the base of two 30 × 20 cm (12 × 8 in) lamington tins (rectangular cake pans). Lightly spray the baking paper with cooking oil, then place in the bottom of the tins, being careful not to get oil on the sides of the tins – this will help the cake rise nice and tall.

Chill the egg whites. Place the egg whites in a stand mixer bowl with the cream of tartar and half the sugar. Using a cupped hand, firmly stir the egg whites against the side of the bowl until the sugar is fully dissolved – there should be no graininess when you rub a bit between your fingers. This 'dump-in' method simplifies the meringue preparation. Once the sugar is completely dissolved, chill the bowl in the fridge for about 20 minutes, or in the freezer for about 10 minutes.

Recipe continues

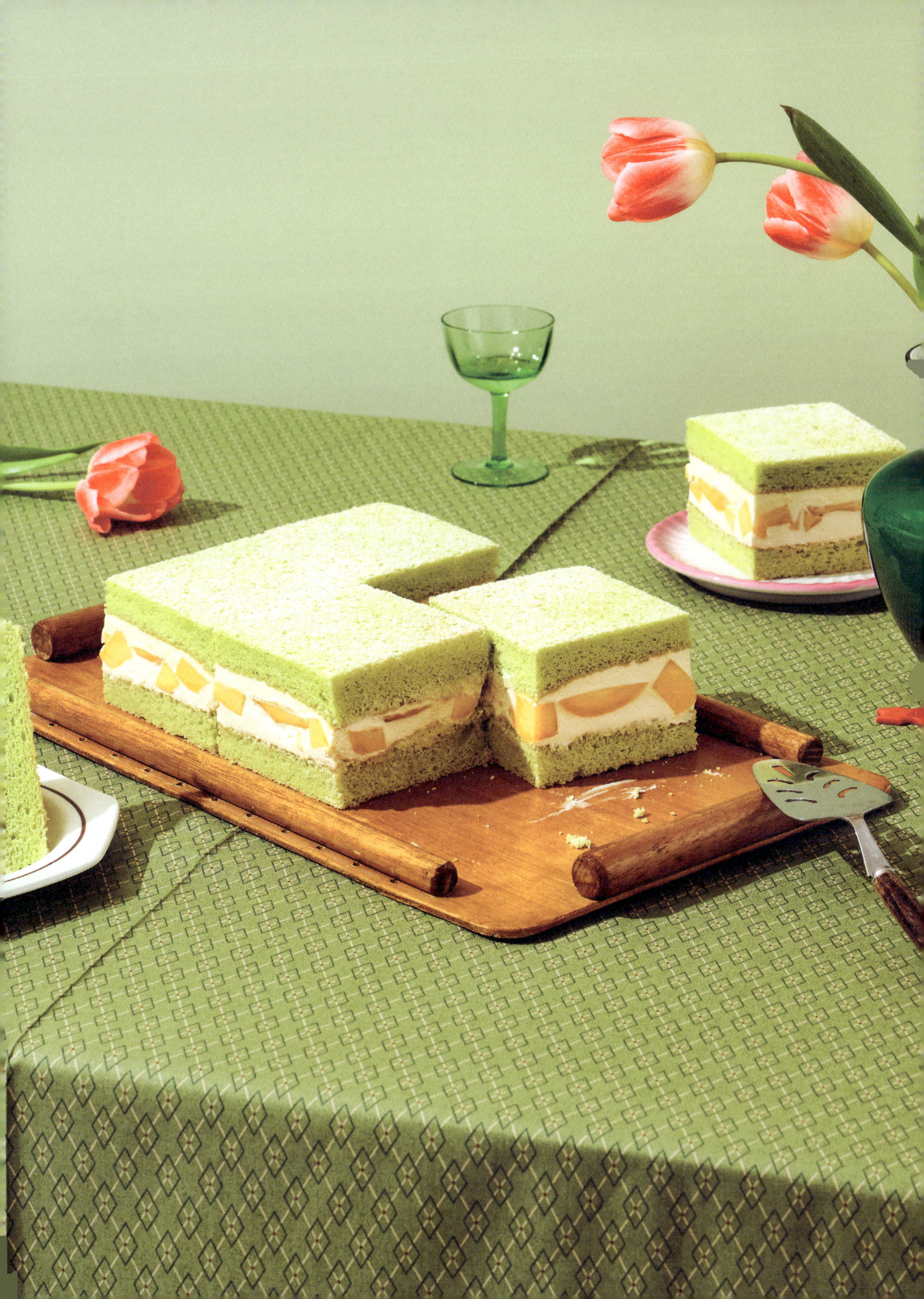

Prepare the pandan extract. Line a strainer with cheesecloth (muslin) and set it over a bowl. Place the pandan leaves and water in a blender (or a small smoothie blender) and blitz until completely pulverised. Strain the mixture into the bowl, squeezing out as much liquid as possible. Measure out 140 g (4.94 oz) of the pandan extract into a small bowl, add the milk powder and stir until most of the powder dissolves. Set aside.

Combine the dry ingredients. In a small bowl, combine the flour, cornflour, baking powder and salt. Set aside with a sieve ready.

Whip the meringue. Attach the chilled bowl of egg white mixture to the stand mixer. Start whipping on low speed, then gradually increase the speed to medium. Whip for about 2 minutes, then increase the speed to medium–high and whip for another 2–3 minutes, or until medium peaks form. The key is to gradually increase the speed – this helps create a stable meringue with fine and even bubbles.

Mix the wet ingredients. While the meringue is whipping, place the remaining caster sugar and the egg yolks in a large bowl. Whisk immediately and vigorously using a hand whisk until the mixture turns pale and the sugar has fully dissolved – be careful not to let the sugar sit in the yolks too long, as this can cause them to harden. Add the pandan extract, oil and food colouring and whisk until fully incorporated.

Whisk the dry ingredients into the wet. Sift the dry ingredients into the egg-yolk mixture in three additions. Whisk until the batter is just combined after each addition, ensuring no lumps of flour remain.

Fold in the meringue. Gently fold one-third of the meringue into the batter using a spatula. Once combined, add the remaining meringue and fold until just incorporated, with no white streaks visible. Take care not to deflate the mixture – use smooth, confident motions, scooping from the bottom and folding over the surface while rotating the bowl with your other hand.

Bake the cake

Fill the tins and bake. Divide the batter evenly between the tins, about 500 g (17.64 oz) each. Gently spread it out to the edges and corners, taking care not to press too hard, to keep the batter nice and airy. Smooth the tops with an angled (offset) palette knife to ensure an even finish. Gently tap the tins on the counter a few times to pop any air pockets and help the batter settle. Bake for 30–35 minutes, or until the tops are golden and spring back when you gently press them in the centre.

Let cool and release from the tins. Remove from the oven and let the cakes cool completely in their tins for about 45 minutes. Lightly spray two cooling racks with cooking oil, gently turn the cakes out onto the racks, then carefully peel off the baking paper.

TO FINISH
3 ripe mangoes
icing (confectioners') sugar, for dusting

Finish preparing the fillings

Whip the infused toasted coconut cream. Set a fine-meshed strainer over a clean stand mixer bowl. Strain the completely chilled infused coconut cream into the bowl, pressing down to extract as much cream as possible. Sift in the icing sugar, then whip on medium speed for 1 minute. Increase the speed to medium–high and continue whipping for another 1–2 minutes, or until stiff peaks form.

Prepare the mangoes. Peel the mangoes, then slice off the two large cheeks set them aside. The thickest part of the cheeks shouldn't be more than 2.5 cm (1 in), or there won't be enough cream to fully cover them, and the cake may end up too tall and difficult to cut. If you're using large mangoes, trim the cheeks slightly to keep the thickness in check. Trim any remaining flesh from the sides of each mango stone, being careful not to cut too close, to avoid the fibrous part. Cut the trimmed mango flesh into 1 cm (½ in) cubes.

Assemble the cake

Build the cake layers. Clean and dry the cake tin you used to bake the sponge cakes and line the bottom and sides of the tin with cling wrap. Place one cake layer inside, with the smooth side facing down. Use an angled (offset) palette knife to spread half the whipped toasted coconut cream evenly over the cake. Arrange the mango cheeks on top, flat side down, and fill any gaps with the diced mango. Spread the remaining coconut cream evenly over the mango pieces. Place the second cake on top, with the smooth green side facing up. Align the edges carefully, then gently press to level the cake and secure the layers.

Chill the cake. Wrap the cake and refrigerate for at least 3 hours or overnight, to allow it to fully set before slicing.

Slice and serve

Trim the edge. Once the cake has chilled and set, turn the cake out on to a chopping board. Use a large sharp knife to trim off about 5 mm (¼ in) from each side to give the cake a neat finish.

Slice into portions. Cut the cake into six or 12 pieces, transfer the cake to a serving plate and finish by dusting the tops with icing sugar and enjoy.

Mandarin cotton cheesecake

MAKES: 1 × 20 cm (8 in) cake
SERVES: 8–10
STORE: in the fridge for up to 2 days

This cheesecake is light, fluffy and airy — all thanks to the meringue folded into the batter. It's the kind of cheesecake I could eat over and over again, so delicate and soft compared to its richer, denser relatives. My take on this classic is gluten free, with a mandarin reduction folded through for a bright citrusy note — because who doesn't love a hint of sunshine in their dessert?

This cake demands patience and precision to achieve a smooth, crack-free top. The key is to whip the meringue gradually and gently to create fine, stable bubbles — rush this step and cracks may appear.

The final hour of baking is just as crucial. You'll need to open the oven door a few times to release steam, as too much trapped moisture can also cause cracking. I know it sounds a little tricky, but once you get the hang of it, you'll want to make this cake again and again!

MANDARIN REDUCTION
200 g (7 oz) mandarin juice, strained (from about 7 mandarins)

COTTON CHEESECAKE
150 g (5.3 oz) egg whites (from about 5 eggs)
2 g (½ teaspoon) cream of tartar
100 g (3.5 oz) caster (superfine) sugar
80 g (2.82 oz) full-cream (whole) milk
60 g (2.17 oz) unsalted butter, cubed
2 g (¼ teaspoon) fine sea salt
1 gram (¼ teaspoon) mandarin zest (from about 1 mandarin)
230 g (8.11 oz) full-fat cream cheese
40 g (1.41 oz) plain (all-purpose) gluten-free flour (or use plain flour if you don't have gluten-free flour on hand)
15 g (0.53 oz) cornflour (corn starch)
80 g (2.82 oz) egg yolks (from about 4 eggs)
30–35 g (1.06–1.23 oz) mandarin reduction (above)
1 teaspoon vanilla extract

INGREDIENTS LIST CONTINUES →

Get ready to bake

Preheat your oven and prepare the tin. Preheat the oven to 170°C (340°F) and position an oven rack in the lower–middle or second-lowest level of the oven. Grease a round 20 cm (8 in) cake tin and line the bottom and side with baking paper. Have a large, deep roasting tray ready to use as a water bath.

Make the mandarin reduction

Reduce the mandarin juice. In a small saucepan, bring the mandarin juice to a simmer over medium heat, then gently cook until the liquid reduces to about one-sixth of the original amount. This will take 13–14 minutes, leaving you with 30–35 g (1.06–1.23 oz) concentrated liquid. Set aside to cool at room temperature until needed.

Prepare the cheesecake batter

Chill the egg whites. Place the egg whites in the bowl of a stand mixer with the cream of tartar and the sugar. Using a cupped hand, firmly stir the egg whites against the side of the bowl until the sugar is fully dissolved — there should be no graininess when you rub a bit between your fingers. This 'dump-in' method simplifies the meringue preparation. Once the sugar is completely dissolved, place the bowl in the fridge for about 20 minutes, or in the freezer for about 10 minutes, to chill the mixture.

Set up a double boiler. Fill a large saucepan with 5 cm (2 in) water and bring to a gentle simmer over medium–high heat. Once simmering, lower the heat to maintain a steady simmer.

Recipe continues

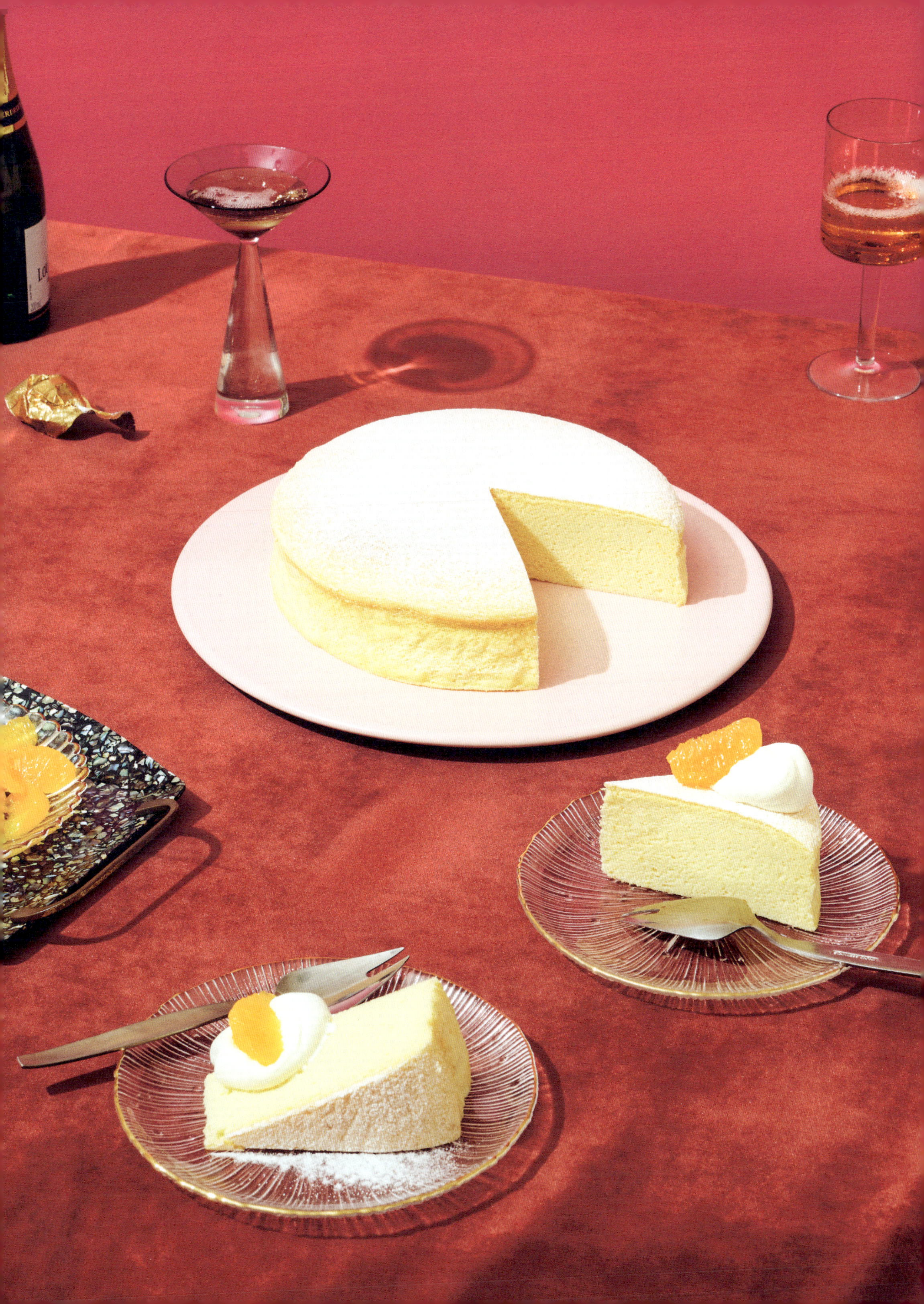

Melt some of the ingredients. In a large heatproof bowl, combine the milk, butter, salt and mandarin zest. Place the bowl over the simmering water, ensuring the base of the bowl doesn't touch the water. Whisk until the butter is fully melted. Add the cream cheese, cover the bowl with a lid, then leave to soften for about 5 minutes.

Combine the dry ingredients. In a small bowl, combine the flour and cornflour. Set aside with a sieve ready.

Whisk in the egg, flour mix and mandarin reduction. Remove the bowl from the heat and whisk the cream cheese mixture vigorously until completely smooth. If lumps remain, return the bowl briefly to the heat and whisk again. While still warm, whisk in the egg yolks until fully combined. Sift in the flour mixture, whisking until smooth. Add the mandarin reduction and vanilla, then whisk again until the batter is uniform.

Sieve the mixture. Pass the batter through a fine-meshed strainer into a large mixing bowl.

Whip the meringue. Attach the chilled bowl of egg white mixture to the stand mixer. Start whipping on low speed, then gradually increase the speed to medium. Whip for about 2 minutes, then increase the speed to medium–high and whip for another 1–2 minutes, or until soft peaks form. It's important to whip the egg whites as gradually as possible to avoid large air bubbles, as these can cause your cheesecake to crack.

Fold in the meringue. Gently fold one-third of the meringue into the cheesecake batter using a spatula. Once combined, add the remaining meringue and fold until just incorporated, with no white streaks visible. Be careful not to deflate the mixture – use smooth, confident motions, scooping from the bottom and folding over the surface while rotating the bowl with your other hand. The key is to be gentle but controlled, avoiding extra air bubbles that could cause cracks in the cake during baking.

Bake the cake

Fill the tin. Pour the cheesecake batter into the cake tin. Run a skewer through the batter to remove any large air pockets, then gently tap the tin on the counter a few times to release any remaining bubbles. If you see air bubbles on the surface, gently pop them with the skewer.

Set up a water bath. Place a wet tea towel in the roasting tray and place the cake tin on top. Pour enough hot water into the roasting tray to come about 1.5 cm (½ in) up the side of the tin. (Don't add more than this, as too much steam can cause the cake to crack.)

TO FINISH
2 mandarins
200 g (7 oz) cream (about 35% fat), chilled
1 g (small pinch) fine sea salt
5 g (1½ teaspoons) icing (confectioners') sugar, plus extra for dusting over the cake

Transfer to the oven. Bake at 170°C (340°F) for 15 minutes, then reduce the oven temperature to 130°C (265°F) and bake for another 15 minutes. Open the oven door for about 5 seconds to release the steam, then gently close the door, reduce the oven temperature to 120°C (250°F) and continue baking for 1 hour. Set a timer and open the oven door briefly every 15 minutes to release excess steam. Once baked, your cheesecake should have a smooth, lightly golden top. A small crack is nothing to worry about – the cake will shrink slightly as it cools, and any small cracks should disappear.

Cool in the oven. Once the cheesecake is ready, turn off the oven, and let the cheesecake rest in the oven for 10 minutes with the door slightly ajar – this helps prevent the cheesecake from shrinking too much.

Cool on a rack. Remove the cheesecake from the oven and place on a cooling rack to cool for another 10 minutes.

Turn the cake out. Place a plate on top of the cake tin and gently flip the cheesecake over. Carefully remove the cake tin and peel off the baking paper. Place a serving plate on top of the cake and flip the cheesecake back over onto the serving plate.

Add the finishing touches

Segment the mandarin. Use a small sharp knife to slice off the top and bottom of each mandarin, creating two flat surfaces. Stand the fruit upright on a chopping board and cut away the peel and pith by following the curve of the fruit. Hold the mandarin over a bowl to catch any juices, then carefully slice along both sides of each membrane to release the fleshy segments.

Whip the cream. Combine the cream, salt and icing sugar in a mixing bowl. Using an electric mixer, whip at medium speed for 1–2 minutes, until soft peaks form – or whisk by hand if you prefer.

Dust with icing sugar. Sift a generous amount of icing sugar over the cake.

Slice and serve. Serve the cheesecake warm or chilled, decorating each slice with a dollop of whipped cream and a fresh mandarin segment on top.

SIMPLE FINISH CAKES

Strawberry & cream olive oil sponge roll

SPECIAL EQUIPMENT: 2 large piping bags; 1 medium round nozzle
MAKES: 1 × roll cake, about 38 cm (15 in) long
SERVES: 6–8
STORE: best eaten immediately

I have a deep obsession with cake rolls — or roulades, to use a fancier term. In my opinion, they're the perfect way to enjoy cake! A light, fluffy sponge swirled with cream and a burst of filling in every bite — it's everything that makes cake so perfect.

This recipe is a classic crowd-pleaser. The cake itself is made with a simple olive oil sponge, but with a special twist — the batter is piped onto the baking tray to create a delicate pattern when sliced, but if you don't feel like piping, you can simply spread the batter onto the baking tray and bake the cake as usual. A generous dusting of icing sugar, both before and after baking, adds a subtle crunch, contrasting the soft, airy texture of the cake.

WHIPPED RICOTTA CREAM
650 g (23 oz) full-fat ricotta
165 g (5.82 oz) cream (about 35% fat), chilled
50 g (1.75 oz) icing (confectioners') sugar
4 g (1 teaspoon) vanilla bean paste
1 g (small pinch) fine sea salt

OLIVE OIL SPONGE
150 g (5.3 oz) egg whites (from about 5 eggs)
140 g (4.94 oz) caster (superfine) sugar
2 g (½ teaspoon) cream of tartar
100 g (3.5 oz) plain (all-purpose) flour
20 g (0.7 oz) cornflour (corn starch)
2 g (½ teaspoon) baking powder
2 g (¼ teaspoon) fine sea salt
100 g (3.5 oz) egg yolks (from about 5 eggs)
40 g (1.41 oz) extra virgin olive oil
30 g (1.06 oz) icing (confectioners') sugar

STRAWBERRY JAM
100 g (3.5 oz) fresh strawberries, hulled and cut into 1 cm (½ in) dice
30 g (1.06 oz) caster (superfine) sugar
1 g (½ teaspoon) lemon zest
15 g (0.53 oz) lemon juice
2 g (1 teaspoon) cornflour (corn starch)

INGREDIENTS LIST CONTINUES →

Start preparing the whipped ricotta cream

Strain the ricotta for at least 8 hours. Line a fine-meshed strainer with cheesecloth (muslin) and set it over a bowl. Add the ricotta, fold the cheesecloth over it and place a small weight on top to press out the excess liquid. Pop the bowl in the fridge and let the ricotta strain for at least 8 hours, or overnight if you can. You should end up with about 450 g (15.88 oz) strained ricotta.

Start the sponge batter

Chill the egg whites. Place the egg whites in the bowl of a stand mixer with the sugar and cream of tartar. Using a cupped hand, firmly stir the egg whites against the side of the bowl until the sugar is fully dissolved — there should be no graininess when you rub a bit between your fingers. This 'dump-in' method simplifies the meringue preparation. Once the sugar is completely dissolved, chill the bowl in the fridge while you work on the jam.

Make the strawberry jam

Warm the strawberries until jammy. Place the diced strawberries in a small saucepan with the sugar and lemon zest. In a small bowl, mix the lemon juice and cornflour until dissolved into a smooth slurry, then stir it through the strawberry mixture. Cook over medium–low heat, stirring constantly, for about 4 minutes, until the strawberries soften and the mixture thickens and takes on a jam-like texture.

Chill until cooled. Transfer the jam to a small bowl and blend using an immersion blender until smooth. Press a piece of plastic wrap directly onto the surface of the jam to prevent a skin forming, then refrigerate for about 1 hour, or until completely cooled.

Recipe continues

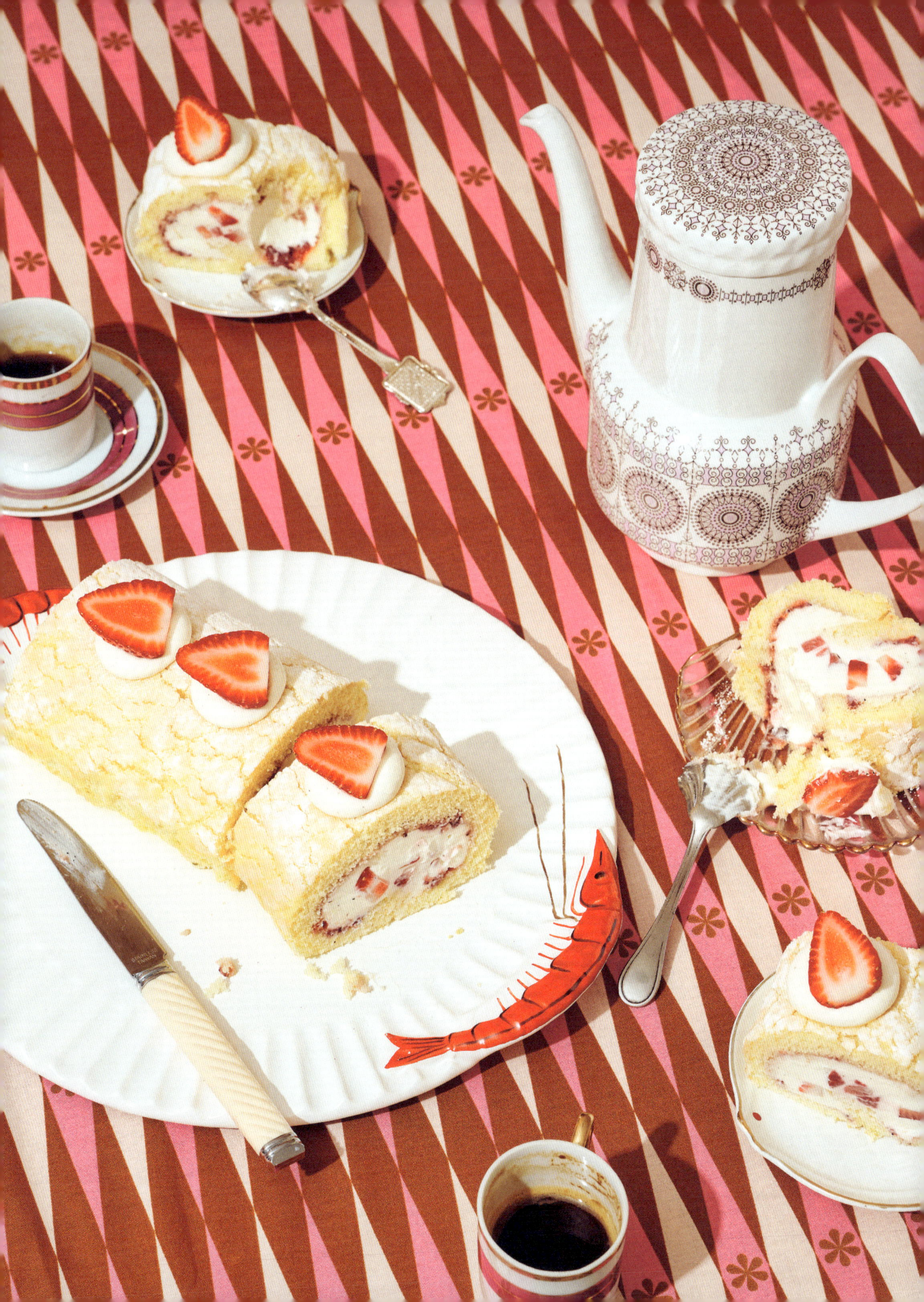

Finish the sponge batter

Preheat your oven and prepare the pan. Preheat the oven to 180°C (350°F) and position an oven rack in the centre of the oven. Cut a sheet of baking paper to fit the base of a 38 × 25.5 cm (15 × 10 in) sheet pan (jelly roll pan), leaving about 2.5 cm (1 in) hanging over the shorter sides, to make it easier to lift the cake out later. Lightly spray the baking paper with cooking oil and press it firmly into the bottom of the pan. Avoid oiling the exposed sides of the pan – this will help ensure the cake rises properly.

Prepare the piping bag. Place a piping bag in a tall sturdy container, then fold the top edge of the bag down around the container rim to hold the bag steady.

Combine the dry ingredients. In a small bowl, combine the flour, cornflour, baking powder and salt. Set aside with a sieve ready.

Whip the meringue. Attach the chilled bowl of egg white mixture to the stand mixer. Start whipping on low speed, then gradually increase the speed to medium. Whip for about 2 minutes, then increase the speed to medium–high and whip for another 3–4 minutes, or until stiff peaks form. The key is to gradually increase the speed – this helps create a stable meringue with fine and even bubbles.

Add the yolks and oil to the meringue. Stop the mixer, then add the egg yolks and oil and mix on high speed for about 5 seconds, until just combined.

Add the dry ingredients. Scrape the meringue mixture into a large mixing bowl. Sift the dry ingredients over the meringue in three additions and use a whisk to gently fold in each addition, mixing until no dry flour remains. Be careful not to deflate the mixture – use smooth, confident folding motions, scooping from the bottom and folding over the surface while rotating the bowl with your other hand.

Bake the sponge

Fill the pan and bake. Fill the piping bag in the container with the batter, then cut an opening about 2.5 cm (1 in) wide at the pointy end. Working in straight diagonal lines, starting at one corner and working to the opposite side, pipe the batter into the roll pan, applying firm, steady pressure to ensure the lines sit neatly next to each other without gaps. (If you prefer, you can simply pour the batter directly into the pan and smooth it out with an angled [offset] palette knife, though this won't create a pattern on the finished cake.) Dust half the icing sugar evenly over the top, then bake for 10 minutes, or until the top is golden and springs back when gently pressed in the centre.

Remove from the pan. Remove the pan from the oven and place on a cooling rack. Run a knife along the long sides of the pan to loosen the cake, then gently lift the sponge out of the pan using the overhanging baking paper. The sponge will get soggy if it sits for too long in the sheet pan. Dust the top with the remaining icing sugar to prevent sticking.

STRAWBERRY FILLING
150 g (5.3 oz) fresh strawberries, hulled and cut into 5 mm (¼ in) dice

TO SERVE
3–4 whole strawberries, hulled

Roll up the sponge

Flip and trim. Place a fresh sheet of baking paper over the cake, then cover it with a tea towel – the baking paper will stop the cake sticking to the tea towel and help preserve the pattern. Place another cooling rack on top of the cake and flip it over carefully. Peel off the baking paper. Using a long serrated knife, trim the long sides of the cake at a slight angle to taper the edges. This helps reduce the bulkiness and makes rolling the cake much easier.

Roll and let cool. While the cake is still warm, start rolling it from one of the longer edges. Gently lift and roll the cake tightly but carefully, using the tea towel to help guide it into a spiral. Avoid pressing too hard, to prevent cracking. Keep the towel and baking paper wrapped inside the roll as you go. Once rolled, place the cake, seam side down, and let it cool completely for about 1 hour to set its shape.

Finish the ricotta cream

Combine and whip. Transfer the strained ricotta to a food processor. Add the cream, icing sugar, vanilla and salt and blend until smooth and thickened. Reserve about 200 g (7 oz) for decorating and use the remaining 450 g (15.88 oz) to fill the sponge.

Fill the sponge roll

Unroll and fill. Gently unroll the cooled cake, leaving the baking paper and tea towel underneath for re-rolling. Spread the strawberry jam evenly over the surface, leaving a 2 cm (¾ in) border on the long edges. Spread the whipped ricotta cream on top of the jam, smoothing it as evenly as possible. Scatter the diced strawberries over the cream, gently pressing them down.

Re-roll the cake. Using the tea towel, gently lift the long edge of the cake and fold it down to create the first turn. Then, continue rolling tightly to form a neat spiral, taking care not to squash the cake. Keep the tea towel and the baking paper outside the roll – it's there to guide and support as you roll. Once fully rolled, place the cake, seam side down, on a serving plate or tray.

Chill and set. Refrigerate the cake for at least 4 hours, or overnight, to set.

Slice and serve

Add the finishing touches. Trim about 5 mm (¼ in) off both ends of the roll for neat edges. Slice the cake into six to eight equal pieces. Fit another piping bag with a round nozzle and pipe a small dollop of the remaining ricotta cream on top of each slice. Halve the strawberries, place one half on top of each dollop, and enjoy.

Vietnamese coffee flan cake

SPECIAL EQUIPMENT: 1 piping bag; instant-read digital thermometer
MAKES: 1 × 20 cm (8 in) layered flan cake
SERVES: 8–10
STORE: best eaten immediately but keeps in the fridge for 1 day

What better way to end a dinner party than with a dessert that whispers of coffee and caramel?

Inspired by the classic Filipino leche flan, this cake is a tribute to my partner Luke and his love for Vietnamese coffee. It has a silky, coffee-kissed flan and a layer of fluffy vanilla sponge that soaks up the flan's excess caramel.

The flan is sweetened with condensed milk instead of traditional sugar, giving it an extra creamy mouthfeel. The best coffee to use here is instant arabica coffee, but whatever instant coffee you have on hand will work just as well.

For the perfect finish, let patience be your guide and a thermometer your compass. At 80°C (175°F), the flan sets into silky perfection.

Get ready to bake

Preheat your oven and prepare the tin. Preheat the oven to 170°C (340°F) and position an oven rack in the centre of the oven. Ensure a round 20 cm (8 in) cake tin is clean and dry, but do not grease it. Have a roasting tray ready to use for a water bath.

Prepare the piping bag. Place a piping bag in a tall sturdy container, then fold the top edge of the bag down around the container rim to hold the bag steady.

Make the caramel

CARAMEL
100 g (3.5 oz) water
200 g (7 oz) caster (superfine) sugar

INGREDIENTS LIST CONTINUES →

Set up your cake tin. Place your cake tin on a cooling rack near the stove so you can pour the caramel in quickly once it's ready. Have a tea towel or oven mitt ready.

Warm the sugar. In a small saucepan, add the water then the sugar, stirring gently until all the sugar is moistened. Place over medium heat and cook for 10–12 minutes, until the sugar turns a medium amber colour. Avoid stirring the caramel as this can cause the sugar to crystallise; gently swirl the pan instead. Be careful not to let the caramel get too dark, as it will continue cooking as it cools.

Caramel-coat the cake tin. As soon as it's ready, quickly pour the caramel into the cake tin. Working quickly, use a heatproof spatula to scrape any remaining caramel from the saucepan. Hold the tin with the tea towel or oven mitt and start swirling the tin to coat the bottom and about 2 cm (¾ in) up the side. Keep swirling until the caramel sets, ensuring the side is coated as thickly as possible. Set the cake tin aside until needed.

Recipe continues

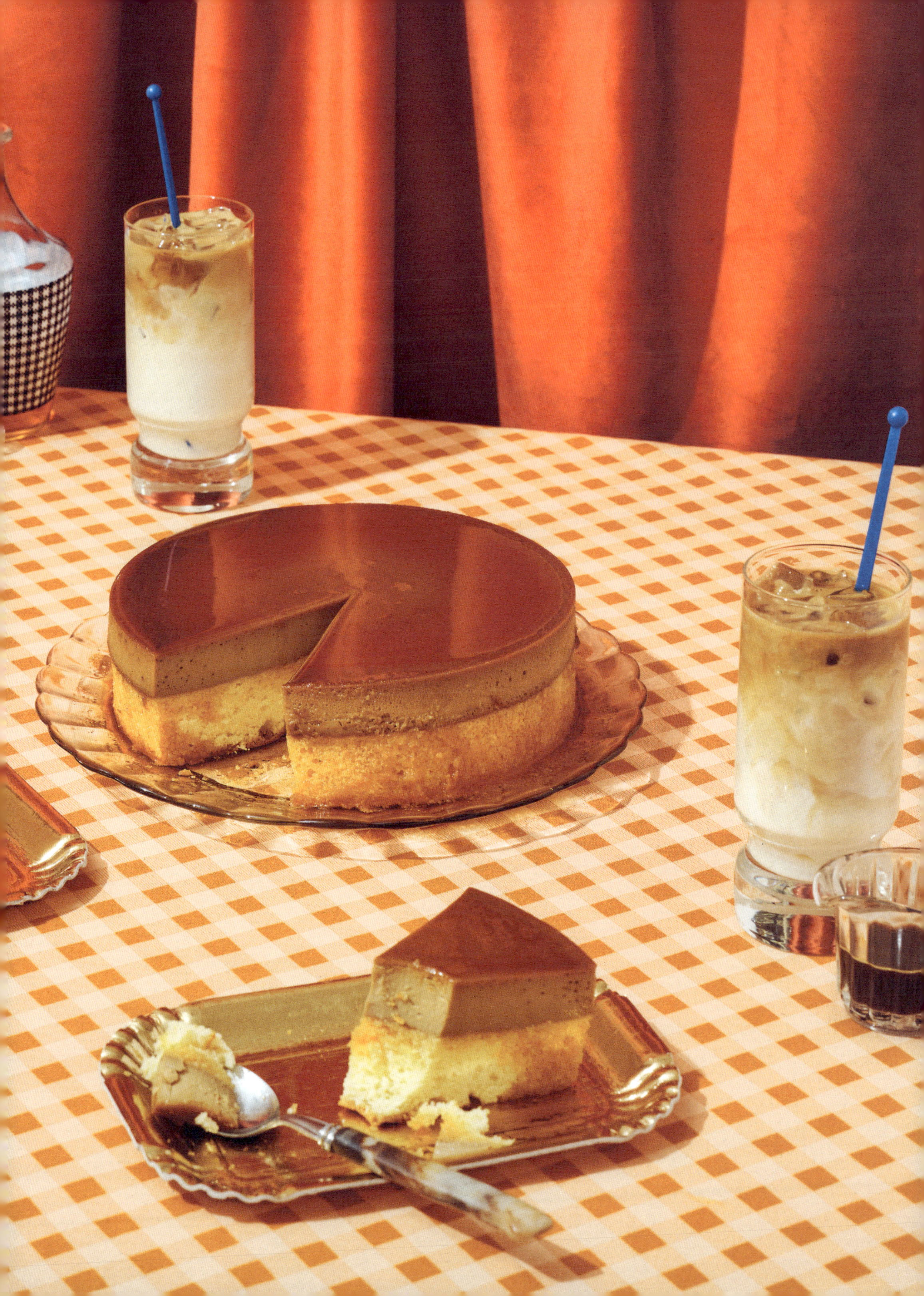

VANILLA SPONGE

90 g (3.17 oz) egg whites (from about 3 eggs)
1 g (¼ teaspoon) cream of tartar
80 g (2.82 oz) caster (superfine) sugar
60 g (2.17 oz) plain (all-purpose) flour
10 g (4 teaspoons) cornflour (corn starch)
1 g (¼ teaspoon) baking powder
1 g (small pinch) fine sea salt
60 g (2.17 oz) egg yolks (from about 3 eggs)
30 g (1.06 oz) vegetable oil
50 g (1.75 oz) evaporated milk
4 g (1 teaspoon) vanilla bean paste

VIETNAMESE COFFEE FLAN

16 g (0.56 oz) instant arabica coffee granules
15 g (0.53 oz) boiling water
400 g (14 oz) evaporated milk
150 g (5.3 oz) sweetened condensed milk
4 g (1 teaspoon) vanilla bean paste
1 g (small pinch) fine sea salt
150 g (5.3 oz) eggs (about 3 eggs)
60 g (2.17 oz) egg yolks (from about 3 eggs)

Start the vanilla sponge batter

Chill the egg whites. Place the egg whites in the bowl of a stand mixer with the cream of tartar and half the sugar. Using a cupped hand, firmly stir the egg whites against the side of the bowl until the sugar is fully dissolved – there should be no graininess when you rub a bit between your fingers. This 'dump-in' method simplifies the meringue preparation. Once the sugar is completely dissolved, place the bowl in the fridge to chill the mixture while you work on the flan mixture.

Prepare the flan

Dissolve and cool the coffee. In a small bowl, whisk together the coffee and boiling water until the coffee granules are fully dissolved. Set aside to cool for about 10 minutes.

Combine the other flan ingredients. Place the evaporated milk, condensed milk, vanilla and salt in a bowl. Gently whisk together using a hand whisk until just combined, being careful not to create air bubbles. Place a fine-meshed strainer over the bowl and strain the eggs and egg yolks directly into the mixture. Use the whisk to gently press the eggs and yolks through the strainer – this step takes a little time, but ensures a perfectly smooth flan.

Gently whisk in the coffee. Add the cooled coffee to the flan mixture and whisk gently until fully incorporated, again taking care to minimise bubbles. Set aside.

Finish the vanilla sponge batter

Combine the dry ingredients. In a small bowl, combine the flour, cornflour, baking powder and salt. Set aside with a sieve ready.

Whip the meringue. Attach the chilled bowl of egg white mixture to the stand mixer. Start whipping on low speed, then gradually increase the speed to medium. Whip for about 2 minutes, then increase the speed to medium–high and whip for another 2–3 minutes, or until medium peaks form. The key is to gradually increase the speed – this helps create a stable meringue with fine and even bubbles.

Mix the wet ingredients. While the meringue is whipping, place the remaining caster sugar and the egg yolks in a large bowl. Whisk immediately and vigorously using a hand whisk until the mixture turns pale and the sugar has fully dissolved – be careful not to let the sugar sit in the yolks too long, as this can cause them to harden. Add the oil, evaporated milk and vanilla and whisk until fully incorporated.

Whisk the dry ingredients into the wet. Sift the dry ingredients into the egg-yolk mixture in three additions. Whisk until the batter is just combined after each addition, ensuring no lumps of flour remain.

Fold in the meringue. Gently fold one-third of the meringue into the batter using a spatula. Once combined, add the remaining meringue and fold until just incorporated, with no white streaks visible. Take care not to deflate the mixture – use smooth, confident motions, scooping from the bottom and folding over the surface while rotating the bowl with your other hand.

Bake the cake

Strain the flan mixture into the cake tin. Strain the flan mixture through a fine-meshed strainer directly onto the set caramel in the cake tin. Tap the tin gently on the counter to release any air bubbles.

Pipe in the sponge batter. Fill the piping bag with the vanilla sponge batter, then cut an opening about 3 cm (1¼ in) wide at the pointy end. Pipe the batter over the flan in a circular motion, starting from the outer edge. Pipe the batter against the side of the tin and work your way inwards until all the batter is used. Smooth the surface gently with an angled (offset) palette knife, then run a skewer through the batter to pop any air bubbles – be careful not to push too deeply into the flan.

Set up a water bath. Place a wet tea towel in a deep roasting tray and place the cake tin on top. Pour enough hot water into the roasting tray to come halfway up the side of the cake tin. Bake for 50–55 minutes, or until the flan's internal temperature reaches 80°C (175°F) on an instant-read digital thermometer – any higher, and the flan will be overcooked.

Leave to cool. Remove the cake tin from the oven, place it on a cooling rack and leave to cool completely for at least 2 hours at room temperature.

Serve and enjoy

Turn the cake out. Run a knife around the inside of the tin to loosen the cake, being careful not to cut into the flan. To help release the caramel, dip the cake tin into a large bowl or pot of hot water for 5 seconds at a time. This softens the caramel, making it easier to unmould.

Slice and serve. Carefully flip the cake tin onto a serving plate and let the flan gently release, allowing the caramel to cascade beautifully over the top. Cut into slices to serve.

Sake cherry & matcha chiffon roll

SPECIAL EQUIPMENT: 1 piping bag; 1 medium star nozzle; a small square container (about 12 cm/4¾ in) to set the jelly in
MAKES: 1 × roll cake, about 25.5 cm (10 in) long
SERVES: 6–8
STORE: best eaten immediately but keeps in the fridge for 1 day

In 2023, we opened a little hole-in-the-wall pop-up in Fitzroy, Melbourne, where this cake quickly became a customer favourite. After tweaking the recipe several times, I've made it even better and easier to prepare. This delicate matcha chiffon cake is filled with a tangy yoghurt cream and sake-roasted cherries. For added texture, the leftover syrup from roasting the cherries is transformed into a silky jelly.

Using fresh matcha powder is essential. Unlike many teas which are oxidised, matcha is made from young, shade-grown leaves that are steamed, dried, then finely ground to preserve their vibrant green colour and fresh, bold flavour. This delicate processing makes matcha highly sensitive to light, air and moisture. If it's not fresh it can lose both its colour and its distinctive taste.

Start preparing the yoghurt cream

YOGHURT CREAM
300 g (10.58 oz) full-fat Greek-style yoghurt
450 g (15.88 oz) cream (about 35% fat), chilled
60 g (2.17 oz) icing (confectioners') sugar
2 g (¼ teaspoon) fine sea salt

Strain the yoghurt for at least 8 hours. Line a fine-meshed strainer with cheesecloth (muslin) and set it over a bowl. Add the yoghurt, fold the cheesecloth over it and place a small weight on top to press out the excess liquid. Pop the bowl in the fridge and let the yoghurt strain for at least 8 hours, or overnight if you can. You should end up with about 200 g (7 oz) yoghurt.

Prepare the sake cherries and jelly

ROASTED SAKE CHERRIES
300 g (10.58 oz) frozen pitted sour cherries
90 g (3.17 oz) caster (superfine) sugar
50 g (1.75 oz) sake
20 g (0.7 oz) lemon juice

Roast the cherries. Preheat your oven to 170°C (340°F). In a small roasting tray, toss together the cherries, sugar, sake and lemon juice, making sure the cherries are well coated. Roast, uncovered, for 20–25 minutes, until the cherries soften and release their deep red juices, and the sugar fully dissolves.

Strain and chill the cherries. Strain the roasted cherries and reserve 200 g (7 oz) of the syrupy cherry liquid for the jelly. Transfer the roasted cherries to the fridge to cool completely.

SAKE CHERRY JELLY
2 sheets titanium-strength gelatine (about 10 g/0.35 oz)
200 g (7 oz) syrup from the roasted sake cherries (above)

Make the sake cherry jelly

Bloom the gelatine. Fill a small bowl with cold water and submerge the gelatine sheets, then leave to soak for 10 minutes.

INGREDIENTS LIST CONTINUES →

Warm the syrup. In a small saucepan, gently heat the reserved cherry roasting syrup over medium heat until it just starts to simmer, then turn off the heat. Squeeze out any excess water from the bloomed gelatine, then whisk it into the warm cherry roasting syrup until fully dissolved.

Chill and set the jelly. Lightly oil a 12 cm (4¾ in) square jelly mould or container with cooking spray. Pour in the cherry syrup mixture and let it set in the fridge while you start on the cake.

Recipe continues

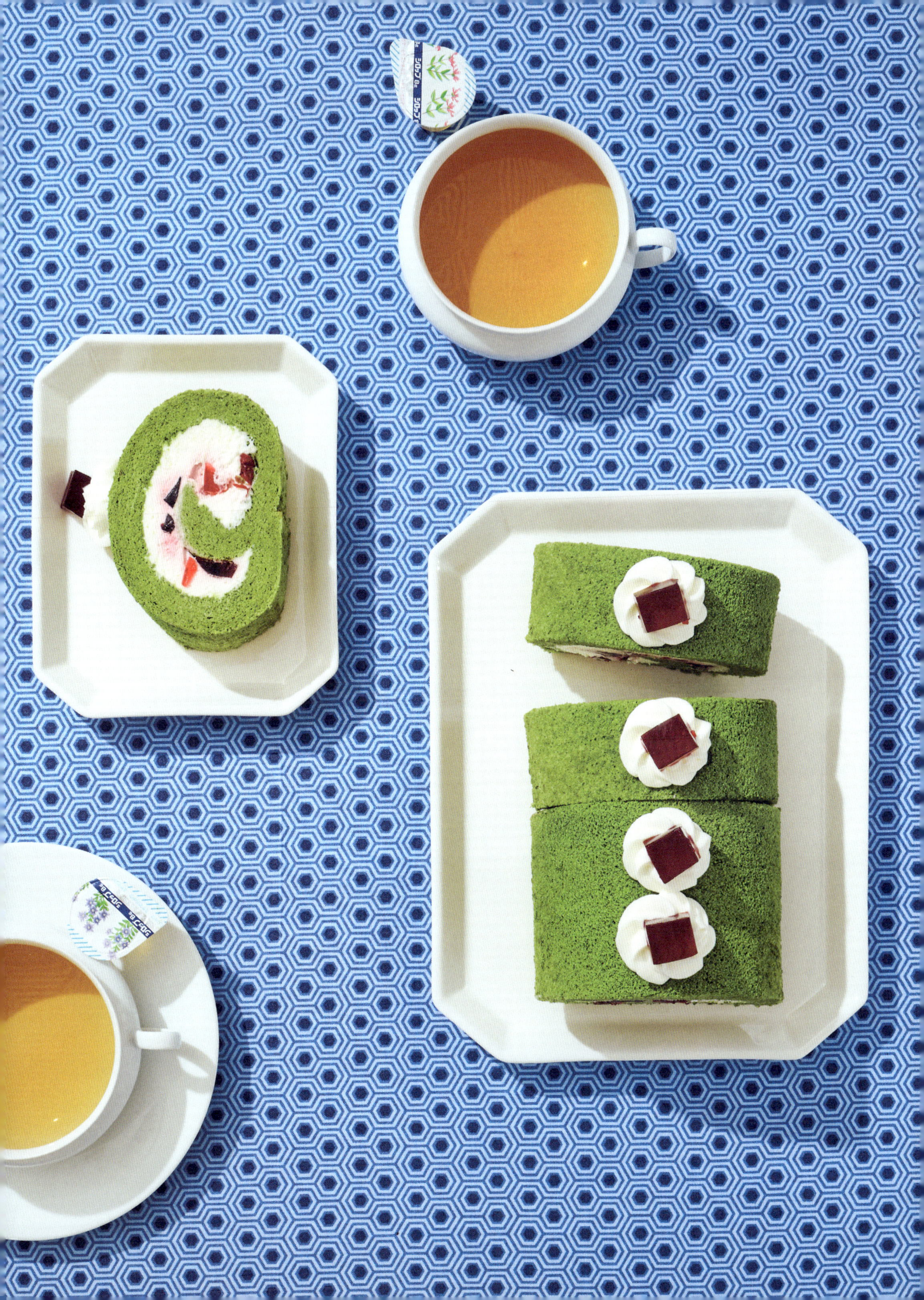

MATCHA CHIFFON SPONGE

10 g (4 teaspoons) matcha powder
120 g (4.23 oz) full-cream (whole) milk
150 g (5.3 oz) egg whites (from about 5 eggs)
2 g (½ teaspoon) cream of tartar
120 g (4.23 oz) caster (superfine) sugar, plus extra for sprinkling
80 g (2.82 oz) plain (all-purpose) flour
15 g (0.53 oz) cornflour (corn starch)
3 g (½ teaspoon) baking powder
2 g (¼ teaspoon) fine sea salt
100 g (3.5 oz) egg yolks (from about 5 eggs)
65 g (2.3 oz) vegetable oil

INGREDIENTS LIST CONTINUES →

Make the chiffon batter

Reset your oven and prepare the pan. Lower the oven temperature to 140°C (275°F) and position an oven rack in the centre of the oven. Cut a sheet of baking paper to fit the base of a 25.5 × 38 cm (10 × 15 in) sheet pan (jelly roll pan). Lightly spray the baking paper with cooking oil and press it firmly into the bottom of the pan. Avoid oiling the exposed sides of the pan – this will help ensure the cake rises properly.

Bloom the matcha. Sift the matcha powder into a small bowl. In a small saucepan, gently warm the milk over medium heat until it's just about to simmer. Pour the hot milk over the matcha powder and whisk vigorously until the powder fully dissolves and the mixture is completely smooth. Leave in the fridge for about 10 minutes to cool down completely.

Chill the egg whites. Place the egg whites in the bowl of a stand mixer with the cream of tartar and half the sugar. Using a cupped hand, firmly stir the egg whites against the side of the bowl until the sugar is fully dissolved – there should be no graininess when you rub a bit between your fingers. This 'dump-in' method simplifies the meringue preparation. Once the sugar is completely dissolved, chill the bowl in the fridge for about 20 minutes, or in the freezer for about 10 minutes.

Combine the dry ingredients. In a small bowl, combine the flour, cornflour, baking powder and salt. Set aside with a sieve ready.

Whip the meringue. Attach the chilled bowl of egg white mixture to the stand mixer. Start whipping on low speed, then gradually increase the speed to medium. Whip for about 2 minutes, then increase the speed to medium–high and whip for another 2–3 minutes, or until medium peaks form. The key is to gradually increase the speed – this helps create a stable meringue with fine and even bubbles.

Whisk the remaining ingredients. While the meringue is whipping, place the remaining caster sugar and egg yolks in a large bowl. Whisk immediately and vigorously using a hand whisk until the mixture turns pale and the sugar has fully dissolved – be careful not to let the sugar sit in the yolks too long, as this can cause them to harden. Add the oil and the cooled bloomed matcha base and whisk until fully incorporated.

Whisk the dry ingredients into the wet. Sift the dry ingredients into the egg-yolk mixture in three additions. Whisk until the batter is just combined after each addition, ensuring no lumps of flour remain.

Fold in the meringue. Gently fold one-third of the meringue into the batter using a spatula. Once combined, add the remaining meringue and fold until just incorporated, with no white streaks visible. Take care not to deflate the mixture – use smooth, confident motions, scooping from the bottom and folding over the surface while rotating the bowl with your other hand.

Bake the chiffon

Fill the pan and bake. Pour the batter into the sheet pan then gently spread it out to the edges and corners, taking care not to press too hard, to keep the batter nice and airy. Smooth the top with an angled (offset) palette knife to ensure an even finish. Gently tap the pan on the counter a few times to pop any large air pockets and help the batter settle. Bake for 30–35 minutes, or until the top springs back when gently pressed in the middle.

Cool the cake tin. Lightly spray two cooling racks with cooking oil. Place the cake pan on one of the sprayed cooling racks and allow to cool slightly for about 10 minutes.

Roll up the chiffon

Flip the cake out. Run a knife along the long sides of the pan to loosen the cake. Place the second sprayed cooling rack on top, then carefully flip the cake over. Peel off the baking paper.

Trim the cake. Using a long serrated knife, trim the short edges at a slight angle – this helps reduce bulk and makes rolling easier. The smooth side will be the outside of your cake roll.

Flip the cake again. Lightly sprinkle caster sugar over the cake surface to prevent sticking. Lay a clean tea towel on top, place the cooling rack back over it, then flip once more. Carefully remove the cooling rack.

Roll and let cool. While the cake is still warm, start rolling it from one of the short edges. Gently lift and roll the cake tightly but carefully, using the tea towel to help guide it into a spiral. Avoid pressing too hard, to prevent cracking. Keep the towel wrapped inside the roll as you go. Once rolled, place the cake, seam side down, and let it cool completely and set its shape for about 1 hour.

Combine the yoghurt cream

Combine and blend. Transfer the strained yoghurt to a tall jug or container. Add the cream, icing sugar and salt and use an immersion blender to blitz until completely smooth.

Divide into two portions. Transfer 450 g (15.88 oz) of the yoghurt cream to a stand mixer bowl and chill in the fridge for filling the cake. Chill the remaining yoghurt cream in a separate container for decorating the finished cake.

Prepare the cherries and jelly

Dry off the cherries. Measure out 100 g (3.5 oz) of the roasted cherries and lay them on paper towel to absorb any excess liquid. This helps stop the cake getting too wet when assembling.

Recipe continues

TO FINISH
20 g (0.71 oz) matcha powder, for dusting

Release and chop the jelly. Place the sake cherry jelly container in hot water for 10–15 seconds, then carefully invert the container onto a chopping board to release the jelly in one piece. Using a sharp knife, slice the jelly in half. Dice one half of the jelly into 7.5 mm (⅓ in) pieces and reserve for the filling. Dice the other half into 1.5 cm (½ in) pieces and reserve for decorating the cake. For the cleanest cuts, dip your knife in warm water and wipe it dry before each slice – this prevents sticking and ensures neat, even pieces. Transfer the garnishing jelly cubes back to the container, keeping them separate so they hold their shape until you're ready to use them.

Whip the yoghurt cream for filling

Whisk to stiff peaks. Once the cake has completely cooled, remove 450 g (15.88 oz) chilled yoghurt cream from the fridge. Using a stand mixer, whisk on medium speed for 1 minute. Increase the speed to medium–high and whip for another 1–2 minutes, or until stiff peaks form.

Fill the chiffon roll

Unroll and fill. Gently unroll the cooled cake, leaving the tea towel underneath for re-rolling. Spread the whipped yoghurt cream evenly over the surface of the cake, leaving a 2 cm (¾ in) border on all sides. Scatter the drained roasted cherries and the small jelly cubes over the cream, gently pressing them down.

Re-roll the cake. Using the tea towel, gently lift the short edge of the cake and fold it down to create the first turn. Now continue rolling tightly to form a neat spiral, taking care not to squash the cake. Keep the tea towel outside the roll – it's there to guide and support as you roll. Once fully rolled, place the cake, seam side down, on a serving plate or tray.

Chill and set. Refrigerate the cake for at least 4 hours, or overnight, to set.

Slice and serve

Add the finishing touches. Trim about 5 mm (¼ in) off both ends of the roll for neat edges. To finish the cake, dust the top with matcha powder. Slice the cake into six to eight equal pieces. Whip the reserved yoghurt cream until stiff peaks form. If the amount is too small for your stand mixer, simply whip it by hand. Transfer to a piping bag fitted with a star nozzle and pipe a small swirl of cream on the top of each slice. Carefully place a jelly piece on top of each swirl and serve immediately.

Hojicha & honey checkerboard cake

SPECIAL EQUIPMENT: checkerboard divider ring set to fit 1 × 23 cm (9 in) cake tin; 2 large piping bags; instant-read digital thermometer; cake board (larger than 23 cm/9 in); turntable; non-slip mat
MAKES: 1 × 23 cm (9 in) three-layer cake
SERVES: 10–20
STORE: in the fridge for up to 3 days; serve at room temperature

I've always loved checkerboard cakes – they're fun to make and have a great vintage feel. But the classic vanilla and chocolate combo has never quite won me over. So, in this version, I've paired the warm, nutty notes of hojicha with the deep sweetness of honey for a flavour that's a little different, but just as comforting. Hojicha, a lesser-known cousin of matcha, is made from roasted tea leaves, giving it a deep, toasty, caramel-like flavour.

To create the cake's signature pattern you'll need a checkerboard cake set, which is easy to find online. It comes with cake tins and a plastic ring with divided sections, making it easy to pipe the batters into place and achieve that graphic look.

HONEY CAKE
- 20 g (0.7 oz) hojicha powder, sieved
- 280 g (9.87 oz) full-cream (whole) milk
- 100 g (3.5 oz) dark honey
- 480 g (16.93 oz) plain (all-purpose) flour
- 80 g (2.82 oz) cornflour (corn starch)
- 400 g (14 oz) caster (superfine) sugar
- 8 g (1½ teaspoons) baking powder
- 6 g (1 teaspoon) bicarbonate of soda (baking soda)
- 9 g (1½ teaspoons) fine sea salt
- 300 g (10.58 oz) eggs (about 6 eggs)
- 50 g (1.75 oz) vegetable oil
- 4 g (1 teaspoon) vanilla extract
- 275 g (9.7 oz) unsalted butter, cubed
- 200 g (7 oz) full-fat sour cream

INGREDIENTS LIST CONTINUES →

Make the cake batter

Preheat your oven and prepare the tins. Preheat the oven to 150°C (300°F) and position an oven rack in the centre of the oven. If all three cake tins won't fit on one rack, arrange one rack in the centre and another in the lower-middle or second-lowest position. Thoroughly spray three round 23 cm (9 in) cake tins with cooking oil and line the bottoms with baking paper, cut to size.

Prepare the piping bags. Place the piping bags in separate tall sturdy containers, then fold the top edge of the bags down around the container rim to hold the bags steady.

Bloom the hojicha. Sift the hojicha powder into a small bowl. In a small saucepan, gently warm 80 g (2.82 oz) of the milk over medium heat until it's just about to simmer. Pour the hot milk over the hojicha powder and whisk vigorously until the powder fully dissolves and the mixture is completely smooth. Set aside to cool down at room temperature.

Make a honey milk. Pour the remaining 200 g (7 oz) milk into a saucepan and add the honey. Gently warm over medium–low heat, whisking until the honey is fully dissolved. Transfer to a bowl and place in the fridge for about 10 minutes to cool to room temperature.

Combine the dry ingredients. Sift the flour, cornflour, sugar, baking powder, bicarbonate of soda and salt into the bowl of a stand mixer. Using the paddle attachment, mix on low speed for about 1 minute, until evenly combined.

Add the eggs, oil and vanilla to the honey milk. Once the honey milk has cooled, lightly whisk in the eggs, oil and vanilla. Set aside.

Add the butter and sour cream to the dry ingredients. Add the butter and sour cream to the dry ingredients. Mix on low speed for about 1 minute, until just evenly moistened. Increase the speed to medium and mix for another minute, until the mixture comes together and becomes slightly paler.

Recipe continues

SIMPLE FINISH CAKES

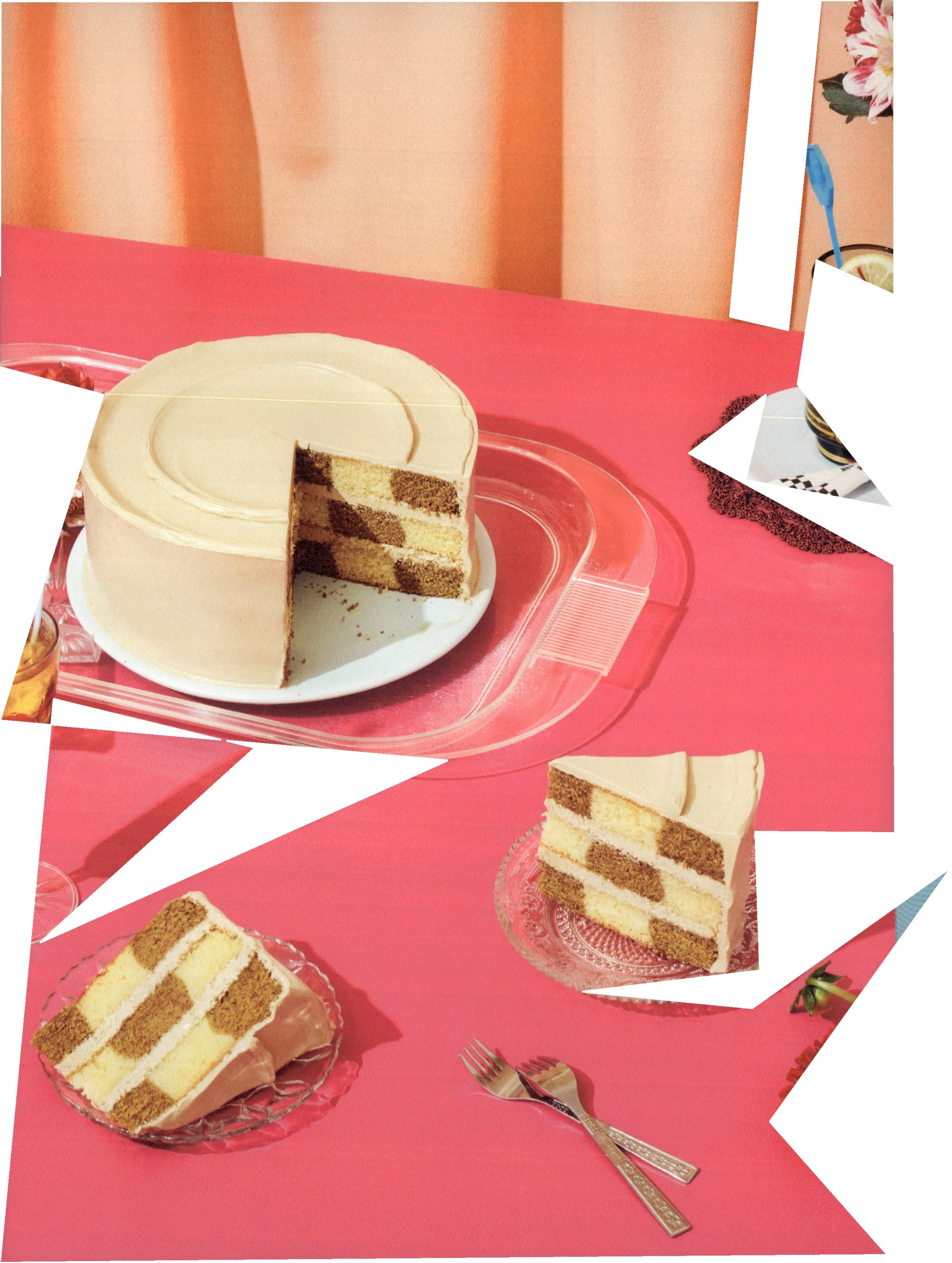

Mix in the honey milk. Add the honey milk mixture in three additions. For each addition, start by mixing on low speed then pour the milk mixture in a thin stream until it starts to combine. Increase the speed to medium–high and mix for about 5 seconds, until just incorporated. After each addition, scrape down the side of the bowl and the paddle attachment, to ensure even mixing. The finished batter should be smooth, thick and custard-like in consistency.

Divide the batter. Measure 1100 g (38.8 oz) of the batter into a large bowl, then fold in the bloomed hojicha base using a spatula, mixing until no streaks remain. Keep the remaining batter plain. Transfer each batter to the piping bags.

Bake the cakes

Fill the tins. Place a cake tin on a digital kitchen scale and place a checkerboard divider ring in the tin. Tare the scale. Cut an opening in both piping bags about 2.5 cm (1 in) wide at the pointy end. Pipe 60 g (2.17 oz) of the hojicha batter into the centre ring. Tare the scale again and pipe 260 g (9.17 oz) of the plain honey batter into the next ring, and tare again and pipe 380 g (13.4 oz) of the hojicha batter into the outermost ring. (To stop the batter flowing out of one piping bag while you're using the other piping bag, twist the cut open end and tuck it back into the bag – this creates a seal, keeping the batter contained and minimising any mess.) Take the cake tin off the scale and, while holding the divider ring in place, gently tap the cake tin on the counter to smooth out the batter.

Carefully lift the divider out of the tin, taking care not to disturb the layers, then wash the divider thoroughly. Repeat the same sequence for the second cake tin.

For the third cake tin, alternate the sequence: start with 60 g (2.17 oz) of the plain honey batter, then 260 g (9.17 oz) of the hojicha batter, and finally 380 g (13.4 oz) of the plain honey batter in the outermost ring.

Transfer to the oven. Bake the cakes for 35–40 minutes, or until a cake tester inserted into the centre comes out clean, or the cakes spring back when gently pressed in the middle. Rotate the tins front to back after 30 minutes to ensure even baking.

Let cool, then turn out. While the cakes are baking, lightly spray at least two cooling racks with cooking oil (make sure there's enough room for all the cakes to fit comfortably). Once the cakes are baked, place the tins on the cooling racks for 7 minutes. Use a straight palette knife to loosen the edge of each cake around the inside of the tins, then gently flip each cake onto the cooling racks and peel off the baking paper. Let the cakes cool completely for at least 2 hours before assembling.

Recipe continues

SIMPLE FINISH CAKES

HOJICHA BUTTERCREAM

60 g (2.17 oz) bittersweet dark chocolate
100 g (3.5 oz) water
230 g (8.11 oz) caster (superfine) sugar
160 g (5.64 oz) egg whites (from about 6 eggs), chilled
6 g (1 teaspoon) fine sea salt
2 g (½ teaspoon) cream of tartar
420 g (14.81 oz) unsalted butter, cubed
12 g (0.42 oz) hojicha powder

Make the hojicha buttercream

Melt the chocolate. Add about 4 cm (1½ in) water to a small saucepan and bring to a gentle simmer over medium heat. Set a heatproof bowl over the saucepan, ensuring the bottom of the bowl doesn't touch the water. Place the chocolate in the bowl and stir constantly until fully melted and smooth. Remove the bowl from the heat, ensuring the chocolate remains fluid for later use. In a cooler kitchen, you can leave the bowl over the saucepan with the heat turned off to maintain its consistency.

Make an Italian meringue buttercream. (For more detailed instructions, see pages 43–46.) In a small saucepan, combine the water and sugar, then gently stir just until the sugar is evenly moistened. Set the pan on the stovetop, ready to heat. Place the chilled egg whites, salt and cream of tartar in the bowl of a stand mixer. Begin whisking on medium speed until the mixture turns foamy and small bubbles form; this should take about 2 minutes. Once the egg whites are ready, and with the mixer running, cook the sugar syrup over medium heat, without stirring, until it reaches 115°C (240°F) on an instant-read digital thermometer. Immediately remove from the heat, increase the mixer speed to high, then slowly pour the hot syrup into the meringue (the egg whites should now be at soft peaks with fine, smooth bubbles), beginning with a thin stream and gradually increasing the flow. When all the syrup is incorporated, whisk on high speed for another 3–4 minutes as the meringue cools slightly. The meringue should turn glossy and hold stiff peaks and should be about 35°C (95°F). While mixing on high speed, gradually add the softened butter cubes one at a time, ensuring each cube is fully incorporated before adding the next. Once all the butter is incorporated, continue beating for 3–4 minutes, until the buttercream changes from a pale yellow to a creamy white, and slightly increases in volume.

Add the melted chocolate and hojicha powder. Once your buttercream is whipped to a silky, airy consistency, pour in the cooled melted chocolate and sift in the hojicha powder. Whip together for an additional 30 seconds, until just fully incorporated.

Assemble the cake

Trim the cakes. Using a long serrated knife, trim the top of each cake, ensuring they are level. Each cake should be about 2.5 cm (1 in) in height.

Set up the first layer. Place the cake board in the centre of your turntable, with the non-slip mat underneath to keep it steady. Using a spatula, add a small dollop of buttercream to the centre of the board to act as an adhesive to anchor the cake in place. Position one of the cakes that has the darker hojicha layer on the outermost ring in the centre of the board, cut side facing up.

Spread the first layer with buttercream. Add a generous dollop of buttercream and spread it evenly with an angled (offset) palette knife, using broad strokes while rotating the turntable. Smooth the surface by holding the palette knife parallel to the cake, with the edge lightly touching. Rotate the turntable until the top is smooth and the buttercream is about 7 mm (¼ in) thick.

Add the next cake layers. Place the cake with the lighter honey layer on the outermost ring on the bottom cake, with the cut side facing up, pressing gently to ensure the cake adheres properly. Quickly check the layer is level and aligned straight. Apply another layer of buttercream in the same way, then repeat with the last cake layer, placing the cut side face down. Use a straight palette knife to smooth out any excess buttercream from the side of the cake.

Set the layers. Refrigerate the cake for about 10 minutes to set the layers.

Crumb coat and frost

Apply a crumb coating. Apply a thin layer of buttercream all over the cake surface to seal in any loose crumbs. Use the same techniques as described on page 53 for frosting, but apply a much thinner layer here and don't worry too much about perfection. The goal is simply to lock in any loose crumbs.

Set the crumb coating. Chill the cake in the fridge for at least 10 minutes to fully set the coating before moving on to frosting.

Frost the cake. Using the remaining buttercream, frost the cake to create a smooth and even finish, following the instructions on page 53.

To create the ridges on top, there's no need to smooth out the top edge of the cake. Place a generous tablespoon of buttercream on the centre of the top of the cake, then use an angled palette knife to spread it evenly, covering roughly 5 cm (2 in) across the top surface. Next, position the knife so the tip rests in the centre of the cake, parallel to your body. The edge closest to you should just touch the surface, while the far edge is slightly raised. Quickly rotate the turntable while gently dragging the tip of the knife outward, stopping about two-thirds of the way to the edge. This motion will create a soft ridge in the centre of the cake.

Slice and serve. Serve the cake at room temperature, cut into slices.

A layer cake is more than just a dessert — it's a beautiful harmony of textures and flavours, with each component contributing its unique note to a sweet symphony. A thoughtfully made layer cake is built on the foundation of its individual elements, each serving a specific purpose.

The cake layers provide structure and stability, while offering a delicate crumb that melts on the tongue. A soak introduces moisture and whispers of complementary flavours, ensuring every bite is as luscious as the last. The filling is where the magic truly happens — a chance to add bursts of fruitiness, the crunch of a crumb, or the luxurious softness of whipped mascarpone that melts away like a dream. The buttercream ties everything together, a flavour carrier that harmonises with the components inside — a canvas for creativity that transforms a collection of ingredients into a work of art.

My approach to creating a layer cake is grounded in the belief that the delight of the opening bite should be as captivating as the moment you first lay eyes on the beautifully decorated exterior. Especially for retro-style cakes generously coated in buttercream, the interior must deliver a layered complexity that balances and enhances the richness of the buttercream.

This chapter has nine complete layer cake recipes. While the components are designed to work beautifully together, feel free to mix and match them to create your own unique combinations.

Layer Cakes

How to use this chapter

Each recipe in this chapter makes an 18 cm (7 in) three-layer cake. You can enjoy the cakes as they are, or use them as a base for the decorating projects in Chapter 5. Some of those projects call for different cake sizes, so you'll find tables at the back of the book (from page 323) to help you adjust the quantities for the various components as needed. The buttercream recipes included with each cake in this chapter are meant for filling and crumb coating these cakes, while the decorating projects in Chapter 5 use the basic Italian meringue buttercream recipe from Chapter 1 (page 43).

If you're not planning to follow the decorating projects, no problem! Each recipe in this chapter makes enough buttercream to frost the cake completely. You will find instructions for assembling a layer cake and creating smooth finishes with buttercream on pages 48–56. Assembling the layer cake should take around 30 minutes, and the assembled cake will need at least 1 hour (or overnight) in the fridge to set before you serve it.

From there, you can add your own finishing touches – perhaps fresh edible flowers or seasonal fruits for a beautifully simple look.

A few tips before you start

Bake in single layers. Each cake layer is baked in its own individual tin – so to make a three-layer cake, you'll need three cake tins, which can all bake in the oven at the same time. Baking each layer in its own tin – rather than baking a thicker cake and slicing it into thinner layers – yields a lighter, fluffier texture and a perfectly tender crumb. It also results in a shorter baking time, as thicker cakes take longer to cook because of their extra batter.

Chill as you go. Make use of your fridge to ensure all components are fully set and chilled before assembling the cake. Any residual warmth can compromise the cake's structure. As you build the cake, pop it into the fridge (or freezer for a quicker set if you have the space) between layers. This helps everything firm up nicely and gives you the freedom to add plenty of filling without the worry of things sliding around or collapsing.

LAYER CAKES 103

LAYER CAKE 1

Sour cream chocolate cake with cinnamon myrtle, raspberry & toasted white chocolate cream cheese buttercream

This was the first cake flavour at Mali Bakes and it's still a favourite. Rich chocolate cake is layered with tangy raspberries and silky toasted white chocolate buttercream. Roasting the raspberries (rather than cooking them down into a jam) keeps their juicy burst, balancing the chocolate's richness. Cinnamon myrtle, a native Australian herb, adds sweet, herbaceous notes and is also used to soak the cake. If unavailable, swap for a pinch of ground cinnamon, ground nutmeg and a bay leaf (simply blend together in a small spice grinder). This cake is very delicate – briefly chilling the layers before handling makes assembly easier.

MAKES	1 × 18 cm (7 in) diameter three-layer cake
SERVES	up to 16
STORE	in the fridge for up to 3 days; do not freeze

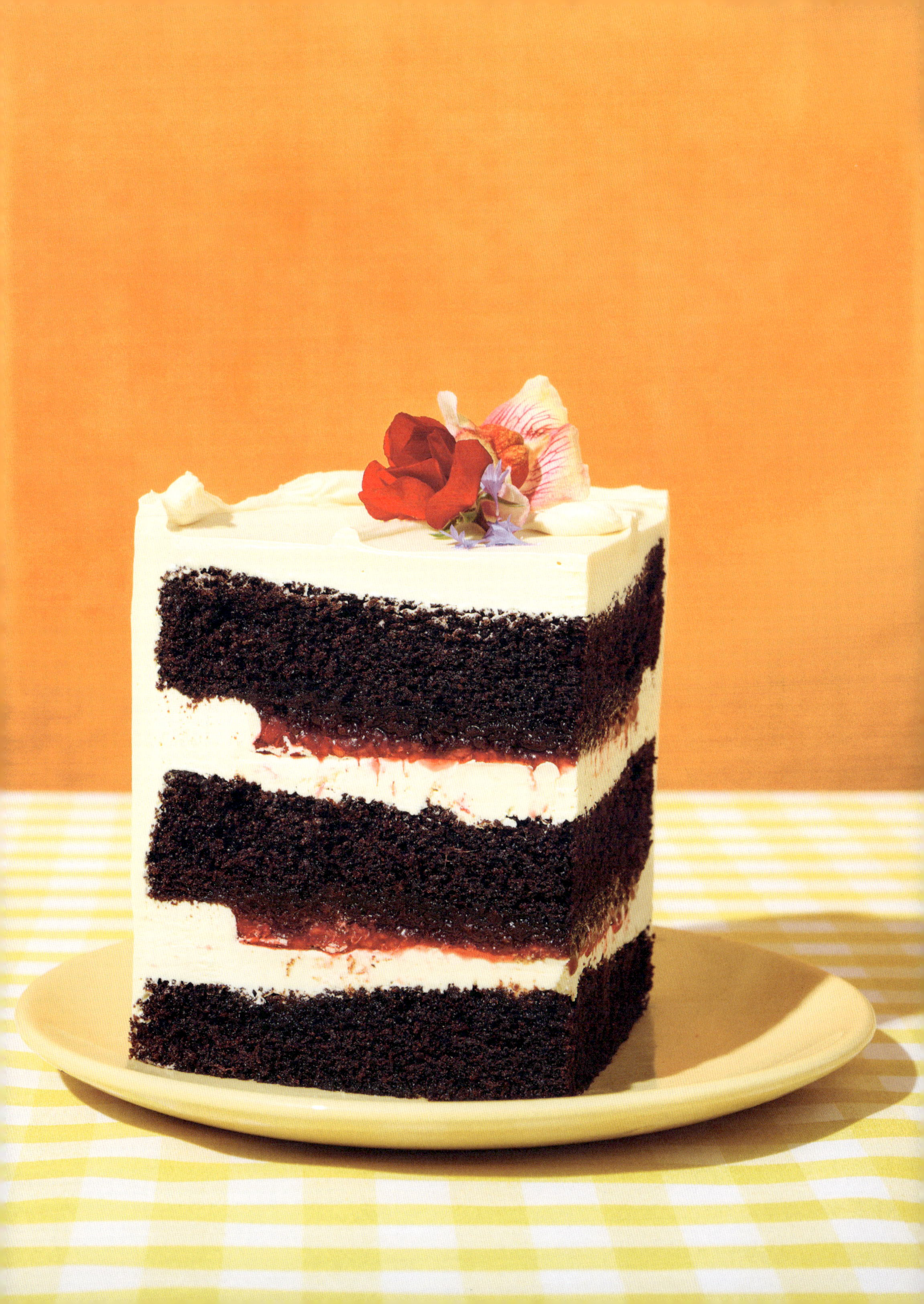

Sour cream chocolate cake with cinnamon myrtle, raspberry & toasted white chocolate cream cheese buttercream

ROASTED RASPBERRIES

750 g (26.46 oz) raspberries, fresh or frozen
225 g (7.94 oz) caster (superfine) sugar
4 g (1½ teaspoons) ground cinnamon myrtle
50 g (1.75 oz) lemon juice

Makes: 500 g (17.64 oz), enough for any of the single-tier Projects
Store: in the fridge for up to 2 weeks, or in the freezer for 3 months

CINNAMON MYRTLE SOAK

100 g (3.5 oz) caster (superfine) sugar
100 g (3.5 oz) water
4 g (1½ teaspoons) ground cinnamon myrtle

Makes: 200 g (7 oz), enough for any of the single-tier Projects
Store: in the fridge for up to 1 month or in the freezer for 6 months

SOUR CREAM CHOCOLATE CAKE

215 g (7.58 oz) plain (all-purpose) flour
35 g (1.23 oz) cornflour (corn starch)
70 g (2.47 oz) Dutch-processed cocoa powder
10 g (1⅔ teaspoons) bicarbonate of soda (baking soda)
6 g (1 teaspoon) fine sea salt
170 g (6 oz) vegetable oil
360 g (12.70 oz) caster (superfine) sugar
240 g (8.47 oz) full-fat sour cream
100 g (3.5 oz) eggs (about 2 eggs)
220 g (7.76 oz) water
4 g (1½ teaspoons) instant coffee granules

Makes: 3 individual 18 cm (7 in) cakes
Store: at room temperature for up to 3 days, or in the freezer for 1 month

Roast the raspberries

Preheat your oven and prepare the raspberries. Preheat the oven to 180°C (350°F). If using fresh raspberries, rinse them thoroughly under cold water and gently pat dry with a clean tea towel.

Toss and roast. In a roasting tray, gently toss the raspberries with the sugar, cinnamon myrtle and lemon juice until well coated. Cover the tray with baking paper, then seal with foil. Roast for about 20 minutes if using fresh raspberries, or 35 minutes if using frozen, stirring halfway through. The raspberries should be tender but still hold their shape once cooked.

Let cool completely. Remove from the oven and discard the baking paper and foil. Allow to cool completely on the tray for about 2 hours. Carefully transfer the raspberries and their juices to a bowl or container. Cover and store in the fridge until ready to use as a filling when assembling the cake.

Prepare the cinnamon myrtle soak

Combine all ingredients. Combine all the soak ingredients in a small saucepan and bring to the boil over medium–high heat. Remove from the heat and cool completely for 2 hours, then refrigerate until required.

Make the sour cream chocolate cakes

Preheat your oven and prepare the cake tins. Preheat the oven to 150°C (300°F) and position an oven rack in the centre of the oven. If all three cake tins won't fit on one rack, arrange two racks near the centre of the oven, ensuring there are at least two levels of space between them. Thoroughly spray three round 18 cm (7 in) cake tins with cooking oil and line the bottoms with baking paper, leaving the sides unlined.

Sift together the dry ingredients. Sift the flour, cornflour, cocoa powder, bicarbonate of soda and salt into a bowl. Set aside.

Mix the wet ingredients together. In the bowl of a stand mixer fitted with a whisk attachment, combine the oil, sugar, sour cream and eggs. Mix on medium–high speed for 30 seconds, scrape down the side of the bowl, then mix for another 30 seconds until well combined.

Add the dry ingredients to the wet. Gradually add the dry ingredients to the wet mixture in three additions. Mix on medium–low speed for 5 seconds after each addition, until just combined, then scrape down the side of the bowl, ensuring no visible lumps of dry flour remain.

Add the boiling coffee. Combine the water and instant coffee in a small saucepan and bring to the boil. With the mixer on medium–low speed, slowly pour the boiling coffee into the batter. Once combined, scrape down the side of the bowl, ensuring the batter is evenly mixed.

Bake the cakes. Divide the batter evenly between the cake tins, or measure 470 g (16.58 oz) per tin. Pop the cakes in the oven, either across one or two racks as necessary.

TOASTED WHITE CHOCOLATE CREAM CHEESE BUTTERCREAM

135 g (4.76 oz) white chocolate, roughly chopped
50 g (1.75 oz) water
150 g (5.3 oz) caster (superfine) sugar
120 g (4.23 oz) egg whites, chilled (from about 4 eggs)
3 g (½ teaspoon) fine sea salt
2 g (½ teaspoon) cream of tartar
250 g (8.82 oz) unsalted butter, cubed
70 g (2.47 oz) full-fat cream cheese, cubed

Makes: 700 g (24.7 oz), enough to fill and frost an 18 cm (7 in) three-layer cake, or fill any single-tier Projects
Store: in the fridge for 1 week or in the freezer for up to 3 months.

Bake for 40–45 minutes, until a cake tester inserted into the centre comes out clean, or the cakes spring back when gently pressed in the middle. Rotate the tins front to back after 25 minutes to ensure even baking.

Let cool, then store. While the cakes are baking, lightly spray at least two cooling racks with oil to prevent sticking. (Make sure there's enough room for all cakes to fit comfortably.) Once the cakes are baked, remove them from the oven and place the tins on the cooling racks for 15 minutes. Use a straight palette knife to loosen the edge of each cake around the inside of the tins, then gently flip each cake onto the cooling racks and peel off the baking paper. Let the cakes cool completely for at least 2 hours before assembling the cake or wrapping them with plastic wrap.

Prepare the toasted white chocolate buttercream

Toast the white chocolate. In a microwave-safe bowl, heat the white chocolate in 15-second intervals, thoroughly stirring with a rubber spatula after each burst to prevent burning. Continue for 3–4 minutes, until the chocolate turns a golden brown with a toasted caramel aroma. Once ready, cool slightly for 1 minute, then stir vigorously to remove any lumps. Cool to room temperature before adding to the buttercream.

Make the IMBC. (For more detailed instructions, see pages 43–46.) In a small saucepan, combine the water and sugar, then gently stir just until the sugar is evenly moistened. Set the pan on the stovetop, ready to heat. Place the chilled egg whites, salt and cream of tartar in the bowl of a stand mixer. Begin whisking on medium speed until the mixture turns foamy and small bubbles form; this should take about 2 minutes. Once the egg whites are ready, and with the mixer running, cook the sugar syrup over medium heat, without stirring, until it reaches 115°C (240°F). Immediately remove from the heat, increase the mixer speed to high, then slowly pour the hot syrup into the meringue (the egg whites should be at soft peaks with fine, smooth bubbles), beginning with a thin stream and gradually increasing the flow. When all the syrup is incorporated, whisk on high speed for another 3–4 minutes as the meringue cools slightly. The meringue should turn glossy and hold stiff peaks and should be about 35°C (95°F). While mixing on high speed, gradually add the softened butter cubes one at a time, ensuring each cube is fully incorporated before adding the next. Once all the butter is incorporated, continue beating for 3–4 minutes until the buttercream changes from a pale yellow to a creamy white, and slightly increases in volume.

Add the cream cheese and white chocolate. Once the buttercream is whipped to a silky and airy consistency, gradually add the softened cream cheese, one cube at a time, while mixing on high. Ensure each cube is fully incorporated before adding the next. Once all the cream cheese is mixed in, pour in the toasted white chocolate and whip for an additional 30 seconds, until well incorporated.

Assemble the cake

Assemble the cake layers, following the instructions on pages 48–56. Set in the fridge for at least 1 hour (or overnight) before serving at room temperature.

LAYER CAKE 2

Buttermilk vanilla cake with brown butter custard & vanilla bean cream cheese buttercream

In Mali Bakes' first year, so many customers asked for a simple, crowd-pleasing flavour, so I decided to create our own version of the classic vanilla cake. Think fluffy vanilla cake loaded with a brown butter custard filling, a crunchy brown butter crumb and silky vanilla bean buttercream. Vanilla and brown butter are a match made in dessert heaven, and this cake is all about celebrating vanilla in the best way possible. It's vanilla-town, and we're here for it!

MAKES	1 × 18 cm (7 in) diameter three-layer cake
SERVES	up to 16
STORE	in the fridge for up to 3 days; do not freeze

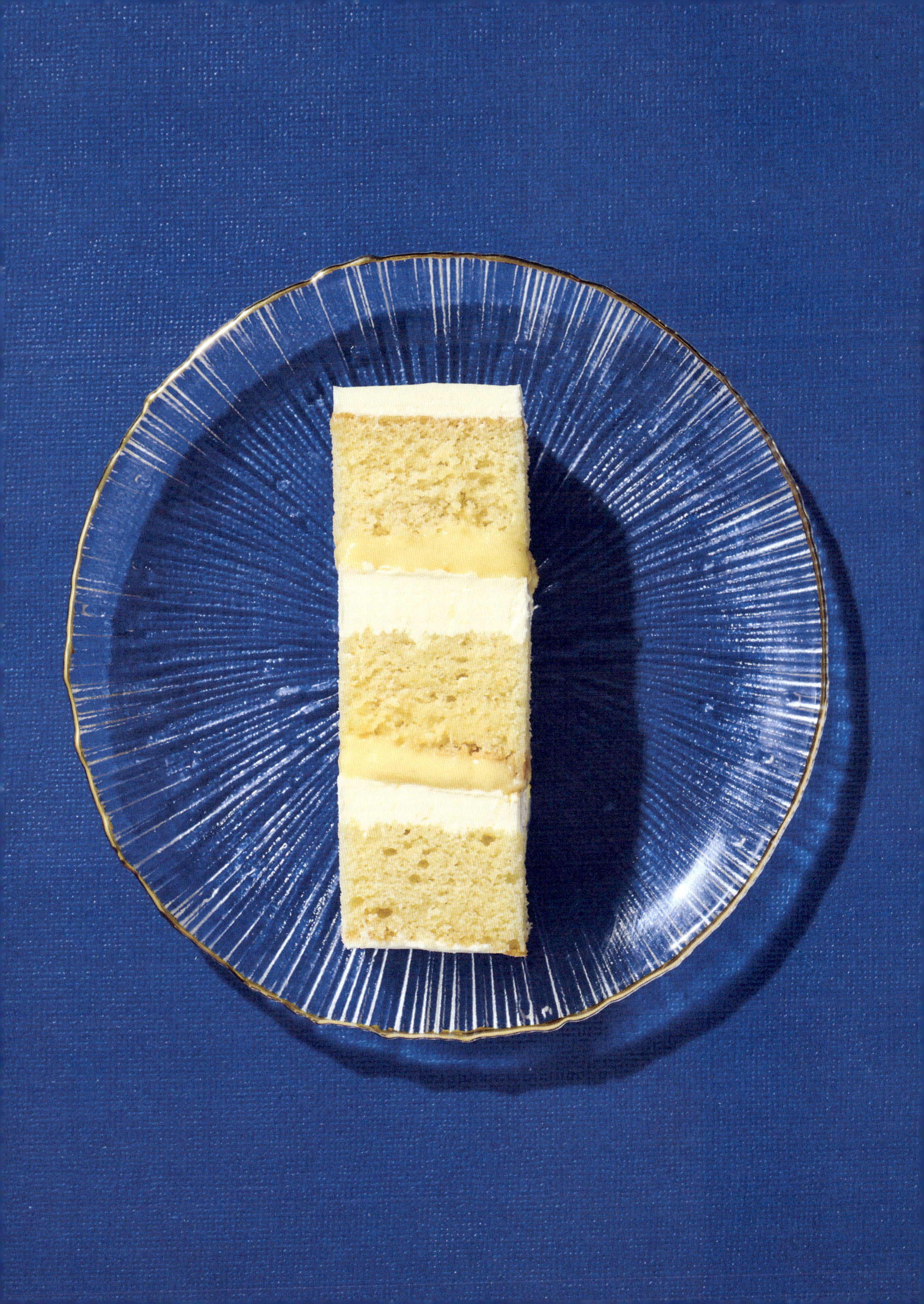

Buttermilk vanilla cake with brown butter custard & vanilla bean cream cheese buttercream

BROWN BUTTER CUSTARD
45 g (1.59 oz) unsalted butter, cubed
60 g (2.17 oz) caster (superfine) sugar
15 g (0.53 oz) cornflour (corn starch)
2 g (¼ teaspoon) fine sea salt
350 g (12.35 oz) full-cream (whole) milk
1 vanilla bean pod, or 4 g (1 teaspoon) vanilla bean paste
70 g (2.47 oz) egg yolks (from about 4 eggs)

Makes: 475 g (16.76 oz), enough for any of the single-tier Projects
Store: in the fridge for up to 4 days, do not freeze

Make the brown butter custard

Brown the butter. Melt the butter in a saucepan over medium heat, stirring occasionally. Continue cooking for another 5–8 minutes. As the butter foams, stir constantly with a heatproof rubber spatula, scraping the bottom of the pan to prevent burning. The butter will release a nutty aroma as the milk solids brown to a golden hue. Once browned, remove from the heat and let cool to room temperature; you should end up with about 35 g (1.23 oz) browned butter.

Set up and combine the dry ingredients. Place a fine-meshed strainer over a bowl and set it aside for later. In a bowl, whisk together the sugar, cornflour and salt, then set aside.

Heat the milk. Pour the milk into a clean saucepan. Split the vanilla bean lengthways, scrape out the seeds and add them to the milk, along with the pod. If using vanilla paste, simply stir it in. Scald the milk over medium–low heat until it reaches 82°C (180°F), or until small bubbles form around the edge. Avoid boiling, as this can affect the custard's texture. Remove the vanilla pod at this stage, if using.

Mix the egg yolks and dry ingredients. While the milk is heating, place the egg yolks in a large bowl. Put a tea towel underneath the bowl to keep it stable while your hands are busy. Thoroughly whisk the eggs using a hand whisk. Add half the sugar mixture and whisk vigorously until it dissolves, then add the remaining sugar mixture and whisk again. The mixture will become slightly paler in colour. Work quickly during this step – sugar can draw moisture from the yolks, which may cause them to seize up and form hard lumps.

Add the milk to the egg yolks. Once the milk is scalded, gradually pour it into the egg-yolk mixture in a slow, steady stream, while whisking constantly to combine.

Cook the custard. Pour the custard mixture back into the saucepan and cook over medium–low heat for about 2 minutes, whisking constantly until it thickens. To check for readiness, stop whisking briefly to see if small bubbles form on the surface, or use a digital thermometer to ensure the temperature reaches 77°C (170°F). Once ready, cook for a further 2 minutes to fully cook the cornflour. Continue whisking constantly, focusing on the bottom and side of the pan to prevent overcooking or burning.

Strain and add the browned butter. Pour the custard through the fine-meshed strainer to remove any egg lumps. Whisk in the room-temperature brown butter, using a hand whisk, until the custard is smooth and glossy. Use a rubber spatula to scrape down the side of the bowl, then press a piece of plastic wrap directly onto the surface of the custard to prevent a skin forming. Refrigerate for at least 2 hours until fully cooled before using. Give the set custard a quick whisk to loosen the texture before using it as a filling when assembling the cake.

BROWN BUTTER CRUMB
80 g (2.82 oz) butter
65 g (2.3 oz) plain (all-purpose) flour
55 g (1.94 oz) caster (superfine) sugar
15 g (0.53 oz) full-cream (whole) milk powder
2 g (¼ teaspoon) fine sea salt

Makes: 150 g (5.3 oz), enough for any of the single-tier Projects
Store: in the fridge for up to 2 weeks, or in the freezer for up to 3 months

BUTTERMILK VANILLA CAKE
340 g (12 oz) caster (superfine) sugar
4 g (1 teaspoon) vanilla bean paste
325 g (11.46 oz) plain (all-purpose) flour
5 g (1 teaspoon) baking powder
4 g (⅔ teaspoon) bicarbonate of soda (baking soda)
4 g (⅔ teaspoon) fine sea salt
40 g (1.41 oz) vegetable oil
270 g (9.52 oz) buttermilk
200 g (7 oz) eggs (about 4 eggs)
135 g (4.76 oz) unsalted butter, cubed

Makes: 3 individual 18 cm (7 in) cakes
Store: at room temperature for up to 3 days, or in the freezer for 1 month

Make the brown butter crumb

Brown the butter. Follow the instructions on the opposite page to brown the butter for the crumb; you should end up with about 65 g (2.3 oz) browned butter. Set aside to cool to room temperature.

Combine the dry ingredients. In a bowl, sift together the flour, sugar, milk powder and salt. Stir well until evenly combined.

Add the melted butter and let set. Pour the cooled brown butter over the mixture and stir with a rubber spatula until evenly moistened. Toss the mixture a few times to form small crumbs. Transfer to an unlined baking tray, spreading the mixture out evenly while keeping the crumbs intact. Let the crumbs firm up in the fridge for 10–15 minutes.

Preheat the oven. While the crumbs are setting, set your oven to 150°C (300°F) and position a rack in the centre of the oven.

Bake and let cool. Bake the brown butter crumbs for 20–25 minutes. Gently stir halfway through, taking care not to break up the crumbs too much. Once done, the crumbs will still appear slightly wet. Remove from the oven and allow the crumbs to cool completely on the tray for at least 2 hours, tossing gently to break up any larger pieces. Store in an airtight container in the fridge until ready to use.

Make the buttermilk vanilla cakes

Preheat your oven and prepare the cake tins. Preheat the oven to 150°C (300°F) and position an oven rack in the centre of the oven. If all three cake tins won't fit on one rack, arrange two racks near the centre of the oven, ensuring there are at least two levels of space between them. Thoroughly spray three round 18 cm (7 in) cake tins with cooking oil and line the bottoms with baking paper, leaving the sides unlined.

Prepare the vanilla sugar. In the bowl of a stand mixer, combine the sugar and vanilla paste. Using your fingertips, rub the mixture together until the vanilla is evenly distributed and the sugar is fully infused with its aroma.

Sift together the dry ingredients. Sift the flour, baking powder, bicarbonate of soda and salt into the stand mixer bowl. Attach the paddle attachment and mix on low speed for about 1 minute, ensuring all the ingredients are thoroughly combined.

Combine the wet ingredients. In a small bowl, stir together the oil and one-quarter of the buttermilk. In a separate bowl, whisk together the eggs and remaining buttermilk. Set both mixtures aside.

Mix in the butter and the oil mixture. Add the butter to the dry ingredients, along with the oil and buttermilk mixture. Mix on low speed for about 1 minute, until just evenly moistened. Increase the speed to medium and mix for another minute, until the mixture comes together and is slightly paler in colour.

Recipe continues

LAYER CAKES

VANILLA MILK SOAK
200 g (7 oz) full-cream (whole) milk
5 g (1 teaspoon) vanilla extract

Makes: 200 g (7 oz), enough for any of the single-tier Projects
Store: in the fridge for up to 4 days, do not freeze

VANILLA BEAN CREAM CHEESE BUTTERCREAM
80 g (2.82 oz) white chocolate, roughly chopped
45 g (1.59 oz) water
150 g (5.30 oz) caster (superfine) sugar
120 g (4.23 oz) egg whites, chilled (from about 4 eggs)
3 g (½ teaspoon) fine sea salt
2 g (½ teaspoon) cream of tartar
250 g (8.82 oz) unsalted butter, cubed
70 g (2.47 oz) full-fat cream cheese, cubed
4 g (1 teaspoon) vanilla bean paste

Makes: 650 g (23 oz), enough to fill and frost an 18 cm (7 in) three-layer cake, or fill any single-tier Projects
Store: in the fridge for 1 week or in the freezer for up to 3 months.

Add the remaining wet ingredients. Add the egg and buttermilk mixture in three additions. Start each addition by mixing on low speed, then pour the wet mixture in a thin stream until it begins to combine. Increase the speed to medium–high and mix for about 5 seconds until fully incorporated. After each addition, scrape down the side and bottom of the bowl, as well as the paddle attachment, to ensure even mixing. The batter should be smooth, thick, and have a custard-like consistency.

Bake the cakes. Divide the batter evenly between the cake tins, or measure 440 g (15.52 oz) per tin. Use an angled (offset) palette knife to smooth the tops of the batter. Pop the cakes in the oven, either across one or two racks as necessary.

Bake for 35–40 minutes, until a cake tester inserted into the centre comes out clean, or the cakes spring back when gently pressed in the middle. Rotate the tins front to back after 25 minutes to ensure even baking.

Let cool, then store. While the cakes are baking, lightly spray at least two cooling racks with oil to prevent sticking. (Make sure there's enough room for all cakes to fit comfortably.) Once the cakes are baked, remove them from the oven and place the tins on the cooling racks for 10 minutes. Use a straight palette knife to loosen the edge of each cake around the inside of the tins, then gently flip each cake onto the cooling racks and peel off the baking paper.

Let the cakes cool completely for at least 2 hours before assembling the cake or wrapping them with plastic wrap.

Prepare the vanilla milk soak

Mix together the milk and vanilla. Refrigerate until required.

Prepare the vanilla bean cream cheese buttercream

Melt the white chocolate. Add about 4 cm (1½ in) water to a small saucepan and bring to a gentle simmer over medium heat. Set a heatproof bowl over the saucepan, ensuring the bottom of the bowl doesn't touch the water. Place the chocolate in the bowl and stir constantly until fully melted and smooth. Remove the bowl from the heat, ensuring the chocolate remains fluid for later use. In a cooler kitchen, you can leave the bowl over the saucepan with the heat turned off to maintain its consistency.

Make the IMBC. (For more detailed instructions, see pages 43–46.) In a small saucepan, combine the water and sugar, then gently stir just until the sugar is evenly moistened. Set the pan on the stovetop, ready to heat. Place the chilled egg whites, salt and cream of tartar in the bowl of a stand mixer. Begin whisking on medium speed until the mixture turns foamy and small bubbles form; this should take about 2 minutes. Once the egg whites are ready, and with the mixer running, cook the sugar syrup over medium heat, without stirring, until it reaches 115°C (240°F). Immediately remove from the heat, increase the mixer speed to high, then slowly pour the hot syrup into the meringue (the egg whites should be at soft peaks with fine, smooth bubbles), beginning with a thin stream and gradually increasing the flow. When all the syrup is incorporated, whisk on high speed for another 3–4 minutes as the meringue cools slightly. The meringue should turn glossy and hold stiff peaks and should be about 35°C (95°F). While mixing on high speed, gradually add the softened butter cubes one at a time, ensuring each cube is fully incorporated before adding the next. Once all the butter is incorporated, continue beating for 3–4 minutes until the buttercream changes from a pale yellow to a creamy white, and slightly increases in volume.

Add the cream cheese, chocolate and vanilla. Once the buttercream is whipped to a silky and airy consistency, gradually add the softened cream cheese, one cube at a time, while mixing on high. Ensure each cube is fully incorporated before adding the next. Once all the cream cheese is mixed in, pour in the melted white chocolate and vanilla, then whip for an additional 30 seconds until well incorporated.

Assemble the cake

Assemble the cake layers, following the instructions on pages 48–56. Set in the fridge for at least 1 hour (or overnight) before serving at room temperature.

Chocolate chip cake with passionfruit curd, dark chocolate crumb & vanilla bean cream cheese buttercream

This cake is all about contrast and balance. You've got soft, chocolate chip–studded cake layers paired with a smooth vanilla bean buttercream – comforting and familiar, like your favourite ice cream. Then comes the passionfruit curd, bright and punchy, which cuts through the sweetness with a tropical kick. A sprinkle of dark chocolate crumb adds a hint of bitterness and a bit of crunch in every bite. Together, these flavours play off each other in the best way – sweet, sharp, rich and refreshing all at once.

MAKES	1 × 18 cm (7 in) diameter three-layer cake
SERVES	up to 16
STORE	in the fridge for up to 3 days; do not freeze

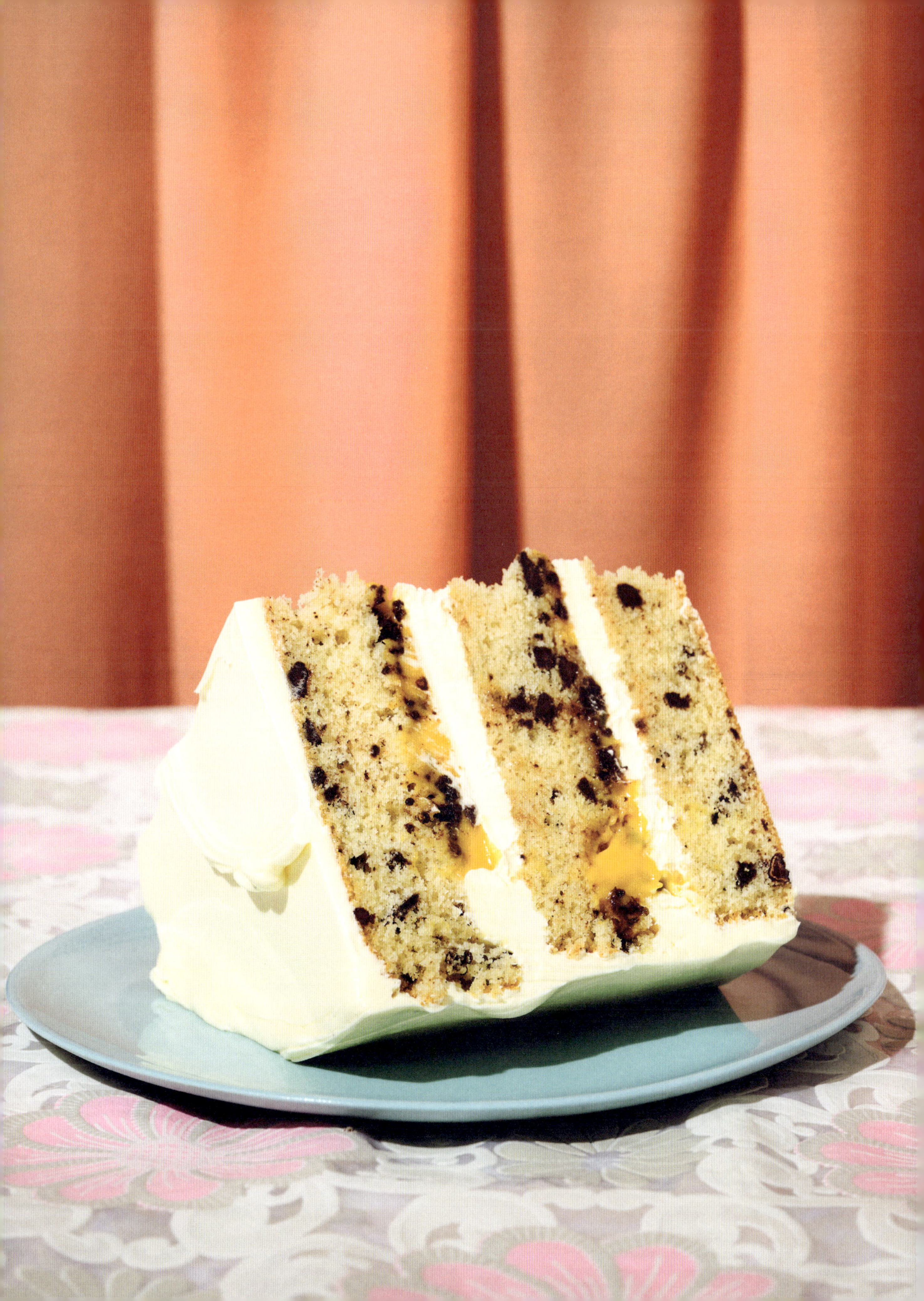

Chocolate chip cake with passionfruit curd, dark chocolate crumb & vanilla bean cream cheese buttercream

PASSIONFRUIT CURD
170 g (6 oz) passionfruit juice and pulp, fresh or frozen and thawed
40 g (1.41 oz) lemon juice
1 g (½ teaspoon) lemon zest
65 g (2.3 oz) caster (superfine) sugar
110 g (3.88 oz) egg yolks (from about 6 eggs)
1 g (small pinch) fine sea salt
120 g (4.23 oz) unsalted butter, cubed

Makes: 500 g (17.64 oz), enough for any of the single-tier Projects
Store: in the fridge for up to 1 week, or in the freezer for 1 month

Make the passionfruit curd

Strain the passionfruit juice and pulp. Set a fine-meshed strainer over a bowl. Add the passionfruit juice and pulp and, using the back of a spoon, press the pulp against the strainer to extract as much juice as possible. Combine the strained passionfruit juice with the lemon juice, and set the remaining passionfruit pulp aside.

Set up a double boiler and strainer. Add about 4 cm (1½ in) water to a large saucepan and place a heatproof bowl on top. Check the fit, ensuring the bowl sits securely without touching the water. Remove the bowl and bring the water to a gentle simmer over medium heat. Meanwhile, set a fine-meshed strainer over another bowl and set it aside for later.

Make the lemon sugar. In the heatproof bowl you're using for the double boiler, combine the lemon zest and sugar. Using your fingertips, rub the zest into the sugar until it's evenly mixed and releases a bright, citrusy aroma.

Whisk the egg yolks and sugar. Add the egg yolks to the sugar mixture and whisk immediately, using a hand whisk, until smooth and well combined. Pour in the lemony passionfruit juice, add the salt then whisk again until fully incorporated. Work quickly during this step – sugar can draw moisture from the yolks, which may cause them to seize up and form hard lumps.

Cook the curd. Reduce the heat to keep the water at a gentle simmer. Place the bowl over the simmering water and stir occasionally with a whisk until the curd thickens, or reaches 80°C (175°F). This should take 7–8 minutes. Avoid increasing the heat, as this can cause the curd to scramble. Keep an eye on the water level, adding more if it begins to evaporate.

Strain, then whisk in the butter. Once the curd is cooked, remove the bowl from the heat and pass the curd through your strainer to remove any egg lumps. Whisk in the reserved passionfruit pulp and butter until fully incorporated. Use a rubber spatula to scrape down the side of the bowl, then press a piece of plastic wrap directly onto the curd surface to prevent a skin forming. Refrigerate for at least 2 hours or until fully chilled before use. Give the set curd a quick whisk to loosen the texture before using it as a filling when assembling the cake.

CHOCOLATE CRUMB

50 g (1.75 oz) plain (all-purpose) flour
5 g (2 teaspoons) cornflour (corn starch)
2 g (¼ teaspoon) fine sea salt
30 g (1.06 oz) coconut sugar
50 g (1.75 oz) Dutch-processed cocoa powder
40 g (1.41 oz) unsalted butter, melted and cooled to room temperature

---

Makes: 175 g (6.17 oz), enough for any of the single-tier Projects
Store: in the fridge for up to 2 weeks, or in the freezer for up to 3 months.

CHOCOLATE CHIP CAKE

340 g (12 oz) caster (superfine) sugar
4 g (1 teaspoon) vanilla bean paste
325 g (11.46 oz) plain (all-purpose) flour
100 g (3.5 oz) bittersweet dark chocolate, chopped into small pieces about 5 mm (¼ in) in size
5 g (1 teaspoon) baking powder
4 g (⅔ teaspoon) bicarbonate of soda (baking soda)
4 g (⅔ teaspoon) fine sea salt
40 g (1.41 oz) vegetable oil
260 g (9.17 oz) buttermilk
200 g (7 oz) eggs (about 4 eggs)
130 g (4.59 oz) unsalted butter, cubed

Makes: 3 individual 18 cm (7 in) cakes
Store: at room temperature for up to 3 days, or in the freezer for 1 month

Make the chocolate crumb

Preheat the oven. Preheat your oven to 150°C (300°F) and position a rack in the centre of the oven.

Combine the dry ingredients. In a bowl, sift together all the dry ingredients. Stir thoroughly to ensure they are well combined and the coconut sugar is fully broken up and evenly mixed in.

Add the melted butter. Add the room temperature melted butter and stir with a rubber spatula until the mixture is evenly moistened. Give the bowl a few quick tosses to help the mixture form small crumbs.

Bake and let cool. Spread the crumbs on an unlined baking tray and bake for 20 minutes. Gently stir halfway through, taking care not to break up the crumbs too much. Once done, the crumbs will still appear slightly wet. Remove from the oven and allow the crumbs to cool completely on the tray for at least 2 hours, tossing gently to break up any larger pieces. Store in an airtight container in the fridge until ready to use.

Make the chocolate chip cakes

Preheat your oven and prepare the cake tins. Preheat the oven to 150°C (300°F) and position an oven rack in the centre of the oven. If all three cake tins won't fit on one rack, arrange two racks near the centre of the oven, ensuring there are at least two levels of space between them. Thoroughly spray three round 18 cm (7 in) cake tins with cooking oil and line the bottoms with baking paper, leaving the sides unlined.

Prepare the vanilla sugar. In the bowl of a stand mixer, combine the sugar and vanilla paste. Using your fingertips, rub the mixture together until the vanilla is evenly distributed and the sugar is fully infused with its aroma.

Sift together the dry ingredients. Take about 1 tablespoon of the flour and mix it thoroughly with the chocolate chips, then set aside. Sift the remaining flour, baking powder, bicarbonate of soda and salt into the stand mixer bowl. Attach the paddle attachment and mix on low speed for about 1 minute, ensuring all the ingredients are thoroughly combined.

Combine the wet ingredients. In a small bowl, stir together the oil and one-quarter of the buttermilk. In a separate bowl, whisk together the eggs and remaining buttermilk. Set both mixtures aside.

Mix in the butter and the oil mixture. Add the butter to the dry ingredients, along with the oil and buttermilk mixture. Mix on low speed for about 1 minute, until just evenly moistened. Increase the speed to medium and mix for another minute, until the mixture comes together and is slightly paler in colour.

Recipe continues

VANILLA MILK SOAK
1 × quantity Vanilla milk soak (page 112)

VANILLA BEAN CREAM CHEESE BUTTERCREAM
1 × quantity Vanilla bean cream cheese buttercream (page 112)

Add the remaining wet ingredients. Add the egg and buttermilk mixture in three additions. Start each addition by mixing on low speed, then pour the wet mixture in a thin stream until it begins to combine. Increase the speed to medium–high and mix for about 5 seconds until fully incorporated. After each addition, scrape down the side and bottom of the bowl, as well as the paddle attachment, to ensure even mixing. The batter should be smooth, thick, and have a custard-like consistency.

Fold in the chocolate chips. Using a spatula, fold the flour-coated chocolate chips into the batter until just evenly distributed, being careful not to overmix.

Bake the cakes. Divide the batter evenly between the cake tins, or measure 470 g (16.58 oz) per tin. Use an angled (offset) palette knife to smooth the tops of the batter. Pop the cakes in the oven, either across one or two racks as necessary.

Bake for 35–40 minutes, until a cake tester inserted into the centre comes out clean, or the cakes spring back when gently pressed in the middle. Rotate the tins front to back after 25 minutes to ensure even baking.

Let cool, then store. While the cakes are baking, lightly spray at least two cooling racks with oil to prevent sticking. (Make sure there's enough room for all cakes to fit comfortably.) Once the cakes are baked, remove them from the oven and place the tins on the cooling racks for 10 minutes. Use a straight palette knife to loosen the edge of each cake around the inside of the tins, then gently flip each cake onto the cooling racks and peel off the baking paper.

Let the cakes cool completely for at least 2 hours before assembling the cake or wrapping them with plastic wrap.

Prepare the vanilla milk soak

Follow the instructions on page 112 to prepare the vanilla milk soak.

Prepare the vanilla bean cream cheese buttercream

Follow the instructions on pages 112–113 to prepare the vanilla bean cream cheese buttercream.

Assemble the cake

Assemble the cake layers, following the instructions on pages 48–56. Set in the fridge for at least 1 hour (or overnight) before serving at room temperature.

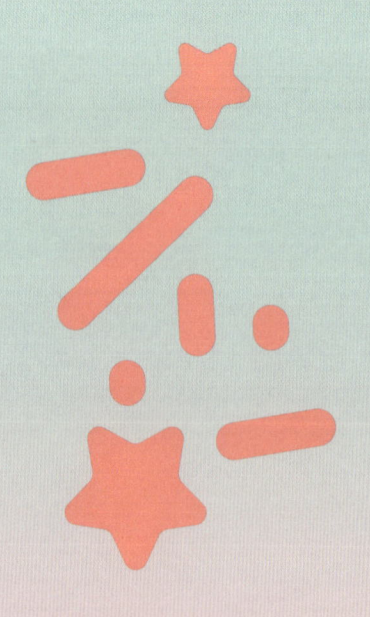

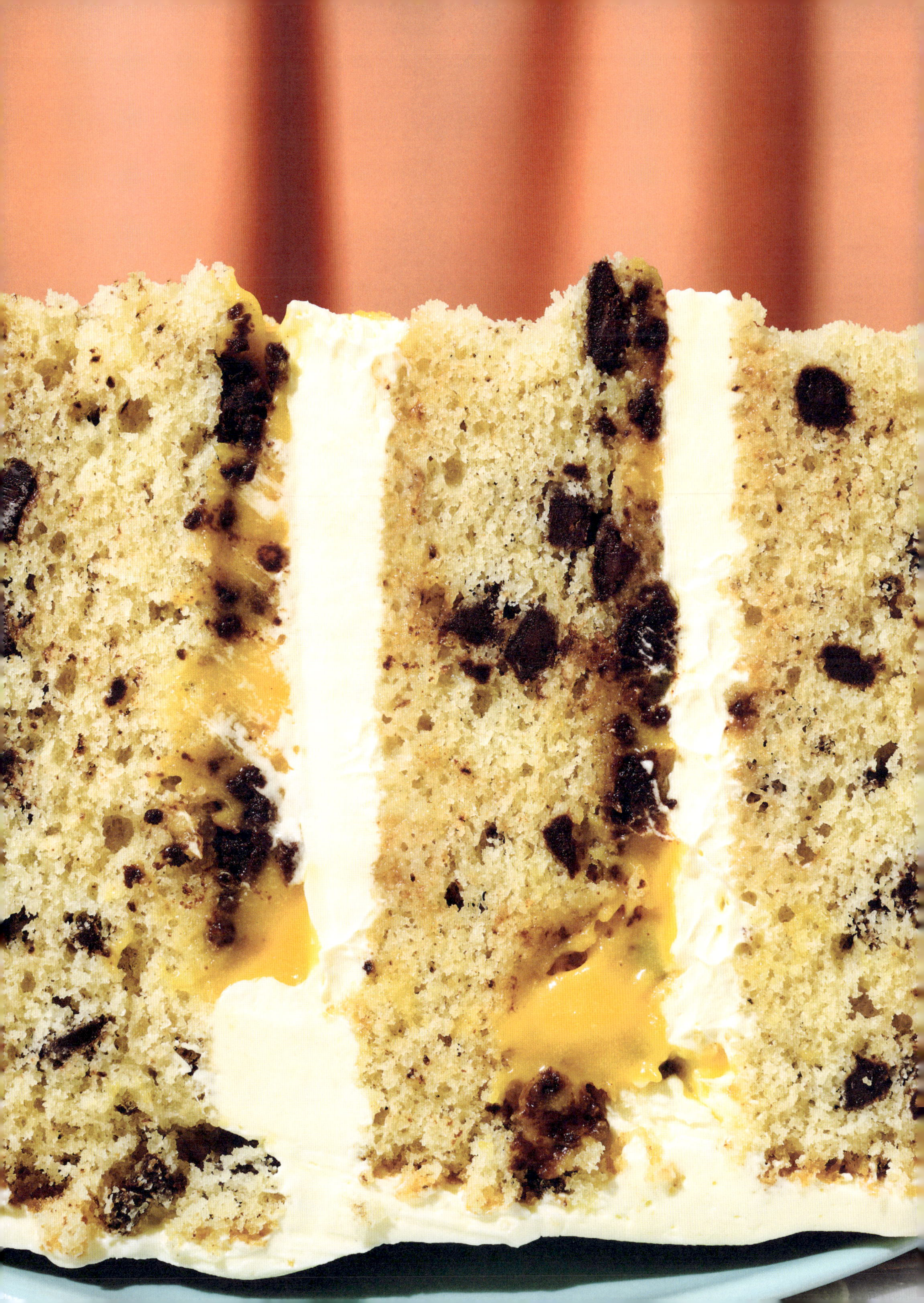

LAYER CAKE 4

Peanut butter cake with roasted strawberries, whipped mascarpone & peanut butter cream cheese buttercream

Peanut butter and strawberries are a classic duo that never gets old. In this cake, the strawberries are roasted to keep their juicy texture, and the extra syrup becomes a quick homemade jammy gel — kind of like a grown-up version of your favourite childhood jam. The whipped mascarpone is light and dreamy and helps tie everything together, but it does need to set overnight, so plan ahead. When it's time to build the cake, there's no wrong way — go heavy on the mascarpone or load up on the strawberries. Either way, it's delicious!

MAKES	1 × 18 cm (7 in) diameter three-layer cake
SERVES	up to 16
STORE	in the fridge for up to 3 days; do not freeze

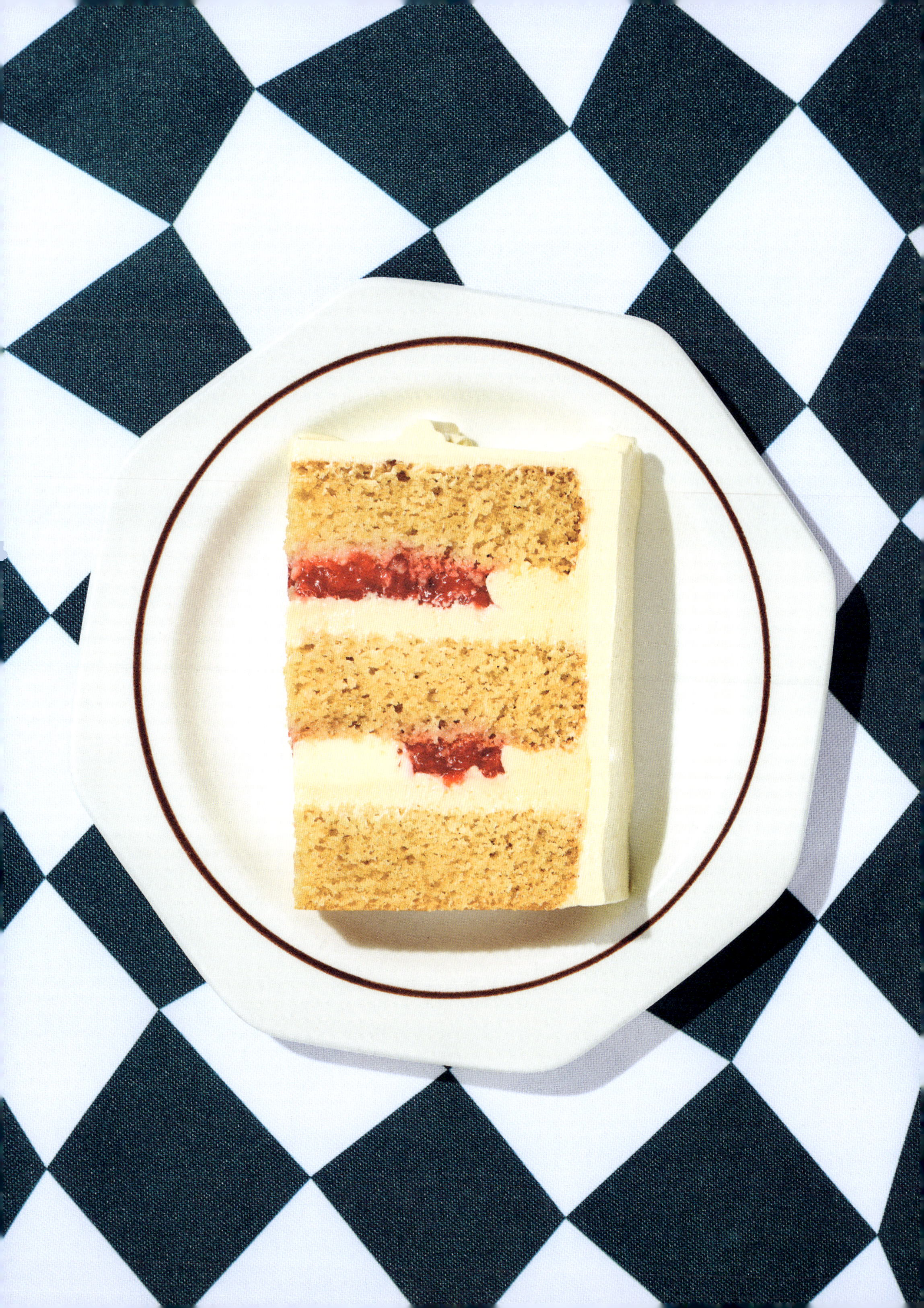

Peanut butter cake with roasted strawberries, whipped mascarpone & peanut butter cream cheese buttercream

ROASTED STRAWBERRIES

550 g (19.4 oz) strawberries, fresh or frozen, hulled and diced into 1 cm (½ in) pieces
165 g (5.82 oz) caster (superfine) sugar
2 g (1 teaspoon) lemon zest
30 g (1.06 oz) lemon juice

Makes: 500 g (17.64 oz), enough for any of the single-tier Projects
Store: in the fridge for 1 week, or in the freezer for 3 months

JAMMY STRAWBERRY GEL (OPTIONAL)

200 g (7 oz) cooked strawberry liquid, from roasting the strawberries (above)
4 g (1 teaspoon) citrus pectin

Makes: 200 g (7 oz), enough for decorating the cake, or mixing into the roasted strawberry filling for the cake
Store: in the fridge for 2 weeks, or in the freezer for 3 months

Roast the strawberries

Preheat your oven and prepare the strawberries. If using frozen strawberries, let them thaw completely in the fridge overnight. Preheat the oven to 180°C (350°F). If using fresh strawberries, rinse them thoroughly under cold water and gently pat them dry with a clean tea towel or paper towel.

Add the other ingredients and roast. In a roasting tray, toss the strawberries with the sugar, lemon zest and juice until well coated. Cover the tray with baking paper, then seal with foil. Roast for about 30 minutes, stirring halfway through to ensure even cooking. The strawberries should be tender throughout, their juices pooling and their shapes gently softening.

Let cool completely. Remove the tray from the oven and discard the baking paper and foil. Allow the strawberries cool completely on the tray for about 2 hours. Carefully transfer the strawberries, along with their juices, to a bowl or container. Cover and refrigerate until ready to use.

Strain the strawberries. Strain any excess juice before using the strawberries as a filling when assembling the cake. The strawberries can be used to fill the cake as is, or can be turned into the jammy strawberry gel (see below).

Make the strawberry gel (optional)

Combine the ingredients. Pour the reserved roasted strawberry juices into a small saucepan, add the pectin and blend with an immersion blender until the pectin is fully dissolved.

Cook the gel. Bring the mixture to the boil over medium–high heat, stirring constantly and scraping the bottom of the pan to prevent burning. Once boiling, cook for a further 2 minutes, or until the liquid becomes translucent. (Cooking the mixture high and fast helps preserve the brightness of the strawberry flavour.)

Let cool and combine with roasted strawberries. Let the gel cool down slightly in the pan for about 10 minutes, then stir in as many of the roasted strawberry pieces as you please. Transfer to a bowl or container, then cover and refrigerate until ready to use as a filling when assembling the cake.

WHIPPED MASCARPONE CREAM

½ sheet titanium-strength gelatine
100 g (3.5 oz) mascarpone
90 g (3.17 oz) white chocolate, roughly chopped
250 g (8.82 oz) cream (about 35% fat)
4 g (1 teaspoon) vanilla bean paste, or 1 vanilla bean pod

Makes: 400 g (14 oz), enough for any of the single-tier Projects
Store: in the fridge for up to 1 week. Do not freeze

PEANUT BUTTER CAKE

165 g (5.82 oz) caster (superfine) sugar
110 g (3.88 oz) brown sugar
230 g (8.11 oz) plain (all-purpose) flour
27 g (0.95 oz) cornflour (corn starch)
10 g (2 teaspoons) baking powder
6 g (1 teaspoon) bicarbonate of soda (baking soda)
3 g (½ teaspoon) fine sea salt
250 g (8.82 oz) full-cream (whole) milk
50 g (1.75 oz) vegetable oil
165 g (5.82 oz) eggs (from about 3 eggs)
4 g (1 teaspoon) vanilla bean paste
90 g (3.17 oz) unsalted butter, cubed
165 g (5.82 oz) smooth peanut butter

Makes: 3 individual 18 cm (7 in) cakes
Store: at room temperature for up to 3 days, or in the freezer for 1 month

Prepare the whipped mascarpone cream

Bloom the gelatine. Fill a small bowl with cold water and submerge the gelatine sheet, then leave to soak for 10 minutes. Once softened, gently squeeze out the excess water.

Prepare the mascarpone and white chocolate. Place the mascarpone, white chocolate and bloomed gelatine in a tall heatproof jug or container tall enough to blend the ingredients with an immersion blender without spilling. Set aside.

Heat the cream and vanilla. Pour the cream into a small saucepan. If using vanilla paste, simply stir it in. If using a vanilla bean pod, split it lengthways, scrape out the seeds, and add both the seeds and the pod to the saucepan. Warm over medium–low heat until the mixture just begins to simmer, or reaches 80°C (175°F), stirring regularly with a heatproof rubber spatula to prevent the bottom burning; this should take 2–3 minutes. Be careful not to let it boil, as this can cause the mixture to split when whipped.

Blend and let set. Remove the vanilla pod, if using, then pour the hot cream mixture over the mascarpone and white chocolate mixture. Let it sit for about 1 minute to soften the chocolate, then blend using an immersion blender until fully incorporated and smooth, with no visible lumps of chocolate. Transfer to a container and press a piece of plastic wrap directly onto the surface of the mascarpone mixture to prevent a skin forming. Refrigerate overnight, or for at least 8 hours, allowing it to fully set.

Whip the cream. Chill the bowl of your stand mixer and whisk attachment in the fridge for 15 minutes. Add the chilled mascarpone mixture and whisk on medium speed until soft peaks form. Increase the speed to medium–high, pausing occasionally to scrape the side of the bowl for even mixing. Whisk until stiff peaks just form; this will take about 5 minutes. Transfer to a piping bag and refrigerate until needed.

Make the peanut butter cakes

Preheat your oven and prepare the cake tins. Preheat the oven to 150°C (300°F) and position an oven rack in the centre of the oven. If all three cake tins won't fit on one rack, arrange two racks near the centre of the oven, ensuring there are at least two levels of space between them. Thoroughly spray three round 18 cm (7 in) cake tins with cooking oil and line the bottoms with baking paper, leaving the sides unlined.

Sift together the dry ingredients. Place the caster sugar and brown sugar in the bowl of a stand mixer. Sift in the flour, cornflour, baking powder, bicarbonate of soda and salt. Attach the paddle attachment and mix on low speed for about 1 minute, ensuring all the ingredients are thoroughly combined.

Combine the wet ingredients. In a bowl, whisk together three-quarters of the milk, the oil, eggs and vanilla until just combined. Set aside.

Recipe continues

LAYER CAKES

VANILLA MILK SOAK
1 × quantity Vanilla milk soak (page 112)

Mix in the butter and peanut butter. Add the butter, peanut butter and remaining milk to the dry ingredients and mix on low speed for about 1 minute, until just evenly moistened. Increase the speed to medium and mix for another minute, until the mixture comes together and is slightly paler in colour.

Add the wet ingredients. Add the wet ingredients in three additions. Start each addition by mixing on low speed, then pour the wet mixture in a thin stream until it begins to combine. Increase the speed to medium–high and mix for about 5 seconds until fully incorporated. After each addition, scrape down the side and bottom of the bowl, as well as the paddle attachment, to ensure even mixing. The batter should be smooth, thick, and have a custard-like consistency.

Bake the cakes. Divide the batter evenly between the cake tins, or measure 420 g (14.81 oz) per tin. Use an angled (offset) palette knife to smooth the tops of the batter. Pop the cakes in the oven, either across one or two racks as necessary.

Bake for 35–40 minutes, until a cake tester inserted into the centre comes out clean, or the cakes spring back when gently pressed in the middle. Rotate the tins front to back after 25 minutes to ensure even baking.

Let cool, then store. While the cakes are baking, lightly spray at least two cooling racks with oil to prevent sticking. (Make sure there's enough room for all cakes to fit comfortably.) Once the cakes are baked, remove them from the oven and place the tins on the cooling racks for 10 minutes. Use a straight palette knife to loosen the edge of each cake around the inside of the tins, then gently flip each cake onto the cooling racks and peel off the baking paper.

Let the cakes cool completely for at least 2 hours before assembling the cake or wrapping them with plastic wrap.

Prepare the vanilla milk soak

Follow the instructions on page 112 to prepare the vanilla milk soak.

PEANUT BUTTER CREAM CHEESE BUTTERCREAM

75 g (2.65 oz) white chocolate, roughly chopped
45 g (1.59 oz) water
135 g (4.76 oz) caster (superfine) sugar
100 g (3.5 oz) egg whites, chilled (from about 4 eggs)
3 g (½ teaspoon) fine sea salt
2 g (½ teaspoon) cream of tartar
225 g (7.94 oz) unsalted butter, cubed
65 g (2.3 oz) cream cheese, cubed
120 g (4.23 oz) smooth peanut butter
4 g (1 teaspoon) vanilla bean paste

Makes: 750 g (26.46 oz), enough to fill and frost an 18 cm (7 in) three-layer cake, or fill any of the single-tier Projects
Store: in the fridge for 1 week or in the freezer for up to 3 months.

Prepare the peanut buttercream

Melt the white chocolate. Add about 4 cm (1½ in) water to a small saucepan and bring to a gentle simmer over medium heat. Set a heatproof bowl over the saucepan, ensuring the bottom of the bowl doesn't touch the water. Place the chocolate in the bowl and stir constantly until fully melted and smooth. Remove the bowl from the heat, ensuring the chocolate remains fluid for later use. In a cooler kitchen, you can leave the bowl over the saucepan with the heat turned off to maintain its consistency.

Make the IMBC. (For more detailed instructions, see pages 43–46.) In a small saucepan, combine the water and sugar, then gently stir just until the sugar is evenly moistened. Set the pan on the stovetop, ready to heat. Place the chilled egg whites, salt and cream of tartar in the bowl of a stand mixer. Begin whisking on medium speed until the mixture turns foamy and small bubbles form; this should take about 2 minutes. Once the egg whites are ready, and with the mixer running, cook the sugar syrup over medium heat, without stirring, until it reaches 115°C (240°F). Immediately remove from the heat, increase the mixer speed to high, then slowly pour the hot syrup into the meringue (the egg whites should be at soft peaks with fine, smooth bubbles), beginning with a thin stream and gradually increasing the flow. When all the syrup is incorporated, whisk on high speed for another 3–4 minutes as the meringue cools slightly. The meringue should turn glossy and hold stiff peaks and should be about 35°C (95°F). While mixing on high speed, gradually add the softened butter cubes one at a time, ensuring each cube is fully incorporated before adding the next. Once all the butter is incorporated, continue beating for 3–4 minutes until the buttercream changes from a pale yellow to a creamy white, and slightly increases in volume.

Add the cream cheese, white chocolate, peanut butter and vanilla. Once the buttercream is whipped to a silky and airy consistency, gradually add the softened cream cheese, one cube at a time, while mixing on high. Ensure each cube is fully incorporated before adding the next. Once all the cream cheese is mixed in, pour in the white chocolate, peanut butter and vanilla, then whip for an additional 30 seconds until well incorporated.

Assemble the cake

Assemble the cake layers, following the instructions on pages 48–56. Set in the fridge for at least 1 hour (or overnight) before serving at room temperature.

LAYER CAKE 5

Orange yoghurt cake with yuzu curd, fresh orange segments & yuzu poppy seed buttercream

I'm all about citrus-on-citrus, and this cake is a total sunshine bomb! It pairs two bold citrus flavours – orange and yuzu – for a fresh, zesty combo. The base is a soft orange yoghurt cake, layered with tangy yuzu curd for that extra punch. Fresh orange segments add juicy pops throughout, and the poppy seed buttercream brings a fun little crunch, giving a wink to the classic poppy seed cake. You can find bottled yuzu juice at most Asian or Japanese grocers, just be sure to grab one that's 100 per cent juice, with no vinegar or sugar added.

MAKES	1 × 18 cm (7 in) diameter three-layer cake
SERVES	up to 16
STORE	in the fridge for up to 3 days; do not freeze

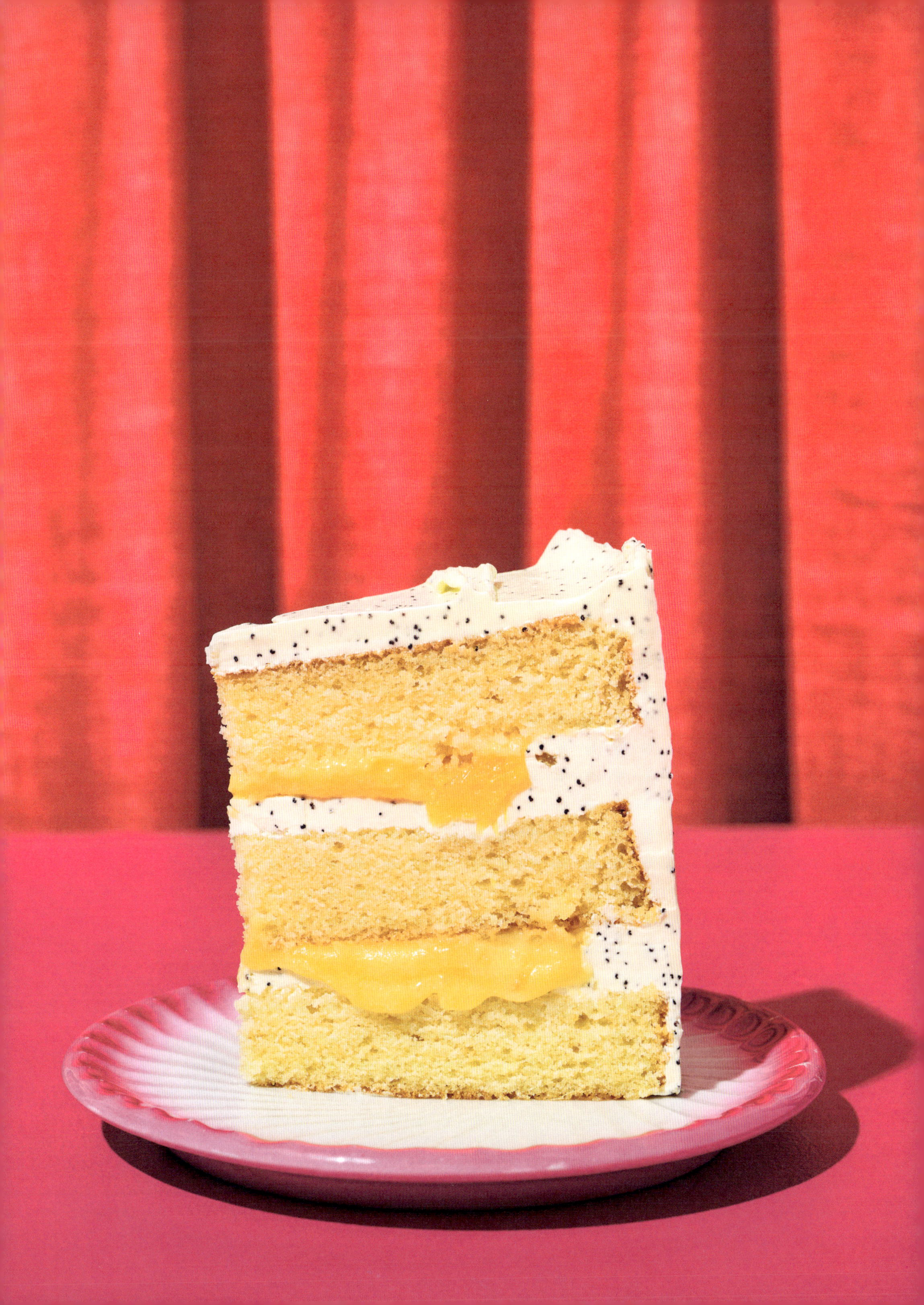

Orange yoghurt cake with yuzu curd, fresh orange segments & yuzu poppy seed buttercream

YUZU CURD

2 g (1 teaspoon) lemon zest
100 g (3.5 oz) caster (superfine) sugar
120 g (4.23 oz) egg yolks (from about 6 eggs)
80 g (2.82 oz) yuzu juice
80 g (2.82 oz) lemon juice
1 g (small pinch) fine sea salt
120 g (4.23 oz) unsalted butter, cubed

Makes: 500 g (17.64 oz), enough for any of the single-tier Projects
Store: in the fridge for up to 1 week, or in the freezer for 1 month

ORANGE SOAK

100 g (3.5 oz) caster (superfine) sugar
50 g (1.75 oz) water
4 g (2 teaspoons) orange zest (from about 1 orange)
50 g (1.75 oz) orange juice (from about 1 orange)

Makes: 200 g (7 oz), enough for any of the single-tier Projects
Store: in the fridge for up to 4 weeks, or in the freezer for 6 months

Prepare the yuzu curd

Set up a double boiler and strainer. Add about 4 cm (1½ in) water to a large saucepan and place a heatproof bowl on top. Check the fit, ensuring the bowl sits securely without touching the water. Remove the bowl and bring the water to a gentle simmer over medium heat. Meanwhile, set a fine-meshed strainer over another bowl and set it aside for later.

Make the lemon sugar. In the heatproof bowl you're using for the double boiler, combine the lemon zest and sugar. Using your fingertips, rub the zest into the sugar until it's evenly mixed and releases a bright, citrusy aroma.

Whisk the egg yolks and sugar together. Add the egg yolks to the sugar mixture and whisk immediately, using a hand whisk, until smooth and well combined. Pour in the yuzu juice, lemon juice and salt, then whisk again until fully incorporated. Work quickly during this step – sugar can draw moisture from the yolks, which may cause them to seize up and form hard lumps.

Cook the curd. Reduce the heat to keep the water at a gentle simmer. Place the bowl over the simmering water and stir occasionally with a whisk until the curd thickens, or reaches 80°C (175°F). This should take 7–8 minutes. Avoid increasing the heat, as this can cause the curd to scramble. Keep an eye on the water level, adding more if it begins to evaporate.

Strain, then whisk in the butter. Once the curd is cooked, remove the bowl from the heat and pass the curd through your strainer to remove any egg lumps. Whisk in the butter until fully incorporated. Use a rubber spatula to scrape down the side, then cover the surface of the curd with plastic wrap, pressing it directly onto the surface to prevent a skin forming. Refrigerate for at least 2 hours or until fully chilled before use. Give the set curd a quick whisk to loosen the texture before using it as a filling when assembling the cake.

Prepare the orange soak

Combine all ingredients. Combine all the orange soak ingredients in a small saucepan and bring to the boil over medium–high heat. Remove from the heat and leave to cool completely for 2 hours, then refrigerate until ready to use. Strain before using.

ORANGE YOGHURT CAKE

325 g (11.46 oz) caster (superfine) sugar
4 g (2 teaspoons) orange zest (from about 1 orange)
310 g (10.94 oz) plain (all-purpose) flour
5 g (1 teaspoon) baking powder
4 g (⅔ teaspoon) bicarbonate of soda (baking soda)
4 g (⅔ teaspoon) fine sea salt
200 g (7 oz) eggs (from about 4 eggs)
100 g (3.5 oz) buttermilk
40 g (1.41 oz) vegetable oil
40 g (1.41 oz) orange juice (from about 1 orange)
130 g (4.59 oz) unsalted butter, cubed
130 g (4.59 oz) full-fat yoghurt

Makes: 3 individual 18 cm (7 in) cakes
Store: at room temperature for up to 3 days, or in the freezer for 1 month

Make the orange yoghurt cakes

Preheat your oven and prepare the cake tins. Preheat the oven to 150°C (300°F) and position an oven rack in the centre of the oven. If all three cake tins won't fit on one rack, arrange two racks near the centre of the oven, ensuring there are at least two levels of space between them. Thoroughly spray three round 18 cm (7 in) cake tins with cooking oil and line the bottoms with baking paper, leaving the sides unlined.

Prepare the orange sugar. In the bowl of a stand mixer, combine the sugar and orange zest. Using your fingertips, rub the zest into the sugar until it's evenly mixed through and releases a bright, citrusy aroma.

Sift together the dry ingredients. Sift the flour, baking powder, bicarbonate of soda and salt into the stand mixer bowl. Attach the paddle attachment and mix on low speed for about 1 minute, ensuring all the ingredients are thoroughly combined.

Combine the wet ingredients. In a bowl, whisk together the eggs, buttermilk, oil and orange juice. Set aside.

Mix in the butter and yoghurt. Add the butter and yoghurt to the dry ingredients and mix on low speed for about 1 minute, ensuring the dry ingredients are evenly moistened. Increase the speed to medium and continue mixing for another minute, until the mixture comes together and is slightly paler in colour.

Add the wet ingredients. Gradually add the wet ingredients in three additions. Start each addition by mixing on low speed, then slowly pour the wet mixture in a thin stream until it begins to combine. Increase the speed to medium–high and mix for about 5 seconds until fully incorporated. After each addition, scrape down the side and bottom of the bowl, as well as the paddle attachment, to ensure even mixing. The batter should be smooth, thick, and have a custard-like consistency.

Bake the cakes. Divide the batter evenly between the cake tins, or measure 430 g (15.17 oz) per tin. Use an angled (offset) palette knife to smooth the tops of the batter. Pop the cakes in the oven, either across one or two racks as necessary.

Bake for 30–35 minutes, until a cake tester inserted into the centre comes out clean, or the cakes spring back when gently pressed in the middle. Rotate the tins front to back after 25 minutes to ensure even baking.

Let cool, then store. While the cakes are baking, lightly spray at least two cooling racks with oil to prevent sticking. (Make sure there's enough room for all cakes to fit comfortably.) Once the cakes are baked, remove them from the oven and place the tins on the cooling racks for 10 minutes. Use a straight palette knife to loosen the edge of each cake around the inside of the tins, then gently flip each cake onto the cooling racks and peel off the baking paper.

Let the cakes cool completely for at least 2 hours before assembling the cake or wrapping them with plastic wrap.

Recipe continues

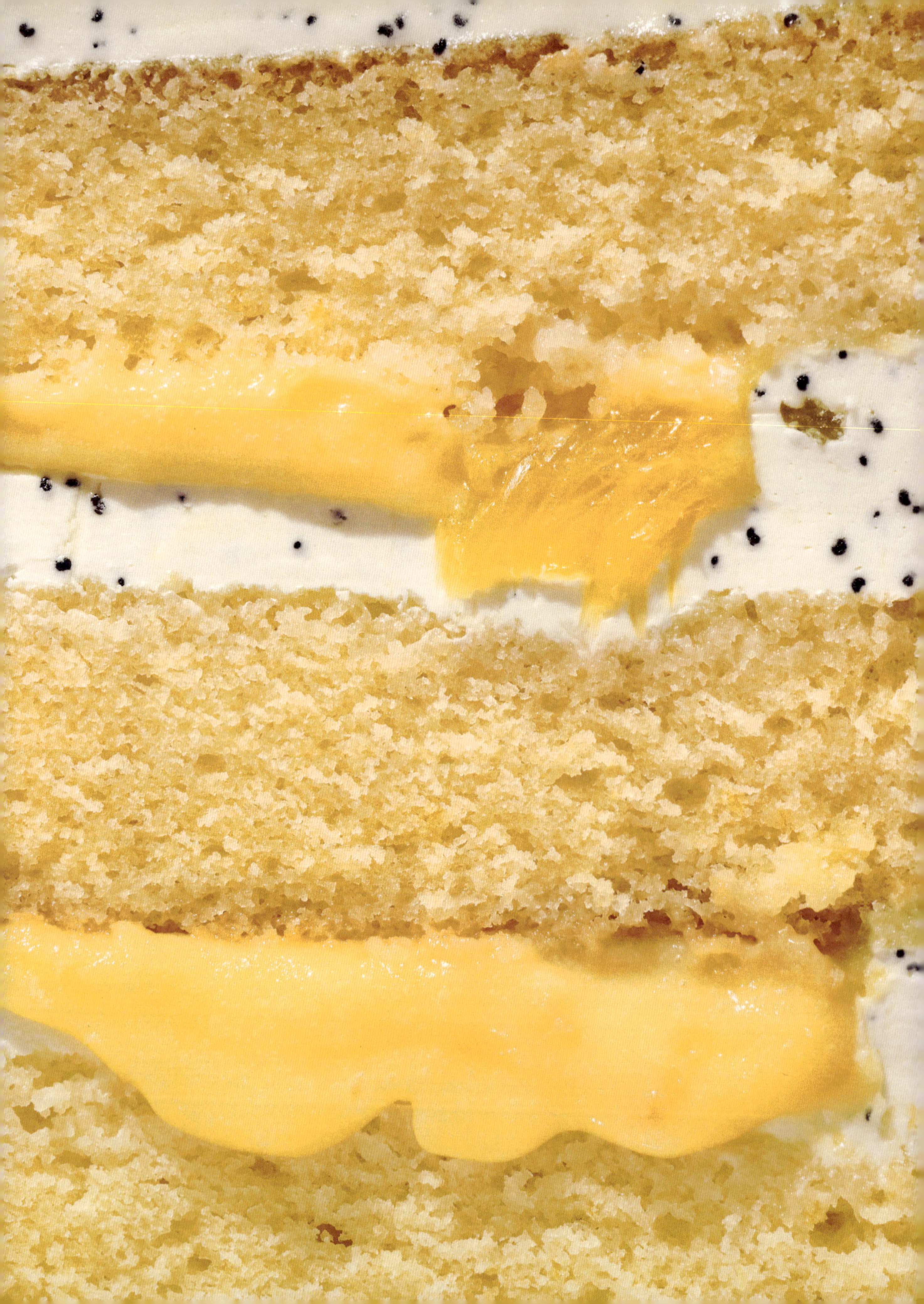

YUZU POPPY SEED BUTTERCREAM

65 g (2.3 oz) water
200 g (7 oz) caster (superfine) sugar
150 g (5.30 oz) egg whites, chilled (from about 5 eggs)
3 g (½ teaspoon) fine sea salt
2 g (½ teaspoon) cream of tartar
300 g (10.58 oz) unsalted butter, cubed
50 g (1.75 oz) yuzu juice
25 g (0.88 oz) poppy seeds

Makes: 700 g (24.7 oz), enough to fill and frost an 18 cm (7 in) three-layer cake, or fill any single-tier Projects
Store: in the fridge for 1 week or in the freezer for up to 3 months.

FRESH ORANGE SEGMENTS

1 orange

Makes: enough for any of the single-tier Projects

Prepare the yuzu poppy seed buttercream

Make the IMBC. (For more detailed instructions, see pages 43–46.) In a small saucepan, combine the water and sugar, then gently stir just until the sugar is evenly moistened. Set the pan on the stovetop, ready to heat. Place the chilled egg whites, salt and cream of tartar in the bowl of a stand mixer. Begin whisking on medium speed until the mixture turns foamy and small bubbles form; this should take about 2 minutes. Once the egg whites are ready, and with the mixer running, cook the sugar syrup over medium heat, without stirring, until it reaches 115°C (240°F). Immediately remove from the heat, increase the mixer speed to high, then slowly pour the hot syrup into the meringue (the egg whites should be at soft peaks with fine, smooth bubbles), beginning with a thin stream and gradually increasing the flow. When all the syrup is incorporated, whisk on high speed for another 3–4 minutes as the meringue cools slightly. The meringue should turn glossy and hold stiff peaks and should be about 35°C (95°F). While mixing on high speed, gradually add the softened butter cubes one at a time, ensuring each cube is fully incorporated before adding the next. Once all the butter is incorporated, continue beating for 3–4 minutes until the buttercream changes from a pale yellow to a creamy white, and slightly increases in volume.

Add the yuzu juice and poppy seeds. Once the buttercream is whipped to a silky and airy consistency, add the yuzu juice and poppy seeds and whip for another 30 seconds, until well incorporated.

Prepare the orange segments

The orange segments will be used as a filling, so it's best to prepare them just before assembling the cake, to keep them fresh and juicy!

Cut off the ends. Using a small sharp knife, slice off the top and bottom of the orange to create flat surfaces.

Remove the peel. Stand the orange upright and cut away the peel and bitter white pith by following the curve of the fruit.

Cut between the membranes. Hold the orange over a bowl to catch the excess juice. Carefully slice along both sides of each membrane to release the fleshy segments. Finally, cut each segment in half.

Assemble the cake

Assemble the cake layers, following the instructions on pages 48–56, scattering the orange segment pieces on top of each layer of yuzu curd. Set in the fridge for at least 1 hour (or overnight) before serving at room temperature.

LAYER CAKE 6

Coffee cake with spiced blueberry jam, whipped mascarpone & coconut sugar buttercream

A few years ago, we opened a tiny pop-up cafe – a cosy little spot in the inner Melbourne suburb of Fitzroy, with just three small tables set up along the footpath serving cake, coffee and matcha. One of the creations from that time was a blueberry cold brew coffee, which quickly became a crowd favourite. That drink was the inspiration for this recipe: a rich coffee cake paired with spiced blueberry jam, creamy whipped mascarpone and a delicate coconut sugar buttercream.

MAKES	1 × 18 cm (7 in) diameter three-layer cake
SERVES	up to 16
STORE	in the fridge for up to 3 days; do not freeze

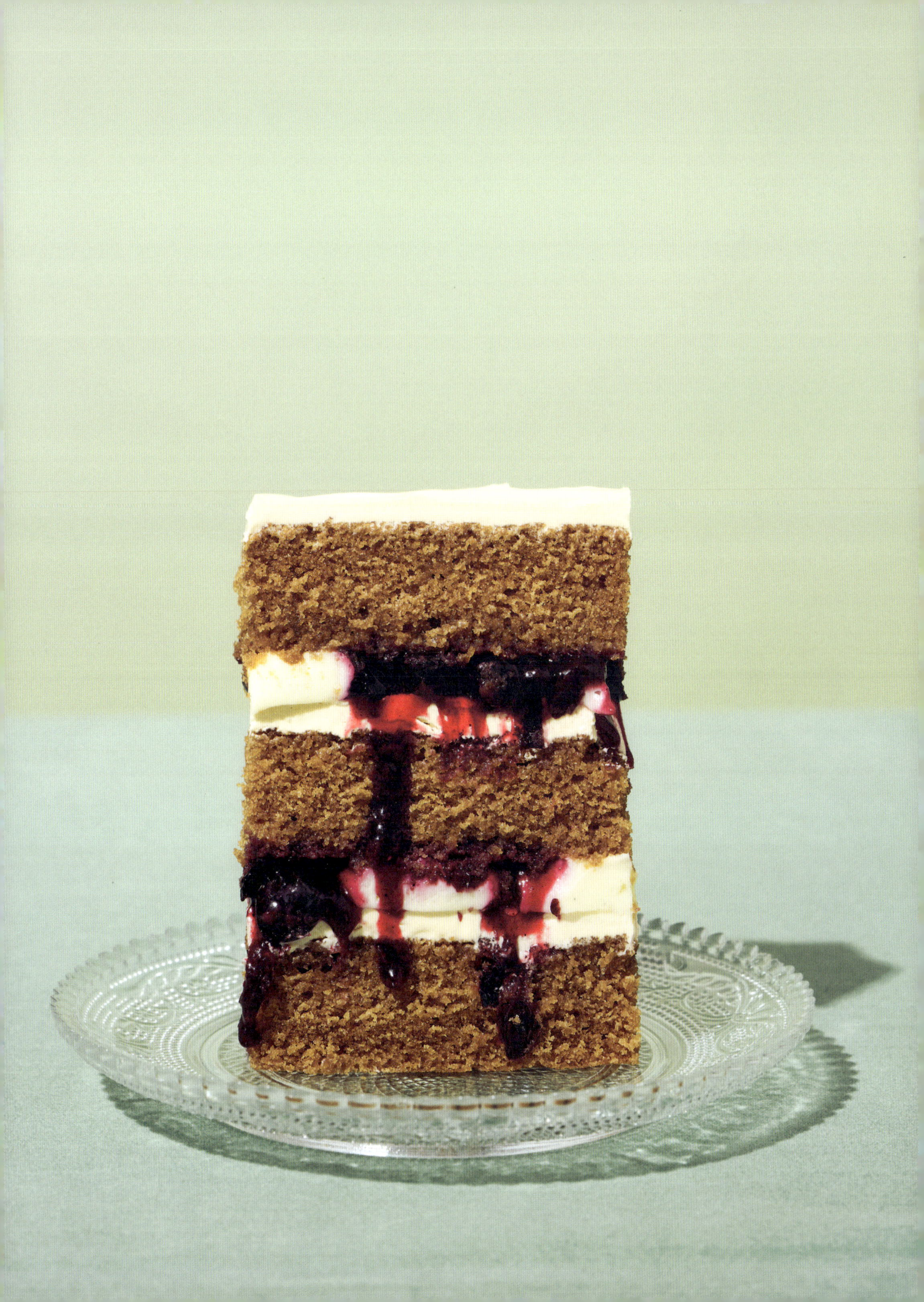

Coffee cake with spiced blueberry jam, whipped mascarpone & coconut sugar buttercream

SPICED BLUEBERRY JAM
500 g (17.64 oz) blueberries, fresh or frozen
150 g (5.30 oz) caster (superfine) sugar
8 g (2½ teaspoons) cornflour (corn starch)
40 g (1.41 oz) lemon juice
4 g (1 teaspoon) vanilla bean paste
1 cinnamon stick
2 star anise
2 g (1 teaspoon) freshly grated nutmeg
peel from ½ orange, peeled into strips

Makes: 500 g (17.64 oz), enough for any of the single-tier Projects
Store: in the fridge for up to 1 week, do not freeze

WHIPPED MASCARPONE CREAM
1 × quantity Whipped mascarpone cream (page 123)

COFFEE SOAK
100 g (3.5 oz) caster (superfine) sugar
100 g (3.5 oz) water
8 g (2 teaspoons) instant coffee granules
4 g (1 teaspoon) vanilla bean paste

Makes: 200 g (7 oz), enough for any of the single-tier Projects
Store: in the fridge for up to 4 weeks, or in the freezer for 6 months

Prepare the blueberry jam

Combine and cook. Combine all blueberry jam ingredients in a saucepan and mix with your hands to ensure the blueberries are evenly coated. Place over medium heat and cook, stirring constantly, for 5–6 minutes until the blueberries soften and release enough liquid to form a pool that comes halfway up the berries. (If using frozen blueberries, cook them directly from frozen, allowing a bit more time.) Scrape the bottom of the pan regularly to avoid sticking or burning.

Strain and break up the blueberries. Once the blueberries have softened and released their vibrant purple juice, strain and reserve the juice from the berries. Remove the cinnamon stick, star anise and orange rind, then use the back of a spoon or a potato masher to break up the blueberries in the strainer to your preferred texture. I like them slightly crushed with soft chunks — it makes slicing the cake easier, while still giving bursts of vibrant berry flavour.

Reduce the liquid. Pour the juice back into the saucepan and bring to the boil over medium–high heat. Stir constantly for 3–4 minutes, or until it thickens and reduces by half. Fast and high cooking helps preserve the bright berry flavour.

Add the blueberries. Once the juice has thickened, reduce the heat to medium and add the mashed blueberries. Cook for another minute, allowing the blueberries to soak up the flavourful liquid, then remove from the heat.

Let cool, then store. Carefully transfer the blueberry jam to a bowl or container and leave to cool completely at room temperature for about 2 hours. Cover and refrigerate until ready to use as a filling when assembling the cake.

Prepare the whipped mascarpone cream

Follow the instructions on page 123 to prepare the whipped mascarpone cream.

Prepare the coffee soak

Combine all ingredients. Combine all the coffee soak ingredients in a small saucepan and bring to the boil over medium–high heat. Remove from the heat and leave to cool completely for 2 hours, then refrigerate until ready to use.

COFFEE CAKE

150 g (5.3 oz) brown sugar
150 g (5.3 oz) caster (superfine) sugar
300 g (10.58 oz) plain (all-purpose) flour
40 g (1.41 oz) cornflour (corn starch)
6 g (1 teaspoon) baking powder
3 g (½ teaspoon) bicarbonate of soda (baking soda)
3 g (½ teaspoon) fine sea salt
100 g (3.5 oz) vegetable oil
350 g (12.35 oz) buttermilk
15 g (0.53 oz) instant coffee granules
150 g (5.3 oz) eggs (from about 3 eggs)
4 g (1 teaspoon) vanilla bean paste
100 g (3.5 oz) unsalted butter, cubed

Makes: 3 individual 18 cm (7 in) cakes
Store: at room temperature for up to 3 days, or in the freezer for 1 month

Make the coffee cakes

Preheat your oven and prepare the cake tins. Preheat the oven to 150°C (300°F) and position an oven rack in the centre of the oven. If all three cake tins won't fit on one rack, arrange two racks near the centre of the oven, ensuring there are at least two levels of space between them. Thoroughly spray three round 18 cm (7 in) cake tins with cooking oil and line the bottoms with baking paper, leaving the sides unlined.

Sift together the dry ingredients. Add the brown sugar and caster sugar to the bowl of a stand mixer. Sift in the flour, cornflour, baking powder, bicarbonate of soda and salt. Attach the paddle attachment and mix on low speed for about 1 minute, ensuring all the ingredients are thoroughly combined.

Combine the wet ingredients. In a small bowl, stir together the oil and one-quarter of the buttermilk. Pour the remaining buttermilk into another bowl, add the instant coffee and use an immersion blender to blend until the coffee fully dissolves, then whisk in the eggs and vanilla. Set both mixtures aside.

Mix in the butter and the oil mixture. Add the butter to the dry ingredients, along with the oil and buttermilk mixture. Mix on low speed for about 1 minute, until just evenly moistened. Increase the speed to medium and mix for another minute, until the mixture comes together and is slightly paler in colour.

Add the remaining wet ingredients. Add the egg and buttermilk mixture in three additions. Start each addition by mixing on low speed, then pour the wet mixture in a thin stream until it begins to combine. Increase the speed to medium–high and mix for about 5 seconds until fully incorporated. After each addition, scrape down the side and bottom of the bowl, as well as the paddle attachment, to ensure even mixing. The batter should be smooth, thick and have a custard-like consistency.

Bake the cakes. Divide the batter evenly between the cake tins, or measure 450 g (15.88 oz) per tin. Use an angled (offset) palette knife to smooth the tops of the batter. Pop the cakes in the oven, either across one or two racks as necessary.

Bake for 35–40 minutes, until a cake tester inserted into the centre comes out clean, or the cakes spring back when gently pressed in the middle. Rotate the tins front to back after 25 minutes to ensure even baking.

Let cool, then store. While the cakes are baking, lightly spray at least two cooling racks with oil to prevent sticking. (Make sure there's enough room for all cakes to fit comfortably.) Once the cakes are baked, remove them from the oven and place the tins on the cooling racks for 10 minutes. Use a straight palette knife to loosen the edge of each cake around the inside of the tins, then gently flip each cake onto the cooling racks and peel off the baking paper.

Let the cakes cool completely for at least 2 hours before assembling the cake or wrapping them with plastic wrap.

Recipe continues

COCONUT SUGAR BUTTERCREAM

75 g (2.65 oz) water
175 g (6.17 oz) caster (superfine) sugar
45 g (1.59 oz) coconut sugar
150 g (5.3 oz) egg whites, chilled (from about 5 eggs)
4 g (⅔ teaspoon) fine sea salt
2 g (½ teaspoon) cream of tartar
330 g (11.64 oz) unsalted butter cubed

Makes: 650 g (23 oz), enough to fill and frost an 18 cm (7 in) three-layer cake, or fill any of the single-tier Projects

Store: in the fridge for 1 week or in the freezer for up to 3 months

Prepare the coconut sugar buttercream

Make the IMBC. (For more detailed instructions, see pages 43–46.) In a small saucepan, combine the water, caster sugar and coconut sugar, then gently stir just until the sugar is evenly moistened. Set the pan on the stovetop, ready to heat. Place the chilled egg whites, salt and cream of tartar in the bowl of a stand mixer. Begin whisking on medium speed until the mixture turns foamy and small bubbles form; this should take about 2 minutes. Once the egg whites are ready, and with the mixer running, cook the sugar syrup over medium heat, without stirring, until it reaches 115°C (240°F). (Keep in mind that syrup made with coconut sugar will bubble more vigorously than syrup made with only caster sugar, so ensure the saucepan is tall enough to prevent splattering.) Immediately remove from the heat, increase the mixer speed to high, then slowly pour the hot syrup into the meringue (the egg whites should be at soft peaks with fine, smooth bubbles), beginning with a thin stream and gradually increasing the flow. When all the syrup is incorporated, whisk on high speed for another 3–4 minutes as the meringue cools slightly. The meringue should turn glossy and hold stiff peaks and should be about 35°C (95°F). While mixing on high speed, gradually add the softened butter cubes one at a time, ensuring each cube is fully incorporated before adding the next. Once all the butter is incorporated, continue beating for 3–4 minutes until the buttercream changes from a pale yellow to a creamy white, and slightly increases in volume.

Assemble the cake

Assemble the cake layers, following the instructions on pages 48–56. Set in the fridge for at least 1 hour (or overnight) before serving at room temperature.

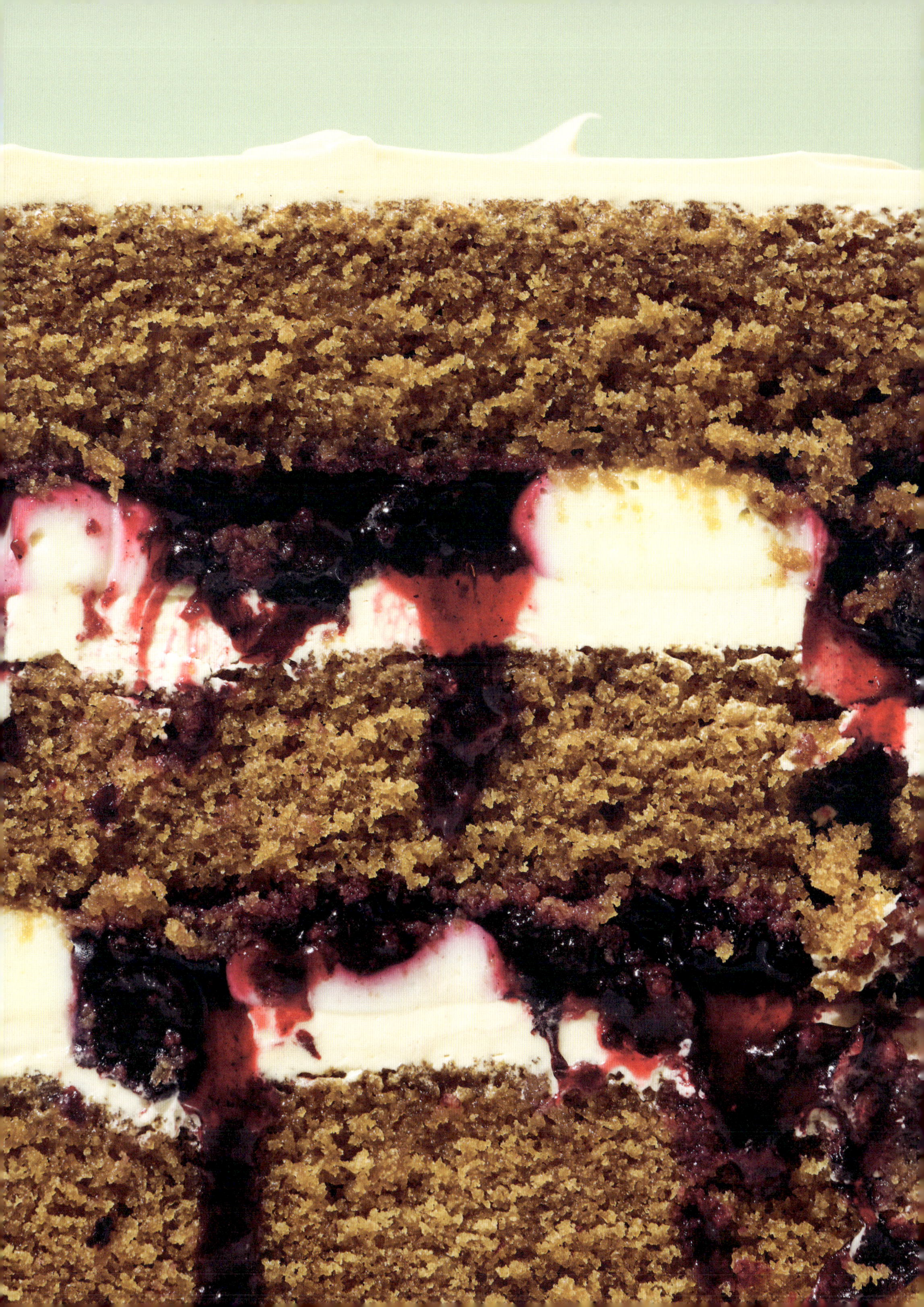

LAYER CAKE 7

Pistachio cake with cardamom-roasted rhubarb, whipped mascarpone & coconut sugar buttercream

Coconut sugar is like a warm, toasty hug. It's got a deep caramel flavour that's not too sweet but so full of character — it adds something special to whatever you're baking. In buttercream, it turns into something rich and complex that somehow works with just about everything. That's exactly why it's the star of this cake. You've got nutty pistachio layers, tangy cardamom-roasted rhubarb, and soft whipped mascarpone — all delicious on their own, but even better together!

MAKES	1 × 18 cm (7 in) diameter three-layer cake
SERVES	up to 16
STORE	in the fridge for up to 3 days; do not freeze

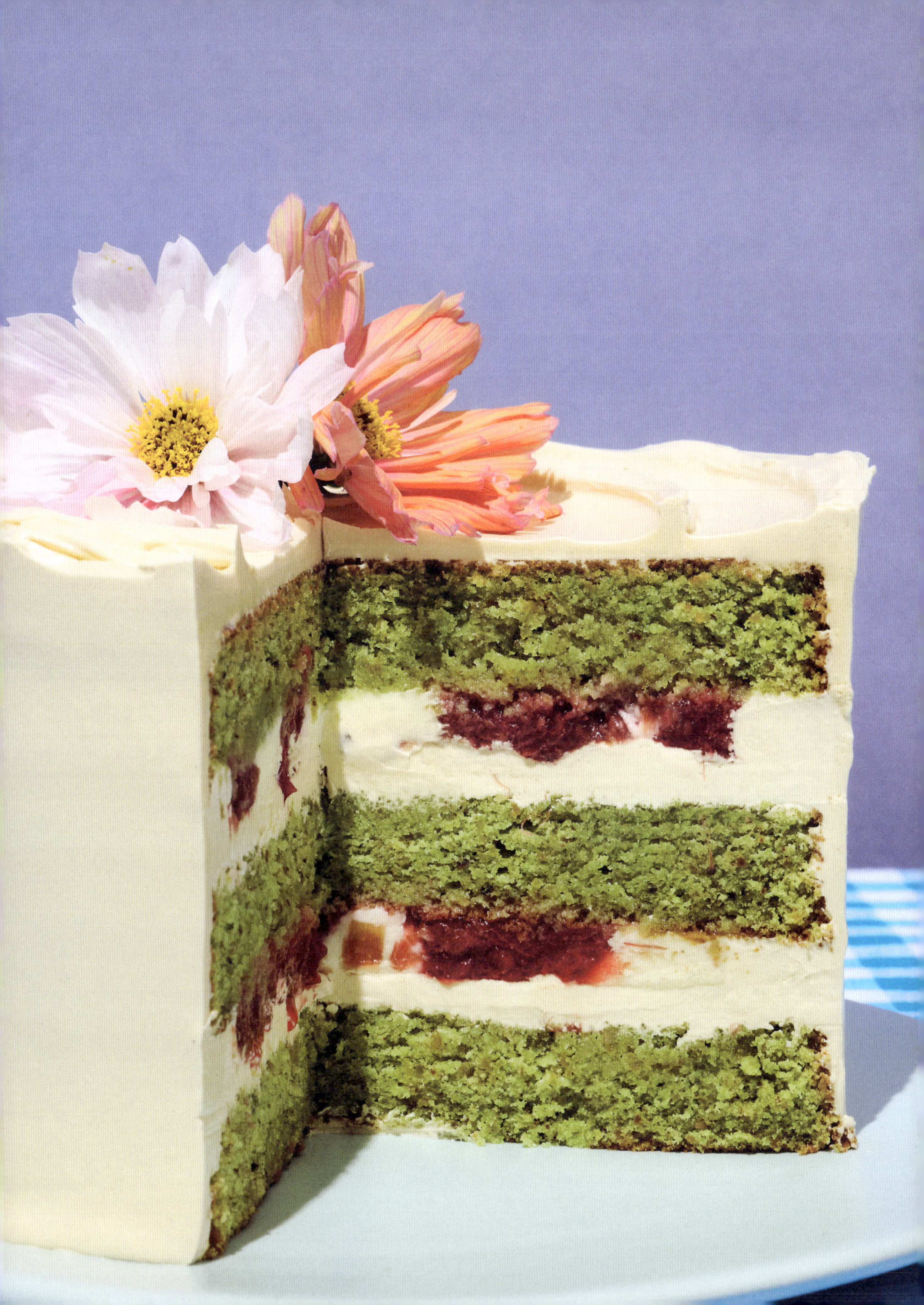

Pistachio cake with cardamom-roasted rhubarb, whipped mascarpone & coconut sugar buttercream

CARDAMOM-ROASTED RHUBARB
450 g (15.88 oz) fresh rhubarb (about 2 bunches)
135 g (4.76 oz) caster (superfine) sugar
2 g (1 teaspoon) ground cardamom
25 g (0.88 oz) orange juice
peel from ½ orange, peeled into strips

Makes: 500 g (17.64 oz), enough for any of the single-tier Projects
Store: in the fridge for up to 2 weeks, or in the freezer for 3 months

CARDAMOM SOAK
100 g (3.5 oz) caster (superfine) sugar
100 g (3.5 oz) water
6 cardamom pods, well crushed

Makes: 200 g (7 oz), enough for any of the single-tier Projects
Store: in the fridge for up to 4 weeks, or in the freezer for 6 months.

WHIPPED MASCARPONE CREAM
1 × quantity Whipped mascarpone cream (page 123)

Roast the rhubarb

Preheat your oven and prepare the rhubarb. Preheat the oven to 180°C (350°F). Trim the top and bottom off each rhubarb stalk, then rinse the stalks thoroughly under cold water. Pat dry with a clean tea towel or paper towel and slice into 1 cm (½ in) pieces.

Add the remaining ingredients and roast. In a roasting tray, toss the rhubarb pieces with the sugar, cardamom, orange juice and orange peel until evenly coated. Cover the tray with baking paper, then seal tightly with foil. Roast for about 20 minutes, stirring halfway through. The rhubarb is ready when it is tender and easily breaks apart when pierced with a fork. If it needs more time, return it to the oven covered with the baking paper and foil, and check every 5 minutes until done.

Let cool completely. Remove the rhubarb from the oven and discard the baking paper and foil. Let the rhubarb cool slightly on the tray for about 5 minutes. Discard the orange peel. Transfer the rhubarb to a bowl and gently break it up with a fork. Don't strain the juices; the rhubarb will reabsorb the liquid as it cools. Once fully cooled, cover and refrigerate until ready to use as a filling when assembling the cake.

Prepare the whipped mascarpone cream

Follow the instructions on page 123 to prepare the whipped mascarpone cream.

Prepare the cardamom soak

Combine all ingredients. Combine all the cardamom soak ingredients in a small saucepan and bring to the boil over medium–high heat. Remove from the heat and leave to infuse for 2 hours, then refrigerate until ready to use. Strain before using.

Make the pistachio cakes

Preheat your oven and prepare the cake tins. Preheat the oven to 150°C (300°F) and position an oven rack in the centre of the oven. If all three cake tins won't fit on one rack, arrange two racks near the centre of the oven, ensuring there are at least two levels of space between them. Thoroughly spray three round 18 cm (7 in) cake tins with cooking oil and line the bottoms with baking paper, leaving the sides unlined.

Prepare the pistachio sugar. In a food processor, blend the pistachios and sugar in 10-second intervals until the mixture achieves a fine, sand-like texture and the pistachios are evenly incorporated into the sugar.

PISTACHIO CAKE

145 g (5.11 oz) raw shelled pistachios
270 g (9.52 oz) caster (superfine) sugar
225 g (7.94 oz) plain (all-purpose) flour
20 g (0.7 oz) cornflour (corn starch)
5 g (1 teaspoon) baking powder
3 g (½ teaspoon) bicarbonate of soda (baking soda)
3 g (½ teaspoon) fine sea salt
270 g (9.52 oz) buttermilk
50 g (1.75 oz) vegetable oil
150 g (5.3 oz) eggs (from about 3 eggs)
6 g (1½ teaspoons) almond extract
6 drops of green food colouring, or adjust as needed (I use Colour Mill's Lime Green)
160 g (5.64 oz) unsalted butter, cubed

Makes: 3 individual 18 cm (7 in) cakes
Store: at room temperature for up to 3 days, or in the freezer for 1 month

COCONUT SUGAR BUTTERCREAM

1 × quantity Coconut sugar buttercream (page 136)

Sift together the dry ingredients. Place the pistachio sugar in the bowl of a stand mixer. Sift the flour, cornflour, baking powder, bicarbonate of soda and salt into the bowl. Attach the paddle attachment and mix on low speed for about 1 minute, ensuring all the ingredients are thoroughly combined.

Combine the wet ingredients. In a small bowl, stir together one-quarter of the buttermilk with the oil. In a separate bowl, whisk the remaining buttermilk with the eggs, almond extract and green food colouring until the mixture is well combined and the food colouring well dissolved. Set both mixtures aside.

Mix in the butter and the oil mixture. Add the butter to the dry ingredients, along with the oil and buttermilk mixture. Mix on low speed for about 1 minute, until just evenly moistened. Increase the speed to medium and mix for another minute, until the mixture comes together and is slightly paler in colour.

Add the wet ingredients. Gradually add the egg and buttermilk mixture in three additions. Start each addition by mixing on low speed, then slowly pour the wet mixture in a thin stream until it begins to combine. Increase the speed to medium–high and mix for about 5 seconds until fully incorporated. After each addition, scrape down the side and bottom of the bowl, as well as the paddle attachment, to ensure even mixing. The batter should come together nicely.

Bake the cakes. Divide the batter evenly between the cake tins, or measure 430 g (15.17 oz) per tin. Use an angled (offset) palette knife to smooth the tops of the batter. Pop the cakes in the oven, either across one or two racks as necessary.

Bake for 35–40 minutes, until a cake tester inserted into the centre comes out clean, or the cakes spring back when gently pressed in the middle. Rotate the tins front to back after 25 minutes to ensure even baking.

Let cool, then store. While the cakes are baking, lightly spray at least two cooling racks with oil to prevent sticking. (Make sure there's enough room for all cakes to fit comfortably.) Once the cakes are baked, remove them from the oven and place the tins on the cooling racks for 10 minutes. Use a straight palette knife to loosen the edge of each cake around the inside of the tins, then gently flip each cake onto the cooling racks and peel off the baking paper.

Let the cakes cool completely for at least 2 hours before assembling the cake or wrapping them with plastic wrap.

Prepare the coconut sugar buttercream

Follow the instructions on page 136 to prepare the coconut sugar buttercream.

Assemble the cake

Assemble the cake layers, following the instructions on pages 48–56. Set in the fridge for at least 1 hour (or overnight) before serving at room temperature.

LAYER CAKE 8

Olive oil ricotta cake with blackberry fennel jam & honey sea salt buttercream

When I was developing recipes for Mali Bakes, I fell in love with the soft, airy texture of a classic sponge. Light as a cloud and beautiful when fresh – but not always practical for wedding cakes that need to be made a few days ahead for decorating. That's where this olive oil ricotta cake came in.

The method is similar to sponge-making, but with warm ricotta folded in at the end. It gives the cake a lasting softness and keeps it moist for days. Paired with a blackberry jam infused with freshly toasted fennel, it quickly became a favourite for summer weddings. It's light, vibrant and full of flavour, just like the best kind of celebration.

Use a good-quality olive oil with bright, citrusy notes. Fresh, unstrained ricotta is best, but a smooth store-bought version works well too. And a dark, floral honey adds a warm depth that ties everything together beautifully.

MAKES	1 × 18 cm (7 in) diameter three-layer cake
SERVES	up to 16
STORE	in the fridge for up to 3 days; do not freeze

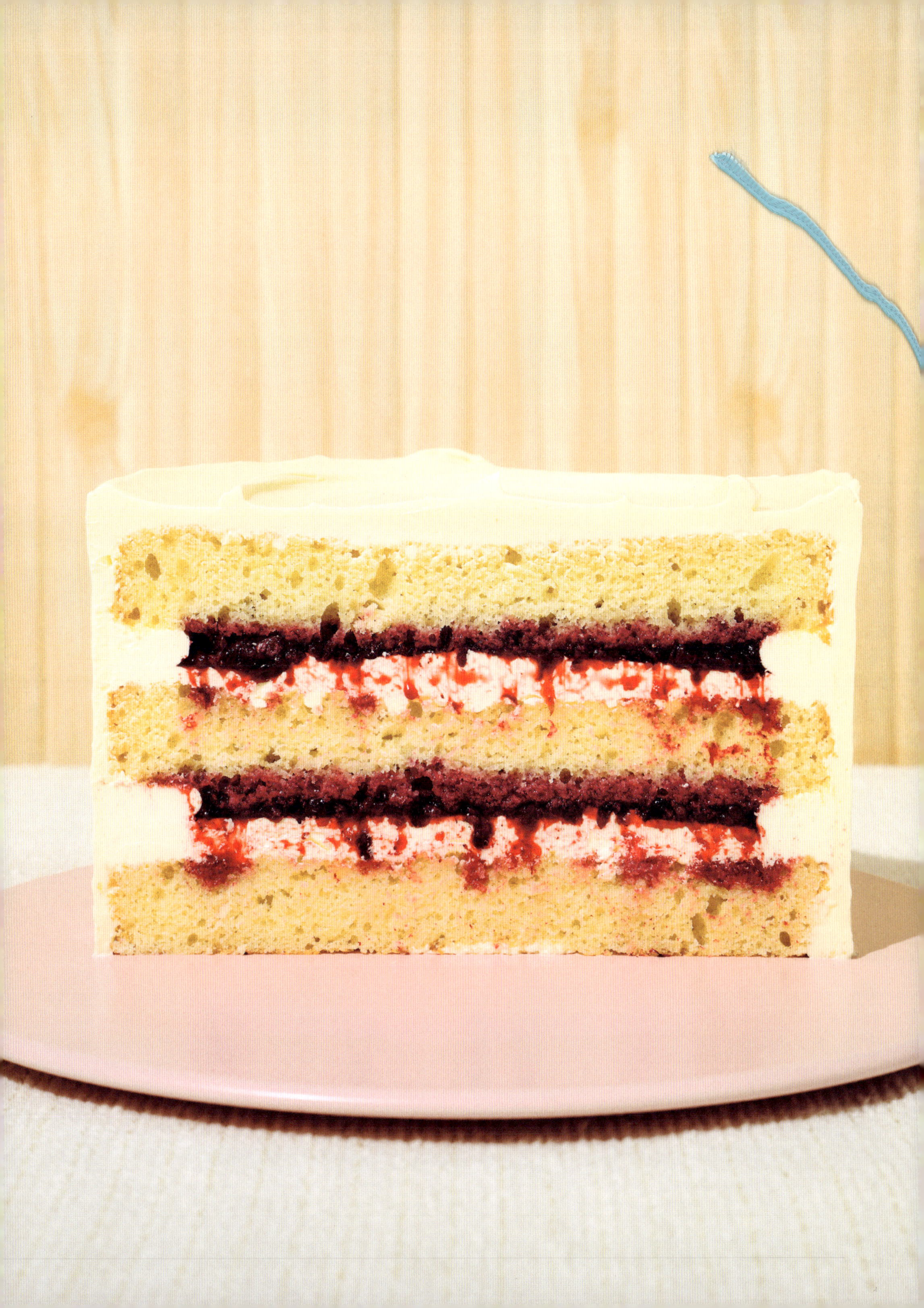

Olive oil ricotta cake with blackberry fennel jam & honey sea salt buttercream

BLACKBERRY FENNEL JAM
2 g (½ teaspoon) fennel seeds
150 g (5.3 oz) caster (superfine) sugar
500 g (17.64 oz) blackberries, fresh or frozen
40 g (1.41 oz) lemon juice
8 g (2½ teaspoons) cornflour (corn starch)

Makes: 500 g (17.64 oz), enough for any of the single-tier Projects
Store: in the fridge for up to 1 week, do not freeze

HONEY SOAK
100 g (3.5 oz) honey
100 g (3.5 oz) water

Makes: 200 g (7 oz), enough for any of the single-tier Projects
Store: in the fridge for up to 4 weeks, or in the freezer for 6 months.

Prepare the blackberry jam

Make the fennel sugar. Toast the fennel seeds in a dry frying pan over medium heat for about 2 minutes, or until they turn a shade darker and release their warm, aromatic fragrance. Let them cool briefly for 2 minutes, then place in a food processor with the sugar. Blend until the fennel seeds are finely ground and evenly incorporated into the sugar.

Combine and cook. Place the fennel sugar in a saucepan with the remaining jam ingredients, mixing with your hands to ensure the blackberries are evenly coated. Place over medium heat and cook, stirring constantly, for 4–5 minutes as the blackberries soften and release enough liquid to form a pool that comes halfway up the berries. (If using frozen blackberries, cook them directly from frozen, allowing slightly more time.) Scrape the bottom of the pan regularly to prevent sticking or burning.

Strain and break up the blackberries. Once the blackberries have softened and released their vibrant purple juices, strain and reserve the juice from the berries. Use the back of a spoon or a potato masher to break up the blackberries in the strainer to your preferred texture. I like them slightly crushed with some soft chunks – it makes slicing the cake easier while still giving bursts of vibrant berry flavour.

Reduce the liquid. Pour the juice back into the saucepan and bring to the boil over medium–high heat. Stir constantly for 3–4 minutes, until it thickens and reduces by half. Cooking the juice high and fast helps preserve the brightness of the berry flavour.

Add the blackberries. Once the juice has thickened, reduce the heat to medium and add the mashed blackberries. Cook for another minute, allowing the blackberries to soak up the flavourful liquid, then remove from the heat.

Let cool, then store. Carefully transfer the blackberry jam to a bowl or container and leave to cool completely at room temperature for about 2 hours. Cover and refrigerate until ready to use as a filling when assembling the cake.

Prepare the honey soak

Combine all ingredients. Combine all the honey soak ingredients in a small saucepan and bring to the boil over medium–high heat, stirring until the honey is fully dissolved. Remove from the heat and leave to cool completely for 2 hours. Refrigerate until ready to use.

OLIVE OIL RICOTTA CAKE

200 g (7 oz) plain (all-purpose) flour
10 g (2 teaspoons) baking powder
3 g (½ teaspoon) fine sea salt
170 g (6 oz) eggs (about 3 eggs)
260 g (9.17 oz) caster (superfine) sugar
75 g (2.65 oz) full-cream (whole) milk
220 g (7.76 oz) smooth, unstrained ricotta
130 g (4.59 oz) extra virgin olive oil

Makes: 3 individual 18 cm (7 in) cakes
Store: at room temperature for up to 3 days, or in the freezer for 1 month

Make the olive oil ricotta cakes

Preheat your oven and prepare the cake tins. Preheat the oven to 150°C (300°F) and position an oven rack in the centre of the oven. If all three cake tins won't fit on one rack, arrange two racks near the centre of the oven, ensuring there are at least two levels of space between them. Thoroughly spray three round 18 cm (7 in) cake tins with cooking oil and line the bottoms with baking paper, leaving the sides unlined.

Combine the dry ingredients. In a bowl, combine the flour, baking powder and salt. Set aside with a fine-meshed strainer ready for later use.

Make the whole egg foam. Combine the eggs and sugar in a stand mixer bowl. Attach the whisk and mix on high speed for 5 seconds to quickly combine, scraping down any sugar on the side of the bowl. Reduce the speed to medium and whisk for 3 minutes to help stabilise the egg foam. Increase the speed to high and whisk for another 8 minutes, until the mixture becomes pale, triples in volume, and reaches the ribbon stage (see page 34). The egg mixture must be at room temperature, around 22°C (72°F), to achieve the ribbon stage. (If you're working in a cooler kitchen, heat some water in a saucepan until it simmers. Place the mixing bowl over the pan and stir constantly with a hand whisk until the mixture warms to 22°C/72°F, then return the bowl to the mixer and continue whisking.) To check the egg foam is at the right consistency, stop the mixer and hover the whisk just above the mixture. Let the foam fall back into the bowl – it should form a line or ribbon that stays visible for a few seconds before dissolving back into the batter.

Warm the wet ingredients. While the eggs are whisking, combine the milk, ricotta and olive oil in a microwave-safe bowl. Heat in the microwave for about 2 minutes, then blend with an immersion blender until smooth. Cover the bowl and set aside. (Alternatively, heat the milk and oil in a saucepan until they come to the boil. Turn off the heat, add the room-temperature ricotta and blend until smooth.) The mixture should be warm – around 45°C (115°F) – when added to the batter.

Sift in the dry ingredients. Once the egg foam reaches the ribbon stage, scrape it into a large mixing bowl using a rubber spatula. Sift the dry ingredients over the batter in three additions, folding in each addition with a hand whisk. Take care not to overmix or deflate the batter. Use confident motions, scooping from the bottom of the bowl and folding over the surface while simultaneously rotating the bowl with your other hand. Mix just until no pockets of dry flour remain visible.

Fold in the wet ingredients. Add the warm ricotta mixture to the batter. Fold it in, using the same folding motion, until just combined.

Bake the cakes. Divide the batter evenly between the cake tins, or measure 350 g (12.35 oz) per tin. Tap the bottom of each tin firmly on the counter three times to release any large air bubbles. Pop the cakes in the oven, either across one or two racks as necessary.

Recipe continues

HONEY SEA SALT BUTTERCREAM

60 g (2.17 oz) water
200 g (7 oz) caster (superfine) sugar
150 g (5.3 oz) egg whites, chilled
2 g (½ teaspoon) cream of tartar
350 g (12.35 oz) unsalted butter, cubed
70 g (2.47 oz) honey
7 g (2 teaspoons) sea salt flakes

Makes: 700 g (24.7 oz), enough to fill and frost an 18 cm (7 in) three-layer cake, or fill any of the single-tier Projects
Store: in the fridge for 1 week or in the freezer for up to 3 months.

Bake for 30–35 minutes, until a cake tester inserted into the centre comes out clean, or the cakes spring back when gently pressed in the middle. Rotate the tins front to back after 20 minutes to ensure even baking.

Let cool, then store. While the cakes are baking, lightly spray at least two cooling racks with oil to prevent sticking. (Make sure there's enough room for all cakes to fit comfortably.) Once the cakes are baked, remove them from the oven and place the tins on the cooling racks for 10 minutes. Use a straight palette knife to loosen the edge of each cake around the inside of the tins, then gently flip each cake onto the cooling racks and peel off the baking paper.

Let the cakes cool completely for at least 2 hours before assembling the cake or wrapping them with plastic wrap.

Prepare the honey sea salt buttercream

Make the IMBC. (For more detailed instructions, see pages 43–46.) In a small saucepan, combine the water and sugar, then gently stir just until the sugar is evenly moistened. Set the pan on the stovetop, ready to heat. Place the chilled egg whites and cream of tartar in the bowl of a stand mixer. Begin whisking on medium speed until the mixture turns foamy and small bubbles form; this should take about 2 minutes. Once the egg whites are ready, and with the mixer running, cook the sugar syrup over medium heat, without stirring, until it reaches 115°C (240°F). Immediately remove from the heat, increase the mixer speed to high, then slowly pour the hot syrup into the meringue (the egg whites should be at soft peaks with fine, smooth bubbles), beginning with a thin stream and gradually increasing the flow. When all the syrup is incorporated, whisk on high speed for another 3–4 minutes as the meringue cools slightly. The meringue should turn glossy and hold stiff peaks and should be about 35°C (95°F). While mixing on high speed, gradually add the softened butter cubes one at a time, ensuring each cube is fully incorporated before adding the next. Once all the butter is incorporated, continue beating for 3–4 minutes until the buttercream changes from a pale yellow to a creamy white, and slightly increases in volume.

Add the honey and sea salt. Once the buttercream is whipped to a silky and airy consistency, add the honey and sea salt and whip for another 30 seconds, until well incorporated.

Assemble the cake

Assemble the cake layers, following the instructions on pages 48–56. Set in the fridge for at least 1 hour (or overnight) before serving at room temperature.

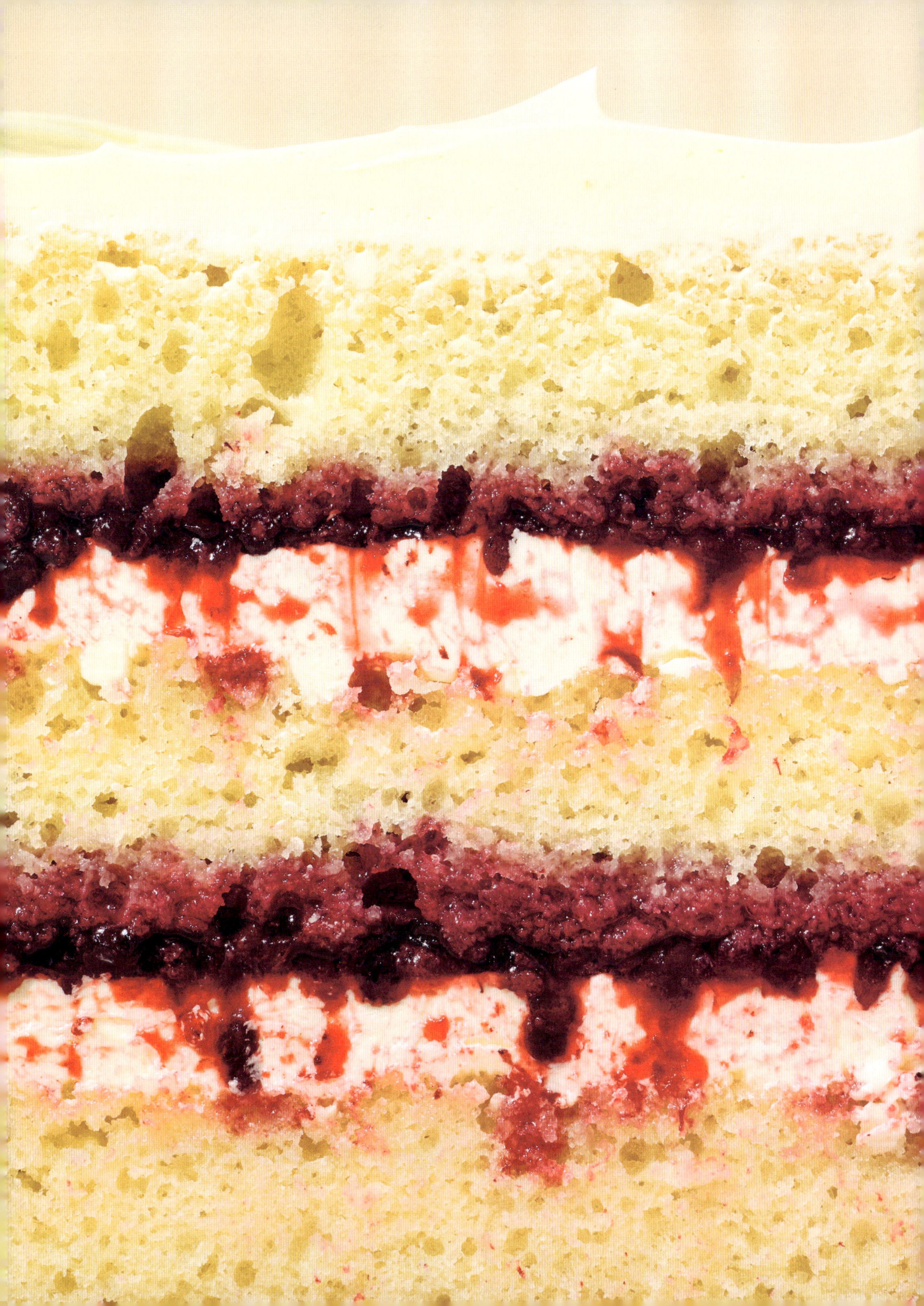

LAYER CAKE 9

Brown sugar cake with stewed apple, sesame crumb & miso caramel buttercream

Brown sugar cake is one of those recipes I tinkered with for ages, but could never quite find the perfect pairing for. The cake itself is light and airy, almost like a sponge, but with a richer crumb, similar to a butter cake. It had so much potential, but nothing seemed to click – until last year. While we were brainstorming new flavours, our brilliant chef, Emma Osborne, came up with a combination that completely blew me away. The cake has a subtle sweetness from the brown sugar, while stewed apples add bursts of freshness and a cosy warmth from a hint of cinnamon. Add the crunch of sesame crumbs and the salty decadence of miso caramel buttercream, and you have a cake that feels like the perfect autumn day!

MAKES	1 × 18 cm (7 in) diameter three-layer cake
SERVES	up to 16
STORE	in the fridge for up to 3 days; do not freeze

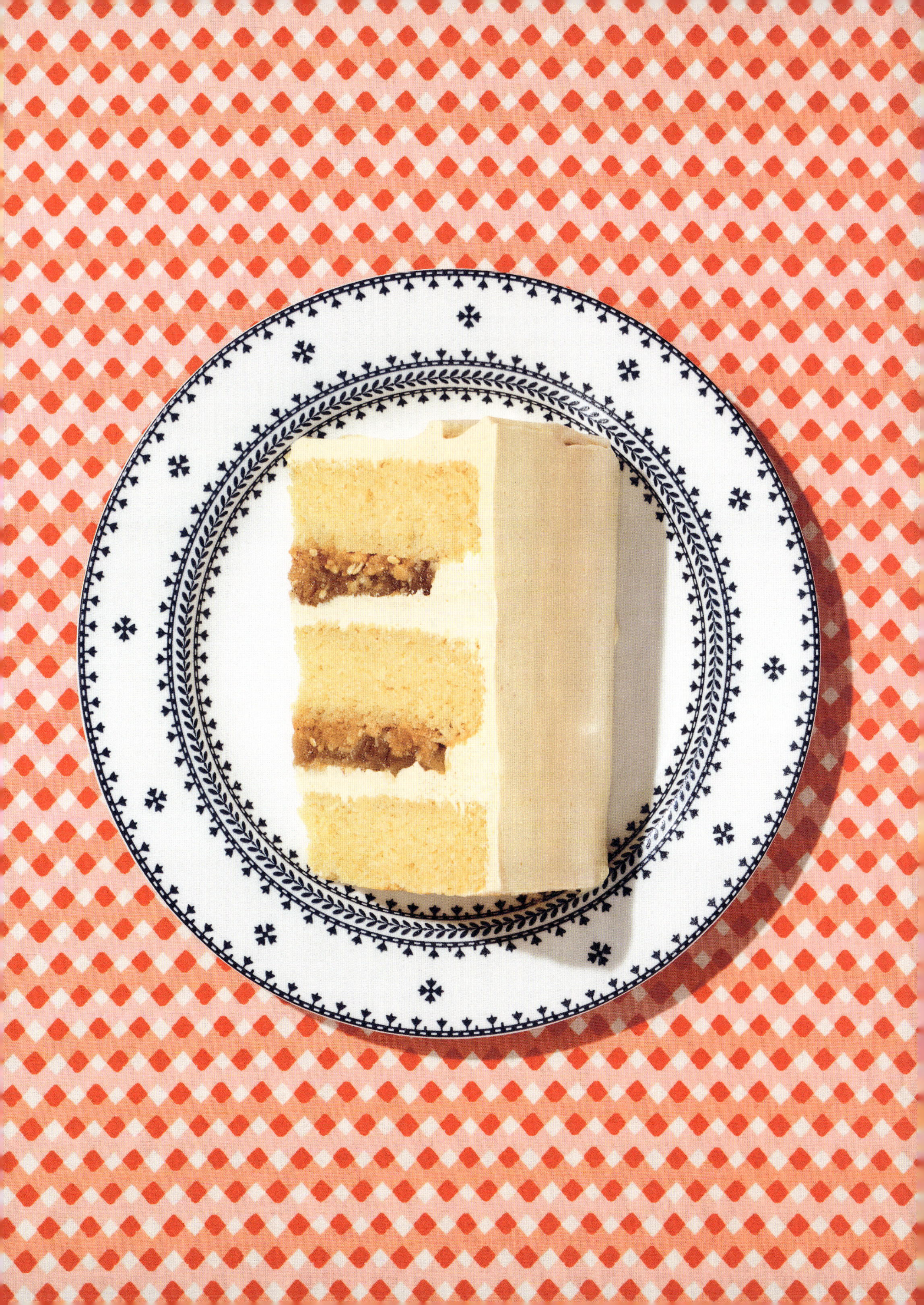

Brown sugar cake with stewed apple, sesame crumb & miso caramel buttercream

STEWED APPLES

550 g (19.4 oz) tart apples, such as Granny Smith (about 5 apples)
150 g (5.3 oz) brown sugar
100 g (3.5 oz) water
75 g (2.65 oz) lemon juice
4 g (1 teaspoon) vanilla bean paste
1 g (½ teaspoon) ground cinnamon

Makes: 600 g (21.16 oz), enough for any of the single-tier Projects
Store: in the fridge for 1 week or in the freezer for up to 3 months.

SESAME CRUMB

20 g (0.7 oz) white sesame seeds
65 g (2.3 oz) almond flour
20 g (0.7 oz) plain (all-purpose) flour
40 g (1.41 oz) caster (superfine) sugar
1 g (small pinch) fine sea salt
25 g (0.88 oz) unsalted butter, melted and cooled to room temperature
10 g (0.35 oz) smooth white miso paste
15 g (0.53 oz) egg white

Makes: 150 g (5.3 oz), enough for any of the single-tier Projects
Store: at room temperature for up to 5 days, or in the freezer for up to 3 months.

Stew the apples

Prepare the apples. Peel and core the apples, then dice into small, uniform 5 mm (¼ in) pieces.

Combine and cook. Place all the ingredients in a large saucepan, mixing well with your hands to ensure the apple is evenly coated. Place over medium–high heat and bring to the boil. Once the mixture begins to bubble, reduce the heat to medium–low, cover with a lid and simmer until the apple is tender, stirring occasionally. This should take about 30 minutes.

Let cool, then store. Carefully transfer to a bowl or container and allow to cool completely at room temperature for about 2 hours. Cover and refrigerate until ready to use as a filling when assembling the cake.

Prepare the sesame crumb

Preheat your oven. Preheat the oven to 140°C (275°F). Position an oven rack in the centre of the oven.

Toast the sesame seeds. In a small dry frying pan, toast the sesame seeds over medium heat, stirring constantly just until they turn a light golden colour. Take care not to let them darken too much, as they will continue to cook in the oven. Set aside to cool completely while you prepare the rest of the crumb mixture.

Combine the remaining ingredients. In a bowl, whisk together the almond flour, flour, sugar and salt until evenly distributed. In a separate small bowl, whisk the room-temperature melted butter with the miso paste and egg white until the miso is fully dissolved. Pour the wet mixture into the dry ingredients and mix well with your hands, tossing the bowl as needed, until small crumbs form.

Bake the crumbs. Spread the crumble mixture evenly on a lined baking tray. Bake for 10 minutes, gently stirring halfway through with a spatula to stop the edges over-browning. Once the crumbs are partially baked, remove the tray from the oven and sprinkle the toasted sesame seeds over the mixture. Mix to coat evenly, then bake for another 20–25 minutes, or until the crumbs are crispy and golden brown, stirring every 3–5 minutes to ensure even baking – be careful not to break the crumbs apart too much while stirring.

Let cool, then store. Remove the sesame crumbs from the oven and leave to cool completely on the tray, then store in an airtight container.

Refresh if needed. If the sesame crumb was made a few days in advance, simply refresh in a 140°C (275°F) oven for about 5 minutes. If frozen, let it thaw overnight at room temperature before refreshing in the oven until crisp.

MISO CARAMEL

90 g (3.17 oz) cream (about 35% fat)
25 g (0.88 oz) smooth white miso paste
30 g (1.06 oz) water
60 g (2.17 oz) caster (superfine) sugar

Makes: 150 g (5.3 oz), enough for the miso caramel buttercream
Store: in the fridge for 1 week or in the freezer for up to 3 months.

BROWN SUGAR CAKE

250 g (8.82 oz) plain (all-purpose) flour
12 g (2½ teaspoons) baking powder
3 g (½ teaspoon) fine sea salt
200 g (7 oz) eggs (from about 4 eggs)
270 g (9.52 oz) brown sugar
180 g (6.35 oz) buttermilk
100 g (3.5 oz) oz) unsalted butter, cubed
20 g (0.7 oz) vegetable oil
4 g (1 teaspoon) vanilla bean paste
140 g (4.94 oz) full-fat sour cream

Makes: 3 individual 18 cm (7 in) cakes
Store: at room temperature for up to 3 days, or in the freezer for 1 month

Make the miso caramel

Warm the cream. In a small saucepan, whisk together the cream and miso paste. Warm over medium heat, whisking constantly until the miso is fully dissolved. When small bubbles form around the edge (about 2–3 minutes), remove from the heat and cover with a lid to keep the mixture warm. This will help prevent the caramel seizing when the cream is added later.

Cook the caramel. Add the water to a another saucepan, followed by the sugar, and gently stir to evenly moisten the sugar. Warm over medium–high heat until the mixture comes to the boil. As the syrup cooks, it will gradually turn light amber. Gently swirl the pan occasionally to ensure even cooking, but avoid stirring to prevent crystallisation. Once the syrup reaches a uniform light amber hue, turn off the heat and allow the caramel to deepen to a rich amber using the residual heat, swirling the pan occasionally. This helps reduce the risk of the caramel burning.

Whisk in the cream. Once the caramel is has reached a deep amber hue, carefully whisk in the warm cream mixture. Be cautious, as the caramel will splatter significantly and release a lot of steam. Whisk vigorously until the cream is fully incorporated, then transfer the mixture to a bowl. Allow to cool completely at room temperature before adding to the buttercream.

Make the brown sugar cakes

Preheat your oven and prepare the cake tins. Preheat the oven to 150°C (300°F) and position an oven rack in the centre of the oven. If all three cake tins won't fit on one rack, arrange two racks near the centre of the oven, ensuring there are at least two levels of space between them. Thoroughly spray three round 18 cm (7 in) cake tins with cooking oil and line the bottoms with baking paper, leaving the sides unlined.

Combine the dry ingredients. In a small bowl, combine the flour, baking powder and salt. Set aside with a fine-meshed strainer ready for later use.

Make the whole egg foam. Combine the eggs and sugar in a stand mixer bowl. Attach the whisk and mix on high speed for 5 seconds to quickly combine, scraping down any sugar on the side of the bowl. Reduce the speed to medium and whisk for 3 minutes to help stabilise the egg foam. Increase the speed to high and whisk for another 8 minutes, until the mixture becomes pale, triples in volume, and reaches the ribbon stage (see page 34). The egg mixture must be at room temperature, around 22°C (72°F), to achieve the ribbon stage. (If you're working in a cooler kitchen, heat some water in a saucepan until it simmers. Place the mixing bowl over the pan and stir constantly with a hand whisk until the mixture warms to 22°C/72°F, then return the bowl to the mixer and continue whisking.) To check the egg foam is at the right consistency, stop the mixer and hover the whisk just above the mixture. Let the foam fall back into the bowl – it should form a line or ribbon that stays visible for a few seconds before dissolving back into the batter.

Recipe continues

HONEY SOAK
1 × quantity Honey soak (page 144)

Warm the wet ingredients. While the eggs are whisking, combine the buttermilk, butter, oil and vanilla in a microwave-safe bowl. Heat in the microwave for about 3 minutes, or until the butter is fully melted. Add the sour cream and blend with an immersion blender until smooth. Cover the bowl and set aside. (Alternatively, heat the buttermilk, butter, oil and vanilla in a small saucepan over medium heat until the butter is fully melted. Remove from the heat, add the sour cream and blend until smooth.) The mixture should be warm – around 45°C (115°F) – when added to the batter.

Sift in the dry ingredients. Once the egg foam reaches the ribbon stage, scrape it into a large mixing bowl using a rubber spatula. Sift the dry ingredients over the batter in three additions, folding in each addition with a hand whisk. Take care not to overmix or deflate the batter. Use confident motions, scooping from the bottom of the bowl and folding over the surface while simultaneously rotating the bowl with your other hand. Mix just until no pockets of dry flour remain visible.

Fold in the wet ingredients. Add the warm sour cream mixture to the batter. Fold it in, using the same folding motion, until just combined.

Bake the cakes. Divide the batter evenly between the cake tins, or measure 390 g (13.76 oz) per tin. Tap the bottom of each tin firmly on the counter three times to release any large air bubbles. Pop the cakes in the oven, either across one or two racks as necessary.

Bake for 30–35 minutes, until a cake tester inserted into the centre comes out clean, or the cakes spring back when gently pressed in the middle. Rotate the tins front to back after 20 minutes to ensure even baking.

Let cool, then store. While the cakes are baking, lightly spray at least two cooling racks with oil to prevent sticking. (Make sure there's enough room for all cakes to fit comfortably.) Once the cakes are baked, remove them from the oven and place the tins on the cooling racks for 10 minutes. Use a straight palette knife to loosen the edge of each cake around the inside of the tins, then gently flip each cake onto the cooling racks and peel off the baking paper.

Let the cakes cool completely for at least 2 hours before assembling the cake or wrapping them with plastic wrap.

Prepare the honey soak

Follow the instructions on page 144 to prepare the honey soak.

MISO CARAMEL BUTTERCREAM
60 g (2.17 oz) water
170 g (6 oz) caster (superfine) sugar
150 g (5.3 oz) egg whites, chilled (from about 5 eggs)
3 g (½ teaspoon) fine sea salt
2 g (½ teaspoon) cream of tartar
300 g (10.58 oz) unsalted butter, cubed
150 g (5.3 oz) miso caramel (from page 151), at room temperature

Makes: 750 g (26.46 oz), enough to fill and frost an 18 cm (7 in) three-layer cake, or fill any of the single-tier Projects
Store: in the fridge for 1 week or in the freezer for up to 3 months.

Prepare the miso caramel buttercream

Make the IMBC. (For more detailed instructions, see pages 43–46.) In a small saucepan, combine the water and sugar, then gently stir just until the sugar is evenly moistened. Set the pan on the stovetop, ready to heat. Place the chilled egg whites, salt and cream of tartar in the bowl of a stand mixer. Begin whisking on medium speed until the mixture turns foamy and small bubbles form; this should take about 2 minutes. Once the egg whites are ready, and with the mixer running, cook the sugar syrup over medium heat, without stirring, until it reaches 115°C (240°F). Immediately remove from the heat, increase the mixer speed to high, then slowly pour the hot syrup into the meringue (the egg whites should be at soft peaks with fine, smooth bubbles), beginning with a thin stream and gradually increasing the flow. When all the syrup is incorporated, whisk on high speed for another 3–4 minutes as the meringue cools slightly. The meringue should turn glossy and hold stiff peaks and should be about 35°C (95°F). While mixing on high speed, gradually add the softened butter cubes one at a time, ensuring each cube is fully incorporated before adding the next. Once all the butter is incorporated, continue beating for 3–4 minutes until the buttercream changes from a pale yellow to a creamy white, and slightly increases in volume.

Add the miso caramel. Once the buttercream is whipped to a silky and airy consistency, add the miso caramel and whip for another 30 seconds, until well incorporated.

Assemble the cake

Assemble the cake layers, following the instructions on pages 48–56. Set in the fridge for at least 1 hour (or overnight) before serving at room temperature.

LAYER CAKES

Just like any craft, creating the perfect cake takes time, dedication and plenty of practice. It's about getting to know your tools, mastering techniques and learning to work intuitively with your materials. I know starting out can feel a little overwhelming – especially if it's your first time holding a piping bag and trying to pipe those perfect shells. Trust me, I've been there. My very first cake had uneven shells, bumpy frosting and looked nothing like the cakes I create today. But that's part of the journey. Don't be discouraged by early attempts; every wonky cake teaches you something valuable.

Decorating a cake is both an art and a science – a dance between precision and creativity. In this section, I've gathered everything I've learned from piping thousands of cakes over the past four years at Mali Bakes. It's packed with tips, techniques and insights to help you master retro-style cakes. Whether you're working through the projects in the next chapter or creating your own designs, this is your go-to guide – a resource you can keep coming back to as you grow.

As you work your way through this chapter, you'll not only pick up essential skills, but also find the inspiration to make every cake uniquely yours. With patience, practice and a little imagination, you'll soon turn even the simplest cake into a stunning centrepiece.

Remember, every great cake starts somewhere – so enjoy the process, have fun and let your creativity shine!

Retro Decorating 101

PIPING PERFECTION

Now that you've already mastered so many skills – baking beautiful cakes, making perfect buttercreams and the art of frosting a cake smoothly – it's time to move on to the truly thrilling part: piping! Before we delve into all the finer points, let's take a step back and get acquainted with the essential tools and some key principles that will set you up for piping success every single time.

Basic piping tools

What is a coupler?

A coupler is a simple plastic tool used in cake decorating that makes it easy to switch between different piping nozzles without needing to change the piping bag. Each coupler has two parts: a coupler base and a coupler ring.

Couplers come in three sizes – standard, medium and large. It's important to make sure that the nozzles you need to use will fit your coupler. If the piping nozzle you're using doesn't fit the coupler, you'll need to use a different piping bag with the correct-sized coupler.

How to use a coupler with a piping bag and nozzle

- Trim about 2.5 cm (1 in) off the tip of the piping bag. Insert the coupler base, adjusting the cut so about 2 mm (5/64 in) of the bag extends past it. If too much sticks out, the buttercream won't flow smoothly; too little, and the coupler won't stay secure.

- Place your chosen nozzle on top of the coupler base and piping bag, then tightly screw the ring onto the base to secure it.

- To change nozzles, unscrew the coupler ring, swap the nozzle, and reattach the ring.

MALI BAKES

Loading the buttercream into the piping bag

- Fit the bag with a coupler and nozzle, then fold the top of the bag over your hand to create a cuff, making it easier to hold open.

- Use a spatula to scoop buttercream into the bag, pressing it down. Scrape the spatula against the side of the bag to keep it tidy. Do not fill the bag more than halfway, as overfilling can make it harder to control the piping pressure.

- Unfold the top of the bag and twist the open end to seal.

How to hold your piping bag

- Hold the top of the piping bag in your dominant hand, with your thumb facing up and fingers on the top side. Twist the open end of the bag and wrap it around your thumb to stop the buttercream pushing back up.

- Squeeze the bag with your dominant hand, while positioning your other hand just above the nozzle to help guide and steady your movements.

- Before starting on the cake, squeeze a small amount of buttercream into a bowl to remove any air bubbles and ensure the buttercream is seated at the nozzle's tip. Repeat this step whenever you change nozzles or refill the bag. As you pipe, twist the bag periodically to keep the buttercream packed at the bottom.

The knack of piping

Learning to make smooth, controlled movements with your piping bag is essential for creating beautiful retro-style cakes. *The Wilton Way of Cake Decorating* (edited by Eugene T and Marilynn C Sullivan with Norman Wilton), highlights three fundamental principles that serve as invaluable guides while you practise decorating: consistency, pressure control and angle.

Consistency

Ensure your buttercream is the right consistency and free of air bubbles. Most piping techniques and cake borders (page 160) require a medium-consistency buttercream, meaning it should be neither too thin nor too stiff. If the buttercream is too thin, borders that feature techniques such as shells or rosettes won't hold their shape, becoming soft or blobby. If the buttercream is filled with air bubbles, string work (page 162) will become impossible, as the strings may break when passing through fine nozzles. On the other hand, overly stiff buttercream can result in rough, uneven designs, with decorations that show gaps and lack smoothness.

To check if your buttercream is at the right consistency, test it by piping a small design on a board or the cake tin. It should flow easily from the bag and hold its shape without sagging.

Too soft | **Correct consistency** | **Too stiff**

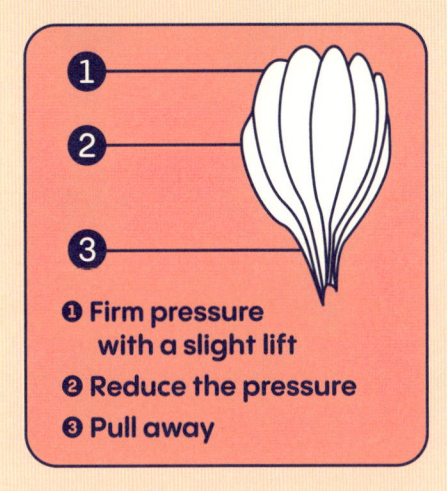

Pressure control

Controlling the pressure you apply when squeezing the piping bag enables you to create uniform and polished decorations. The basic rule is simple: more pressure releases more buttercream, while less pressure releases less buttercream.

Many borders require a combination of pressures to achieve the desired shape. For instance, when piping shells (pages 161–162), begin with firm pressure to create a thick, rounded base, then gradually reduce the pressure as you taper off, finishing with a complete stop for a clean, tapered edge without pulling or unevenness.

You can also vary the size of your design by adjusting the pressure – a firmer squeeze creates larger shells, for example, while a lighter touch produces smaller ones, all with the same nozzle.

❶ Firm pressure with a slight lift
❷ Reduce the pressure
❸ Pull away

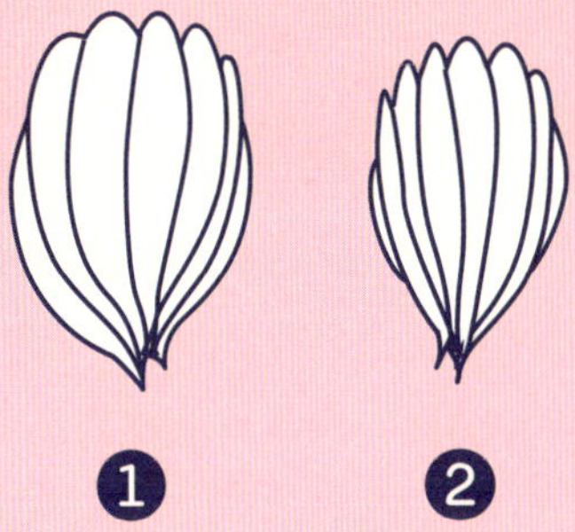

Angle and elevation

Angle and elevation refer to the positioning of the piping bag or nozzle in relation to the cake surface, and whether the nozzle lightly touches it or hovers just above. Different piping techniques will require different angles and elevations; for example, to pipe a rosette or drop string, hold the bag at a 90-degree angle to the cake surface you are piping on. For shells or ruffles, position the bag at a 45-degree angle to the cake surface.

It's important to note that some nozzles, like those for ruffles, petals, leaves or basket weave designs, have an asymmetrical opening, so it's essential to pay attention to the direction the nozzle faces and to take this into account when you are figuring out the ideal angle you need to be working at.

Certain techniques also benefit from being worked from a slight elevation, such as piping circular blobs or shells. For instance, when piping shells, applying firm pressure with a slight lift allows the buttercream to build up nicely.

Similarly, when using a round nozzle to create a blob, holding the nozzle just above the cake surface helps achieve a smooth, perfectly rounded shape.

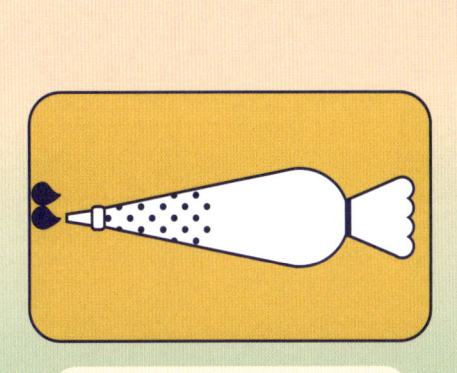

❶ Shell piped with firmer squeeze
❷ Shell piped with lighter touch

90° angle to side of cake

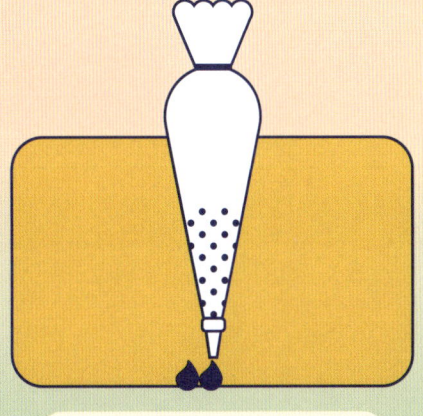

90° angle to top of cake

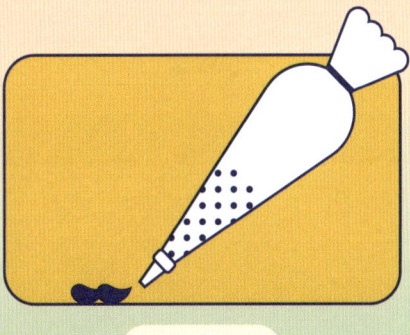

45° angle

RETRO DECORATING 101

Basic piping techniques

In cake decorating, borders are continuous piped decorations, made using one or more piping techniques, that sit along the edges or sides of a cake. At Mali Bakes, we love making tall cakes, which means we often decorate both the upper and lower sides too! Borders serve a dual purpose: they add beautiful, detailed designs and help hide any imperfections, giving the cake a polished, professional finish.

This section offers an overview to the basic piping techniques you can use to create different border designs on your cakes. It includes some guidance for using different nozzles (though you can apply these techniques with other nozzles too), along with the recommended buttercream consistency, pressure and piping angle for each one.

Applying the motions of these techniques with different nozzles creates an endless variety of border designs. These can also be layered to form intricate, eye-catching patterns. You'll see some of these styles in the next chapter's projects.

Before diving in, however, it's advisable to practise these techniques using the practice buttercream on page 169. This will help build confidence and ease any nerves before piping on your actual cake.

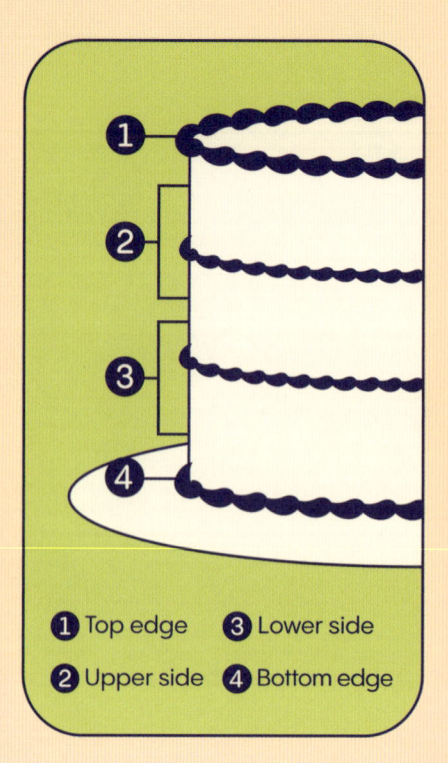

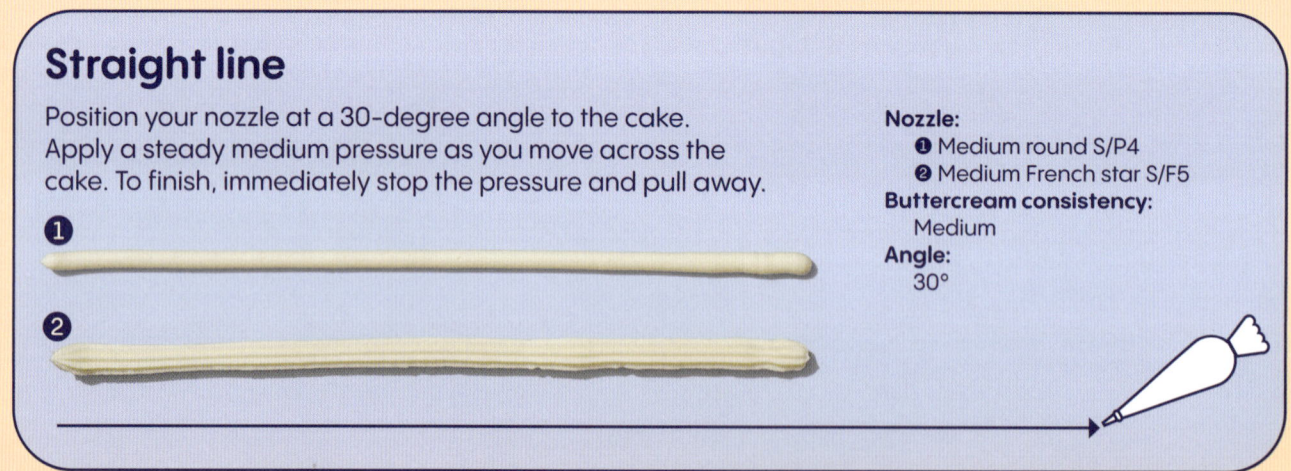

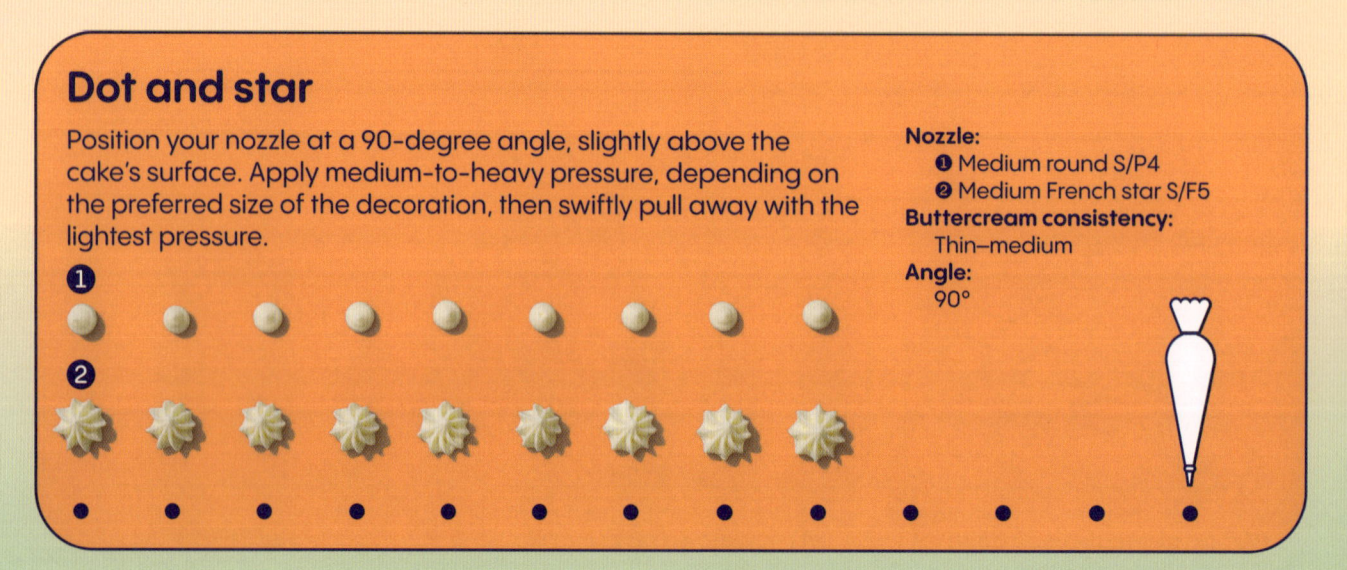

❶ Top edge   ❸ Lower side
❷ Upper side   ❹ Bottom edge

Straight line

Position your nozzle at a 30-degree angle to the cake. Apply a steady medium pressure as you move across the cake. To finish, immediately stop the pressure and pull away.

❶
❷

Nozzle:
❶ Medium round S/P4
❷ Medium French star S/F5
Buttercream consistency:
Medium
Angle:
30°

Dot and star

Position your nozzle at a 90-degree angle, slightly above the cake's surface. Apply medium-to-heavy pressure, depending on the preferred size of the decoration, then swiftly pull away with the lightest pressure.

❶
❷

Nozzle:
❶ Medium round S/P4
❷ Medium French star S/F5
Buttercream consistency:
Thin–medium
Angle:
90°

160   MALI BAKES

Rosettes

Nozzle:
① Medium French star S/F5
② Medium star S/S5
Buttercream consistency: Medium
Angle: 90°

Position your nozzle at a 90-degree angle, just touching the cake's surface. Apply medium-to-heavy pressure, depending on the desired size of the decoration, as you move clockwise or counterclockwise to form a rosette. To finish, release the pressure and swiftly pull away.

Shells

Nozzle:
① Medium French star S/F5
② Medium star S/S5
③ Large French star S/F11
Buttercream consistency: Medium
Angle: 45°
Note:
I've worked from left to right in the examples below, but you can pipe in either direction and achieve the same look. Pipe in the direction that feels most natural to you. With practice you will be able to pipe shells in either direction.

Position your nozzle at a 45-degree angle to the cake's surface, with the nozzle pointing away from the direction you want to move in (for example, if you are working from left to right, point your nozzle towards the left). Ensure the nozzle is just touching the cake's surface.

Begin by applying heavy pressure to build up the buttercream, forming the thicker base of the shell. Gradually lift the nozzle slightly to allow the buttercream to mound naturally. Then, smoothly reduce the pressure to medium as you pull the nozzle down and forward, finishing with light pressure to taper off the shell. If you finish at this point you have piped a single shell.

If you want to pipe a row of continuous shells simply continue without pausing, continuing directly into the next shell and repeat to create a seamless, continuous line.

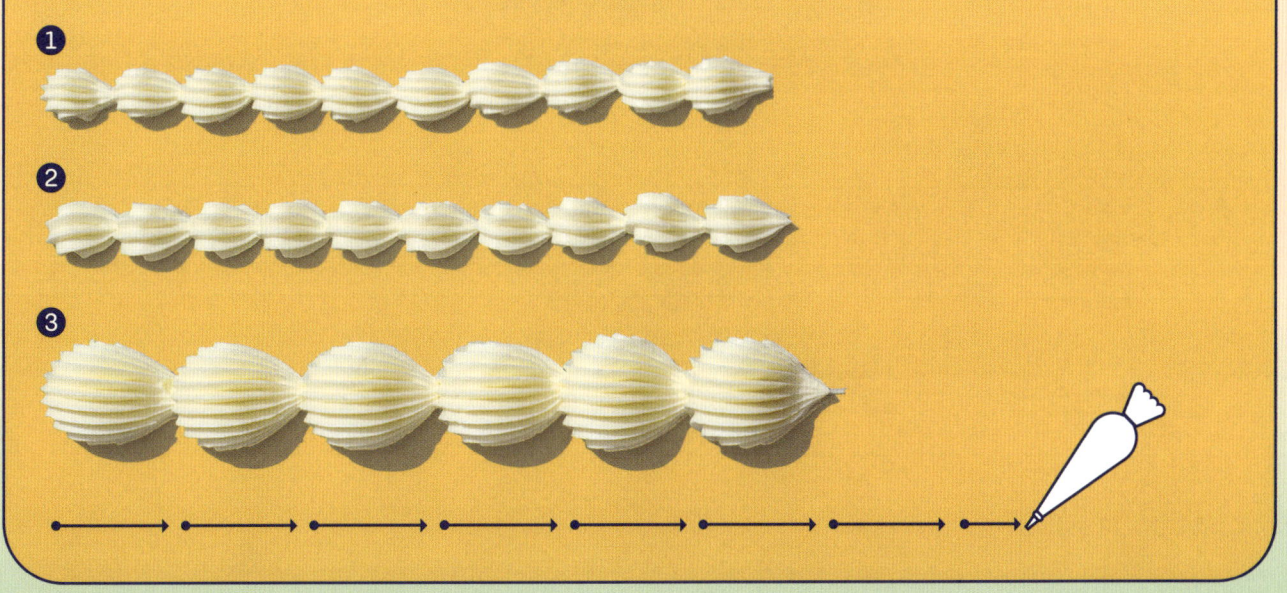

RETRO DECORATING 101

Reverse shells

Position your nozzle at a 45-degree angle to the cake surface, with the nozzle pointing away from the direction you want to move in (for example, if you are working from left to right, point your nozzle towards the left). Ensure the nozzle is just touching the cake's surface. Apply heavy pressure, then slightly lift the nozzle to allow the buttercream to build up as you move it in a clockwise direction, creating the first curve. As you reach the end of the curve, swiftly reduce the pressure to taper off the shell. Then pause, reset the nozzle just above the finishing point on the previous shell and guide the nozzle in the opposite direction to form a reverse curve, creating an 'S' shape while increasing the pressure back to heavy. Gradually reduce the pressure as you complete the reverse curve, tapering off to a fine point. Continue this alternating motion in a continuous line, ensuring each reverse shell connects smoothly to the next.

Nozzle:
❶ Medium star S/S5
❷ Medium French star S/F5
❸ Large French star S/F11

Buttercream consistency: Medium

Angle: 45°

Note:
I've worked from left to right in the examples below, but you can pipe in either direction and achieve the same look. Pipe in the direction that feels most natural to you. With practice you will be able to pipe in either direction.

Drop strings

Position your nozzle at a 90-degree angle to the cake's surface, ensuring it just touches the surface. Apply steady, medium pressure to adhere the buttercream to the cake, and continue squeezing while gently moving the nozzle away from the cake and horizontally across the surface, allowing gravity to naturally guide the string downwards. Once the string drops to the desired position, apply slightly more pressure to attach the end securely to the cake. Avoid lowering the piping nozzle during the drop, as this may create uneven strings. For best precision, work with the cake at eye level.

Nozzle:
❶ Standard round 5
❷ Standard star 16

Buttercream consistency: Medium–stiff

Angle: 90°

Note:
Drop strings can also be piped before adding ribbons, swags or garland designs, serving as a helpful guideline.

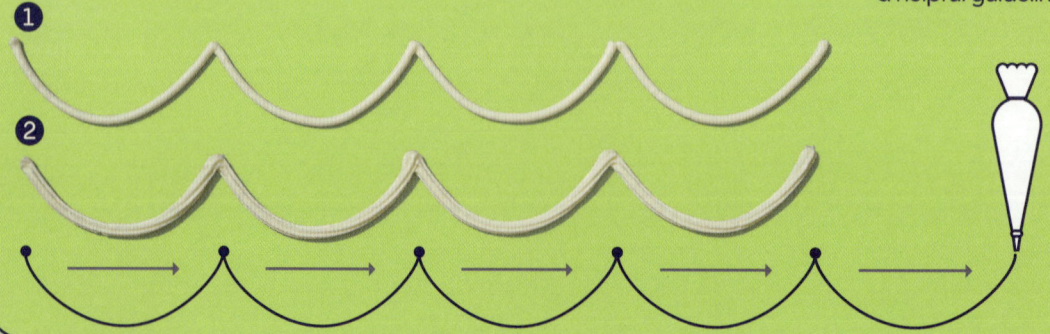

Loop garland

Nozzle:
❶ Medium round S/P4
❷ Medium French star S/F3
Buttercream consistency:
Medium
Angle:
90°
Note:
I've worked from left to right in the examples below, but you can pipe in either direction and achieve the same look. Pipe in the direction that feels most natural to you.

Position your nozzle at a 90-degree angle to the cake's surface, ensuring it just touches the surface. With a steady, medium pressure, pipe a continuous loop by moving the nozzle upwards around and down, working your way across the cake creating a garland shape. As you reach the lowest part of the garland, increase the pressure slightly to create thicker, wider loops, then ease off as you move upwards to complete the loop.

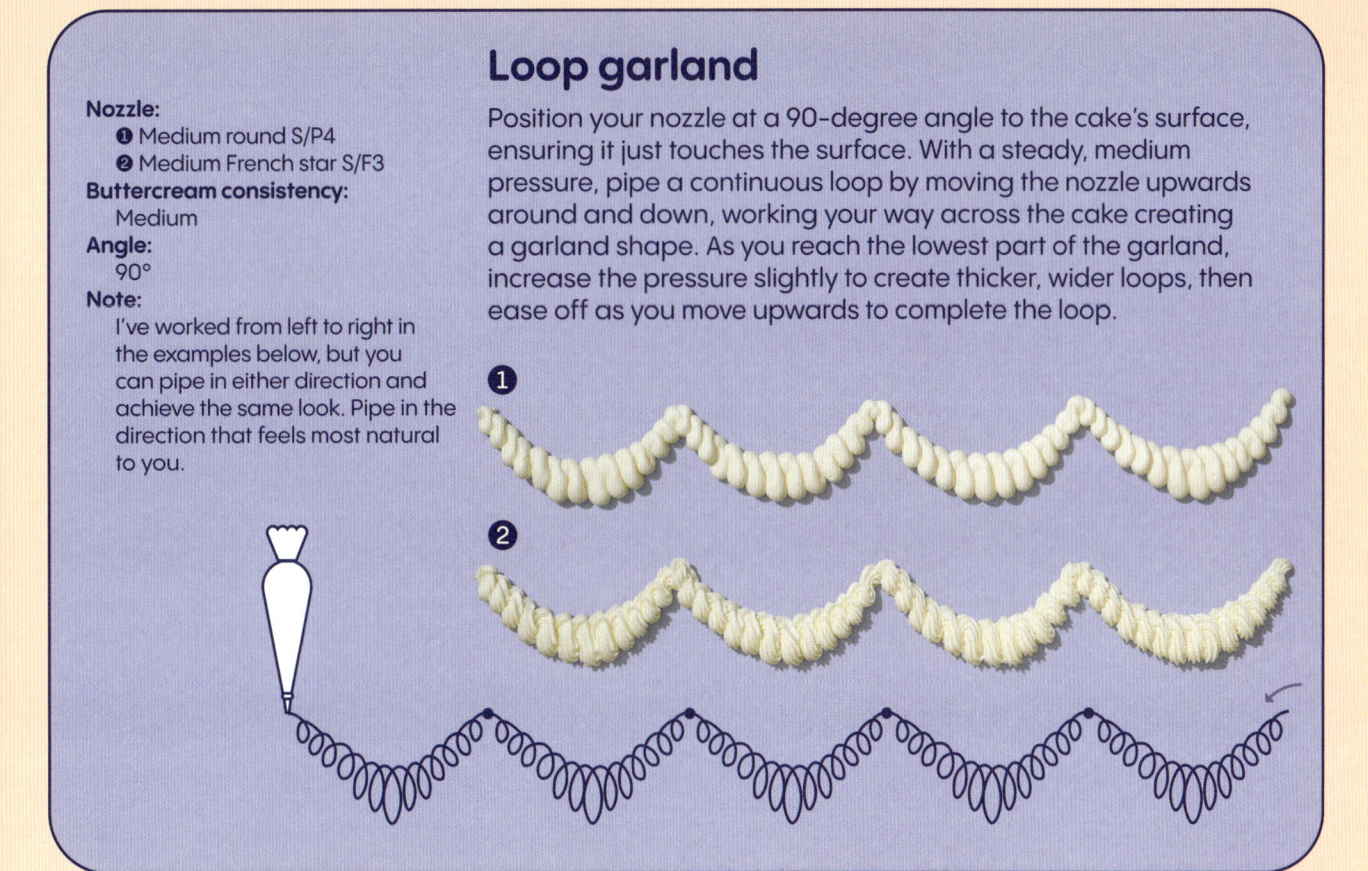

❶

❷

Ribbon

Nozzle:
❶ Standard petal 104W
❷ Medium petal 124K
Buttercream consistency:
Medium
Angle:
45°
Note:
I've worked from right to left in the examples below, but if you are right handed you will need to pipe from left to right.

Position your nozzle at a 45-degree angle to the cake's surface, with the nozzle pointing away from the direction you want to move in (for example, if you are working from left to right, point your nozzle towards the left). The wider part of the nozzle should just touch the cake, with the narrow end pointing away from it. Apply steady, medium pressure as you move the nozzle down, then curve it upwards across the cake to create a drape. Without stopping, repeat this motion to create continuous ribbon drapes around the cake.

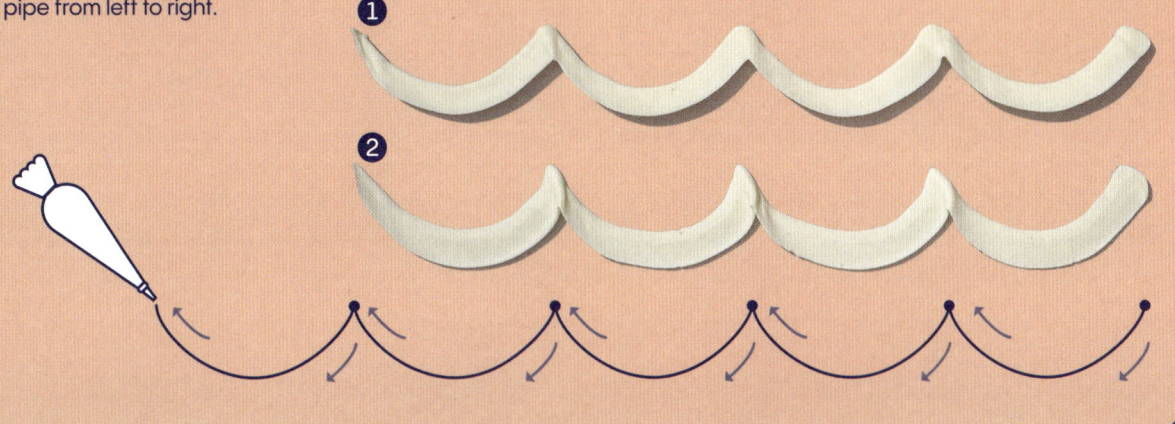

❶

❷

RETRO DECORATING 101

Swag

Position your nozzle at a 45-degree angle to the cake's surface, with the nozzle pointing away from the direction you want to move in (for example, if you are working from left to right, point your nozzle towards the left). The wider part of the nozzle should just touch the cake, with the narrow end pointing away from it. Apply steady, medium pressure as you move the nozzle down, then curve it upwards across the cake to create a drape. When you are back at the highest point of the drape, and without stopping, move the nozzle up and down in two small motions before starting the next drape, maintaining constant steady pressure throughout. Repeat this motion to create continuous swag drapes around the cake.

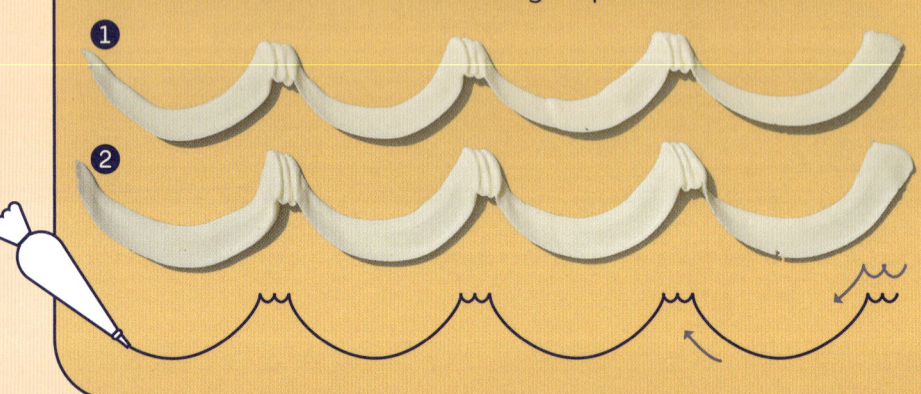

Nozzle:
❶ Standard Petal 104W
❷ Medium petal 124K
Buttercream consistency: Medium
Angle: 45°
Note:
I've worked from right to left in the examples below, but if you are right handed you will need to pipe from left to right.

Fluted ruffles

Position your nozzle at a 45-degree angle to the cake's surface, with the nozzle pointing away from the direction you want to move in (for example, if you are working from left to right, point your nozzle towards the left). The wider part of the nozzle should just touch the cake, with the narrow end pointing away from it. Apply steady, medium pressure while moving the nozzle in small curved motions, going down then up to create ruffles. You can also pipe in a curved line to create fluted ruffle garlands. Pipe drop strings first as a guide to keep the garlands evenly spaced.

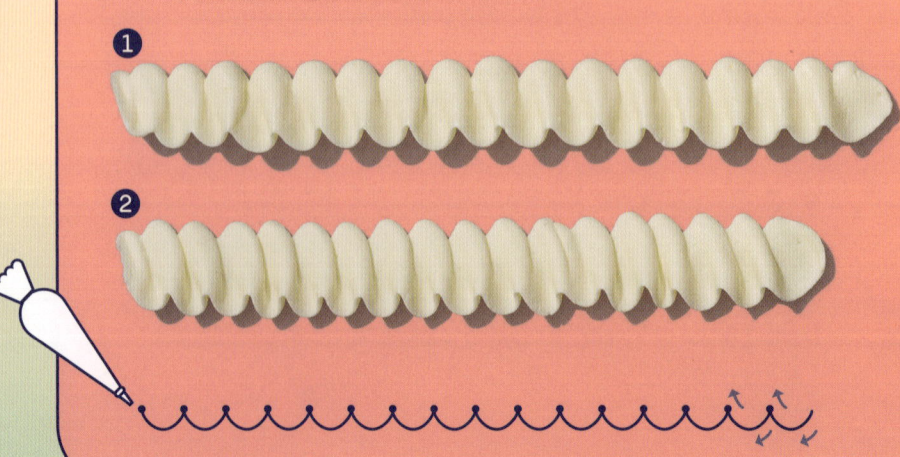

Nozzle:
❶ Standard petal 104W
❷ Medium petal 124K
Buttercream consistency: Medium
Angle: 45°
Note:
I've worked from right to left in the examples below, but if you are right handed you will need to pipe from left to right.

164

MALI BAKES

Folded ruffles

Nozzle:
  ❶ Medium leaf 115
  ❷ Medium petal 126K
Buttercream consistency:
  Medium
Angle:
  45°
Note:
  I've worked from right to left in the examples below, but if you are right handed you will need to pipe from left to right.

Position your nozzle at a 45-degree angle to the cake's surface, with the nozzle pointing away from the direction you want to move in (for example, if you are working from left to right, point your nozzle towards the left). If you are using petal nozzles, the wider part of the nozzle should just touch the cake, with the narrow end pointing away from it. Apply steady, medium pressure as you move the nozzle forwards, then fold it backwards halfway, repeating this motion as you guide the nozzle across the cake. You can also pipe in a curved line to create folded ruffle garlands. Pipe drop strings first as a guide to keep the garlands evenly spaced.

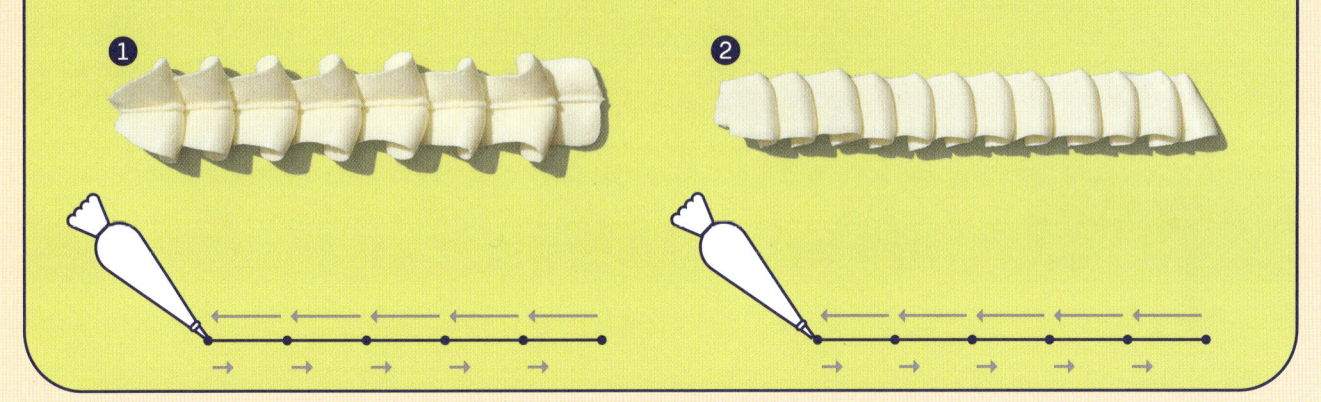

Leaf

Nozzle:
  ❶ Standard leaf 352
  ❷ Standard leaf 70
  ❸ Medium leaf 115
Buttercream consistency:
  Thin
Angle:
  45°
Note:
  I've worked from right to left in the examples below, but you can work this technique in either direction depending on the look you want.

Flat leaf (top row). Position your nozzle at a 45-degree angle to the cake's surface, with the nozzle pointing towards the direction the leaf base will start from. Begin with heavy pressure to let the buttercream fan out, forming the base of the leaf. Gradually pull the nozzle away while easing the pressure to shape the narrow middle section. To finish, stop applying pressure and quickly pull away to create the pointed tip of the leaf.

Curvy leaf (bottom row). Follow the same technique as for a flat leaf, but add a slight jiggle as you pull the nozzle away. This motion will create subtle waves in the leaf.

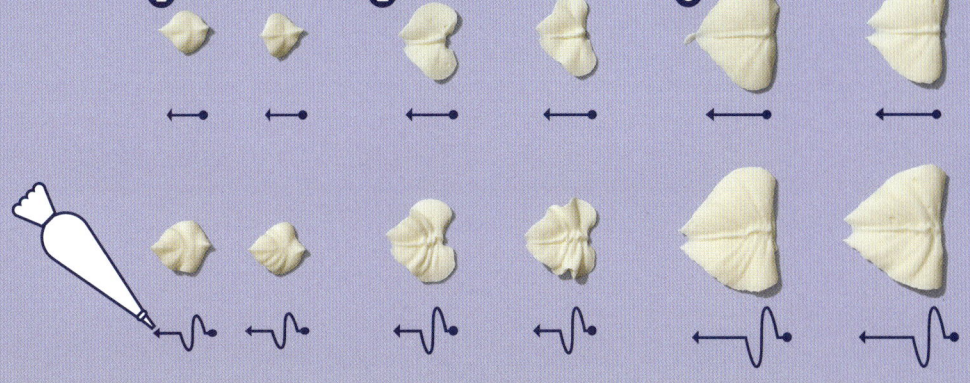

RETRO DECORATING 101

OTHER DECORATING MATERIALS

While the Italian meringue buttercream on page 43 is the go-to for most cake-decorating projects, some designs and techniques benefit from using different piping materials to achieve specific effects. Just as a potter never uses the same clay for every creation, the same is true for cake decorating. Stabilised buttercream, for instance, is perfect for creating buttercream roses, holding their beautiful structure even after hours on display. Meanwhile, royal icing, with its ability to air dry, lends itself to crisp, delicate designs, making decorations like drop flowers both a joy to handle and simple to add to your creation.

This section includes recipes for the additional decorating materials featured in this book. While each project specifies the amount required, I always recommend making a full batch rather than halving or dividing the recipe. Leftovers can be easily frozen or stored, so you'll always have some ready for your next decorating project.

You'll also find a recipe for practice buttercream in this section. It's inexpensive to make and extremely shelf-stable, allowing you to practise piping techniques before working on your actual cake. This way, you can refine your skills without wasting ingredients or worrying about mistakes!

These three buttercreams will see you through every stage of your retro cake decorating journey!

L–R: Stabilised buttercream; Royal icing; Italian meringue buttercream (structurally similar to Practice buttercream)

Stabilised buttercream

Makes: 500 g (17.64 oz)
Store: Refrigerate for 1 week, or freeze for 3 months in an airtight container. Allow to defrost in the fridge at least 8 hours or overnight before use. Once defrosted, do not freeze again.

This buttercream is a lovely marriage of Italian meringue and American buttercream, made with meringue powder instead of fresh egg whites. Meringue powder, which is mainly made of dried egg whites, sugar and stabilisers, gives this buttercream a stiff consistency, making it perfect for creating detailed decorations like drop flowers or flowers using a flower nail. It's great at holding its shape and is more resistant to warm weather, so your decorations stay intact. However, because it's made with icing sugar, it tends to be quite sweet and has a slight grainy texture. While it's fantastic for making buttercream flowers, it's not the best choice for frosting an entire cake.

75 g (2.65 oz) caster (superfine) sugar
3 g (½ teaspoon) fine sea salt
50 g (1.75 oz) boiling water
15 g (0.53 oz) meringue powder
230 g (8.11 oz) icing (confectioners') sugar, sifted
230 g (8.11 oz) unsalted butter, cubed
2.5 g (½ teaspoon) vanilla extract

Make the sugar syrup. Start by dissolving the sugar and salt in the boiling water, stirring until fully dissolved. Allow the syrup to cool completely to room temperature before moving on to the next step.

Make the meringue. In a clean, grease-free bowl of a stand mixer, combine the cooled sugar syrup and meringue powder. Attach the whisk attachment and whisk on high speed until soft peaks form. This should take 5–7 minutes.

Add the icing sugar. Once your meringue reaches soft peaks, start adding the icing sugar, one heaped tablespoon at a time. For each addition, begin beating on low speed, gradually increasing to high speed until the sugar is fully incorporated. After all the icing sugar has been added, increase the speed to high and whisk until stiff peaks form. This should take about 2 minutes.

Add the butter and vanilla. Reduce the mixer speed to medium and start adding the softened butter, one cube at a time. Ensure each cube is fully incorporated before adding the next. Once all the butter is added, add the vanilla and mix for another 30 seconds until fully incorporated. Then, switch to the paddle attachment and whip on high speed for about 2 minutes, until the buttercream becomes pale and smooth.

Remove air bubbles. Turn the mixer down to the lowest speed and continue mixing for a further 2 minutes. Your stabilised buttercream is now ready to use.

Re-whipping made-ahead buttercream

Just like IMBC, if you've prepared stabilised buttercream in advance, it will need a quick re-whip before use. Follow the instructions on page 40 to give it a quick re-whip before use.

Royal icing

Makes: 500 g (17.64 oz)
Store: Room temperature for 5 days in an airtight container. Dried decorations will keep at room temperature for up to 6 months in an airtight container.

Royal icing is an exceptionally versatile choice for cake decoration. Its light, fluffy texture makes it a dream to pipe through a nozzle, while its ability to hold its shape ensures your designs stay crisp and defined.

What sets royal icing apart is its ability to air-dry to a firm finish, giving it exceptional durability and a long shelf life — perfect for creating intricate decorations like drop flowers that can be prepared well in advance. When thinned with a bit of water, royal icing transforms into a smooth, self-levelling icing, ideal for creating plaques or toppers using the flooding technique (see page 311).

When adding colour to your royal icing, to ensure the best results, always opt for a gel food colouring, as oil-based colours can cause the icing to separate and stop it drying properly.

30 g (1.06 oz) meringue powder
450 g (15.88 oz) pure icing (confectioners') sugar, sifted
1.5 g (¼ teaspoon) fine sea salt
70 g (2.47 oz) warm water
2.5 g (½ teaspoon) vanilla extract

Combine all the ingredients. In a clean, grease-free stand mixer bowl, beat all the ingredients on medium speed using the paddle attachment for about 5 minutes or until stiff peaks form.

Check the consistency. Once ready, this royal icing will have a stiff consistency, making it ideal for piping borders or creating drop flowers. If a thinner consistency is needed for flooding, simply add a few drops of water at a time until the preferred consistency is achieved.

Storing royal icing

Transfer the icing to an airtight container and place a wet cloth or clean paper towel directly on the surface to prevent it drying out.

Store dried royal icing decorations in an airtight container at room temperature in a cool, dry area for up to 6 months. To maintain their appearance, keep them away from direct sunlight to avoid fading.

Practice buttercream

Makes: 800 g (28.22 oz)
Store: Room temperature for 3 months, or fridge for 6 months in an airtight container.

Butter – the star ingredient of buttercream – is an expensive ingredient, and you certainly don't want to waste it when you're just starting out with cake decorating. It's important to take the time to build confidence in your piping skills before working on an actual cake. This simple buttercream recipe is made with vegetable shortening. Its consistency closely mimics real buttercream, making it an excellent practice material, and it also has an incredibly long shelf life, so you can pipe, scrape and re-pipe it as much as you like without worrying about waste, and you can then store it away for future practice sessions.

300 g (10.58 oz) solid vegetable shortening, chopped into pieces
450 g (15.88 oz) icing (confectioners') sugar, sifted
30 g (1.06 oz) water
20 g (0.7 oz) glucose syrup

Beat the shortening. Using a large stand mixer bowl and the paddle attachment, beat the shortening on medium speed for 1–2 minutes, until smooth and creamy.

Add the icing sugar. Gradually add the sifted icing sugar, one-third at a time, mixing on low speed after each addition until completely combined.

Add the liquid. Add the water and glucose syrup. Beat on medium speed until the mixture is smooth and creamy. If the buttercream feels too stiff, add an extra teaspoon of water at a time until you reach the desired consistency.

If you've made the buttercream fresh, chill it in the fridge for 10–15 minutes before piping to allow it to firm up slightly.

Re-whipping made-ahead buttercream

If your practice buttercream has been stored in the fridge, let it soften at room temperature for 30–60 minutes, then re-whip it in a stand mixer using the paddle attachment on medium speed until it's smooth and pipeable again. If your buttercream has been stored at room temperature, you may need to briefly chill it in the fridge – especially while practising – to firm it up as needed.

Adjusting the consistency

To soften the practice buttercream, add 1 teaspoon water and 1 teaspoon glucose syrup at a time until it reaches a thinner consistency. To firm it up, add 1 tablespoon icing sugar at a time until it reaches a stiff consistency.

Drop flowers

Drop flowers are a quick and easy way to add beautiful floral details to your creations. There are many types of drop flower nozzles available, most of which resemble star nozzles with various openings. For best results, use Stabilised buttercream (page 167) or Royal icing (page 168), as both hold their shape well.

If using stabilised buttercream, allow the flowers to set in the freezer for about 30 minutes, or until completely firm, before applying them to your cake. If using royal icing, let the flowers air-dry at least 8 hours or overnight, to ensure they are firm and ready to use.

Set up

Thoroughly grease a tray with cooking spray and line it with baking paper, ensuring that the paper is securely adhered to stop it lifting away during piping.

Let's begin!

Position your piping bag at a 90-degree angle to the tray, with the tip touching the baking paper. Hold the piping bag firmly with both hands (image 1).

Twist your hands as far to the left as possible, then, as you start applying pressure, rotate your hands as far to the right as possible to allow the buttercream to fan out and form the petals (image 2). The twist is what gives the petals their shape – if you don't twist enough, the flowers can end up looking more like stars.

Pull the nozzle away from the tray swiftly, maintaining a perfect 90-degree angle throughout.

To finish, pipe the centre of the flower using your preferred small round nozzle (image 3) and allow it to dry or set before using.

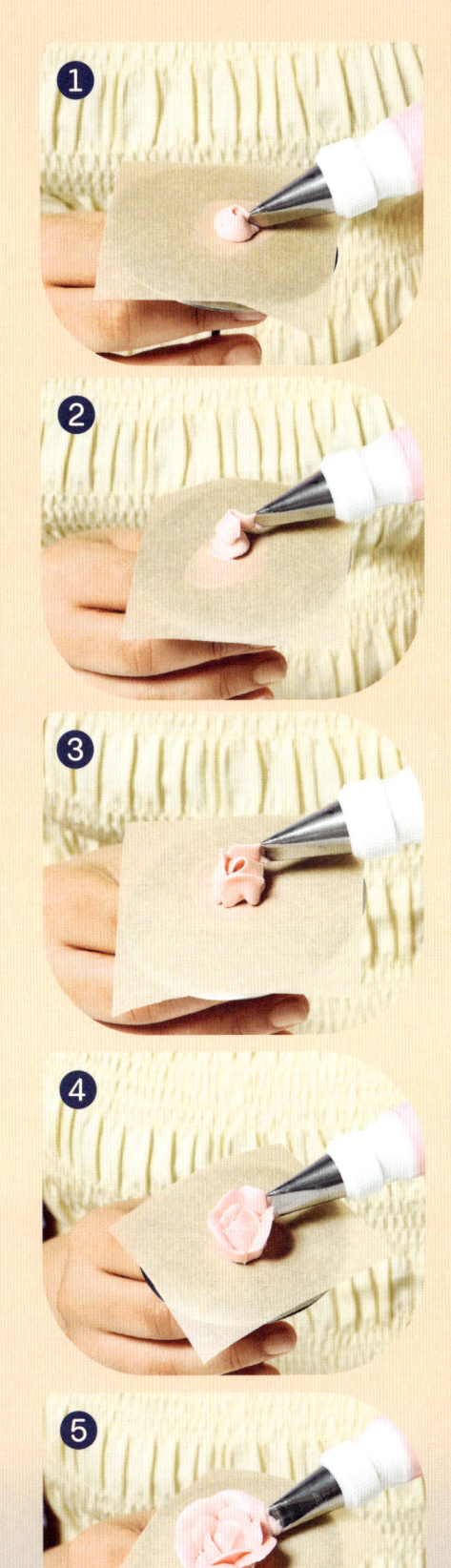

Buttercream roses

Beautiful three-dimensional roses are much easier to create than you might think. All you need is a petal nozzle and a flower nail – a small handheld tool that works like a mini turntable. You can use Italian meringue buttercream (page 43), Stabilised buttercream (page 167) or Royal icing (page 168).

Ensure your buttercream has a stiff consistency and allow the flowers to set in the freezer for about 30 minutes, or until completely firm, before applying them to your cake. For royal icing, let the flowers air-dry overnight to ensure they are firm and ready to use.

Set up

Prepare small squares of baking paper, cut to sizes large enough to fit your flower nail. Cut enough squares for the number of flowers you plan to create.

Let's begin!

Hold the flower nail between your thumb and index finger, ensuring you can rotate it smoothly with your fingers. Dab a small amount of buttercream onto the nail to securely adhere the baking paper to the flower nail.

Using a petal nozzle, apply a small dot of buttercream or royal icing to the centre of the baking paper, this will help to secure your flower in place. Now position the nozzle with the narrow end facing upwards and the wider end resting on the baking paper. Tilt the nozzle slightly inwards to create a dome shape (image 1). Apply consistent pressure while rotating the flower nail to pipe a wide base cone.

Pipe the inner bud by positioning the nozzle with the narrow end facing up and tilted inwards again (image 2). Pipe a ribbon of buttercream or icing, wrapping it around the top of the base cone to form the bud.

With the nozzle tip slightly tilted outwards, pipe three inner petals by drawing the nozzle up and down in a large curved motion, while rotating the flower nail (image 3).

Pipe a second row of four petals (image 4). This time, tilt the nozzle slightly more outwards than before and position these petals just below the first row. Use the same up-and-down curved motion while rotating the flower nail.

Pipe the outermost row of petals, consisting of about seven petals (image 5). Tilt the nozzle even further outwards so the petals fan out naturally. Use the same motion as before, but position this row at the base of the flower. Overlap each petal slightly for a realistic, natural look.

Transfer each rose with its baking paper to a tray and freeze or let dry until needed.

MARKING YOUR DECORATIONS

Marking and measuring decorations evenly is essential for retro cake decorating, as it ensures symmetry, balance and precision. The intricate patterns, clean lines and repetitive elements of vintage cakes often rely on consistent spacing. Proper preparation eliminates guesswork, reduces errors and will save you time. This section offers simple tricks to help you mark your next creation with ease. Always work on a fully set, frosted cake to prevent surface damage while marking.

Round cakes

Marking sections for the top or bottom edge. Cut a round piece of baking paper to match the size of your cake by tracing around the cake tin (image 1). To divide the cake into sections, fold the paper in half, then into quarters, sixths, eighths or more, depending on the number of sections you need (image 2, and see the diagram below).

Once folded, unfold the paper and place it on the top surface of the cake. Use a pointed palette knife to make small marks along the top or bottom edge of the cake where the folded lines meet the edge (image 3).

Marking sections for the side borders. Once you've divided the edge of the cake into equal sections, it's time to mark the starting points for the side borders. Set a wing caliper to the distance you want the border to begin from either the top or bottom edge (image 4). Then, gently measure and create a light mark at each sectioned point to guide your design (image 5).

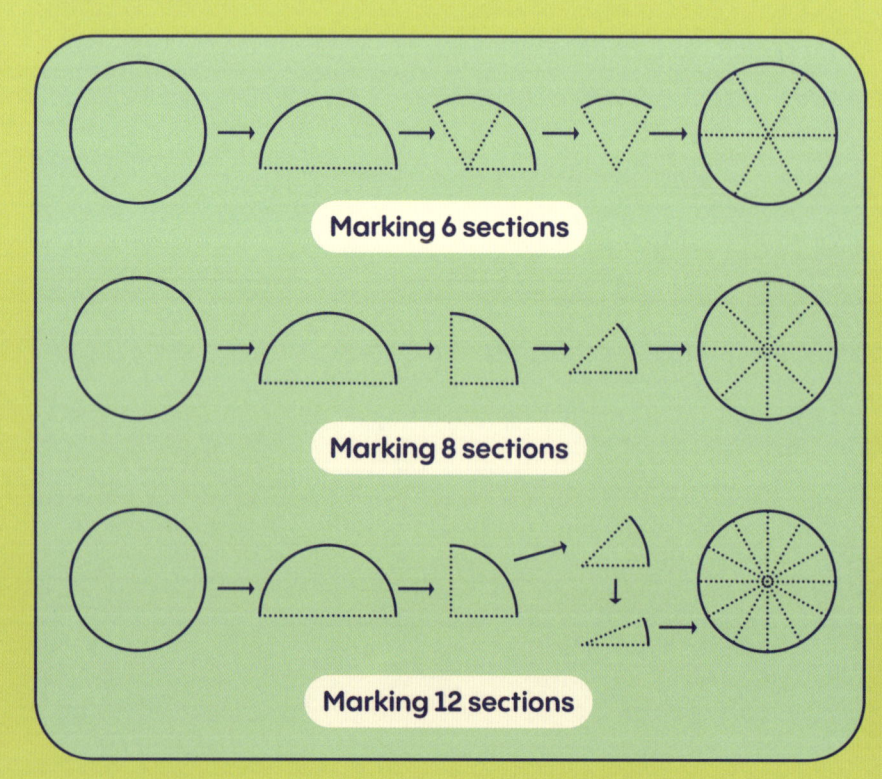

Marking 6 sections

Marking 8 sections

Marking 12 sections

172

MALI BAKES

Heart-shaped cakes

Marking sections for the top or bottom edges. Cut a long strip of baking paper and wrap it around the cake, trimming it to match the total circumference (image 1). Measure the length of the strip and divide it by the number of sections you want (image 2, and see the diagram below). You can use a clean tailor's measuring tape for this step.

Once folded, unfold the paper and place it around the cake (image 3). Use a pointed palette knife to make small marks along the top or bottom edges of the cake where the folded lines meet the edges (image 4). Alternatively, you can set a wing caliper to the length of the equal sections from the folded piece of baking paper and use it to mark equal intervals along the top or bottom edges of the cake.

For heart-shaped cakes, always measure from the point to the centre of the back curve on each side.

Marking sections for the side borders. Use the same method as you would for a round cake.

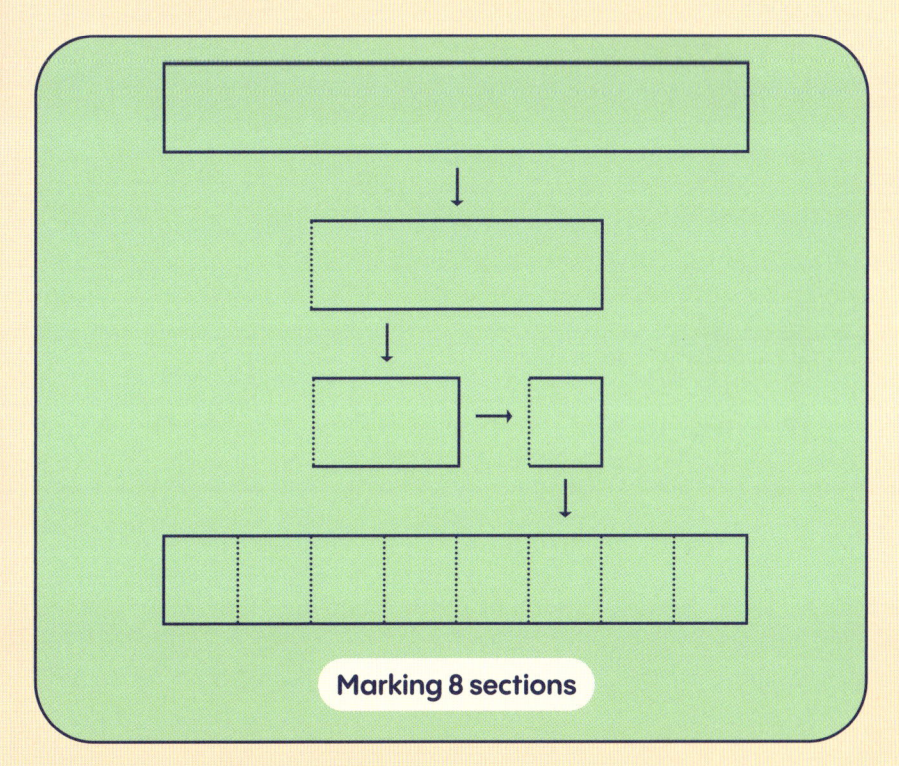

Marking 8 sections

Square cakes

Marking sections for the top or bottom edges. Simply use a ruler to measure the length of each side, then divide it by the number of sections you want. Use a wing caliper to mark evenly along the top and bottom edges.

Marking sections for the side borders. Use the same method as you would for a round cake.

RETRO DECORATING 101

CREATING TIERED CAKES

There aren't many things that make a statement quite like a tiered cake, with its striking, multi-layered design. But what's the difference between a layer cake and a tiered cake? A layer cake refers to a single cake with multiple layers of cake and filling stacked inside one tier. A tiered cake, on the other hand, is made by stacking several individual layer cakes – often of different widths, shapes or heights – on top of each other to build a tall, show-stopping centrepiece.

What excites me most isn't just the height – it's the endless opportunities to get creative with different shapes, sizes, designs, and, of course, flavours. Imagine stacking a square base with a heart-shaped tier, or mixing a tall cake with a shorter base. The larger surface area opens up countless decorative options – not all tiers have to look the same. You can experiment with different base colours, piping designs or beautiful floral arrangements. Best of all, you get to enjoy multiple flavours in one stunning creation.

Assembling a tiered cake is a bit like constructing a building. Each tier has its own weight, but you don't want that weight pressing directly on the cake underneath. That's where support dowels and sturdy cake boards come in. The dowels provide multiple points of contact, distributing the weight evenly onto the cake board below, so no tier directly bears the weight of the one above it. For extra stability, a central dowel running through all the tiers can prevent any sliding or shifting.

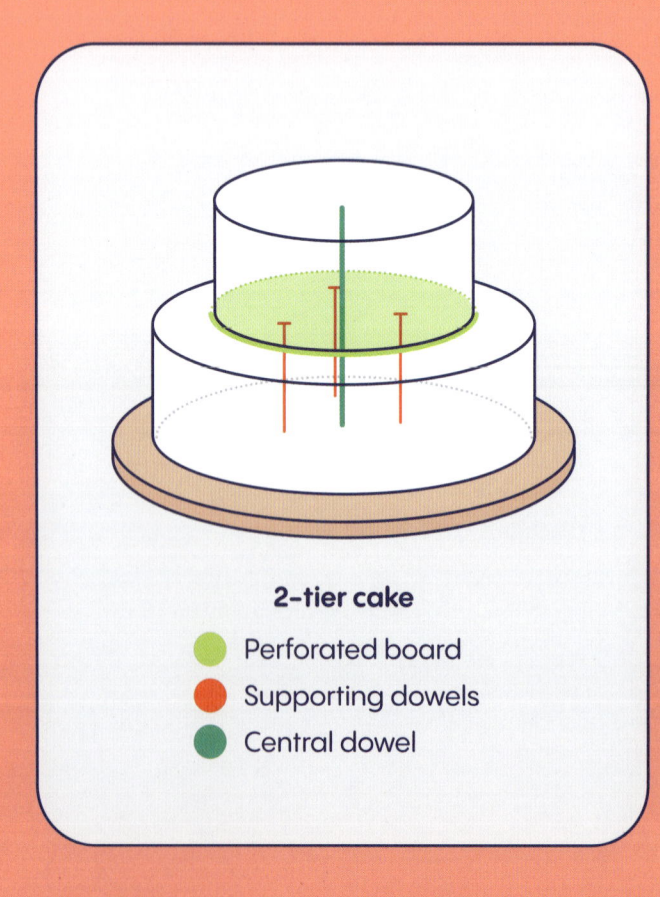

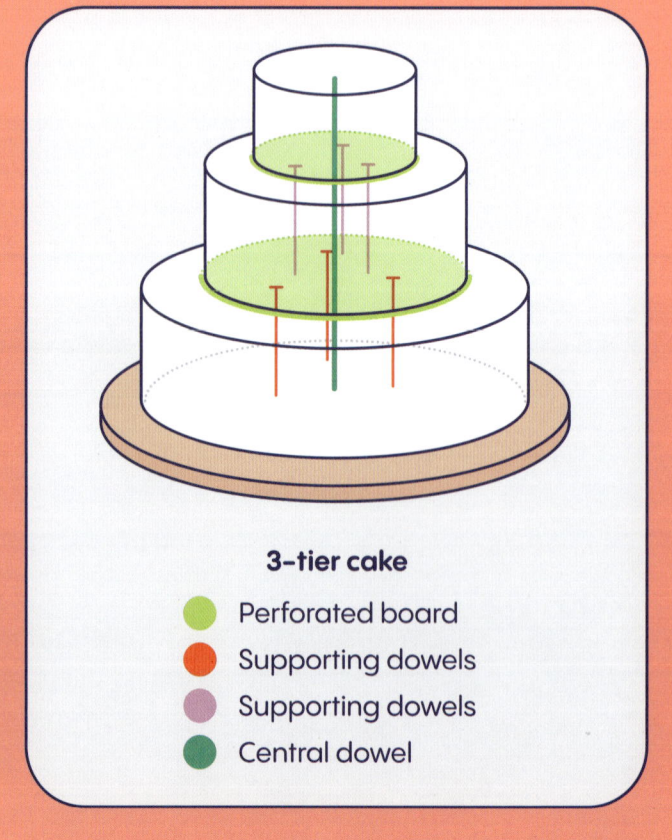

2-tier cake
- Perforated board
- Supporting dowels
- Central dowel

3-tier cake
- Perforated board
- Supporting dowels
- Supporting dowels
- Central dowel

How to stack a tiered cake

This section provides a step-by-step guide for building a stable tiered cake. Keep in mind that you want the borders on each tier to align properly, so always check the markings before stacking the tiers together.

You'll need

Large cake board, at least 1 cm (½ in) thick, for the bottom tier

Perforated cake board(s) sized to match each upper tier. (These boards have a hole in the centre that is designed to fit a dowel.)

Temporary cake boards, larger than each upper tier

Long central dowel, tall enough to span the entire cake's height

Small supporting dowels, three per tier for internal support

Baking paper

Edible marker

Masking tape

Dowel cutter or cutting pliers

Small angled (offset) palette knife or skewer for marking

Set up

The top surface of each tier needs to be perfectly level to make sure your finished cake will be straight. I recommend frosting each tier individually, as this helps create a cleaner finish, especially around the edges and corners between tiers. Just ensure the frosting is fully set and chilled before you start stacking the tiers.

You'll need to assemble each upper tier on a perforated cake board which is the same size as the cake. To make handling these cakes easier, I like to place any upper tiers on a temporary cake board. A temporary cake board can be any board you have on hand (such as a chopping board), or even a flat plate with no raised edge. Once the tier is assembled, frosted and set, carefully lift the tier – along with the perforated board – off the temporary board and place it on top of the tier below.

Let's begin!

Assemble and frost the tiers separately. The bottom cake tier can be placed directly onto your large cake board. Place each upper tier on a perforated cake board matching the exact size of each tier, which will ensure the perforated board remains concealed when stacked. To simplify frosting and handling, temporarily attach each perforated board to a larger temporary board using a folded piece of masking tape before assembly.

After frosting all the tiers, chill them in the fridge until the buttercream is completely set and firm.

Mark the centre of each tier. Using an edible marker, trace the outline of your cake tins onto baking paper and cut out circles that exactly match the size of each tier. To locate the centre, fold each circle in half, then fold it in half again, and carefully snip a small notch at the pointed tip. Unfold the paper and place it neatly on top of the chilled cake. Use a small palette knife or toothpick to gently mark the centre of each tier.

Measure the height of the cake. Carefully insert one of the supporting dowels into the bottom cake tier, positioning it halfway between the centre of the cake and the edge where the next tier will sit. Mark the dowel at the exact point where it meets the surface of the cake using an edible marker, then carefully remove the dowel.

Trim the dowels. Place the marked dowel next to two additional dowels. Align all three against a flat surface to ensure uniform height. Use the edible marker to mark the other dowels at the same height as the first. Trim them to size using a dowel cutter.

Instructions continue

MALI BAKES

Insert the dowels. Reinsert the first dowel into the original hole. Then insert the other two dowels into the cake, positioning them to form a triangle around the centre mark. Use an off-cut from the dowel to gently press each dowel until it rests securely on the cake board. Ensure that the dowels are level with the surface of the cake top.

Place the second tier on top. Apply a small amount of buttercream around the dowel area using an angled palette knife, keeping it within the size of the top tier. This will help the tiers adhere together. Take the second tier out of the fridge. Warm up a dry palette knife in warm water and gently slide it around the bottom edge of the second cake to loosen it from the temporary board, making sure the perforated cake board stays attached. Holding the cake securely from the bottom, remove the masking tape and carefully place the second cake on top of the bottom tier, ensuring it is perfectly centred. If adjustment is needed, gently shift the cake by touching only the bottom edge, which will later be hidden by decorations.

Repeat for additional tiers. For cakes with three or more tiers, repeat the process above for each additional tier. There's no need to insert dowels into the topmost tier, as it won't be supporting any weight. Be sure to mark and cut the dowels for each tier separately, as the height of each cake layer may differ slightly.

Insert the centre dowel. After stacking and centring all the tiers, trim the centre dowel to be slightly shorter than the cake's total height. Insert it into the centre of the top tier, using an off-cut dowel to push it firmly against the bottom cake board.

Cover the hole, chill and decorate. Apply a small amount of buttercream to the hole on the top tier. Use an angled palette knife to smooth it out, blending it seamlessly with the rest of the frosting. Chill the cake in the fridge for 15 minutes to set the buttercream, ensuring a firm surface that's easier to decorate.

How to stack an elevated tier using pillars

Have you ever admired a stunning cake with tiers elevated by elegant pillars? This classic, eye-catching design not only looks beautiful but also allows you to get creative with the space between the tiers, perfect for adding flowers, figurines or other decorations.

This method is similar to stacking a regular tiered cake, except it uses supporting dowels that extend above the cake's surface. The pillars are then inserted over these dowels, allowing the tier above to sit securely on top.

A tool I've found incredibly helpful is a cake separator set, which you can find online. It includes a plastic disc with three pointed feet on the bottom and dowels that can click into the feet. With this easy-to-use tool, you can decorate each tier on its own board and transport the tiers separately. When it's time to assemble, simply attach the top tier to the disc using double-sided tape to hold it securely in place.

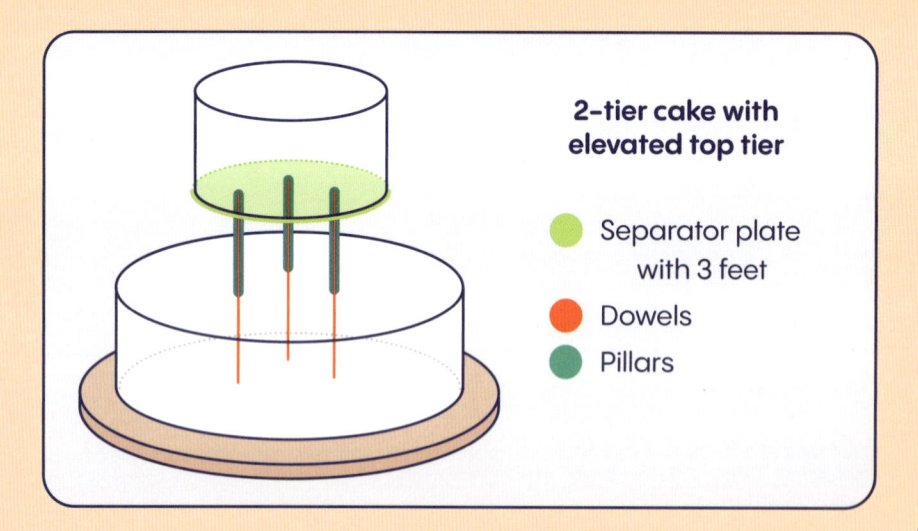

2-tier cake with elevated top tier

- 🟢 Separator plate with 3 feet
- 🟠 Dowels
- 🟢 Pillars

Let's begin!

Assemble and frost the tiers. For a two-tier cake with the top tier elevated, assemble both cake tiers on standard (non-perforated) cake boards. (If you're building a three-tier cake where only the topmost tier is elevated, assemble the bottom two tiers as described on pages 175–177.) Also assemble the elevated top tier on a standard cake board – there's no need for a perforated or temporary board for the elevated tier, as it will sit directly on the separator disc.

After frosting all the tiers, chill them in the fridge until the frosting is fully set and firm. This ensures that each tier is stable and ready for stacking and assembly.

Mark the centre of each bottom tier. Using an edible marker, trace the outline of your cake tins onto baking paper and cut out circles that exactly match the size of the bottom tiers. (There's no need to mark the centre of the top of an elevated tier.) To locate the centre, fold each circle in half, then fold it in half again and carefully snip a

You'll need

Cake board for each tier

A separator set; ensure that the plate size is smaller than the top tier cake board so it remains hidden

Edible marker

Baking paper

Dowel cutter or cutting pliers

Small angled (offset) palette knife or skewer for marking

Double-sided tape

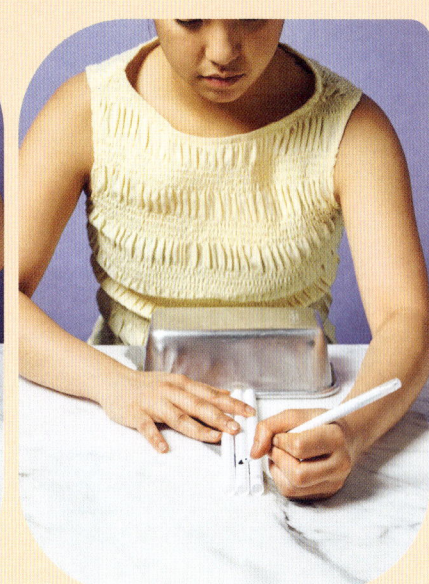

small notch at the pointed tip. Unfold the paper and place it neatly on top of the chilled cake. Use a small palette knife or toothpick to gently mark the centre of each bottom tier.

Mark the dowel positions. Gently position a plastic separator plate on the bottom tiers to mark where the dowels should be placed. Press down lightly so the plate's feet leave indentations as a guide for the dowel positions. (This step is unnecessary for the top tier of an elevated tier.) Ensure the centre of the separator plate is aligned with the centre mark of your bottom tier/s. Keep in mind that each plastic plate should be slightly smaller than the tier it will support, ensuring it stays concealed once the cake is assembled.

Measure the height of the cake and pillar. Push a plastic dowel into the cake at one of the marks you created earlier, making sure it reaches the cake board to provide solid support for the upper tier. Next, position the pillar over the dowel so it rests flush with the cake's surface. Use a marker to draw a line on the dowel where it aligns with the top of the pillar. (The dowel height should be equal to the cake height plus the pillar height.) Carefully remove both the pillar and dowel from the cake.

Trim the dowels. Place the marked dowel next to two additional dowels. Align all three against a flat surface to ensure uniform height. Use the edible marker to mark the other dowels at the same height as the first. Trim them to size using a dowel cutter.

Insert the dowels. Reinsert the first dowel into its original hole. Then, insert the other two dowels into the remaining indentations you marked earlier. Push each dowel down firmly until it rests against the cake board. Pipe a small bead of buttercream around the base of each dowel to help secure the pillars. Place the pillars over the dowels, ensuring they are flush with the cake surface, and chill the cake for at least 10 minutes to set the buttercream.

Instructions continue

RETRO DECORATING 101

Attach the plate. Attach three pieces of double-sided tape to the top of the separator plate to secure the upper tier later. Place the plate over the pillars, clicking the feet into place with the dowels inside. You can do this after decorating to keep the plate out of the way, but it's recommended to test it first to ensure it sits level on the pillars.

Repeat for additional tiers. For cakes with three or more tiers, repeat the process for each additional tier. There's no need to insert dowels into the topmost tier, as it won't be supporting any weight. Be sure to mark and cut the dowels for each tier separately, as the height of each cake layer may differ slightly.

Final assembly. Transport each tier on its own, with the plate already attached to the bottom tier. When you're ready to put the cake together, remove the plastic backing from the double-sided tape on the separator plates, stack the next tier on top, and do the same for any additional tiers. Make sure the cake is aligned just the way you want it from front to back.

CHOOSING COLOUR FOR YOUR CAKES

The first taste of a cake is experienced by sight. Colour is visual flavour and adds emotion and character to everything we see. When colour, form and flavour come together perfectly, they can complement and contrast one another, creating a whole journey of anticipation — from the moment the cake is first seen, to cutting and, finally, tasting.

The best way to learn about colour is through observation. Open yourself up to the colours around you and take note of the objects in your life, and which colour combinations feel good to you and which ones don't. Keep these observations as inspiration for your colour schemes. Some people have an intuitive feel for colour mixing and matching. But if this isn't you, there's no need to be afraid of colour. Once you understand why certain combinations work, it's easy to create harmonious colour schemes and really have fun with your cake designs.

> *'One can speak poetry just by arranging colours well.'*
> **VINCENT VAN GOGH**

Understanding the colour wheel and colour mixing

The colour wheel is an essential guide to understanding the relationships between colours – it's your map to help you create a harmonious colour palette on your cakes. Once you grasp how the colour wheel works, colour pairing and mixing becomes second nature. The following section will take you through some basic concepts in colour theory, such as primary, secondary and tertiary colours, as well as colour temperature and lightening and darkening colours.

With this knowledge, you'll see that you don't need every bottle of food colouring under the sun – just a few key colours that work for you, allowing you to create endless unique hues. Understanding how colours relate to each other can also be a fantastic way to reduce buttercream waste. For instance, leftover pink buttercream can be turned into peach by simply adding a small amount of yellow. The possibilities are endless!

The colour wheel

MALI BAKES

Primary colours: your building blocks

Red, yellow and blue are the foundational colour trio from which every shade and tone is born. By blending two of these primary colours, you create a secondary colour.

Although these three primary colours can be combined to achieve any other colour, I recommend using ready-made secondary or tertiary colours straight from the bottle, as they will deliver a cleaner, more vibrant intensity than hand-mixed versions.

Tertiary colours

Mixing a secondary colour with a primary colour gives you six tertiary colours: yellow–orange, red–orange, red–violet, blue–violet, blue–green and yellow–green.

These six tertiary colours bridge the gaps between primary and secondary hues, adding depth and variety to your palette.

RETRO DECORATING 101

Colour temperature

Colour temperature refers to the warmth or coolness of a colour. Shades in the yellow, orange and red spectrum are perceived as warm, evoking energy and vibrancy, while greens, blues and violets are cool, suggesting calmness and depth.

Sometimes, colours straight from a bottle can feel flat or unrefined. Shifting the temperature slightly can make the colour feel more natural, adding subtle complexity and richness. For example, if you're working with a pink straight from the bottle, adding a touch of yellow can give it a warm, sunlit quality, while a hint of blue shifts it to a cooler, more serene tone. Be cautious when tweaking – adding too much blue could take you into violet territory! Start with a small amount, adjust gradually, and stop when the colour feels just right.

When mixing cool colours, it's important to remember that buttercream, with its naturally warm, yellowish tint, can subtly shift cool hues like blue towards a blue-green. To counter this, add a small amount of violet colouring before mixing in the blue. This will neutralise the yellow undertone in the buttercream, allowing the cool colour to stay true to its intended shade.

Lightening and darkening colours

To create a light or muted pastel tone, simply start by adding tiny amounts of food colouring to your buttercream, letting the natural hue of the buttercream soften and pastelise the colour. Gradually build the shade until you're satisfied with the result.

To deepen a colour, the simplest method is to add more of the same food colouring. For example, gradually increasing red in your buttercream will shift it from a light pinkish tone to a bold, vibrant red. Just be mindful that too much food colouring can affect the buttercream's consistency, making it harder to work with.

If you want to shift a colour to a darker tone, you can add a small amount of black – but this can sometimes lead to a muddied tone. Another method is to use the colour directly opposite on the colour wheel to darken the shade you are working with. For instance, to turn red into a rich burgundy, try adding small amounts of green until you reach the desired depth. This approach creates a cleaner tone of colour.

✦

While these techniques provide valuable insights into understanding and manipulating colour, experimentation is the best way to discover your own unique style. Rules are helpful, but staying open to exploration allows you to develop your own methods to find your unique voice and vision when working with colour.

Basic colour schemes

A colour scheme is much like a musical score – notes can either work together in harmony, or sound like chaos. Too many colours can overwhelm the eye, making a cake design feel dissonant. The key is to find a balance, creating a palette that is harmonious but has enough contrast to be interesting.

Monochromatic palettes

A monochrome palette is classic and minimises the chance of clashing combinations. A single colour palette is the easiest to execute, and can give your cake designs a polished and sophisticated finish. Whether it's the pure white of a traditional wedding cake, a passionate red or an earthy pastel terracotta, a monochrome palette is always a safe and visually stable option.

If you would like to create more dimension with a monochromatic colour scheme, you can also use multiple variations of a single colour. The palette can span from light to dark and from the more vibrant to muted tones of one colour. For example, when red is used sparingly, it can create a soft salmon pink, which works beautifully as a base. Layer it with lighter pink details and accents of bright, bold red for depth and contrast – all without stepping outside one colour family.

One colour plus white palettes

Much like a monochromatic scheme, using a single colour in combination with white (or untinted) buttercream is one of the simplest and most effective ways to introduce colour into your cake designs. White pairs effortlessly with any hue, offering a clean contrast that draws attention without overwhelming the overall look. For added interest, you can incorporate a chromatic scheme – using two or more tones of the same colour alongside white. This adds subtle depth while keeping the palette harmonious. Even with just one bottle of food colour, you can create a beautifully balanced cake by playing with tints, tones and contrast. Imagine a cheerful yellow cake paired with white accents – perfect for your next spring celebration.

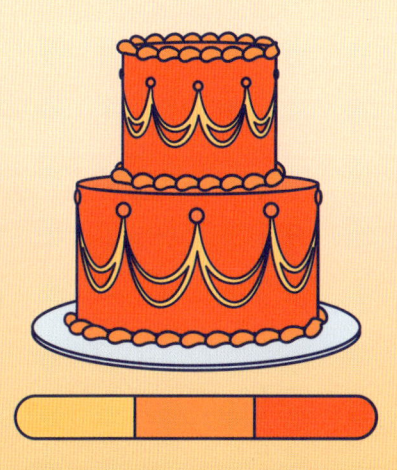

Analogous palettes

Analogous colours are closely related hues that sit next to each other on the colour wheel. Utilising them creates a seamless gradient of shades that flow into each other. The colours remain slightly different, but the harmony is easy on the eyes. This approach is simple to plan and almost always delivers stunning results. Picture a tangerine cake with soft orange and warm yellow accents. It's the essence of summer, simple and striking.

RETRO DECORATING 101

Complementary palettes

Complementary colours sit directly opposite each other on the colour wheel – think red and green, blue and orange, or yellow and violet. When used together, they create a bold contrast that makes each colour pop. To get the best results, it's all about balance – too much of both can be overwhelming, but the right ratio creates a vibrant, eye-catching effect.

You can also mix complementary colours with other schemes for more nuance. For example, pairing a chartreuse cake with lilac, its complementary colour, then softening the look with a pastel version of lilac. It's a playful, party-ready combo that still feels cohesive.

Nature-based palettes

Like all artists and designers, cake decorators can find some of the most delightful colour schemes by drawing inspiration from nature. Picture a pastel blue spring sky with white, fluffy clouds as the backdrop to soft pink cherry blossoms, accented by the fresh lime green of newly sprouted leaves.

This harmonious combination, beyond the confines of any colour wheel formula, is a perfect example of how nature's palette can inspire stunning cake designs. Step outside, observe and let nature spark your creativity.

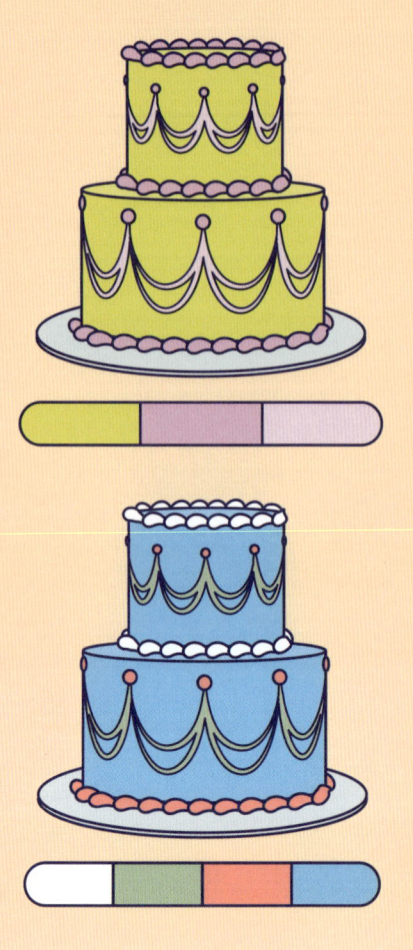

Colour ratio

The ratio of colours in your chosen palette is crucial for achieving harmony in your design. The character of one colour can significantly change depending on the colours placed next to it in different quantities.

With such a vast array of colour combinations available, finding the right ratio is often best accomplished through visualising how the colours will interact with each other in different amounts. Sometimes just a lick of a bright colour is enough to make the whole cake sing.

If you're finding this challenging, I suggest using the 60/30/10 rule. According to this handy guide, 60 per cent of the cake's decoration should feature the dominant colour as the base, setting the overall tone. The secondary colour should make up 30 per cent, while the remaining 10 per cent is reserved for accent colours, adding small but impactful details.

MALI BAKES

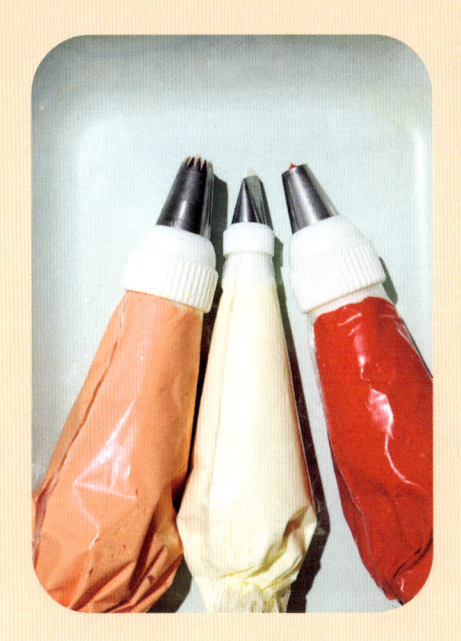

Type of food colourings – and how to use them

There are many types of food colouring available, but at Mali Bakes, we primarily use oil-based and gel food colourings. Liquid food colouring that you can purchase from supermarkets is too thin and doesn't produce vibrant results, while paste colouring, though highly concentrated, is much harder to blend into buttercream. It can also dry out quickly, leaving streaks or flecks of unblended colour on your cake, which is far from ideal.

Oil-based food colouring

This is the main type of colouring we use at Mali Bakes, as it is specifically designed for use with oil- or fat-based products, making it perfect for buttercream as it blends seamlessly and mixes effortlessly. However, it's worth noting that this type of food colouring is typically more expensive, and achieving bright, intense colours such as red can sometimes be tricky. Adding too much oil-based colouring can loosen the buttercream's consistency, making it harder to work with. Also, this type of colouring isn't suitable for royal icing – the oil can cause the mixture to split and stop it drying properly.

Gel food colouring

Ideal for most decorating mediums, including buttercream and royal icing, gel-based food colouring is highly concentrated, so you only need a small amount to achieve vibrant hues. However, gel-based food colouring can take a bit more effort to blend smoothly into buttercream. It also isn't suitable for mixing with chocolate. Heat can help 'bloom' the colour – simply melt the gel with a small amount of buttercream and use an immersion blender to mix it in thoroughly. This type of colouring is ideal for creating bright, bold reds or deep, intense forest greens.

A few final things to keep in mind when mixing colours

Colour will develop over time. When mixing colours, always start with a small amount at a time. Colours often deepen as they sit, so if you're unsure, let the mixture rest for a few minutes before deciding whether to add more.

Make more, rather than trying to match. When mixing a specific shade, it's always a good idea to make a little extra. It's better to have leftover buttercream than to try to match the exact colour again.

✧

Now that you've got the retro cake basics under your belt, it's time to grab that piping bag and get decorating! Don't stress about making it perfect from the get-go – this is your time to play. Try out colours, test a few piping techniques and, most importantly, have fun with it.

Now that you've got the basics of retro decorating under your belt, it's time for the fun part – decorating the cakes! You can use any of the layer cake recipes from Chapter 3 (and check out page 321 for tips on how to adjust the recipe for different shaped cakes or larger projects).

The projects at the start of this chapter are here to ease you in – beginning with simple techniques and gradually building up to more advanced piping skills. Think of it as a little cake-decorating journey: each project is a chance to try something new, have some fun and grow your confidence along the way.

Each project includes a simple day-by-day guide, from preparing and baking the cake layers to assembling and decorating the cake. Carefully read all the instructions for your chosen project, take notes and give yourself plenty of time to decorate without feeling rushed. You can decorate the cake either on the day of serving, or the day before.

A piping practice section is included with each cake project in this chapter. I highly recommend practising on a cake tin (to replicate the motions of piping on the sides of your cake) using the Practice buttercream on page 169 before decorating the actual cake. Refer back to the basic piping and border techniques on pages 160–165, and always keep in mind the three key piping principles: consistency, pressure and angle.

The buttercream and icing amounts provided in each project are measured by weight and include a little extra to make piping easier and account for any mishaps. Any leftovers can be stored in the fridge or freezer for future use.

I invite you to start wherever feels right, but if you're just setting out on your cake-decorating journey, the first project is a great place to begin.

Decorating Projects

Some final tips

Work surface and turntable position. Working on a flat, level surface is essential. If your work surface isn't flat, your turntable might start spinning on its own due to gravity, making it difficult to pipe accurately.

It's also important to adjust the height of your turntable as you work so you stay comfortable and don't have to bend down all the time. When piping side borders, it's much easier if the cake is at eye level. But when piping the top border, it's best if the cake is slightly below eye level. You can use blocks or sturdy large cake tins of different heights to securely position your turntable on top, then add or remove the supporting blocks or tins to adjust the turntable height to suit your needs. Always place a non-slip mat between the bottom of the turntable and the surface it's sitting on.

Start from the back seam. Whether you're working on the top, bottom or side borders of your cake, always start piping at the same point, so it can act as the 'back seam'. Most border designs, such as shells or ruffles — which are piped continuously around the cake — will always have a spot where the border begins and ends. This join is often a little less neat than the rest of the piping. By designating one side of the cake as the back seam and starting each border from there, you can keep the rest of your cake looking seamless.

Be mindful of temperature. The temperature of your kitchen can affect both the buttercream and your cake. A warm room can cause buttercream to soften quickly, while a colder room can make it too firm. If air conditioning isn't available, you may need to frequently adjust the buttercream's consistency following the simple tips on page 40. Warm hands can also soften buttercream in your piping bag.

Chilling the cake at various stages helps to firm up the decorations, making them easier to handle and reducing mess. Whenever your buttercream starts to feel too soft or the design needs more stability, simply pop the cake in the fridge for a quick chill.

Fix mistakes. Mistakes happen, and that's okay! The key to fixing any mistakes is to always work on a cold, frosted cake. Not only are you less likely to damage the cake when the buttercream is cold and set, but the chilled frosting also acts like a protective shell. This prevents the piped decoration from blending into the frosting layer — it simply sits on the surface. This makes it much easier to fix small details without disturbing the frosting underneath. If something goes wrong, simply chill the cake further until the piped decoration is completely firm, then gently pop it off using a small, pointed palette knife.

If you pipe directly onto a soft, unset frosted cake, your decoration will stick and blend into the frosted layer. Even if you chill the cake to set the piped decoration, removing it could still pull up the frosting layer underneath.

Get creative. The details in each project are meant as a guide, so feel free to make the cake your own by changing colours or piping designs. If any piping element feels too challenging, refer back to the basic borders on pages 160–165 and choose a design you're more comfortable with.

A NOTE ON IMAGES

Every project includes step-by-step images to help guide you through each stage of the process.

I'm left-handed, so if you are right-handed, some of the piping techniques might require you to position your hands slightly differently to how I am positioned, or to move in the opposite direction to me.

The basic piping techniques section (from page 160) outlines which specific techniques this will apply to.

Practise each technique before beginning on your cake to find the direction and movements that feel most comfortable to you.

Set yourself up for success

Before you begin any of the projects in this chapter, take some time to make sure everything you need is clean and ready before you start decorating. Go through this checklist and make sure you have:

- Organised all your decorating tools on your workbench, so you won't have to search for them midway through a task;

- Filled a container with warm water to keep your scraper and palette knives warm;

- Placed a small saucepan with about 5 cm (2 in) of water on the stovetop, to adjust the buttercream consistency;

- Assembled and crumb coated your cakes on the correct-sized cake boards (see the project opener pages for specific dimension and minimum thickness requirements);

- Chilled your cake in the fridge; and

- Your Italian meringue buttercream at a medium consistency, with any air bubbles removed.

DECORATING PROJECTS

PROJECT 1

Birthday Confetti

A cake that radiates joy and fun! This design is the perfect starting point if you're new to retro-style cake decorating. It uses basic piping techniques with simple nozzles, making it a perfect project to build your foundational skills.

There's something undeniably charming about decorating with untinted buttercream – it looks gloriously delicious and lets the colourful sprinkles and bright red cherries take centre stage. If you're feeling creative, though, you can always add a touch of colour to the buttercream. A soft buttery yellow or a pastel blue works beautifully. Just remember to stick to a single pastel shade to keep the focus on the vibrant sprinkles and cherries.

This is one of those cakes that's simple to make, yet when it's finished, it looks like you've spent hours creating it!

Project timeline

○ **DAY 1**
Prepare the fillings and bake the cake layers

○ **DAY 2**
Prepare the buttercream and assemble the cake

○ **DAY 3**
Decorate the cake

You'll need

Project basics
Cake: 18 cm (7 in) three-layer round cake, crumb coated and chilled
Cake board: 28 cm (11 in) round cake board, at least 5 mm (¼ in) thick
Buttercream: 700 g (24.7 oz) Italian meringue buttercream (pages 43–46), medium consistency, bubbles removed
Decorations: 6 maraschino cherries (with stems), plus about 15 g (0.53 oz) rainbow sprinkles

Frosting tools
Angled palette knife
Straight palette knife
Stainless steel cake scraper, at least 10 cm (4 in) tall
Bench scraper with plastic handle (for smoothing the top of the cake)
Heatproof container or jug, taller than the scraper and palette knives
Turntable and non-slip mat

Decorating tools
4 piping nozzles:
  Medium petal 126K;
  Medium French star S/F5;
  Medium French star S/F13;
  Large round S/P15
2 large piping bags
1 medium coupler
1 large coupler
Small pointed palette knife for marking

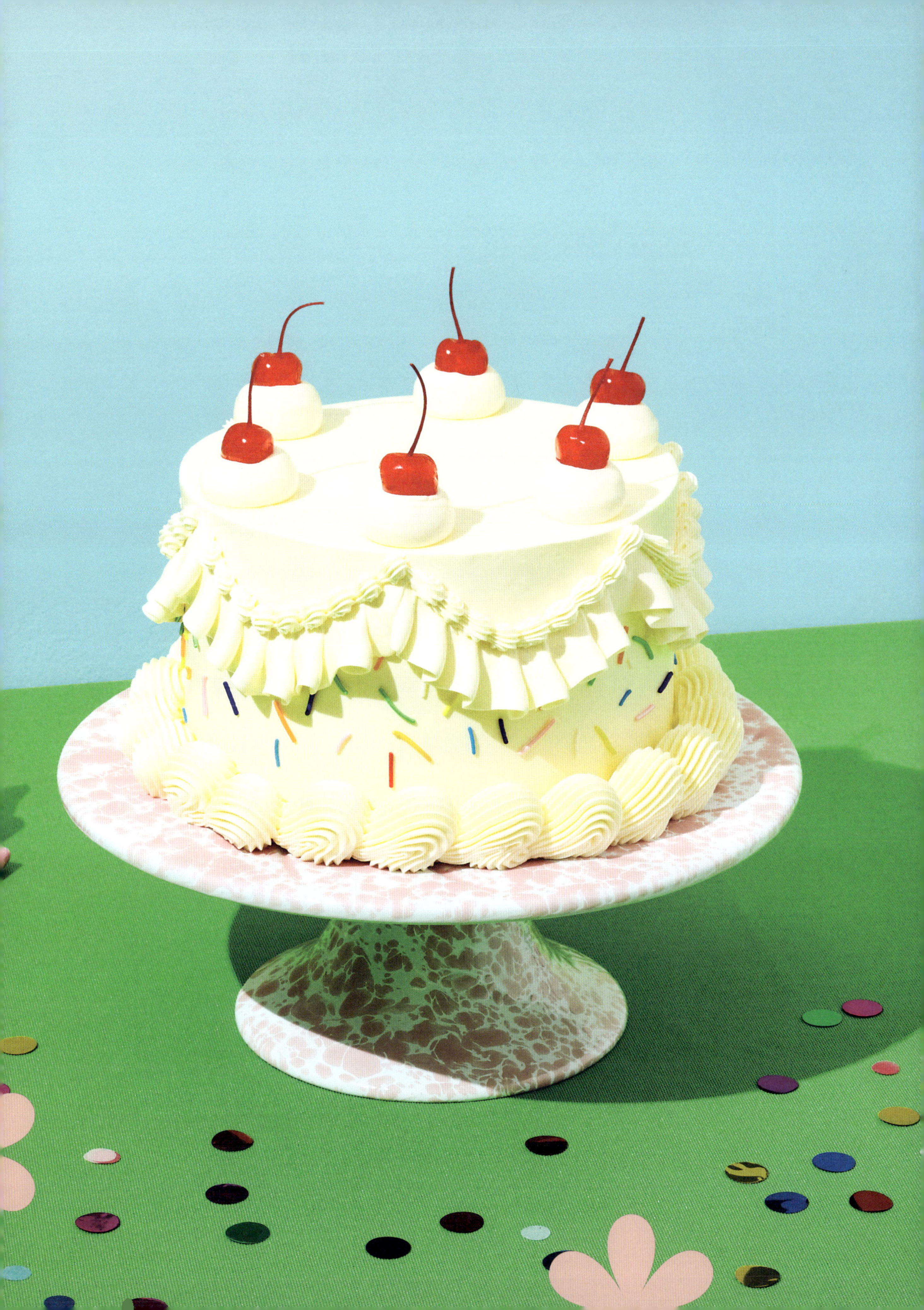

Piping Practice

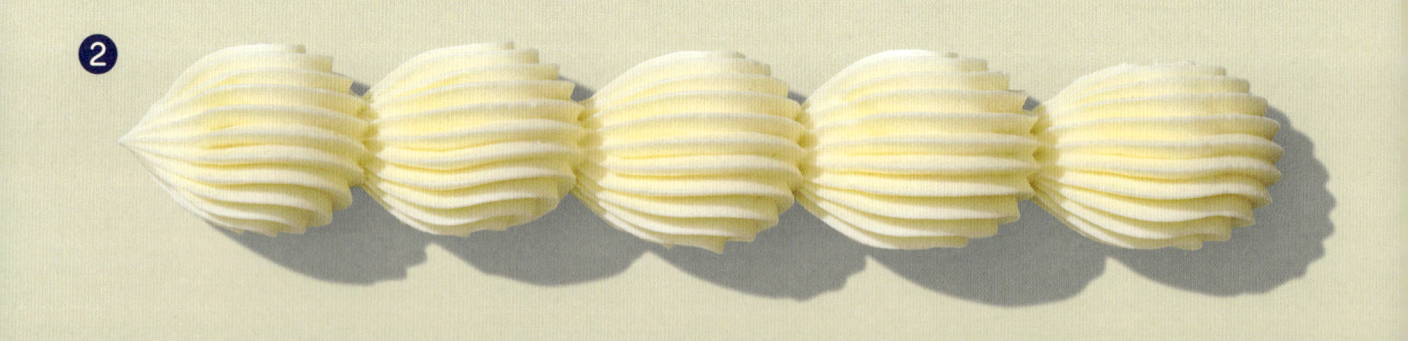

1. **Folded ruffle garland with shell trim**
   Nozzle (folded ruffle garland): Medium petal 126K · **Angle:** 45°
   Nozzle (shells): Medium French star S/F5 · **Angle:** 45°
   Pipe a folded ruffle garland (page 165), then finish with a row of continuous shells (page 161) along the top edge of the ruffle.

2. **Large continuous shells**
   Nozzle: Medium French star S/F13 · **Angle:** 45°

3. **Large blob**
   Nozzle: Large round S/P15 · **Angle:** 90°
   Hold the nozzle 1 cm (½ in) above the cake surface, apply heavy pressure to form a blob, then gradually release the pressure and swiftly pull away.

PROJECT 1   BIRTHDAY CONFETTI

Set up

Make sure you have followed the set-up checklist on page 191 before starting.

Let's begin!

Frost the cake. Start by adjusting 300 g (10.58 oz) of the buttercream to a thin but spreadable consistency (page 40). Follow the instructions on pages 51–53 to frost the cake until a neat smooth base is achieved.

Add the sprinkles. While the frosting is still soft, apply the sprinkles onto the side of the cake, leaving about a 4 cm (1½ in) border around the top edge clear for piping later (image 1). Let the frosted cake chill in the fridge for at least 15 minutes until the frosting is fully set.

Mark the side border into six sections. Start by cutting a round piece of baking paper to match the size of the cake by tracing around an 18 cm (7 in) cake tin. Follow the instructions on page 172 to create a template for marking six sections from the baking paper.

Gently place the paper on top of the cold, frosted cake, aligning the edges. Use a pointed palette knife to gently make small marks about 5 mm (¼ in) below where the folded lines meet the cake top edge. (Avoid marking along the top edge, as this part will remain exposed.) Gently remove the baking paper. You'll now have six even sections marked on the side of the cake, ready for the border.

Pipe the side border. Fit the first piping bag with a medium coupler and a 126K petal nozzle, then fill halfway with buttercream. Start by piping folded ruffles around the top of the cake from one mark point to the next, working your way around the cake (image 2). Each ruffle should drop about 2.5 cm (1 in) below the marked level. If needed, make small marks to indicate the lowest point of each ruffle garland for added precision.

Next, using the same piping bag, switch to the French star S/F5 nozzle and pipe continuous shells in a curved line along the top edge of the ruffles (image 3).

Project continues

DECORATING PROJECTS

PROJECT 1 BIRTHDAY CONFETTI

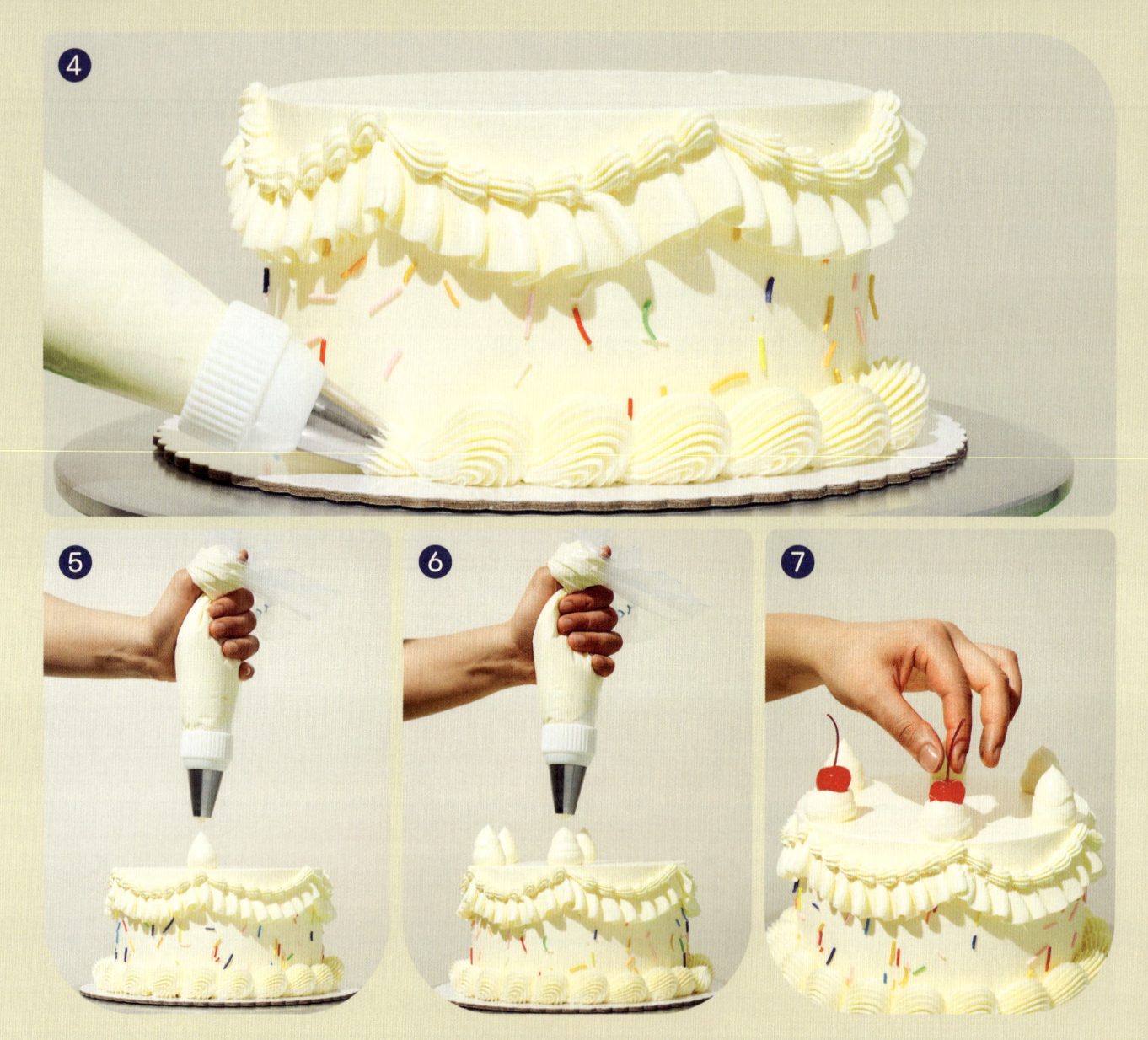

Pipe the bottom border. Switch to the French star S/F13 nozzle and pipe continuous shells along the bottom edge of the cake (image 4).

Pipe six large blobs on top. Attach the large coupler and round S/P15 nozzle to the second piping bag and fill halfway with buttercream. Pipe six large round blobs evenly spaced all around the top edge of the cake, positioning each blob at the points where the garlands meet (images 5 & 6). These blobs will act as the base for the cherries.

Finish with the cherries. Trim off the knotty part of each cherry stem, leaving the stem as long as possible. Pat the cherries dry with paper towels to remove any excess syrup. Once dry, place each cherry directly on top of a buttercream blob, pressing down slightly to secure it in place (image 7).

Chill the cake. Pop your beautifully decorated cake in the fridge for at least 2 hours before party time. This will help set the decorations in place, keeping everything secure so your cake looks picture-perfect when it's ready to shine!

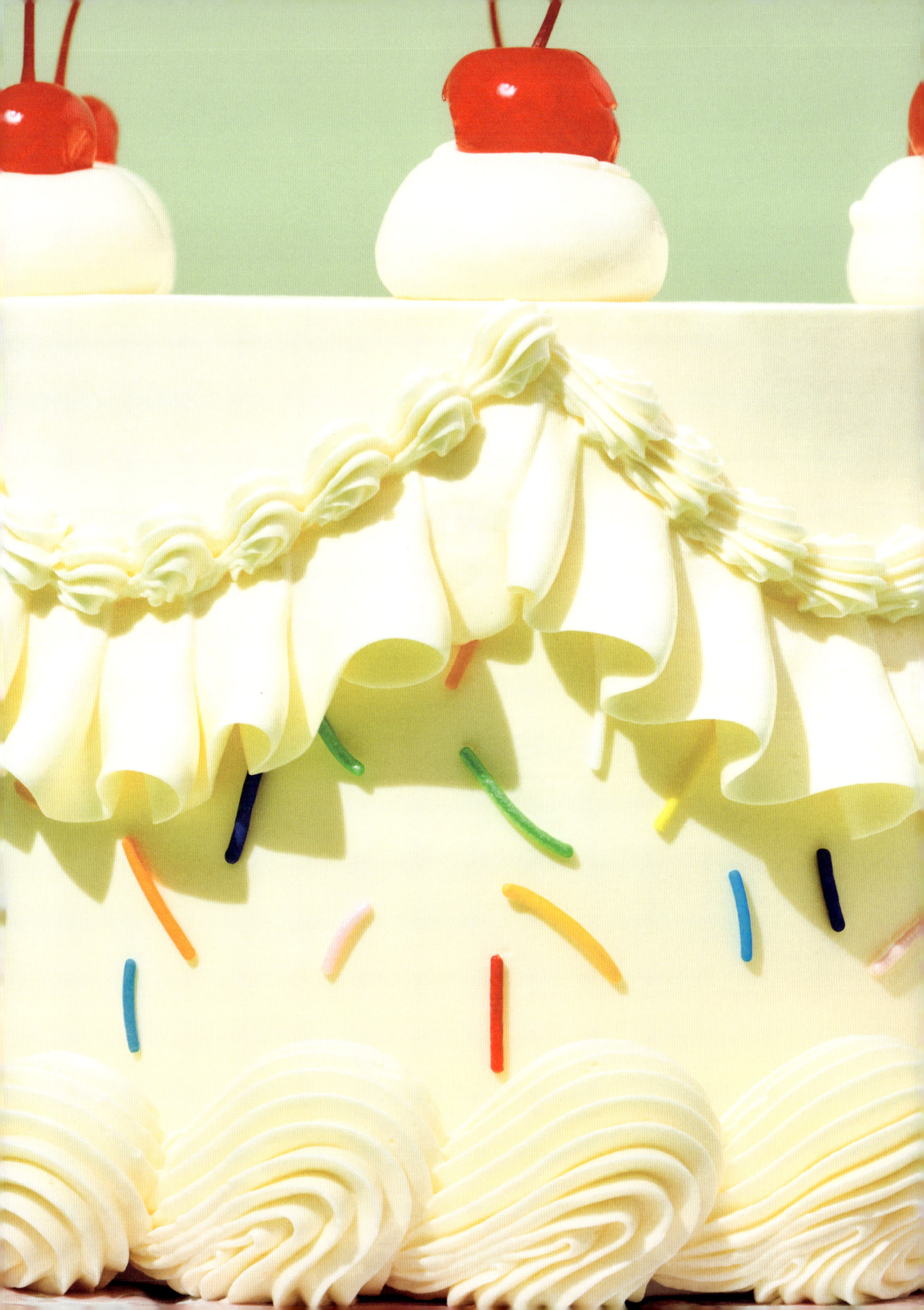

PROJECT 2

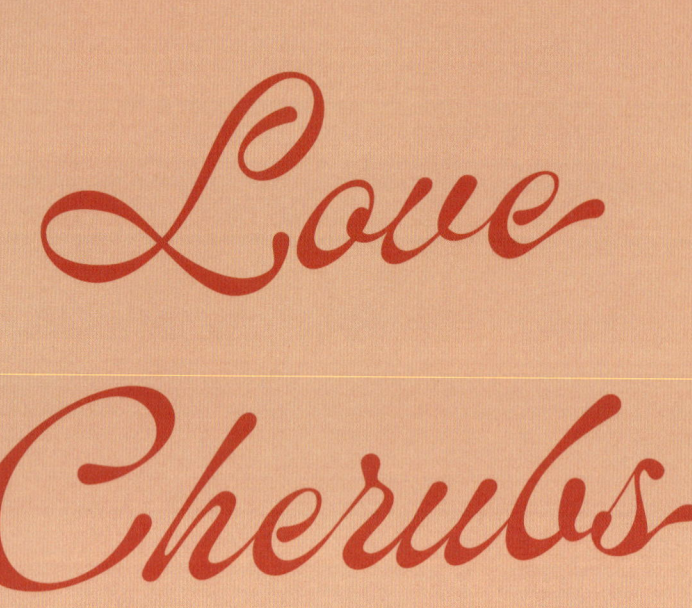

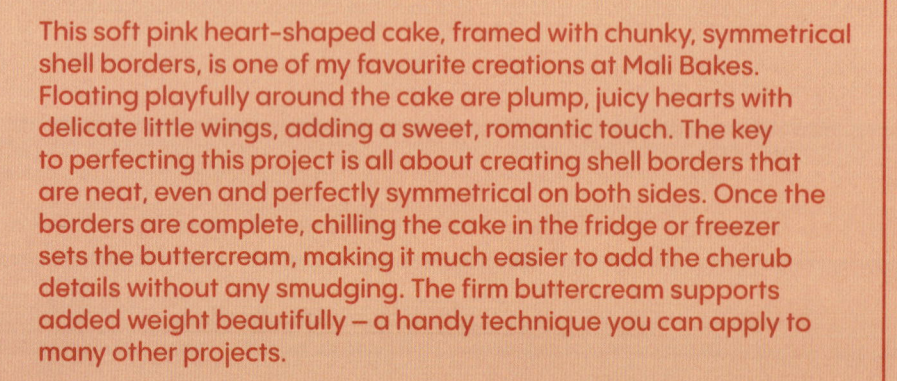

Love Cherubs

This soft pink heart-shaped cake, framed with chunky, symmetrical shell borders, is one of my favourite creations at Mali Bakes. Floating playfully around the cake are plump, juicy hearts with delicate little wings, adding a sweet, romantic touch. The key to perfecting this project is all about creating shell borders that are neat, even and perfectly symmetrical on both sides. Once the borders are complete, chilling the cake in the fridge or freezer sets the buttercream, making it much easier to add the cherub details without any smudging. The firm buttercream supports added weight beautifully – a handy technique you can apply to many other projects.

Project timeline

○ **DAY 1**
Prepare the fillings and bake the cake layers

○ **DAY 2**
Prepare the buttercream and assemble the cake

○ **DAY 3**
Decorate the cake

You'll need

Project basics
Cake: 20 cm (8 in) three-layer heart-shaped cake, crumb coated and chilled
Cake board: 30 cm (12 in) round cake board, at least 5 mm (¼ in) thick
Food colouring: Red, yellow
Buttercream: 1000 g (35.25 oz) Italian meringue buttercream (pages 43–46), medium consistency, bubbles removed

Frosting tools
Angled palette knife
Straight palette knife
Stainless steel cake scraper, at least 10 cm (4 in) tall
Bench scraper with plastic handle (for smoothing the top of the cake)
Heatproof container or jug, taller than the scraper and palette knives
Turntable and non-slip mat

Decorating tools
5 piping nozzles:
　Large French star S/F15;
　Medium French Star S/F13 and S/F5;
　Medium round S/P12;
　Standard petal 104W
4 large piping bags
1 large coupler
2 medium couplers
1 standard coupler
Small pointed palette knife for marking

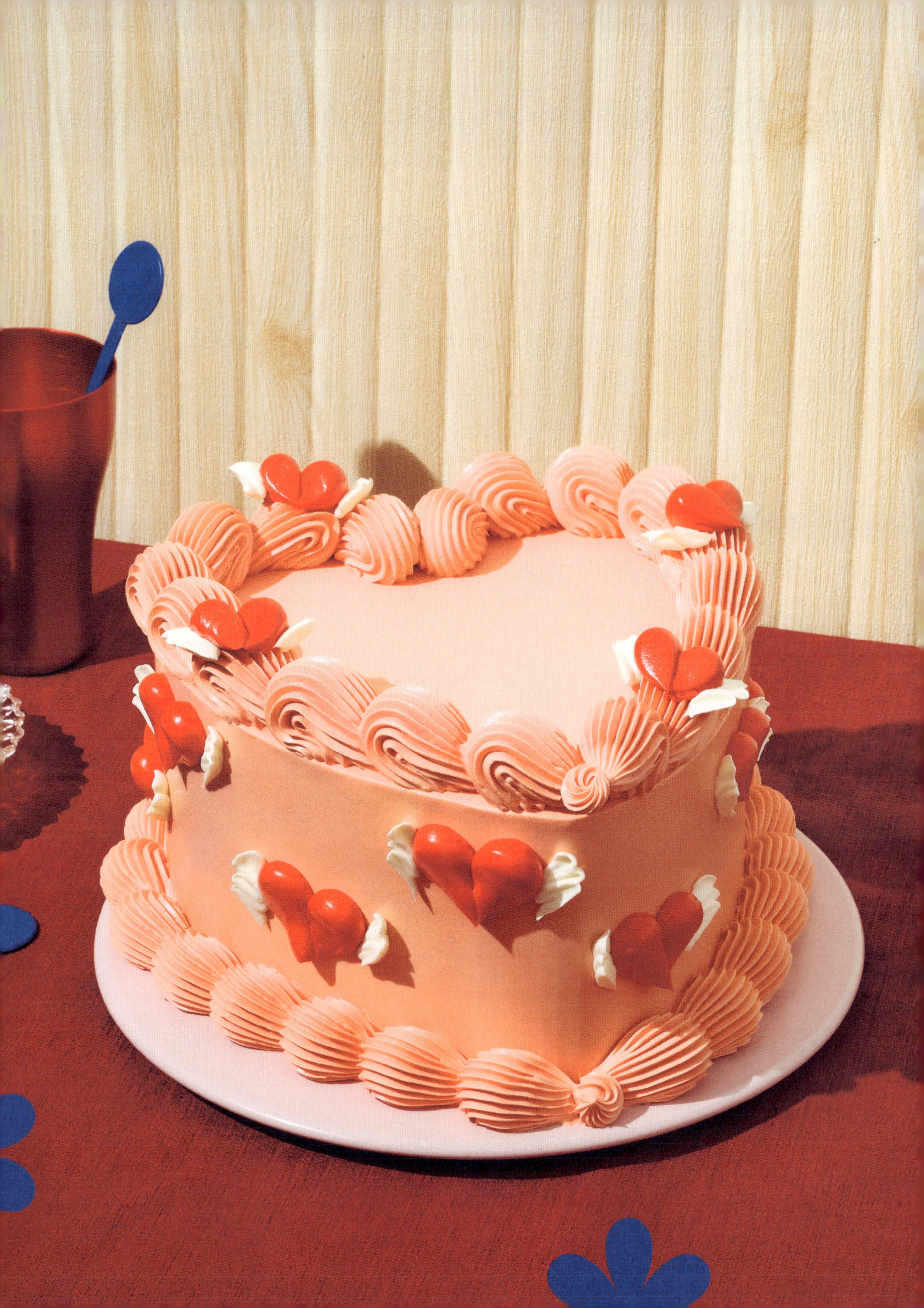

Piping Practice

1

2

3

1. **Large continuous shells (page 161)**
   Nozzles: Large French star S/F15 & Medium French star S/F13 · **Angle:** 45°

2. **Rosettes (page 161)**
   Nozzle: Medium French star S/F5 · **Angle:** 90°

3. **Love cherubs**
   Nozzle (heart): Medium round S/P12 · **Angle:** 45°
   Nozzle (wings): Standard petal 104W · **Angle:** 45°

   Pipe the two halves of the heart with the round nozzle, following the technique for piping a single shell (page 161). For the wings, position the wider end of the petal nozzle against the heart and, using the fluted ruffle technique on page 164, gradually pull away to create a pointed wingtip. Flip the nozzle to repeat on the other side.

PROJECT 2　　　　　　　　　　　　　　　　　　　　　　　　　　　　LOVE CHERUBS

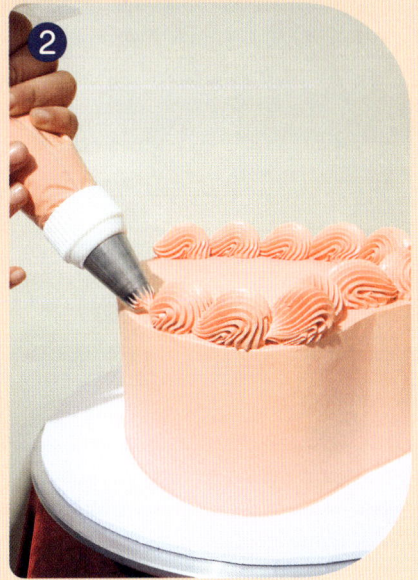

Set up

Make sure you have followed the set-up checklist on page 191 before starting.

Let's begin!

Tint the buttercream: Prepare the buttercream in three shades for decorating. Start by tinting 800 g (28.22 oz) of buttercream with small drops of red food colouring and a touch of yellow until a soft peachy pink tone is achieved. Next, tint 100 g (3.5 oz) of buttercream with red food colouring to create a deep and vibrant red. Leave the remaining 100 g (3.5 oz) of buttercream untinted.

Frost the cake. Start by adjusting 350 g (12.35 oz) of the soft pink buttercream to a thin but spreadable consistency (page 40). Follow the instructions on pages 51–54 to frost the cake until a neat smooth base is achieved. Allow the frosted cake to chill in the fridge for at least 15 minutes until the frosting is fully set.

Pipe the top border. Fit the first piping bag with a large coupler and French star S/F15 nozzle, then fill halfway with the soft pink buttercream. Pipe large continuous shells along the top edge of the cake, starting at the centre of the heart's back curve and working counterclockwise towards the front point (image 1). Repeat in the opposite direction, moving clockwise from the back curve to the front point (image 2). Keep both sides symmetrical, ensuring the shells sit neatly along the edge to conceal it.

Pipe the bottom border. Fit a second piping bag with a medium coupler and French star S/F13 nozzle, and fill halfway with the same soft pink buttercream. Pipe a shell border along the bottom edge of the cake, using the same technique as for the top border (image 3). Ensure both sides meet symmetrically at the front point of the heart.

Project continues

DECORATING PROJECTS

PROJECT 2   LOVE CHERUBS

Finish with rosettes and let set. Replace the nozzle on the same piping bag with a French star S/F5 nozzle. Pipe a small pink rosette at the heart's pointed front, where the shells meet on both the top and bottom borders (image 4). Place the cake in the fridge and allow the decoration to set fully for at least 15 minutes before proceeding to add the heart cherubs.

Pipe the love cherubs. Fit a third piping bag with the other medium coupler and round S/P12 nozzle, then fill halfway with red buttercream. Pipe four love hearts on the top of the cake (image 5). Ensure each heart rests neatly atop the shell border. After finishing the top, move to the sides of the cake (image 6). Pipe about six love hearts, spacing them randomly around the sides.

Pipe the wings. Fit the final piping bag with a standard coupler and a 104W petal nozzle, then fill halfway with the plain untinted buttercream. Pipe small ruffles on the left and right sides of each heart (image 7). Start with the hearts on the top of the cake first, then move to the ones on the sides.

Chill the cake. Pop your beautifully decorated cake in the fridge for at least 2 hours before party time. This will help set the decorations in place, keeping everything secure so your cake looks picture-perfect when it's ready to shine!

PROJECT 3

Daisy Dreams

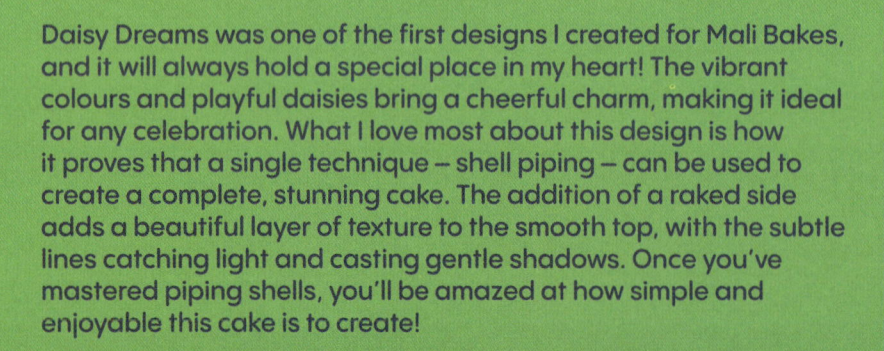

Daisy Dreams was one of the first designs I created for Mali Bakes, and it will always hold a special place in my heart! The vibrant colours and playful daisies bring a cheerful charm, making it ideal for any celebration. What I love most about this design is how it proves that a single technique – shell piping – can be used to create a complete, stunning cake. The addition of a raked side adds a beautiful layer of texture to the smooth top, with the subtle lines catching light and casting gentle shadows. Once you've mastered piping shells, you'll be amazed at how simple and enjoyable this cake is to create!

Project timeline

○ **DAY 1**
Prepare the fillings and bake the cake layers

○ **DAY 2**
Prepare the buttercream and assemble the cake

○ **DAY 3**
Decorate the cake

You'll need

Project basics
Cake: 18 cm (7 in) four-layer round cake, crumb coated and chilled
Cake board: 28 cm (11 in) round cake board, at least 5 mm (¼ in) thick
Food colourings: Forest green, red, hot pink
Buttercream: 1100 g (38.8 oz) Italian meringue buttercream (pages 43–46), medium consistency, bubbles removed
Topping: 6 maraschino cherries, with stems

Frosting tools
Angled palette knife
Straight palette knife
Stainless steel cake scraper, at least 15 cm (6 in) tall
Rake scraper, at least 15 cm (6 in) tall
Bench scraper with plastic handle (for smoothing the top of the cake)
Heatproof container or jug, taller than the scraper and palette knives
Turntable and non-slip mat

Decorating tools
5 piping nozzles:
   Medium star S/S5 and S/S3;
   Medium open star 172;
   Medium French star S/F13;
   Large French star S/F15
3 large piping bags
2 medium couplers
1 large coupler
Small pointed palette knife for marking
Metal scraper

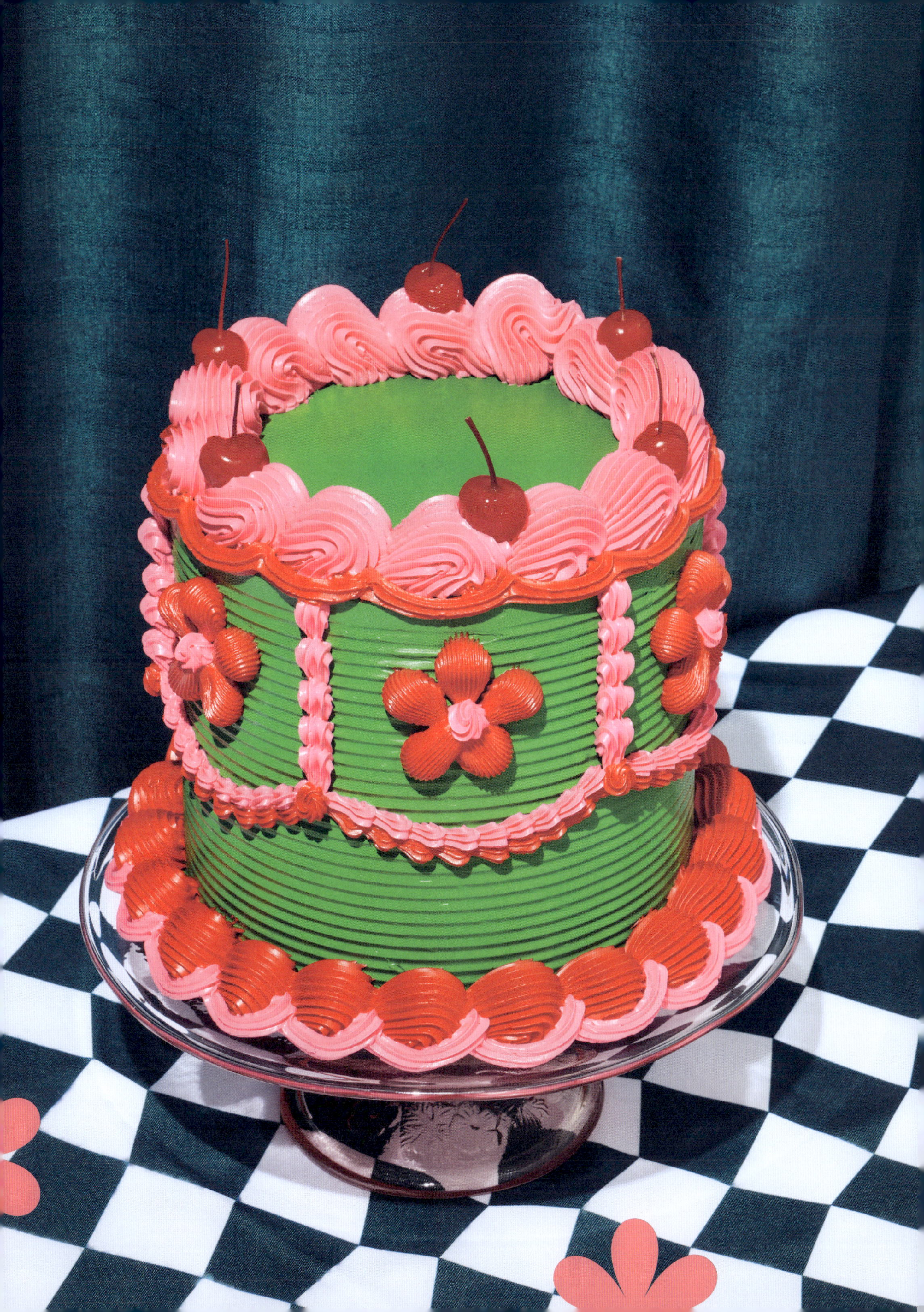

Piping Practice

1.

2.

3.

4.

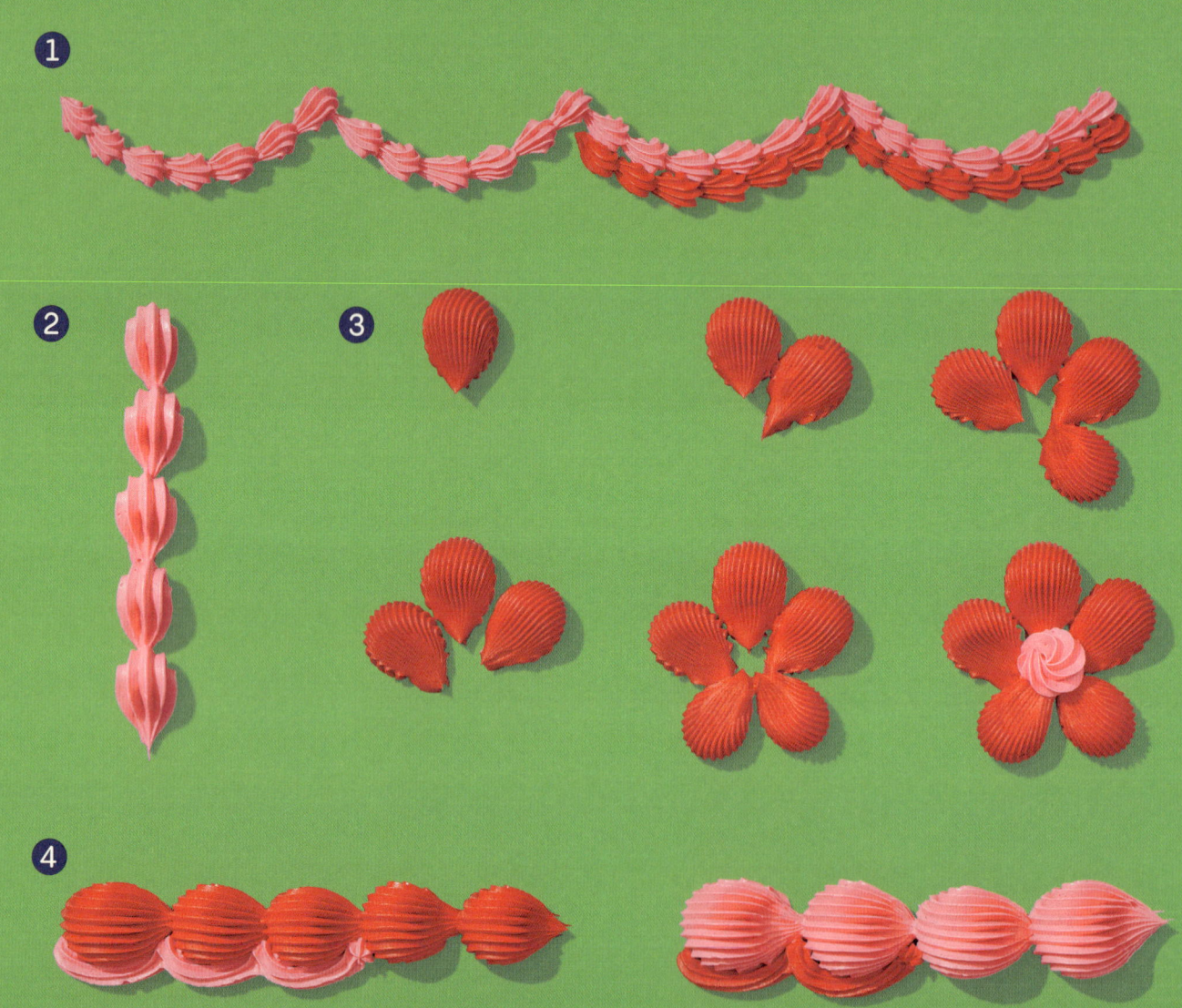

1. **Continuous shells in curve (page 161).**
   Nozzle: Medium star S/S3 · **Angle:** 45°
   Follow the method for continuous shells, but pipe in curved lines instead of straight lines.

2. **Vertical continuous shells**
   Nozzle: Medium star S/S5 · **Angle:** 45°

3. **Daisy**
   Nozzle (petals): Medium open star 172 · **Angle:** 45°
   Nozzle (rosette): Medium star S/S5 · **Angle:** 90°
   For the petals, pipe five single shells (following the technique on page 161), ensuring the tails point towards the same central point. Cover the centre of the daisy with a rosette (page 161) to finish.

4. **Large continuous shells with scallop trim**
   Nozzle (shells): Medium French star S/F13 (red) & Large French star S/F15 (pink) · **Angle:** 45°
   Nozzle (red and pink scallop trim): Medium star S/S5 · **Angle:** 90°
   Pipe continuous shells using a French star nozzle. For the trim, use the star nozzle. Start at the narrowest point of each shell, squeeze to adhere the trim, then apply pressure to pipe around the shell, and release at the next narrow point. Repeat for all shells.

Set up

Make sure you have followed the set-up checklist on page 191 before starting.

Let's begin!

Tint the buttercream. Prepare the buttercream in three shades for decorating. Start by tinting 300 g (10.58 oz) of the buttercream with forest green food colouring to achieve a deep green shade. Divide the remaining buttercream in half, tinting one portion with red food colouring for a bright red shade, and the other with hot pink food colouring for a vibrant hot pink shade.

Frost and rake the cake. Start by adjusting the forest green buttercream to a thin but spreadable consistency (page 40). Follow the instructions on pages 51–56 to frost and rake the cake until a neat base is achieved. Allow the frosted cake to chill in the fridge for at least 15 minutes until the frosting is fully set.

Mark the side border into six sections. Start by cutting a round piece of baking paper to match the size of the cake by tracing around an 18 cm (7 in) cake tin. Follow the instructions on page 172 to create a template for marking six sections from the baking paper.

Gently place the paper on top of the cold, frosted cake, aligning the edges. Use a pointed palette knife to carefully make small marks right along the top edge of the cake where the folded lines meet the edge. Gently remove the baking paper. You'll now have six even sections marked on the side of the cake, ready for the border.

To create vertical guides for the shells, dip a metal scraper in warm water, dry it with a tea towel, then press it gently against the cake to make a straight vertical line. Each line should be 7 cm (2¾ in) long and extend downwards from each marked point on the top edge.

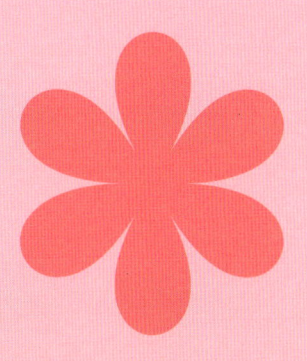

Project continues

PROJECT 3   DAISY DREAMS

Pipe the daisy frames. Fit the first piping bag with a medium coupler and star S/S5 nozzle, then fill halfway with the pink buttercream. Using the marked vertical lines as guides, pipe a continuous row of small shells along each line, starting at the top and working down to the bottom (image 1). After completing all six vertical rows, switch to star S/S3 nozzle and pipe a horizontal curved row of small pink shells, connecting the bottom of each vertical row to the next, ensuring each row curves evenly (image 2).

Next, prepare a second piping bag with a medium coupler and a clean star S/S3 nozzle, then fill halfway with red buttercream. Pipe a second horizontal row of red curved shells directly below the pink ones (image 3). To finish, use the same nozzle to pipe a small rosette at each point where the vertical and horizontal shells meet.

Pipe the daisies. Switch the nozzle on the red buttercream piping bag to an open star 172 nozzle. Pipe daisy petals in the centre of each window (image 4). To complete the flowers, switch to the piping bag filled with pink buttercream and fit it with a star S/S5 nozzle. Pipe a small pink rosette in the centre of each red daisy to finish the design (image 5).

Pipe the bottom border. Take the piping bag with red buttercream, switch to a French star S/F13 nozzle and pipe a continuous row of medium-sized red shells along the bottom edge of the cake for a border (image 6). To pipe the scallop trim, use pink buttercream and star S/S5 nozzle to pipe the trim along the bottom of the shells (image 7).

Pipe the top border. Fit the final piping bag with a large coupler and French star S/F15 nozzle, and fill halfway with pink buttercream. Pipe a continuous row of large shells along the top border of the cake, staying as close to the edge as possible. To complete the border, switch to the piping bag filled with red buttercream, fit it with a clean star S/S5 nozzle, and pipe a red scallop trim along the outer edge of the top shells (image 8).

Finish with the cherries. Trim off the knotty part of each cherry stem, leaving the stem as long as possible. Pat the cherries dry with paper towels to remove any excess syrup. Once dry, arrange the cherries evenly along the top pink border, positioning each cherry directly above a daisy to keep the spacing consistent (image 9).

Chill the cake. Pop your beautifully decorated cake in the fridge for at least 2 hours before party time. This will help set the decorations in place, keeping everything secure so your cake looks picture-perfect when it's ready to shine!

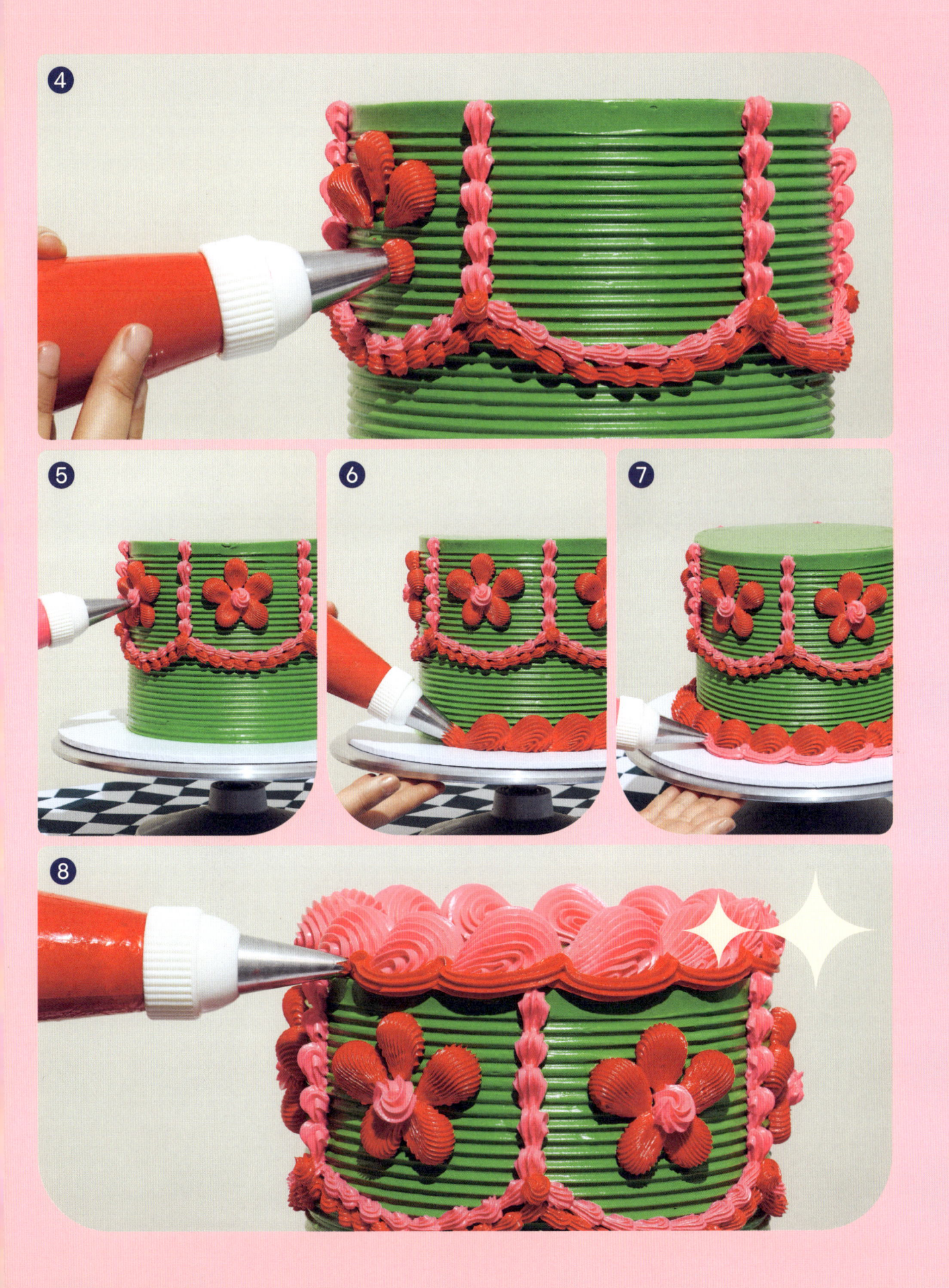

DECORATING PROJECTS 209

9

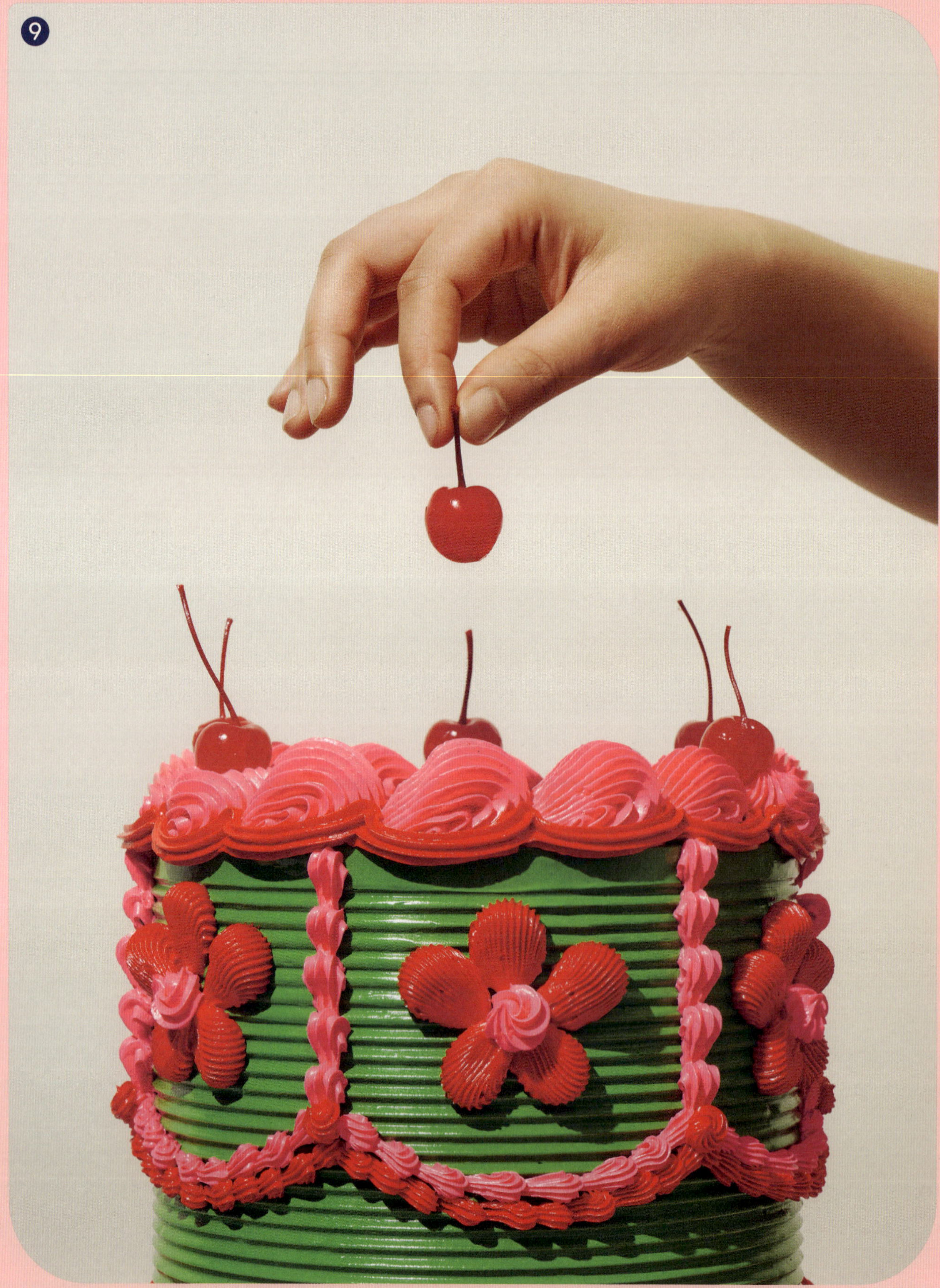

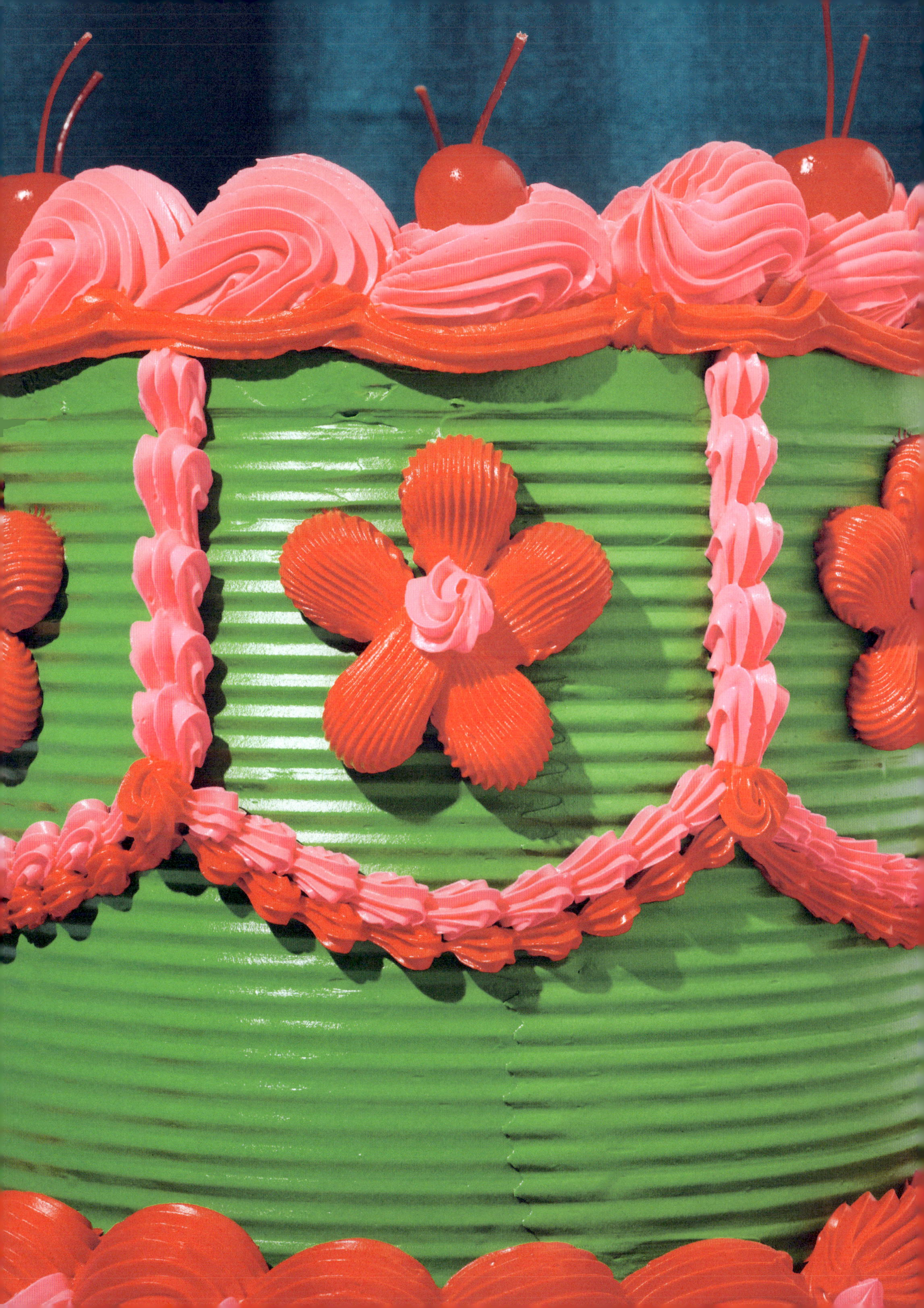

PROJECT 4

Pressed Flowers

This cake design is all about embracing ruffles, from layered borders to elegant vertical cascades, different ruffle techniques come together here to create a truly stunning cake. The top borders feature two styles of ruffles for a dramatic effect, while vertical ruffles frame the beautiful edible pressed flowers on the sides. Keeping the buttercream a single colour allows the pressed flowers to really stand out. You can easily find edible pressed flowers online – just ensure they are specifically labelled as edible and are free from harmful dyes or chemicals. Don't be afraid to play around with your buttercream colour – choose a shade that complements the flowers and brings the whole design together.

Project timeline

○ **DAY 1**
Prepare the fillings and bake the cake layers

○ **DAY 2**
Prepare the buttercream and assemble the cake

○ **DAY 3**
Decorate the cake

You'll need

Project basics
Cake: 20 cm (8 in) three-layer heart-shaped cake, crumb coated and chilled
Cake board: 30 cm (12 in) round cake board, at least 5 mm (¼ in) thick
Food colouring: Hot pink, sky blue
Buttercream: 1100 g (38.8 oz) Italian meringue buttercream (pages 43–46), medium consistency, bubbles removed
Decorations: 20–25 edible pressed flowers, in mixed sizes and colours

Frosting tools
Angled palette knife
Straight palette knife
Stainless steel cake scraper, at least 10 cm (4 in) tall
Bench scraper with plastic handle (for smoothing the top of the cake)
Heatproof container or jug, taller than the scraper and palette knives
Turntable and non-slip mat

Decorating tools
5 piping nozzles:
 Standard leaf 70;
 Medium open star 1M;
 Medium Petal 126K;
 Medium leaf 115;
 Medium French star S/F5
2 large piping bags
1 standard coupler
1 medium coupler
Wing caliper
Small pointed palette knife for marking
Metal scraper

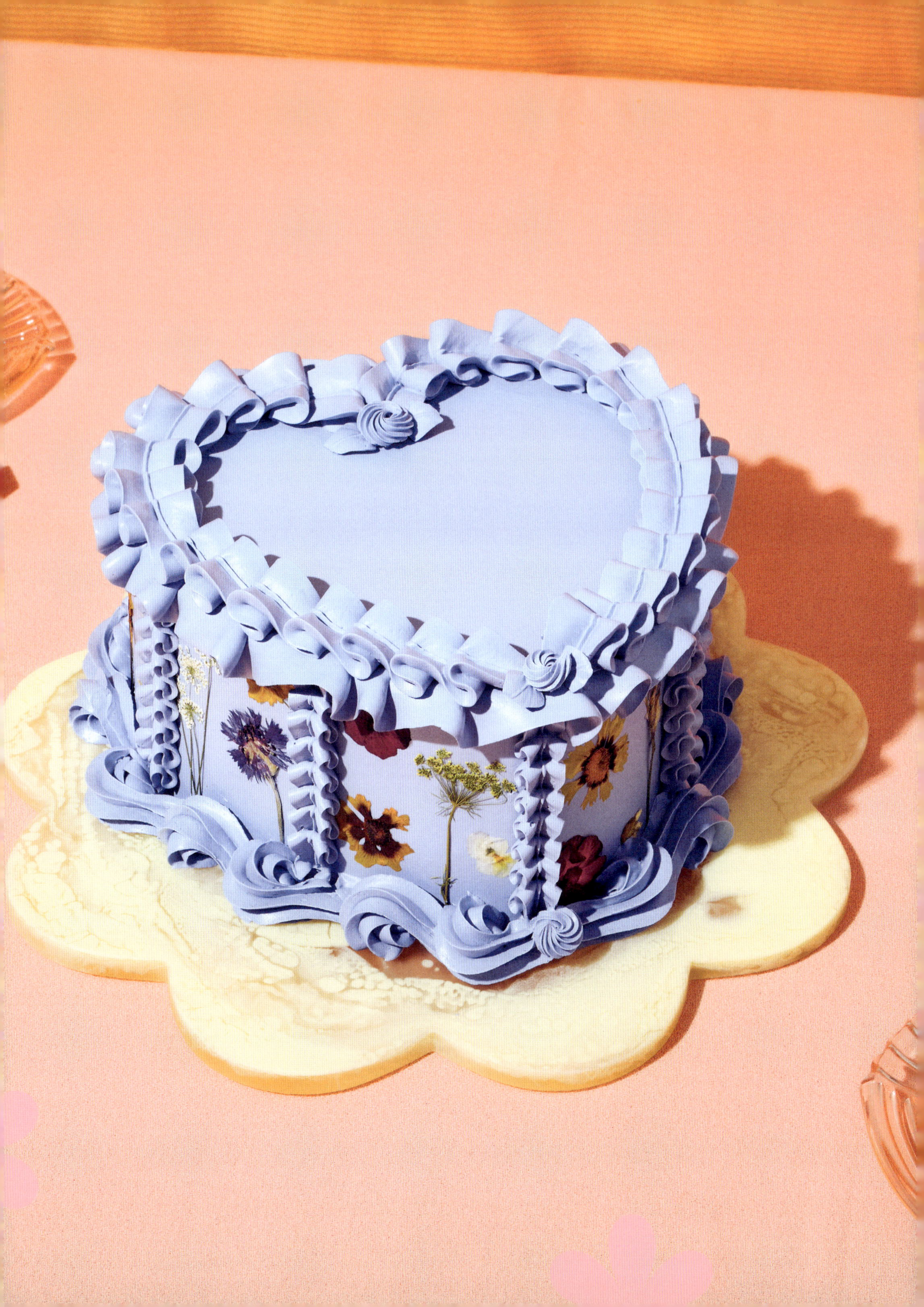

Piping Practice

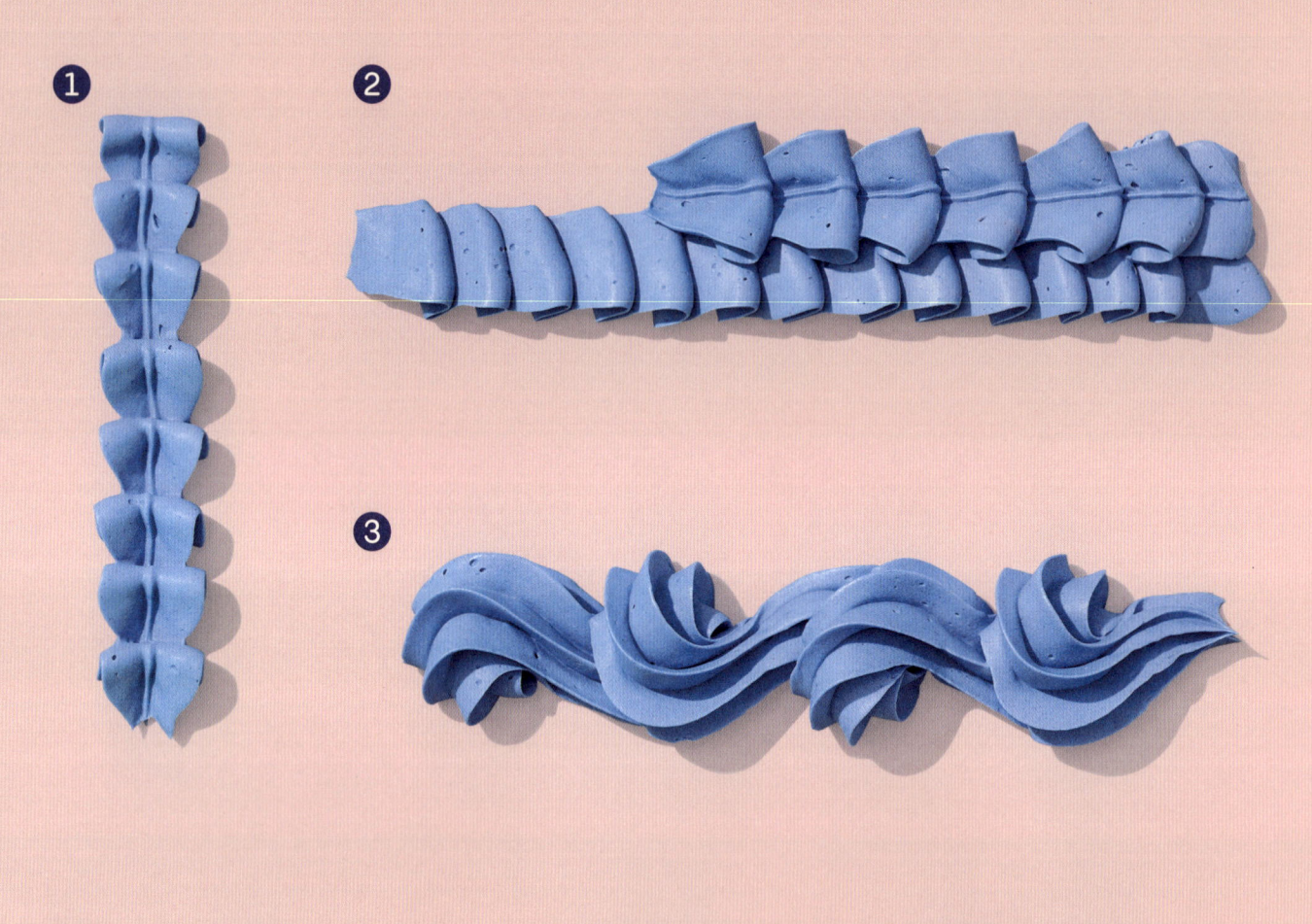

1. **Vertical folded ruffles (page 165)**
   Nozzle: Standard leaf 70 · **Angle:** 45°

2. **Folded ruffles (top border)**
   Nozzle (first layer): Medium petal 126K · **Angle:** 45°
   Nozzle (top ruffle layer): Medium leaf 115 · **Angle:** 45°

3. **Reverse shells (page 162)**
   Nozzle: Medium open star 1M · **Angle:** 45°

4. **Rosette with leaves (pages 161 & 165)**
   Nozzle (rosettes): French star S/F5 · **Angle:** 90°
   Nozzle (leaves): Standard leaf 70 · **Angle:** 45°

PROJECT 4 PRESSED FLOWERS

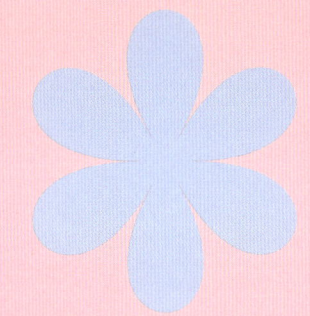

Set up

Make sure you have followed the set-up checklist on page 191 before starting.

Let's begin!

Tint the buttercream: Tint all the buttercream with small amounts of hot pink and sky blue food colouring until a pastel purple shade is achieved. To create a softer lilac tone, add more pink; for a cooler periwinkle hue, add a touch more blue. This tinted buttercream will be used for both frosting and piping.

Frost the cake. Start by adjusting 350 g (12.35 oz) of the buttercream to a thin but spreadable consistency (page 40). Follow the instructions on pages 51–54 to frost the cake until a neat smooth base is achieved.

Mark the side decoration into eight sections. Follow the instructions on page 173 to create a template for marking eight sections for a heart-shaped cake. Alternatively, use a wing caliper set to 8 cm (3¼ in) to mark just below the top edge of the cake, dividing the left and right sides of the heart into four equal sections. Begin at the pointed front of the cake and work towards the curved back on each side. Any slight size differences in the back sections will not be noticeable. To create guides for the vertical ruffles, dip a metal scraper in warm water, dry it, and press straight vertical lines down the cake from each marked spot.

Project continues

DECORATING PROJECTS   215

PROJECT 4 PRESSED FLOWERS

2

3

Apply the pressed flowers and let set. While the frosting is still soft, press your dried flowers onto the sides of the cake inside each marked section, keeping them flat against the surface and leaving a 1 cm (½ in) gap from each marked line for the piped ruffles (image 1).

Arrange the flowers naturally, mixing larger and smaller blooms in each window. As you're applying the flowers, trim long stems as needed, leaving some stems reaching the bottom edge of the cake, which will later be piped over to create the illusion of flowers growing from the base (image 2). Refrigerate the cake for 15 minutes to set the frosting.

Pipe the vertical folded ruffles. Fit the first piping bag with a standard coupler and leaf 70 nozzle, then fill halfway with buttercream. Using the marked vertical lines as guides, begin piping folded ruffles from the top edge down, leaving about a 1.25 cm (½ in) gap at the bottom of the cake to avoid a bulky bottom border (image 3). Keep the ruffles even and straight as you work. Continue until all eight vertical ruffles are complete.

Pipe the bottom border. Fit the second piping bag with a medium coupler and open star 1M nozzle, then fill halfway with buttercream. Pipe reverse shells along the bottom edge of the cake, starting at the centre of the back curve and working towards the pointed front of the heart on both sides (image 4).

Pipe the top border. Using the same piping bag, switch to a petal 126K nozzle. Position the nozzle halfway over the top edge of the cake, with the wider end facing the cake's centre. This placement ensures the ruffles will drape nicely over the edge. Pipe folded ruffles, starting at the centre of the back curve of the heart and work your way around the cake (image 5). Maintain the nozzle position halfway over the edge for even, consistent ruffles. Chill the cake for at least 10 minutes to set this first layer of ruffles before starting the second layer.

Pipe the top ruffle layer. Switch to a leaf 115 nozzle and refill the buttercream if necessary. Position the nozzle directly on the edge of the cake so the new ruffles will slightly overlap the first layer that drapes over the edge (image 6). This time, start from the centre of the back curve to the pointed front of the heart on both sides.

Finish with rosettes and leaves. To complete the top of the cake, switch the piping bag with the medium coupler to a French star S/F5 nozzle. Pipe a rosette at the pointed front of the heart on both the top and bottom edges (images 7 & 8), and another at the centre back curve of the heart, where the left and right ruffles meet (image 9). Position the back rosette slightly closer to the centre of the cake to emphasise the heart shape.

To pipe the leaves, add thinned buttercream to the piping bag fitted with the standard coupler and the leaf 70 nozzle. Pipe one leaf on the left and right side of each rosette to complete the design, except for the rosette on the bottom front edge (image 10).

Chill the cake. Pop your beautifully decorated cake in the fridge for at least 2 hours before party time. This will help set the decorations in place, keeping everything secure so your cake looks picture-perfect when it's ready to shine!

Images continue

DECORATING PROJECTS

218

MALI BAKES

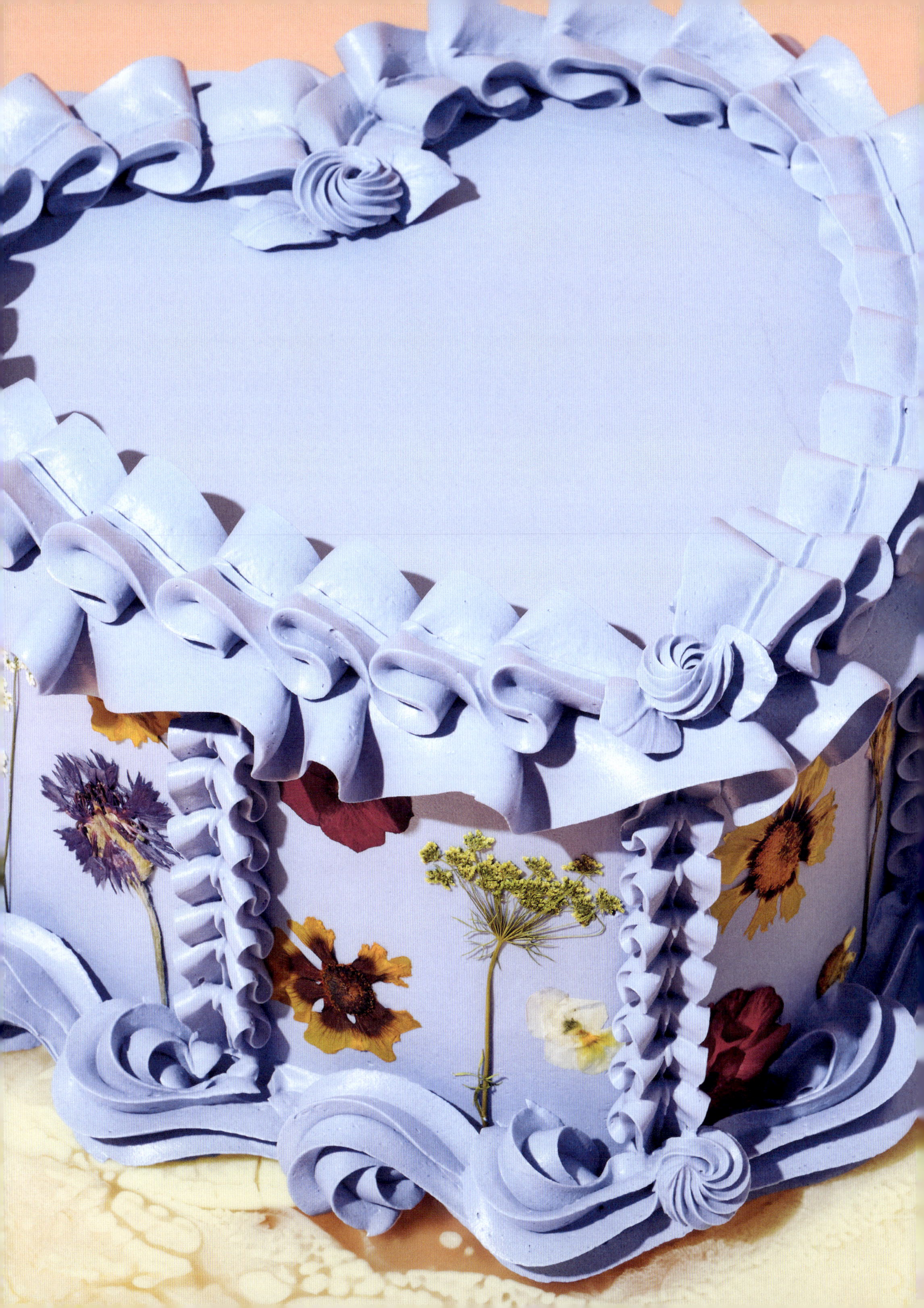

PROJECT 5

Scribbly Bloom

The Scribbly Bloom cake has a child-like charm and pop. It's such an easy and fun design to create. It features simple shell borders and uses a round nozzle to add scribbles to the side of the cake, so there's no need to pre-mark the decoration beforehand. One of my favourite elements is the bubble text – it's a great way to add lettering without worrying about it being crooked or off-centre. Simply make the bubble base separately, freeze it and then place it on the cake before piping the text onto each bubble. You can change the text to fit the occasion, but keeping it short works best for a clean and minimal look.

Project timeline

- **DAY 1** Prepare the fillings and bake the cake layers
- **DAY 2** Prepare the buttercream and assemble the cake
- **DAY 3** Decorate the cake

You'll need

Project basics
Cake: 18 cm (7 in) three-layer round cake, crumb coated and chilled
Cake board: 23 cm (9 in) round cake board, at least 5 mm (¼ in) thick
Food colouring: Red, orange
Buttercream: 800 g (28.22 oz) Italian meringue buttercream (pages 43–46), medium consistency, bubbles removed

Frosting tools
Angled palette knife
Straight palette knife
Stainless steel cake scraper, at least 10 cm (4 in) tall
Bench scraper with plastic handle (for smoothing the top of the cake)
Heatproof container or jug, taller than the scraper and palette knives
Turntable and non-slip mat

Decorating tools
3 piping nozzles:
    Medium round S/P14;
    Medium French star S/F7;
    Medium round S/P4
2 large piping bags
2 medium couplers
Angled palette knife
Small pointed palette knife

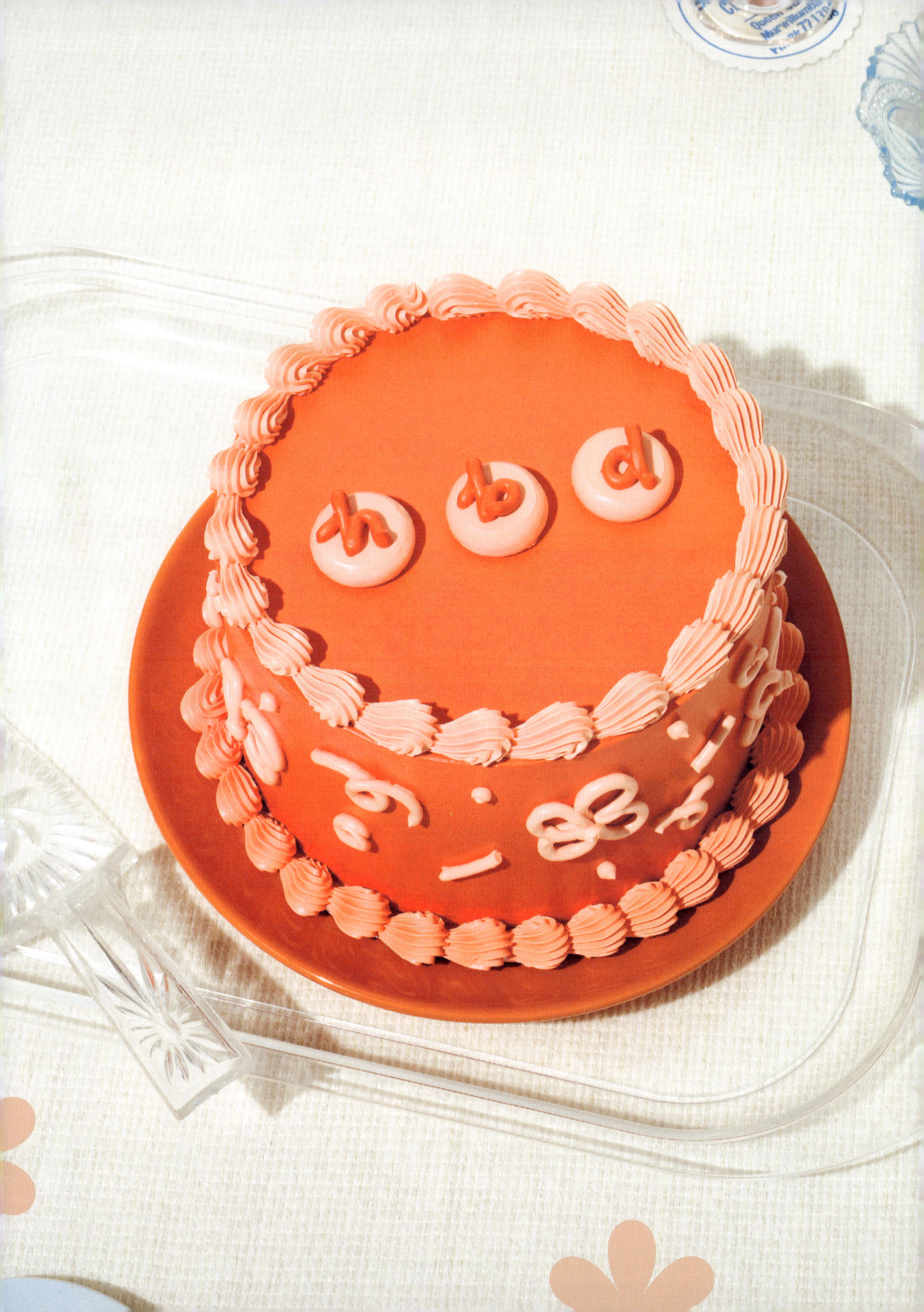
h b d

Piping Practice

1. Blobs (see opposite)
Nozzle: Medium round S/P14 · Angle: 90° with elevation

2. Small dots (page 160)
Nozzle: Medium round S/P4 · Angle: 90°

3. Small circles
Nozzle: Medium round S/P4 · Angle: 90°

4. Sprinkles
Nozzle: Medium round S/P4 · Angle: 90°

5. Confetti
Nozzle: Medium round S/P4 · Angle: 90°

6. Flowers
Nozzle: Medium round S/P4 · Angle: 90°

7. Continuous medium shells (page 161)
Nozzle: Medium French star S/F7 · Angle: 45°

8. Text
Nozzle: Medium round S/P4 · Angle: 90°

PROJECT 5 SCRIBBLY BLOOM

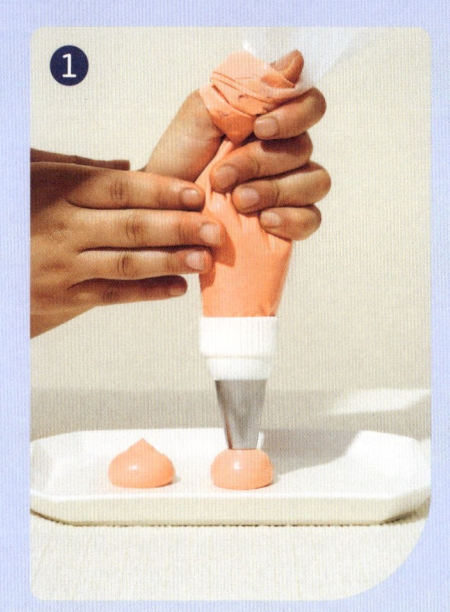

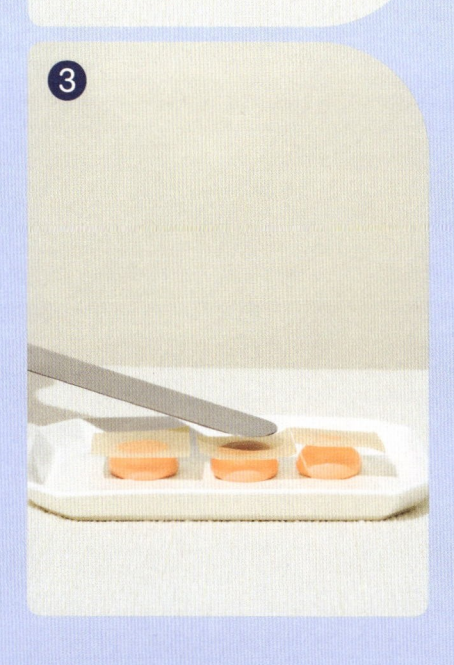

Set up

Make sure you have followed the set-up checklist on page 191 before starting.

Let's begin!

Tint the buttercream. Prepare the buttercream in two shades for decorating. Tint 400 g (14 oz) of the buttercream with equal parts red and orange food colouring until a bright burnt orange shade is achieved. Add a small dollop of this tinted buttercream to the remaining buttercream to create a softer, pale orange shade.

Frost the cake. Adjust the bright burnt orange buttercream to a thin but spreadable consistency (page 40). Follow the instructions on pages 51–53 to frost the cake, ensuring a smooth and even base. Once frosted, chill the cake in the fridge for at least 15 minutes until the frosting is fully set. Reserve the remaining bright burnt orange buttercream for adding decorative text later.

Prepare the bubble base for the text. Grease a tray that fits in your freezer and line with baking paper. Cut out small squares of baking paper, about 4 cm (1½ in) across, one for each letter.

To pipe the bubbles, fit the first piping bag with a medium coupler and round S/P14 nozzle, then fill with the pale orange buttercream. Pipe evenly sized blobs onto the lined tray, spacing them out (image 1).

Place a baking paper square on each blob and press gently with an angled palette knife to flatten them evenly (images 2 & 3). Put the tray in the freezer with the papers still on the bubble blobs to let them set firm while you're decorating the cake.

Project continues

DECORATING PROJECTS

PROJECT 5   SCRIBBLY BLOOM

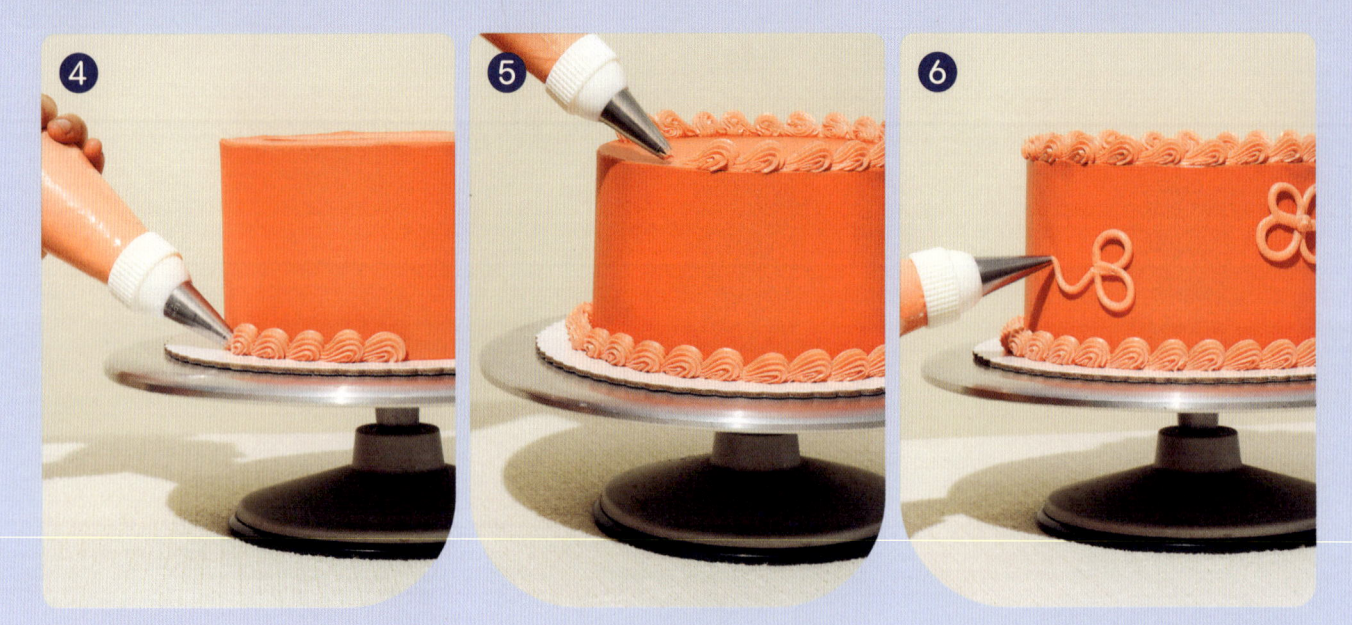

Pipe the top and bottom borders. Using the same piping bag, switch to a French star S/F7 nozzle and pipe continuous shells along the bottom and top edge of the cake (images 4 & 5).

Pipe the side scribbles. Using the same piping bag, switch to a round S/P4 nozzle. Pipe flower shapes randomly around the side of the cake (image 6). Then, using the same nozzle, fill the negative space with small dots, circles, sprinkles and confetti details (image 7).

Position the bubble bases. Work on a stable surface instead of a turntable for better precision as you work through these final steps. Use a pointed palette knife to lightly mark the spots for each bubble on top of the cake, centring and spacing them evenly (image 8). Using the round S/P4 nozzle, pipe a small buttercream dot at each mark to secure the bubbles (image 9). Remove the bubble bases from the freezer, peel off the baking paper and quickly transfer them to the marked buttercream spots using the pointed palette knife (image 10). Adjust the positioning if needed before the buttercream sets (image 11).

Pipe the text. Fit the second piping bag with the other medium coupler and a clean round S/P4 nozzle, then fill with the bright orange buttercream, ensuring it is at a thin consistency. Carefully pipe one letter onto each bubble, keeping the letters as even in size as possible (image 12).

Chill the cake. Pop your beautifully decorated cake in the fridge for at least 2 hours before party time. This will help set the decorations in place, keeping everything secure so your cake looks picture-perfect when it's ready to shine!

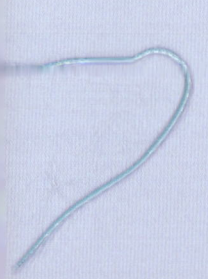

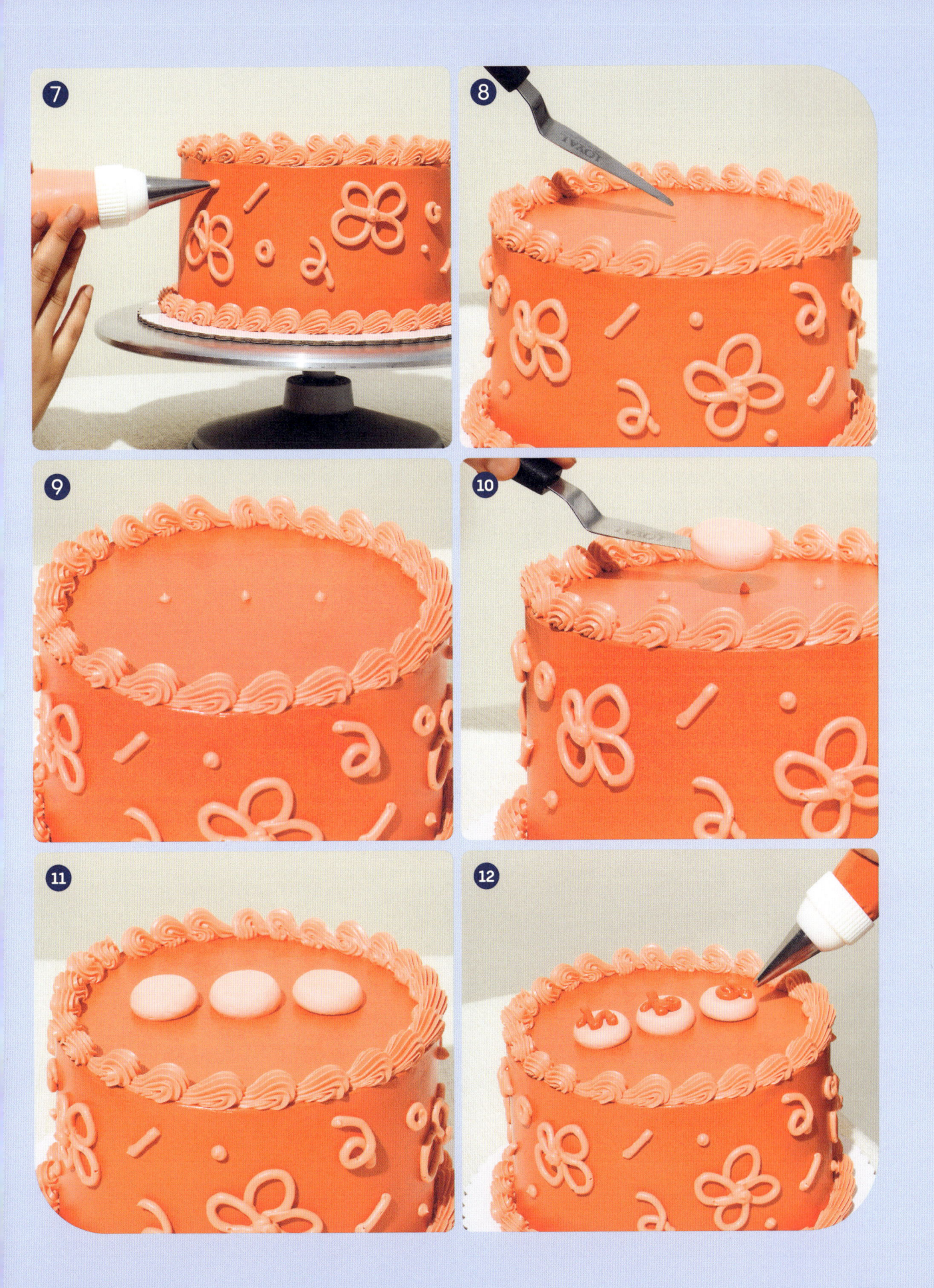

DECORATING PROJECTS 225

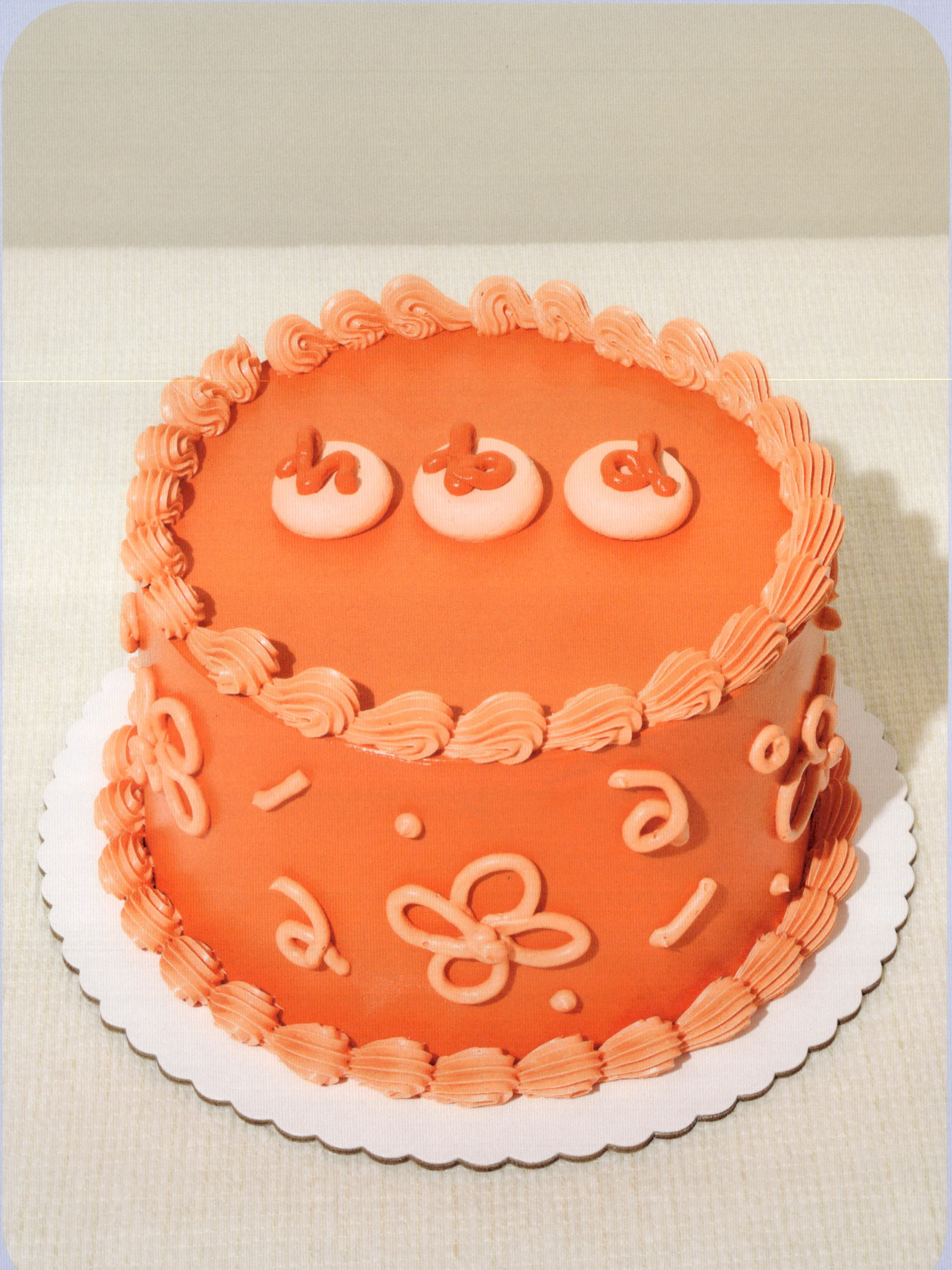
hbd

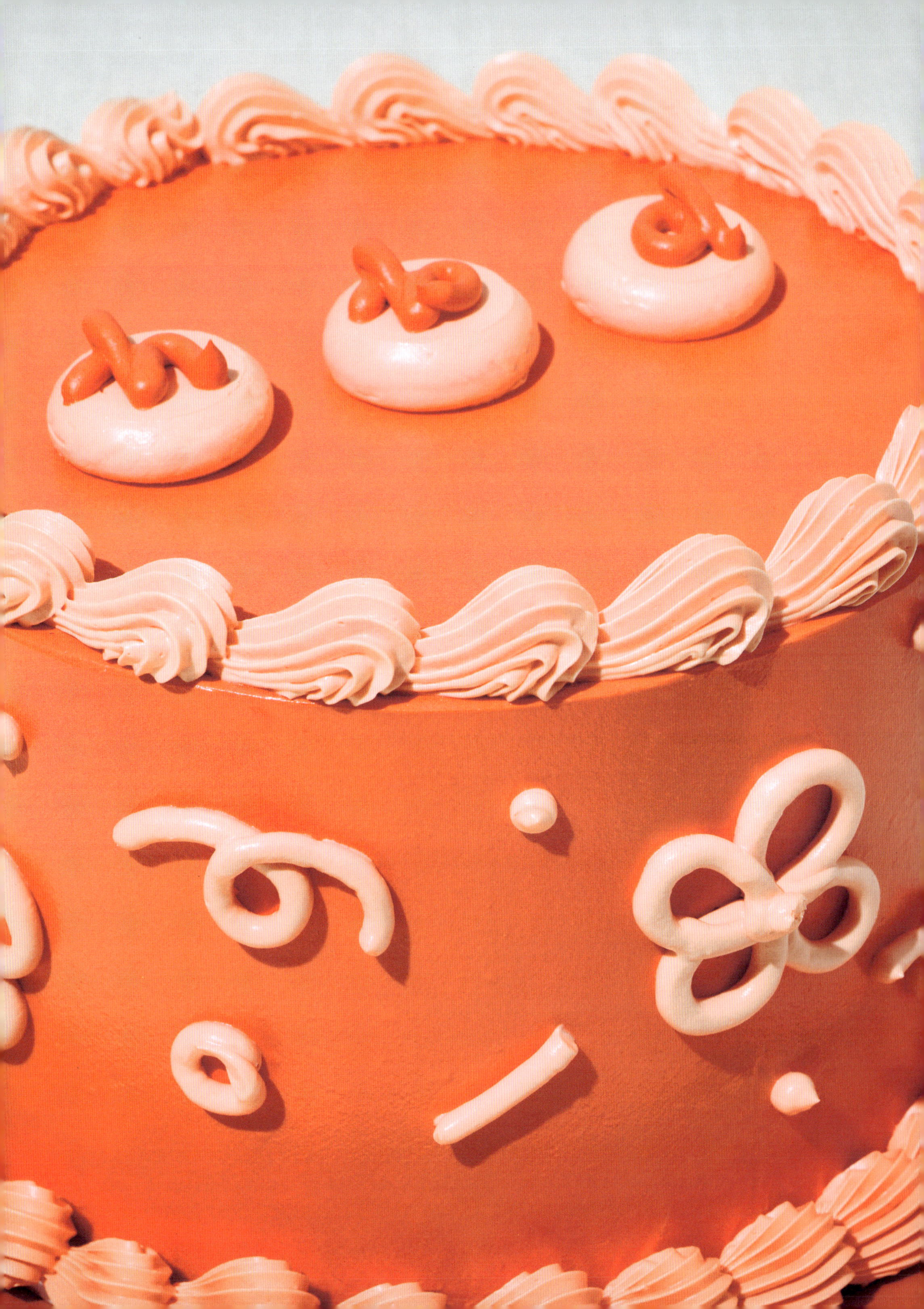

PROJECT 6

Rosy Plaid

This colourful plaid design, reminiscent of a classic picnic basket, is brought to life with vibrant red, soft peach and light blue hues. It's framed with chunky, glossy bead boarders, and adorned with delicate red buttercream roses and pale blue leaves. Rosy Plaid is a fun little step up from previous projects. Its ribbon garland details may take some practice to perfect, as they require confidence in controlling the pressure and flow of your hand movements to achieve an even, symmetrical drape. The plaid design on top is delightfully simple, but it's important to focus on applying steady pressure to ensure your lines are perfectly straight and unbroken.

Project timeline

DAY 1
Prepare the fillings and bake the cake layers

DAY 2
Prepare the buttercream and assemble the cake

DAY 3
Decorate the cake

You'll need

Project basics
Cake: 18 cm (7 in) three-layer round cake, crumb coated and chilled
Cake board: 23 cm (9 in) round cake board, at least 5 mm (¼ in) thick
Food colouring: Hot pink, cobalt blue, red, yellow
Buttercream: 700 g (24.7 oz) Italian meringue buttercream (pages 43–46), medium consistency, bubbles removed
Topping: 8 maraschino cherries, with stems

Frosting tools
Angled palette knife
Straight palette knife
Stainless steel cake scraper, at least 10 cm (4 in) tall
Rake scraper, at least 10 cm (4 in) tall
Bench scraper with plastic handle (for smoothing the top of the cake)
Heatproof container or jug, taller than the scraper and palette knives
Turntable and non-slip mat

Decorating tools
6 piping nozzles:
    Medium basketweave 2B;
    Standard basketweave 44;
    Standard round 5;
    Medium French star S/F5;
    Standard leaf 70;
    Medium round S/P 14;
4 large piping bags
2 medium couplers
2 standard couplers
Small pointed palette knife for marking
Metal scraper

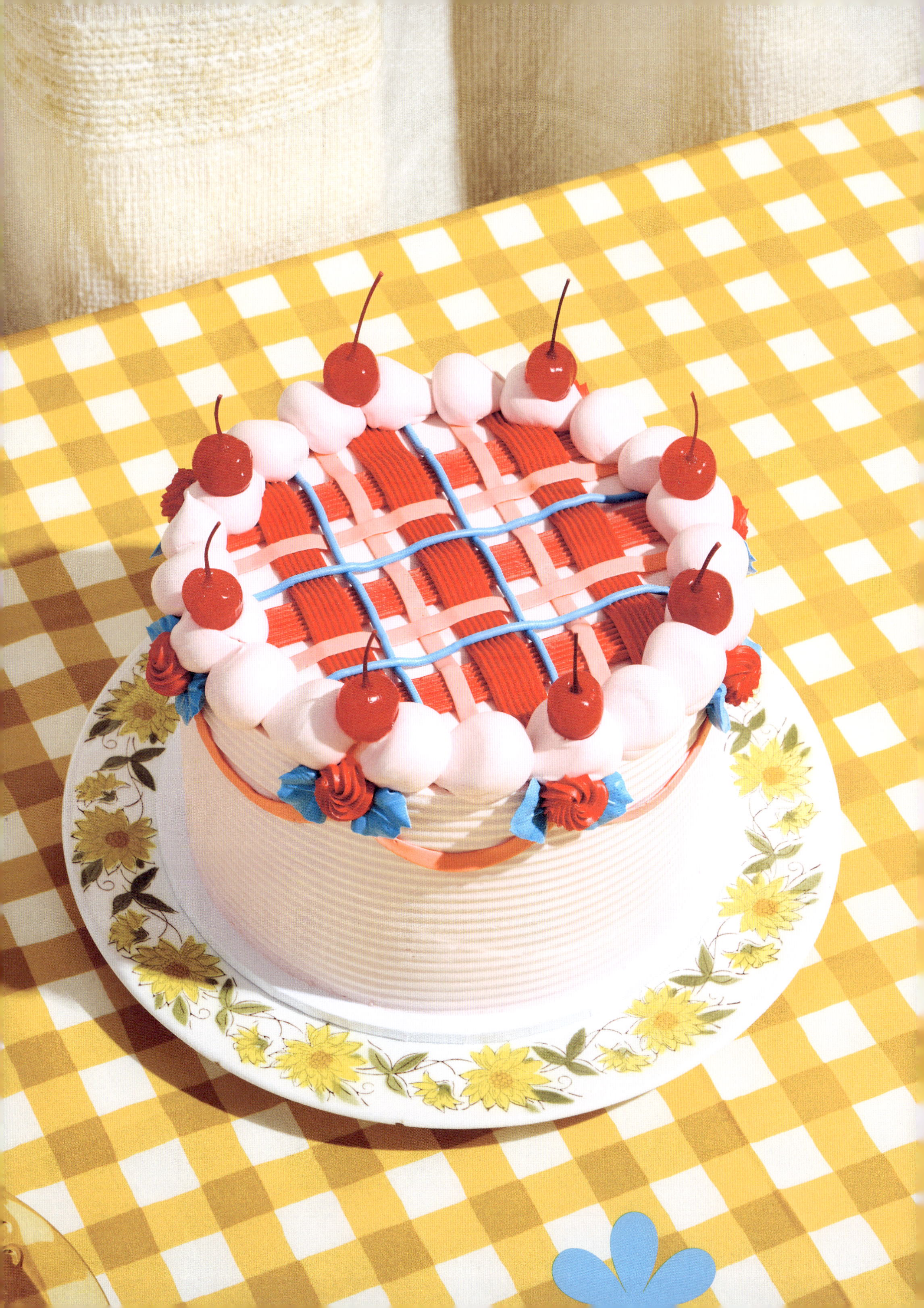

Piping Practice

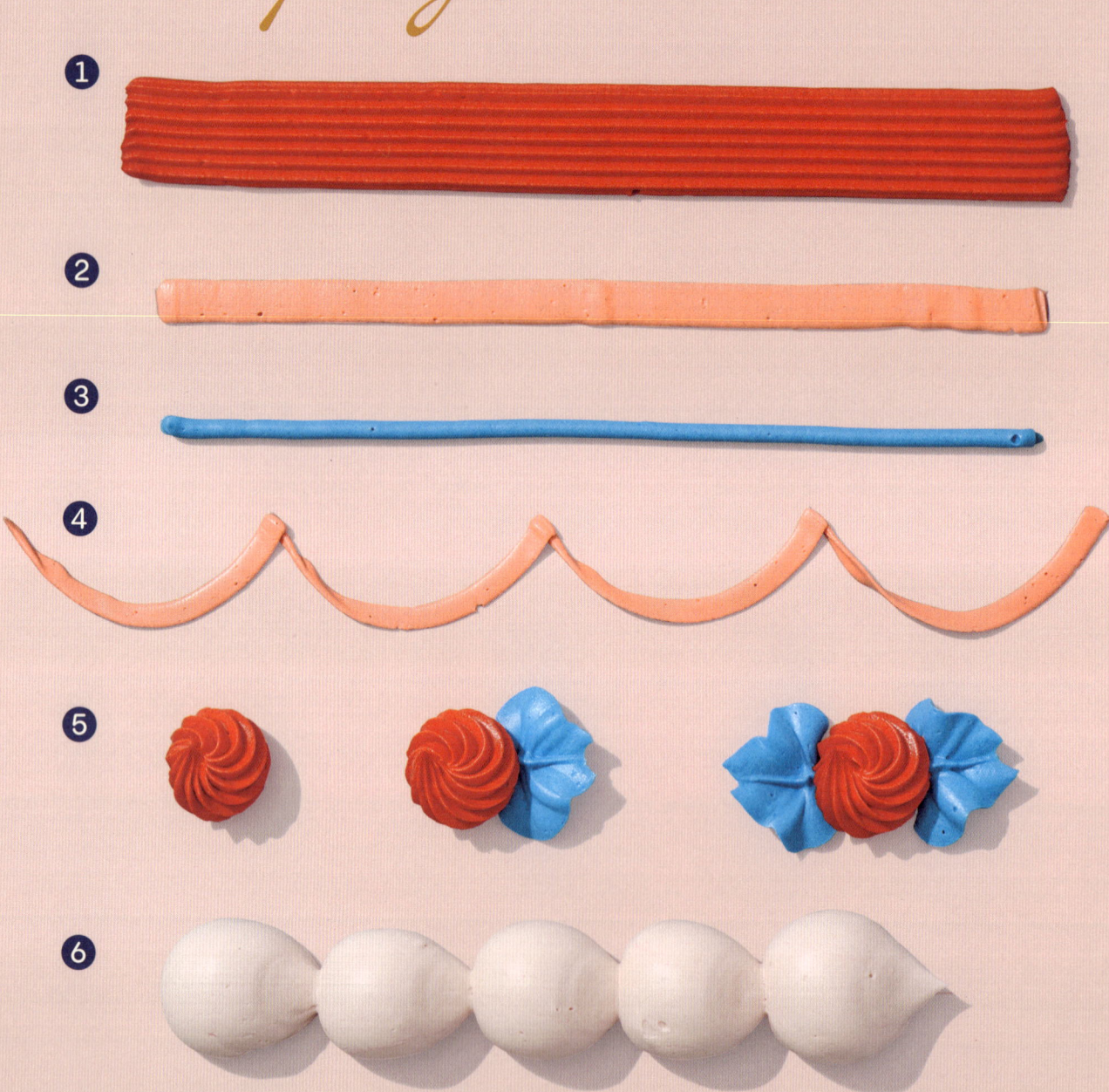

1. **Straight line with large basketweave (page 160)**
   Nozzle: Medium basketweave 2B · **Angle:** 30°

2. **Straight line with small basketweave**
   Nozzle: Standard basketweave 44 · **Angle:** 30°

3. **Straight line with small round nozzle**
   Nozzle: Standard round 5 · **Angle:** 30°

4. **Ribbon (page 163)**
   Nozzle: Standard basketweave 44 · **Angle:** 45°

5. **Large rosette with leaves (pages 161 & 165)**
   Nozzle (rosettes): Medium French star S/F5 · **Angle:** 90°
   Nozzle (leaves): Standard leaf 70 · **Angle:** 45°

6. **Continuous beads**
   Nozzle: Medium round S/P 14 · **Angle:** 45°
   Use a large round nozzle and follow the technique for piping continuous shells (page 161) to pipe continuous beads.

Set up

Make sure you have followed the set-up checklist on page 191 before starting.

Let's begin!

Tint the buttercream. Prepare the buttercream in four shades for decorating. Tint 500 g (17.64 oz) with small drops of hot pink and a touch of blue food colouring to achieve a pale pink tone. Tint 100 g (3.5 oz) with red food colouring for a bright red shade, 50 g (1.75 oz) with cobalt blue and a touch of hot pink for a vibrant soft blue, and the remaining 50 g (1.75 oz) with equal parts hot pink and yellow for a light peachy tone.

Frost and rake the cake. Adjust 150 g (5.30 oz) of the pale pink buttercream to a thin but spreadable consistency (page 40). Follow the instructions on pages 51–56 to frost and rake the cake until a neat base is achieved. Allow the frosted cake to chill in the fridge for at least 15 minutes until the frosting is fully set.

Mark the top plaid. For this step, ensure the frosting is fully set at all times to prevent damage. Chill the cake as needed, and also work on a stable surface instead of a turntable. To mark the top plaid, cut out an 18 cm (7 in) circle of baking paper by tracing the outline of your cake tin. Fold the paper in half, then again lengthways to create four equal sections running lengthways. Unfold the paper into a half-circle and place it on the cake, aligning the curved edge of the paper with the cake's edge to find the horizontal line across the centre of the cake. Dip a metal scraper in warm water, dry it, then lightly press along the folded edge of the paper to mark the buttercream underneath.

Repeat on the folded parallel lines above and below the centre line so that you have three horizontal markings across the cake.

Remove the baking paper and rotate the cake 90 degrees. Gently reposition the baking paper on the cake again, and repeat the steps above to create a grid pattern with three lines each running vertically and horizontally (image 1).

Mark the side border into eight sections. Reposition the cake so the grid marks are on a diagonal to you. Cut another round piece of baking paper to match the size of the cake. Follow the instructions on page 172 to create a template for marking eight sections from the baking paper.

Gently place the paper on top of the cold frosted cake, aligning the edges, ensuring one of the marks is centred at the front, as this will be the front of the cake. Use a pointed palette knife to gently make small marks about 1 cm (½ in) below where the folded lines meet the cake's top edge. Gently remove the baking paper. You'll now have eight even sections marked on the side of the cake, ready for the side border.

Project continues

PROJECT 6 ROSY PLAID

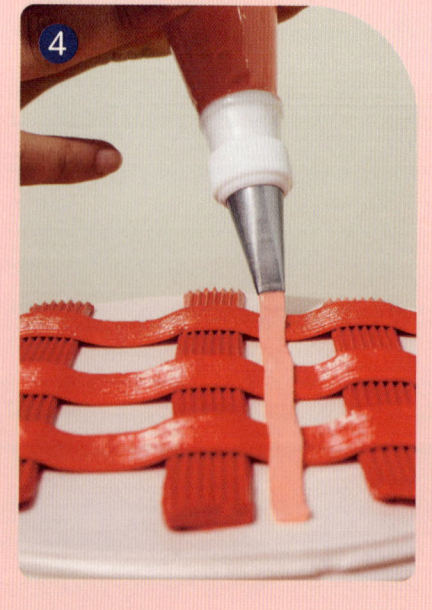

Pipe the top plaid. To create a lovely plaid pattern, work on a stable surface instead of a turntable for better precision. Pipe one colour at a time, starting with the red lines, maintaining the same sequence and leaving about a 1.5 cm (½ in) gap from the edge, to keep the tartan ends invisible.

Fit the first piping bag with a medium coupler and basketweave 2B nozzle, then fill halfway with red buttercream. Position the nozzle 'teeth' facing up and pipe three straight lines, using the marked grid as a guide (image 2). Rotate the cake 90 degrees and pipe another set of three red lines across the first set (image 2 & 3).

To pipe the peach-coloured lines, rotate the cake back to the starting position and fit a second piping bag with a standard coupler and a basketweave 44 nozzle, then fill halfway with peach buttercream. Pipe two lines across, positioned just above the bottom two red lines. Rotate the cake 90 degrees and repeat on the intersecting grid (image 4).

To pipe the blue lines, rotate the cake back again. Fit a third piping bag with the other standard coupler and round 5 nozzle, then fill halfway with blue buttercream. Pipe two more lines across, positioned closer to the top red lines this time (image 5). Rotate 90 degrees and repeat (image 6).

MALI BAKES

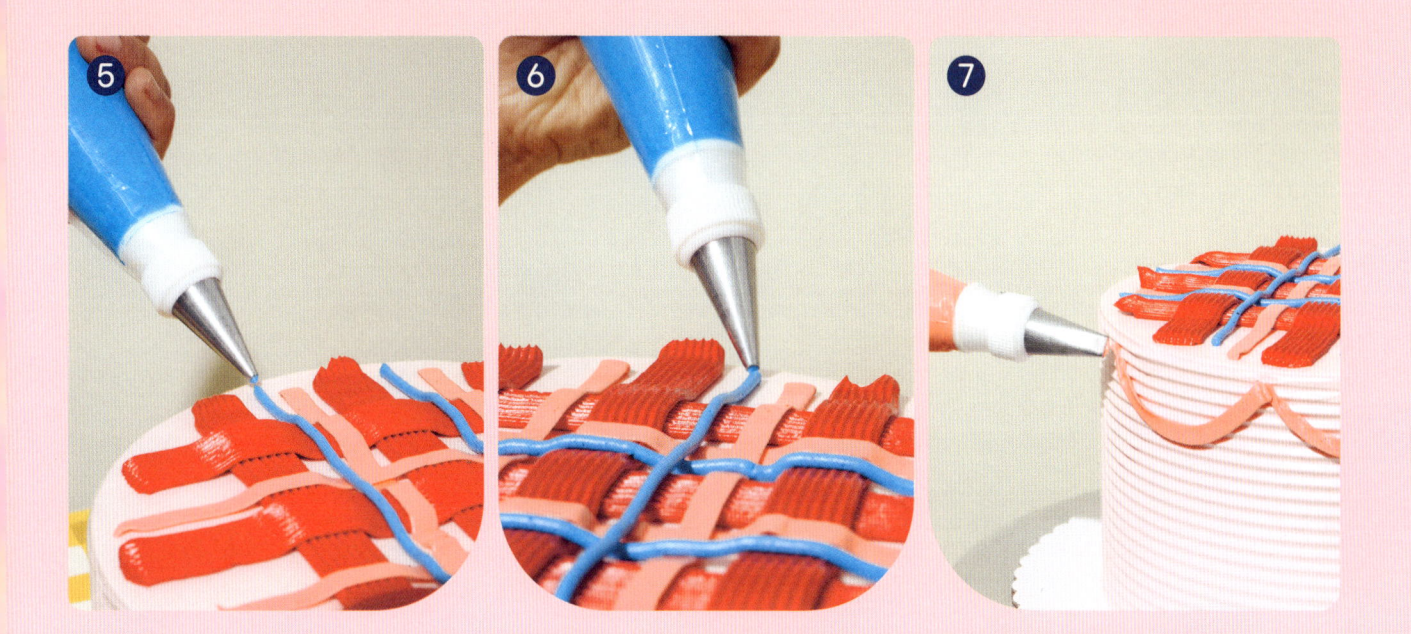

Pipe the side border. Take the piping bag with the peach buttercream and basketweave 44 nozzle. Pipe eight ribbon garlands around the side of the cake, starting from one marked point to the next. Allow each ribbon to drop about 2.5 cm (1 in) below the marked level (image 7).

Pipe the top border. Fit the final piping bag with the other medium coupler and round S/P14 nozzle, then fill halfway with pale pink buttercream. Pipe a continuous row of large beads along the top edge of the cake so they neatly cover the ends of the plaid pattern (images 8 & 9).

Pipe chunky rosettes. Switch the nozzle on the piping bag with red buttercream to a French star S/F5 nozzle. Pipe a rosette at each point where the ribbon garlands meet around the side of the cake, positioning them slightly higher so the top of each rosette aligns with the top of the cake (image 10).

Once all eight rosettes are piped, switch to the piping bag with the blue buttercream. Ensure the blue buttercream is thinned to the right consistency, then attach the leaf 70 nozzle and pipe a single leaf on both sides of each rosette (image 11).

Finish with the cherries. Trim off the knotty part of each cherry stem, leaving the stem as long as possible. Pat the cherries dry with paper towels to remove any excess syrup. Once dry, arrange the cherries evenly on the top border, positioning each cherry directly above a rosette to keep the spacing consistent (image 12).

Chill the cake. Pop your beautifully decorated cake in the fridge for at least 2 hours before party time. This will help set the decorations in place, keeping everything secure so your cake looks picture-perfect when it's ready to shine!

Images continue

DECORATING PROJECTS

234

MALI BAKES

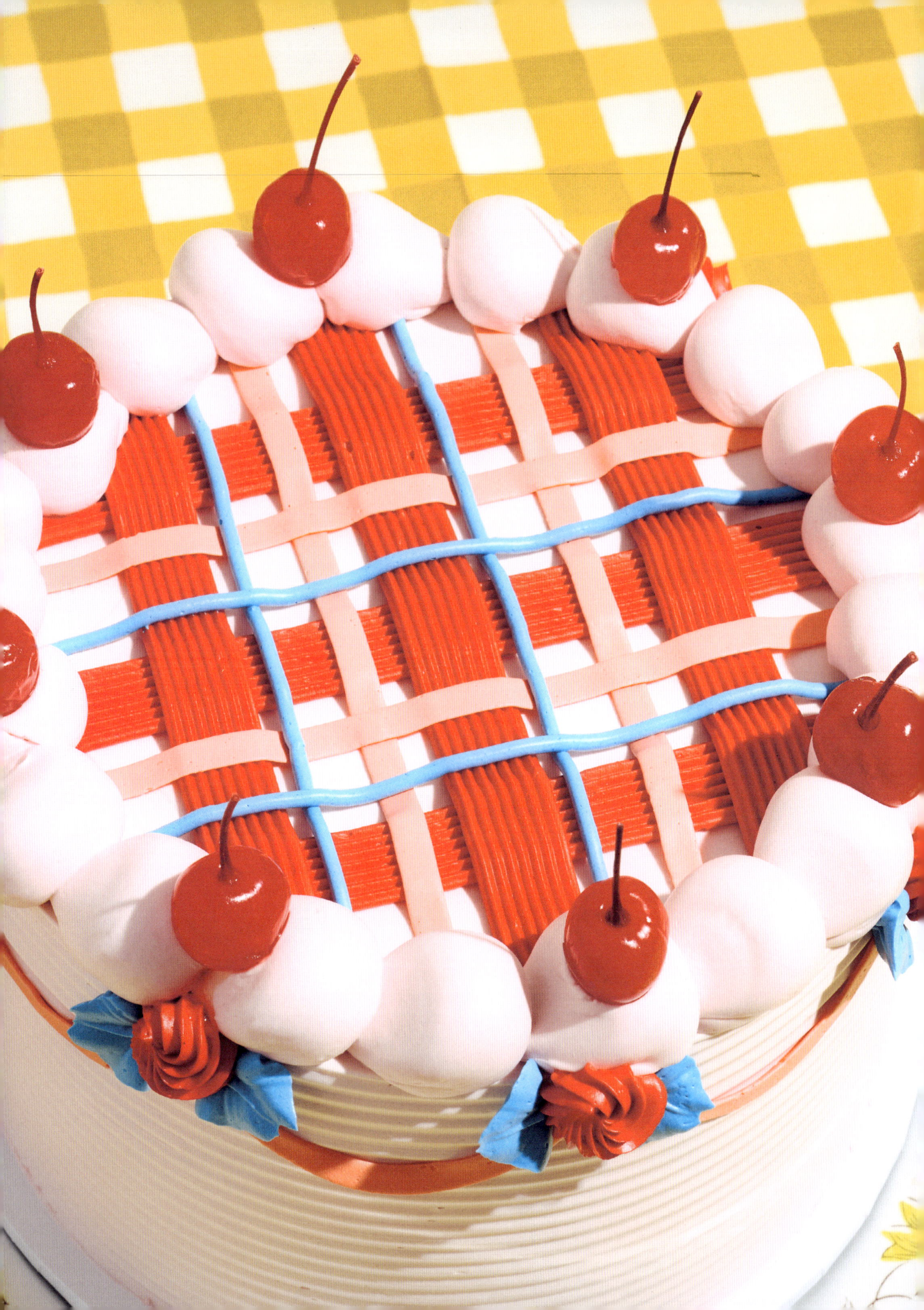

PROJECT 7

Retro Love

Retro Love is, without a doubt, the most beloved design at Mali Bakes – and it's easy to see why. It has all the flair you could want: the shells, the ruffles, and those elegant strings! When I think of retro-style cakes, this is exactly what comes to mind. For this design, vibrant red is paired with a hot pink accent and a soft peachy-beige base, creating a combination that feels both classic and fun. This project is also the perfect opportunity to master the drop string technique. Admittedly, it's the skill that took me the longest to feel comfortable with, but once you've perfected it, you'll find it's an absolute game-changer. You can use it to outline drapes or garlands, ensuring the border design is even and flawless around the cake. Pay close attention to the consistency of your buttercream – it must be smooth with absolutely no air bubbles, otherwise the string will break.

Project timeline

DAY 1
Prepare the fillings and bake the cake layers

DAY 2
Prepare the buttercream and assemble the cake

DAY 3
Decorate the cake

You'll need

Project basics
Cake: 18 cm (7 in) four-layer round cake, crumb coated and chilled
Cake board: 28 cm (11 in) round board, at least 5 mm (¼ in) thick
Food colouring: Yellow, hot pink, mustard, red
Buttercream: 1100 g (38.8 oz) Italian meringue buttercream (pages 43–46), medium consistency, bubbles removed
Topping: 8 maraschino cherries, with stems

Frosting tools
Angled palette knife
Sraight palette knife
Stainless steel cake scraper, at least 15 cm (6 in) tall
Bench scraper with plastic handle (for smoothing the top of the cake)
Heatproof container or jug, taller than the scraper and palette knives
Turntable and non-slip mat

Decorating tools
7 piping nozzles:
   Standard round 5;
   Medium French star S/F9;
   Medium petal 126K;
   Standard star 16;
   Medium French star S/F13 and S/F5;
   Large French star S/F15
3 large piping bags
1 standard coupler
1 medium coupler
1 large coupler
Wing caliper
Small pointed palette knife for marking

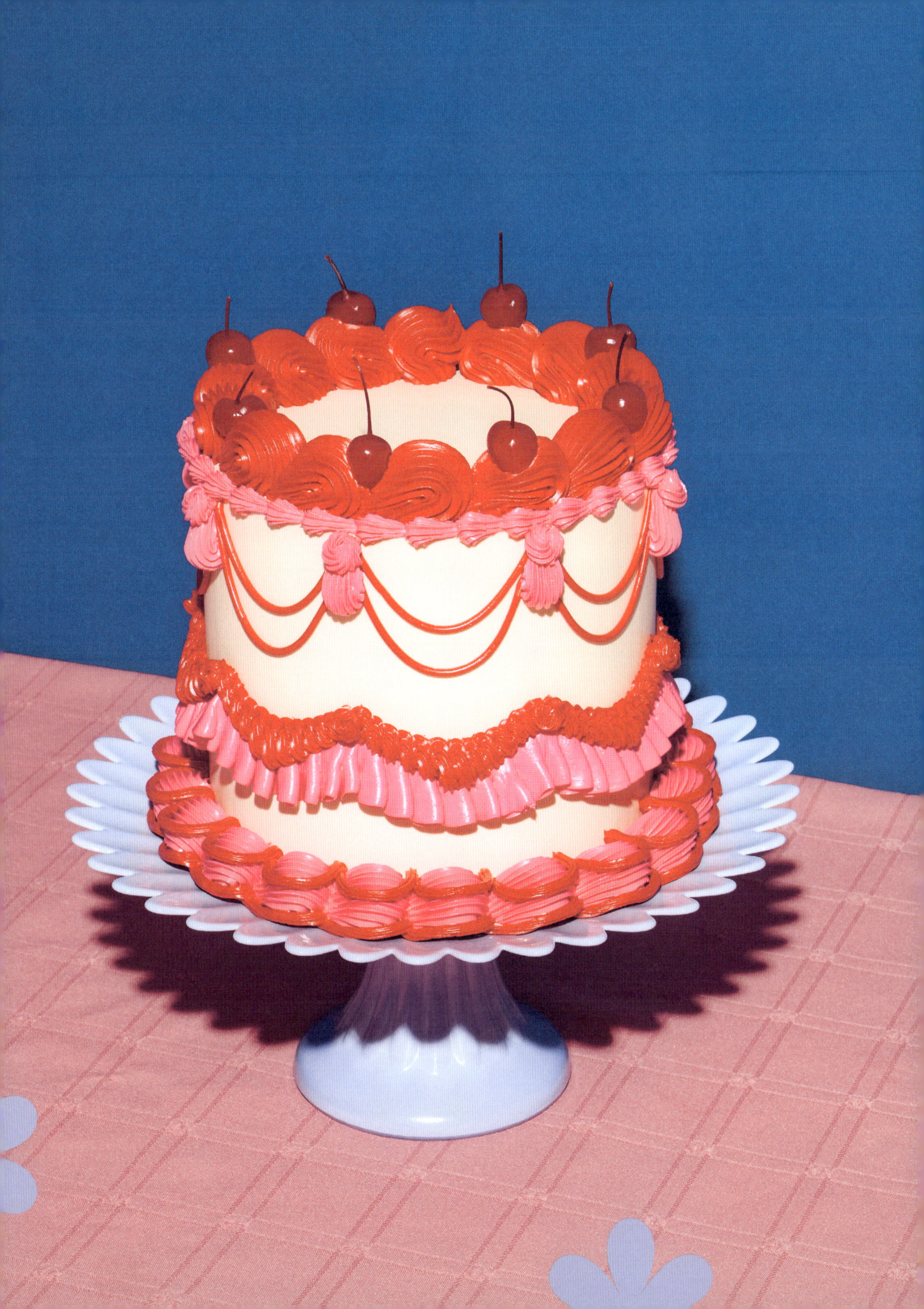

Piping Practice

1.

2.

3.

4.

5.

6.

7.

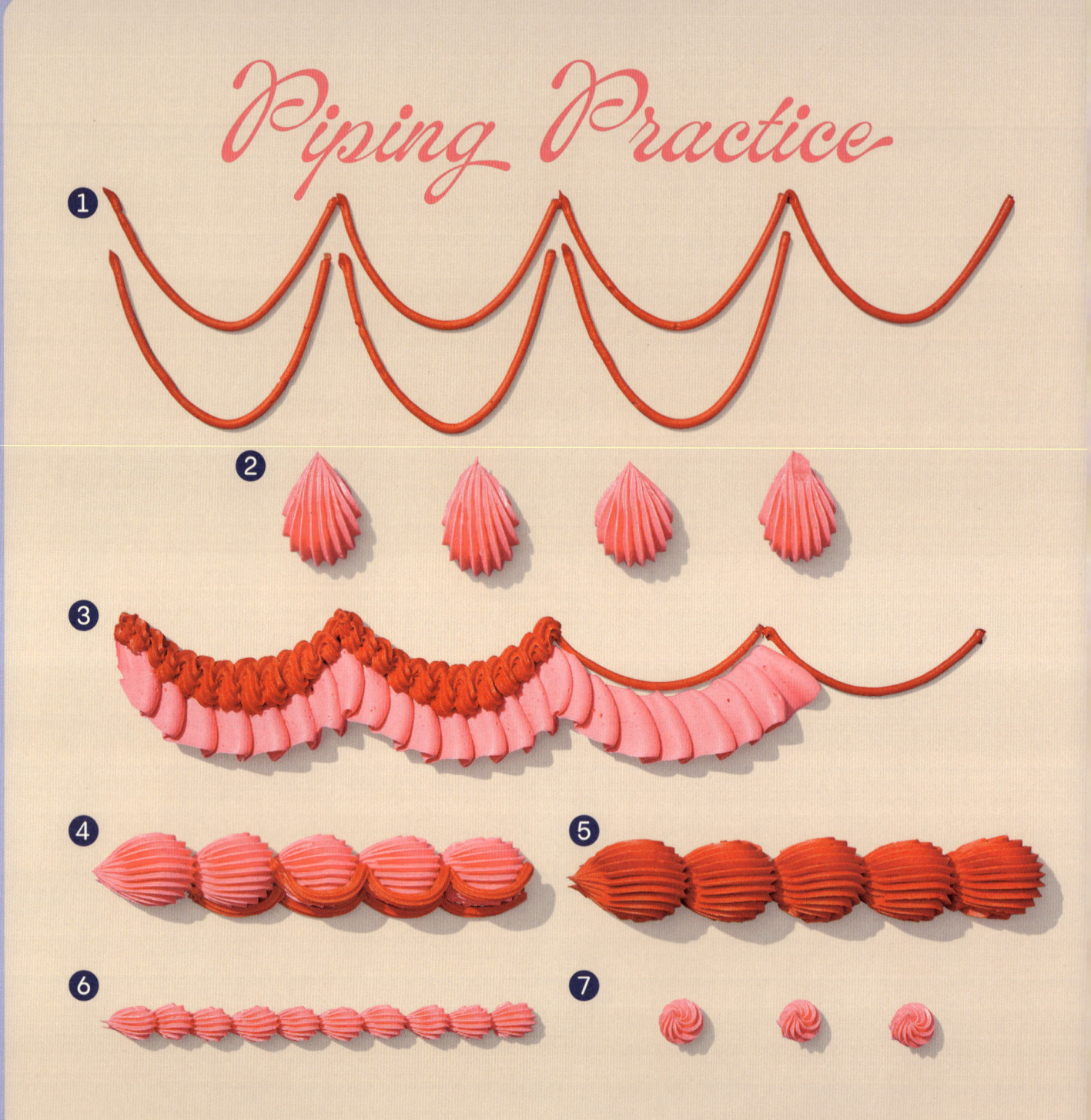

1. **Double drop strings (page 162)**
   Nozzle: Standard round 5 · **Angle:** 90°

2. **Upward shells (page 161)**
   Nozzle: Medium French star S/F9 · **Angle:** 45°

3. **Fluted ruffle with loop garland**
   Nozzle (drop string): Standard round 5 · **Angle:** 90°
   Nozzle (fluted ruffle garland): Medium petal 126K · **Angle:** 45°
   Nozzle (loop garland): Standard star 16 · **Angle:** 90°
   Pipe a drop string as an outline, then pipe the fluted ruffle garland (page 164) just below the drop string. Finish by piping the loop garland (page 163) on the top edge of the fluted ruffle.

4. **Shell border with double scallop trim**
   Nozzle (shells): Medium French star S/F13 · **Angle:** 45°
   Nozzle (scallop trim): Standard star 16 · **Angle:** 90°
   See instructions on page 206, but add a second scallop trim halfway up the shells.

5. **Large continuous shells (page 161)**
   Nozzle: Large French star S/F15 · **Angle:** 45°

6. **Small continuous shells**
   Nozzle: Medium French star S/F5 · **Angle:** 45°

7. **Rosettes (page 161)**
   Nozzle: Medium French star S/F5 · **Angle:** 90°

Set up

Make sure you have followed the set-up checklist on page 191 before starting.

Let's begin!

Tint the buttercream. Prepare the buttercream in three shades for decorating. For the frosting, tint 300 g (10.58 oz) with small drops of equal parts yellow, hot pink and mustard food colouring until a soft peachy-beige hue is achieved. Divide the remaining buttercream into two equal portions. Tint one portion with hot pink food colouring for a bright pink shade and the other with red for a bold red shade.

Frost the cake. Adjust all the peachy-beige buttercream to a thin but spreadable consistency (page 40). Follow the instructions on pages 51–53 to frost the cake until a neat smooth base is achieved. Allow the frosted cake to chill in the fridge for at least 15 minutes until the frosting is fully set.

Mark the upper side border into eight sections. Start by cutting a round piece of baking paper to match the size of the cake by tracing around an 18 cm (7 in) cake tin. Follow the instructions on page 172 to create a template for marking eight sections from the baking paper.

Gently place the paper on top of the cold frosted cake, aligning the edges. Use a pointed palette knife to gently make small marks about 5 mm (¼ in) below where the folded lines meet the cake's top edge. Gently remove the baking paper. You'll now have eight even sections marked on the upper side of the cake, ready for the borders.

Mark the lower side border. Set a wing caliper to 7.5 cm (3 in) and measure straight down from each mark on the top edge, creating gentle marks around the cake. You will now have eight even sections marked on the lower side of the cake, perfectly aligning with the upper ones.

Project continues

PROJECT 7   RETRO LOVE

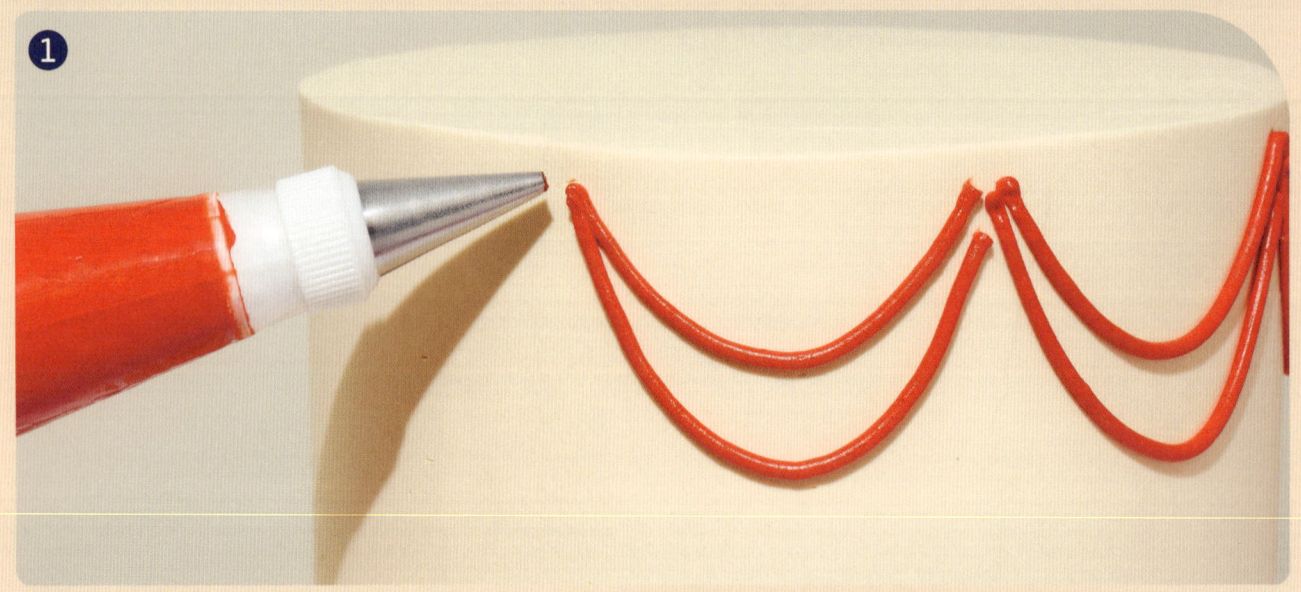

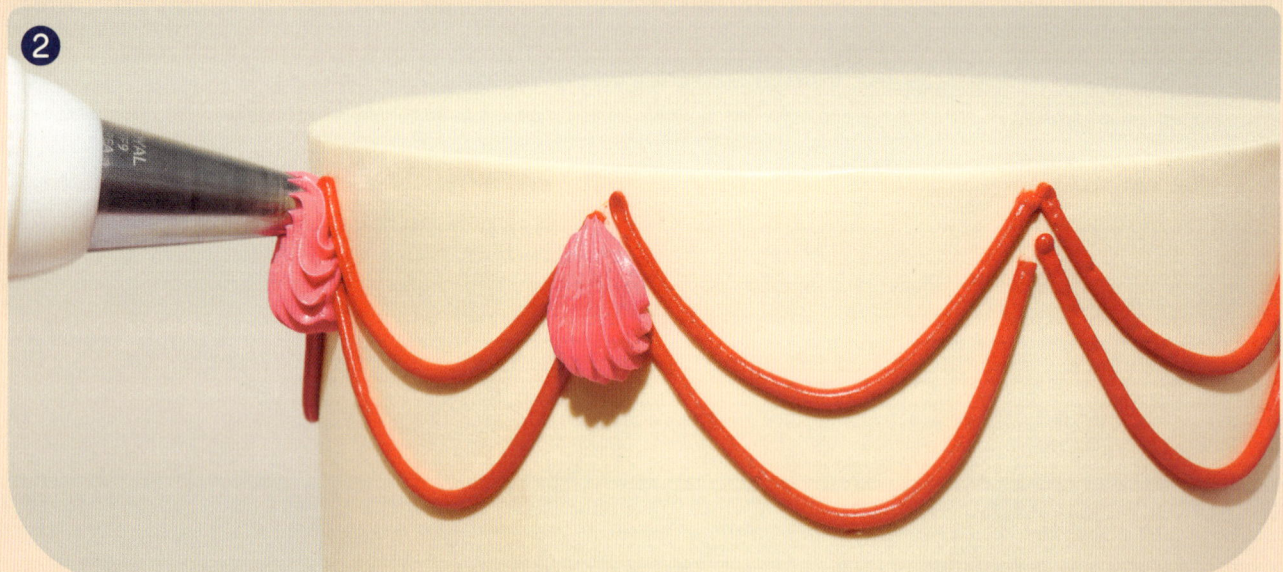

Pipe the upper side border. Fit the first piping bag with the standard coupler and round 5 nozzle, then fill halfway with red buttercream. Pipe double drop strings, connecting each marked point to the next around the cake (image 1). Let the top string drop about 4 cm (1½ in) and the bottom string about 6 cm (2½ in).

To finish the border, use a second piping bag fitted with the medium coupler and French star S/F9 nozzle, then fill halfway with pink buttercream. Pipe upward shells at each point where the drop strings meet, creating a total of eight shells (image 2).

Pipe the lower side border. Start by piping drop strings with the red buttercream and round 5 nozzle, connecting each lower mark and allowing each string to drop about 2 cm (¾ in) (image 3).

240   MALI BAKES

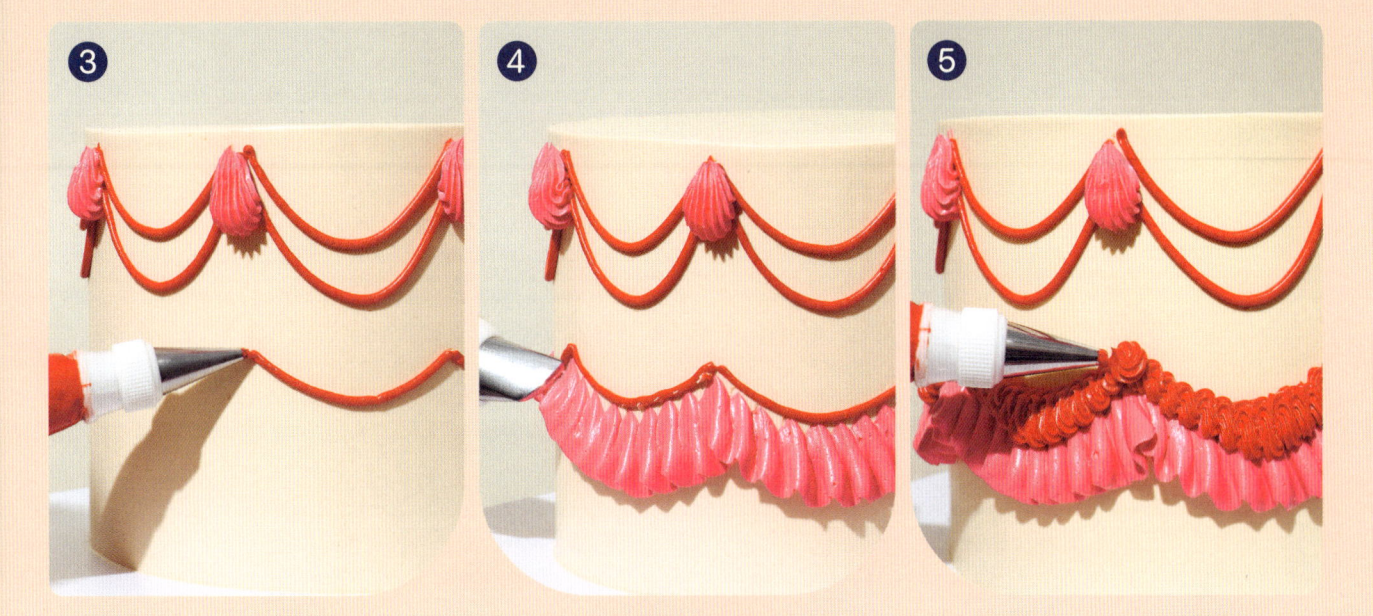

Next, switch to the piping bag filled with pink buttercream and use a petal 126K nozzle to pipe fluted ruffle garlands, using the outline string as a guide (image 4).

Then, take the piping bag with the red buttercream and switch to a star 16 nozzle to pipe loop garlands along the top edge of the ruffles, concealing the outline string. To finish, use the same nozzle to pipe a small red rosette at each point where the garlands meet (image 5).

Pipe the bottom border. Switch the nozzle on the pink buttercream piping bag to a French star S/F13 nozzle. Pipe a continuous row of pink shells neatly along the bottom edge of the cake (image 6). Next, take the piping bag with the red buttercream and the star 16 nozzle and pipe a scalloped trim along the bottom edge of the shell border (image 7). Then pipe a second scalloped trim along the top edge of the shell border (image 8).

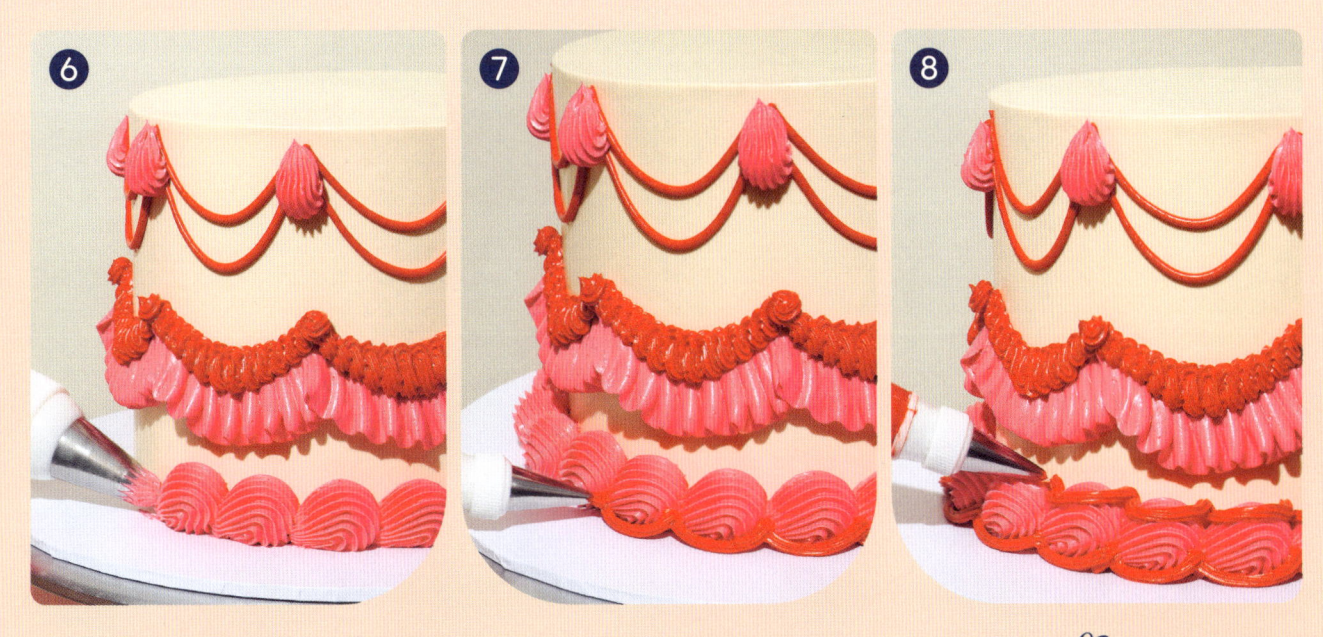

Project continues

DECORATING PROJECTS

PROJECT 7   RETRO LOVE

9

Pipe the top borders. Using the piping bag with the pink buttercream, switch to a French star S/F5 nozzle and pipe a continuous row of small shells around the top of the cake, along the edge (image 9). Next, fit the final piping bag with the large coupler and a French star S/F15 nozzle, then fill halfway with red buttercream. Working in the opposite direction to the pink shells, pipe a row of large continuous red shells around the top of the cake, as close to the edge as possible (image 10). The red and pink shells will be facing opposite directions.

Pipe the rosettes. Using the piping bag with pink buttercream and the French star S/F5 nozzle, pipe a small rosette on top of each upward shell, where it meets the pink shell border, to give you eight evenly spaced rosettes around the cake (image 11).

Finish with the cherries. Trim off the knotty part of each cherry stem, leaving the stem as long as possible. Pat the cherries dry with paper towels to remove any excess syrup. Once dry, place each cherry along the top red border, spacing them evenly around the cake, and positioning each one directly above a rosette or at the points where the double drop strings meet (image 12).

Chill the cake. Pop your beautifully decorated cake in the fridge for at least 2 hours before party time. This will help set the decorations in place, keeping everything secure so your cake looks picture-perfect when it's ready to shine!

10

11   **12**

MALI BAKES

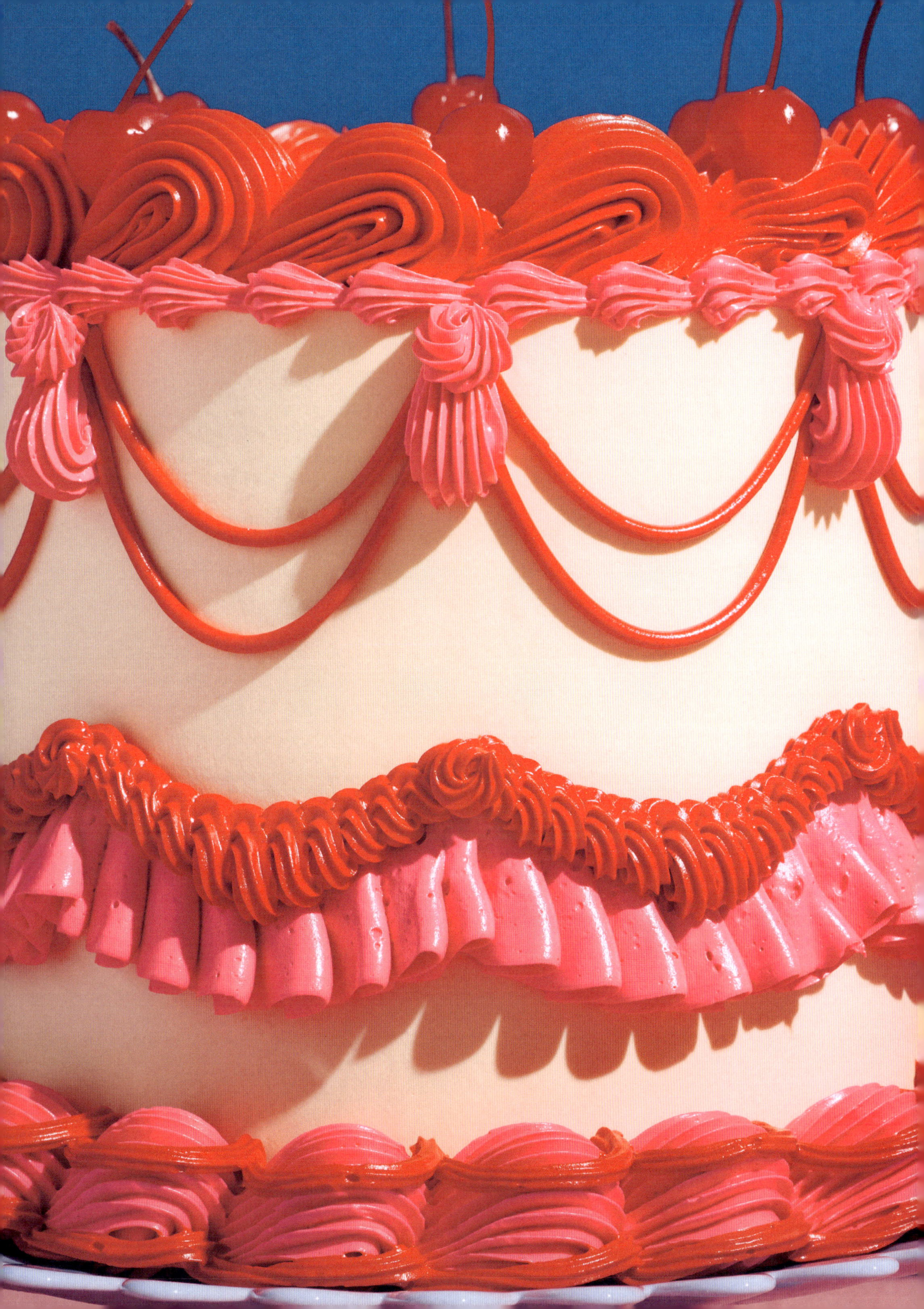

PROJECT 8

Garden Strawberry

In this project, a humble heart-shaped cake is transformed into a stunning strawberry, making it the perfect centrepiece for your next summer gathering. While the cake looks exquisite, it's actually a very simple design that requires only two types of piping nozzles!

A flower nail is an incredibly versatile tool for cake decorating – not just for creating flowers, but also other intricate details that might be tricky to pipe directly onto a cake. To gain some practice using a flower nail, we'll start with shaping simple leaves. For best results, I recommend using stabilised buttercream for the leaves, as it provides excellent structure and holds its shape beautifully. However, if you're working in a cool, dry environment, a stiff-consistency Italian meringue buttercream will work just as well.

Project timeline

○ **DAY 1**
Prepare the fillings and bake the cake layers

○ **DAY 2**
Prepare the buttercream and assemble the cake

○ **DAY 3**
Decorate the cake

You'll need

Project basics
Cake: 20 cm (8 in) three-layer heart-shaped cake, crumb coated and chilled
Cake board: 30 cm (12 in) round board, at least 5 mm (¼ in) thick
Food colouring: Red, forest green, yellow, black
Buttercream: 700 g (24.7 oz) Italian meringue buttercream (pages 43–46), medium consistency, bubbles removed – plus 100 g (3.5 oz) Stabilised buttercream (page 167), medium consistency

Frosting tools
Angled palette knife
Straight palette knife
Stainless steel cake scraper, at least 10 cm (4 in) tall
Bench scraper with plastic handle (for smoothing the top of the cake)
Heatproof container or jug, taller than the scraper and palette knives
Turntable and non-slip mat

Decorating tools
4 piping nozzles:
    Medium petal 126K;
    Standard round 4;
    Medium round S/P4 and S/P12
4 large piping bags
3 medium couplers
1 standard coupler
1 large flower nail, number 14
Wing caliper
Small pointed palette knife for marking

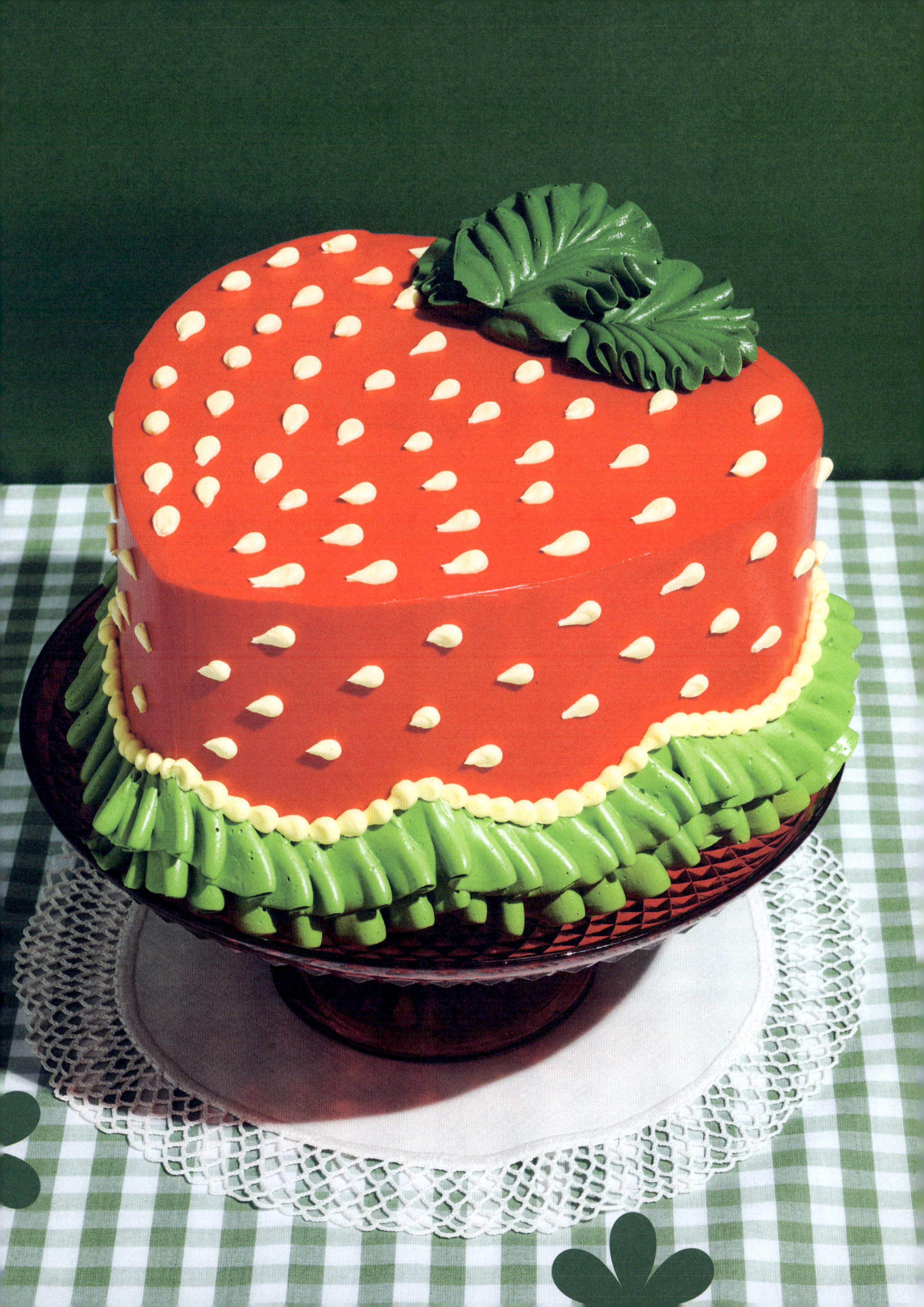

Piping Practice

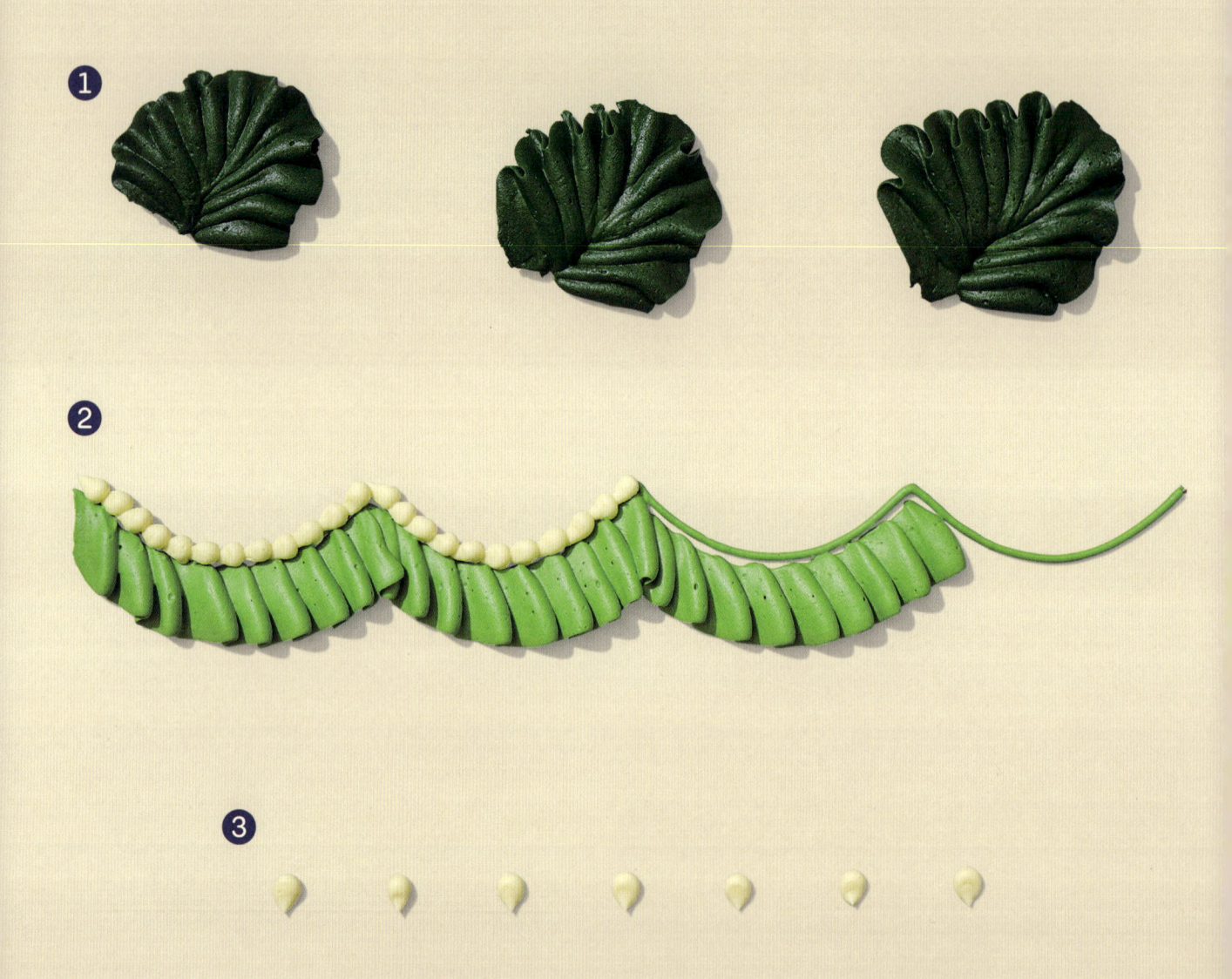

1

2

3

1. Strawberry leaf
Nozzle: Medium petal 126K · **Angle:** 45°

With the wider end of the nozzle touching the paper and the narrower end lifted slightly, start piping from the base of the leaf. Move the nozzle back and forth to create the leaf's curve – begin with larger motions, then gradually slow down as you spin the flower nail toward the pointed tip. Continue around to the other side of the leaf, widening your motion again as you return to the base.

2. Folded ruffle garland with bead trim
Nozzle (drop string): Medium round S/P4 · **Angle:** 90°
Nozzle (folded ruffle): Medium petal 126K · **Angle:** 45°
Nozzle (beads): Medium round S/P4 · **Angle:** 45°

Pipe a drop string (page 162) as an outline. Pipe two rows of folded ruffle garlands (page 165) below the drop string. Finish with a row of continuous beads (follow the technique for continuous shells, page 161, but use a round nozzle) to cover the drop string.

3. Teardrop-shaped seeds
Nozzle: Medium round S/P4 · **Angle:** 45°

PROJECT 8   GARDEN STRAWBERRY

Set up

Make sure you have followed the set-up checklist on page 191 before starting.

Let's begin!

Tint the buttercream. Prepare the Italian meringue buttercream in three shades for decorating. For the frosting, tint 350 g (12.35 oz) with red food colouring to achieve a bold red shade. Tint another 250 g (8.82 oz) with small drops of equal parts forest green and yellow to create a lime green shade. Tint the remaining 100 g (3.5 oz) with a small drop of yellow food colouring to achieve a pale yellow shade for the strawberry seeds.

Frost the cake. Adjust the red buttercream to a thin but spreadable consistency (page 40). Follow the instructions on pages 51–54 to frost the cake until a neat smooth base is achieved. Allow the frosted cake to chill in the fridge for at least 15 minutes until the frosting is fully set.

Prepare the strawberry leaves. Cut out three 8 cm (3¼ in) squares of baking paper as bases.

Tint the stabilised buttercream with forest green and a touch of black food colouring to create a deep green leaf shade. Fit the first piping bag with a medium coupler and 126K petal nozzle and fill the piping bag halfway with the deep green stabilised buttercream. Dab some of the buttercream onto a flower nail, press a baking paper square onto it, and pipe one large leaf onto the paper (image 1). Place the paper square on a tray, with the leaf still on it. Repeat to make a second large leaf and a third smaller leaf, transferring each square of paper with its piped leaves to the tray. Pop the tray in the freezer until ready to use.

Mark the bottom border into eight sections. Once the frosting on the cake is fully set, use a wing caliper set to 8 cm (3¼ in) to gently mark along the bottom edge of the cake, dividing the left and right sides of the heart into four equal sections. Start at the pointed front and work towards the curved back on each side; slight size differences in the back sections will not be noticeable.

Next, adjust the wing caliper to 3.75 cm (1½ in) and measure directly above each marked spot to indicate the starting points for each ruffle garland.

Pipe the double folded ruffles around the base. Fit a second piping bag with the standard coupler and a round 4 nozzle, then fill halfway with the lime green buttercream. Pipe a drop string from one marked point to the next, to outline the ruffle border, letting each string drop about 2 cm (¾ in) below the marked level (image 2).

Project continues

DECORATING PROJECTS

PROJECT 8 GARDEN STRAWBERRY

Next, fit the third piping bag with a medium coupler and a clean 126K petal nozzle, then fill halfway with the lime green buttercream. Pipe a folded ruffle just below the drop string, following it as a guide and working your way around the cake (image 3). Then, pipe another row of folded ruffles just above the drop string, to overlap the bottom ruffle nicely (image 4).

Pipe the bead trim. To finish the bottom border, attach the final piping bag with the other medium coupler and a round S/P4 nozzle, then fill half way with pale yellow buttercream. Pipe continuous small beads in a curved line along the top edge of the double ruffle (image 5).

Pipe the strawberry seeds. Take the same piping bag with the round S/P4 nozzle and the pale yellow buttercream. Empty the bag to remove the buttercream, thin it slightly for smoother piping, then refill the bag. On the top surface, pipe small teardrop-shaped seeds, in vertical rows. Begin from the left and right sides, working towards the centre, and offset each row slightly from the one before it (image 6). Gradually lessen the curve of the rows towards the middle to create a realistic strawberry look (images 7 & 8).

Now pipe some seeds on the red frosting all around the side of the cake, tapering the ends of the seeds so they point in the same direction as those on top of the cake (image 9).

Finish with the leaves. Switch the nozzle on the piping bag with the leaf green buttercream to a round S/P12 nozzle. Place the cake on a flat, stable surface. Pipe a rounded blob of buttercream around 3 cm (1¼ in) in diameter at the top centre of the cake (image 10).

Remove the firmly set leaves from the freezer. Carefully peel the baking paper off the smallest leaf and place it on the buttercream base, angling it slightly to the left. Add the second leaf, positioning it slightly to the right. Finish by placing the third leaf in the centre (image 11).

Chill the cake. Pop your beautifully decorated cake in the fridge for at least 2 hours before party time. This will help set the decorations in place, keeping everything secure so your cake looks picture-perfect when it's ready to shine!

MALI BAKES

DECORATING PROJECTS 249

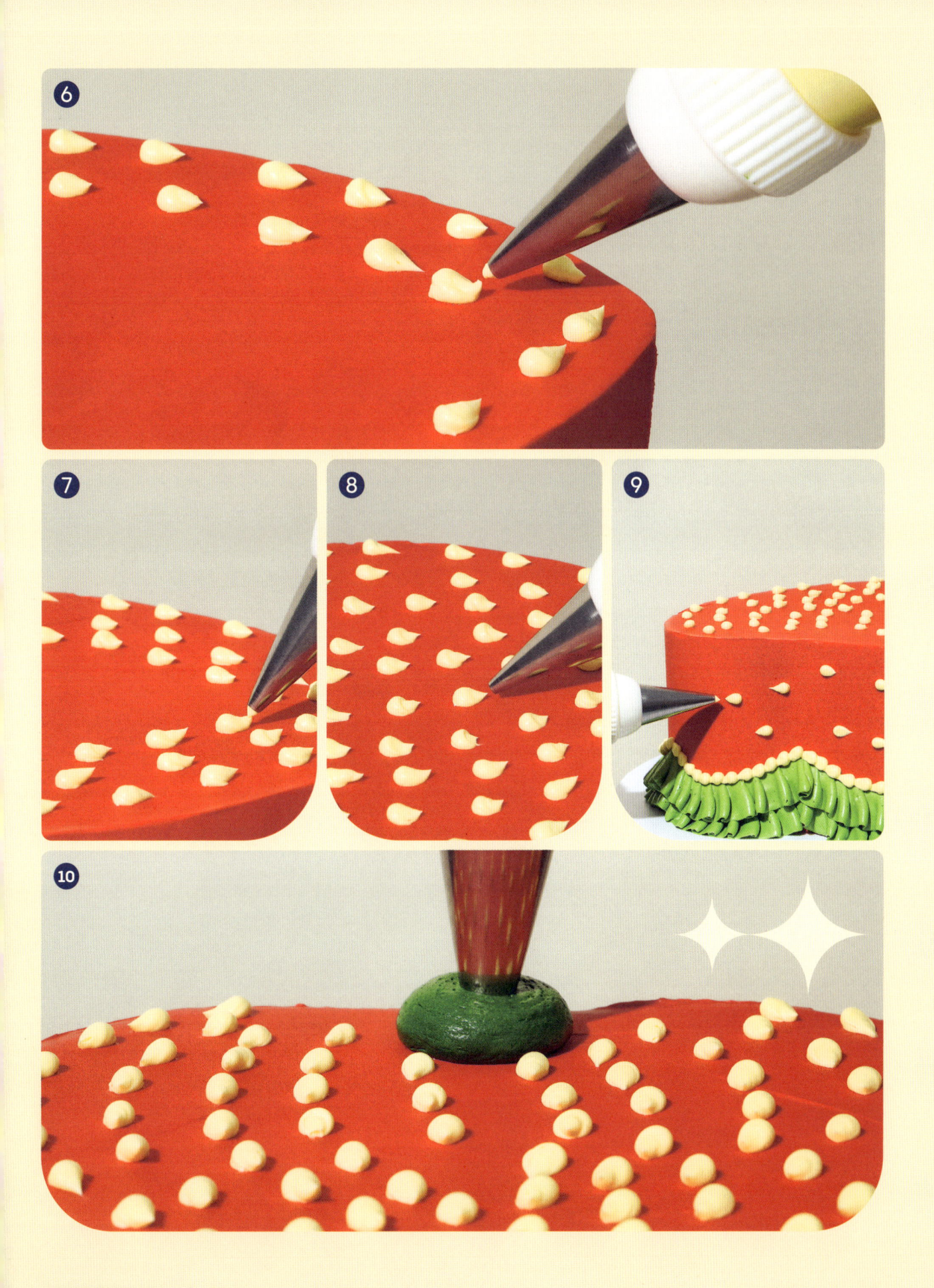

11

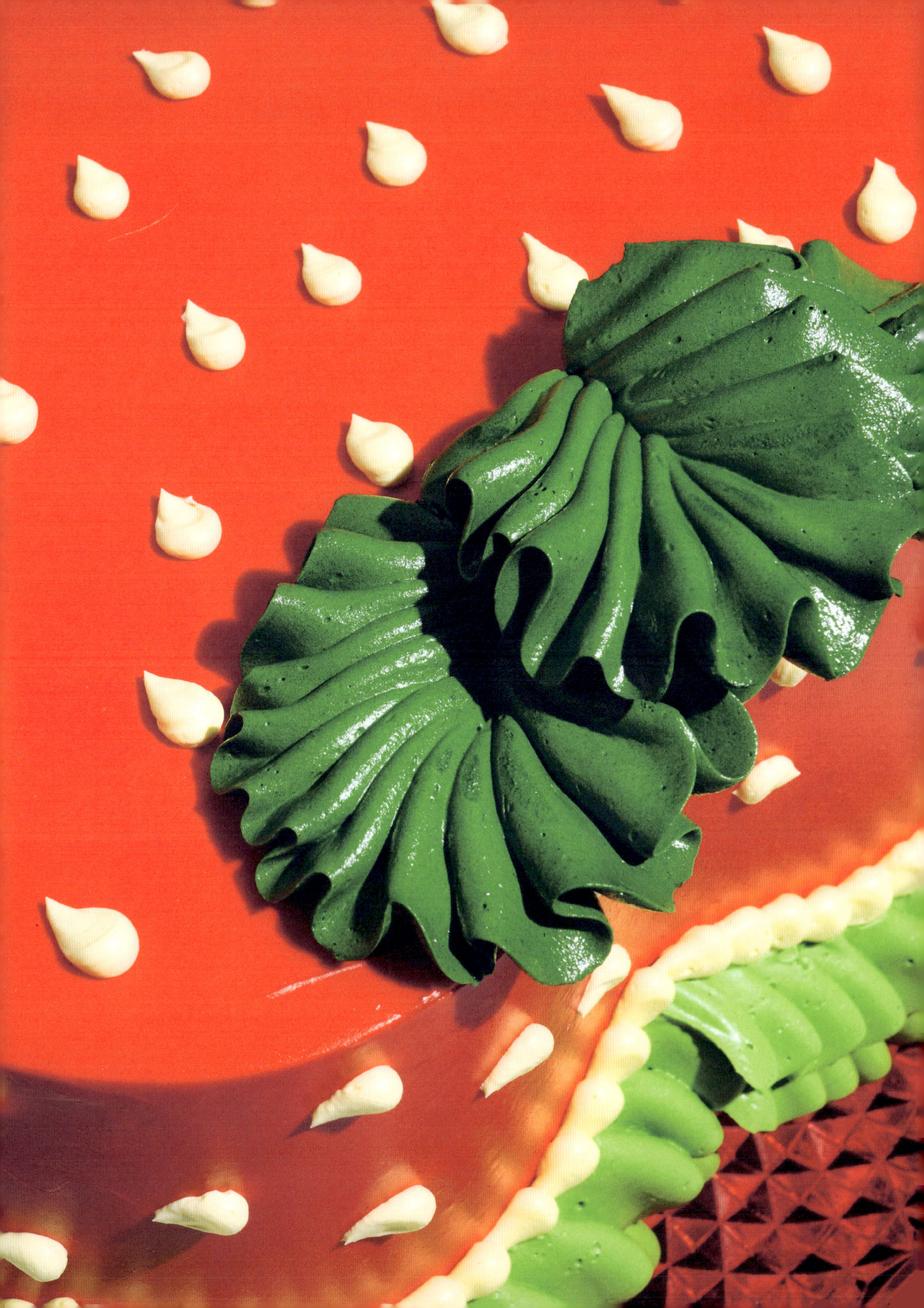

PROJECT 9

Minted Rose

This cake is a stunning tribute to vintage elegance, blending soft colours and timeless details to create a design that feels classic and romantic. Creating a retro cake can sometimes be all about balance – adding intricate touches while keeping the overall look refined and not overly busy. One of my favourite tricks is to focus on a single piping nozzle and explore its versatility to create a cohesive design. For this project, we're using petal nozzles to create beautiful buttercream roses, elegant ruffles and ribbon-like borders.

I recommend using stabilised buttercream for the roses – it's easy to handle and holds its shape beautifully. Be sure to keep the buttercream at a stiff consistency, especially when adding food colouring for the vibrant red. Don't forget to pop the bowl in the fridge from time to time to maintain the ideal consistency.

Project timeline

DAY 1
Prepare the fillings and bake the cake layers

DAY 2
Prepare the buttercream and assemble the cake

DAY 3
Decorate the cake

You'll need

Project basics
Cake: 20 cm (8 in) three-layer heart-shaped cake, crumb coated and chilled
Cake board: 30 cm (12 in) round board, at least 5 mm (¼ in) thick
Food colouring: Sky blue, forest green, mustard, black, red
Buttercream: 900 g (31.75 oz) Italian meringue buttercream (pages 43–46), medium consistency, bubbles removed – plus 150 g (5.3 oz) Stabilised buttercream (page 167), stiff consistency

Frosting tools
Angled palette knife
Straight palette knife
Stainless steel cake scraper, at least 10 cm (4 in) tall
Bench scraper with plastic handle (for smoothing the top of the cake)
Heatproof container or jug, taller than the scraper and palette knives
Turntable and non-slip mat

Decorating tools
6 piping nozzles:
    Standard petal 104 and 101;
    Standard round 3;
    Medium petal 124K;
    Medium round S/P4;
    Standard leaf 352
4 large piping bags
3 standard couplers
1 medium coupler
Wing caliper
Medium flower nail, number 13
Small pointed palette knife for marking

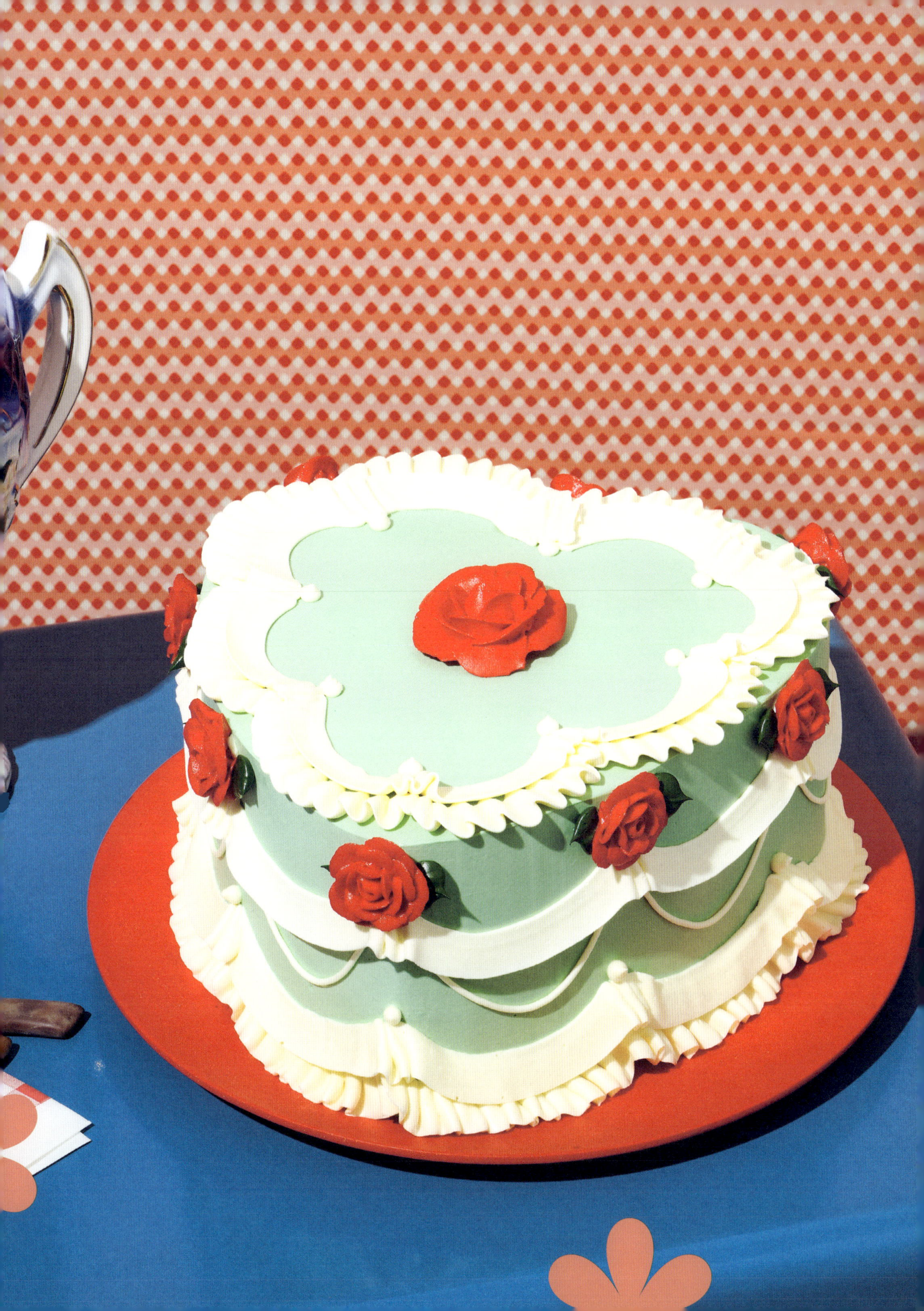

Piping Practice

1.

2.

3.

1. **Double drop strings with swag**
   Nozzle (double drop strings): Standard round 3 · **Angle:** 90°
   Nozzle (swag): Medium petal 124K · **Angle:** 45°
   Pipe two rows of drop strings (page 162), then top the highest row of drop strings with a swag (page 164).

2. **Fluted ruffle with swag and bead**
   Nozzle (drop string): Standard round 3 · **Angle:** 90°
   Nozzle (ruffles & swag): Medium petal 124K · **Angle:** 45°
   Nozzle (beads): Medium round S/P4 · **Angle:** 90°
   Pipe a drop string (page 162) as an outline. Pipe a fluted ruffle garland (page 164) below the drop string, then pipe a swag (page 164) on the top edge of the fluted ruffle. Finish with beads (page 160) above the highest point of the swag.

3. **Leaves (page 165)**
   Nozzle: Standard leaf 352 · **Angle:** 45°

PROJECT 9   MINTED ROSE

Set up

Make sure you have followed the set-up checklist on page 191 before starting.

Let's begin!

Tint the buttercream. Prepare the Italian meringue buttercream in three shades for decorating. For the frosting, tint 350 g (12.35 oz) with a few drops of equal parts sky blue and forest green, and a touch of mustard food colouring, to achieve a pastel mint green. Tint 100 g (3.5 oz) with forest green and a touch of black for a deep green shade to pipe the leaves. Leave the remaining buttercream untinted for the borders.

Frost the cake. Adjust the mint green buttercream to a thin but spreadable consistency (page 40). Follow the instructions on pages 51–54 to frost the cake until a neat smooth base is achieved. Allow the frosted cake to chill in the fridge for at least 15 minutes until the frosting is fully set.

Pipe the roses. While the frosted cake sets in the fridge, tint the stabilised buttercream with red food colouring to create a bold red. Ensure the buttercream has a stiff consistency for the roses to hold their shape, adjusting if needed.

Cut out at least nine 8 cm (3¼ in) squares of baking paper as bases. Fit the first piping bag with a standard coupler and a 104 petal nozzle. Dab some of the buttercream onto a flower nail, press a baking paper square onto it, and pipe one large rose onto the paper, following the instructions on page 171 (image 1). Place the paper square on a tray, with the rose still on it. Switch to a 101 petal nozzle and pipe eight smaller roses using the same technique, transferring each square of paper with its piped rose to the tray. Prepare a few extra roses as spares and freeze until ready to use.

Mark the top border into eight sections. Once the frosting on the cake is fully set, use a wing caliper set to 8 cm (3¼ in) to gently mark along the top edge of the cake, dividing the left and right sides of the heart into four equal sections. Start at the pointed front and work towards the curved back on each side; slight size differences in the back sections will not be noticeable. Adjust the wing caliper to 2.5 cm (1 in) and mark inwards from each top-edge mark towards the centre of the cake to indicate the starting point of the top border.

For the side border, keep the wing caliper set to 2.5 cm (1 in) and mark straight down from each top-edge mark along the side of the cake.

Mark the bottom border. Reset the wing caliper to 8 cm (3¼ in) and mark along the bottom edge, as you did for the top. Now adjust the wing caliper to 3 cm (1¼ in) and mark upwards from each bottom-edge point to set the starting points for the ruffle border.

Project continues

DECORATING PROJECTS   255

Pipe the side border. Fit a second piping bag with another standard coupler and a round 3 nozzle, then fill halfway with the untinted buttercream. Starting at the upper side decoration marks, pipe a double drop string from one mark to the next around the cake (image 2). The first string should drop about 2 cm (¾ in), and the second string should extend about 5 cm (2 in) below the mark level.

Once the drop strings are complete, fit a third piping bag with the medium coupler and a petal 124K nozzle, then fill halfway with more untinted buttercream. Work your way around the cake and pipe a swag over the top drop strings (image 3).

Pipe the bottom border. Take the piping bag fitted with the round 3 nozzle and pipe a drop string between the lower side decoration marks, letting it drop about 1.5 cm (½ in) below the marked level as a guide for the ruffle border. Switch to the piping bag fitted with the 124K petal nozzle and pipe fluted ruffles just below the drop string, ensuring the bottom edge of the ruffle touches the cake board to conceal the base of the cake (image 4). Using the same nozzle, pipe a swag detail above the drop string for a layered double-ruffle effect (image 5). To finish, switch to a round S/P4 nozzle and pipe small bead details above each highest point of the swag to complete the border (image 6).

Pipe the top border. Use the same technique as for the bottom border, but without the string outline. Starting at each inner marked point, use the 124K petal nozzle to pipe a fluted ruffle from one point to the next around the cake (image 7). Using the same nozzle, add the swag detail above the ruffle. Finish by piping a small bead at each garland peak using the round S/P4 nozzle (image 8).

Add the roses. Remove the buttercream roses from the freezer. Using the piping bag with the round S/P4 nozzle and untinted buttercream, pipe a small dot of buttercream at the points where the upper side garlands meet and securely attach a small flower to each (images 9 & 10).

Position the large flower on top of the cake, in the centre (image 11). If the flowers begin to soften while you're working with them, briefly place them back in the freezer before continuing, to ensure they remain firm and easy to handle.

Pipe the leaf details. Fit the fourth piping bag with the other standard coupler and a leaf 352 nozzle, then fill with the deep green buttercream. Ensure the buttercream has a thin consistency. Pipe a leaf on the left and right sides of each side rose, leaving the top flower without any leaves (image 12).

Chill the cake. Pop your beautifully decorated cake in the fridge for at least 2 hours before party time. This will help set the decorations in place, keeping everything secure so your cake looks picture-perfect when it's ready to shine!

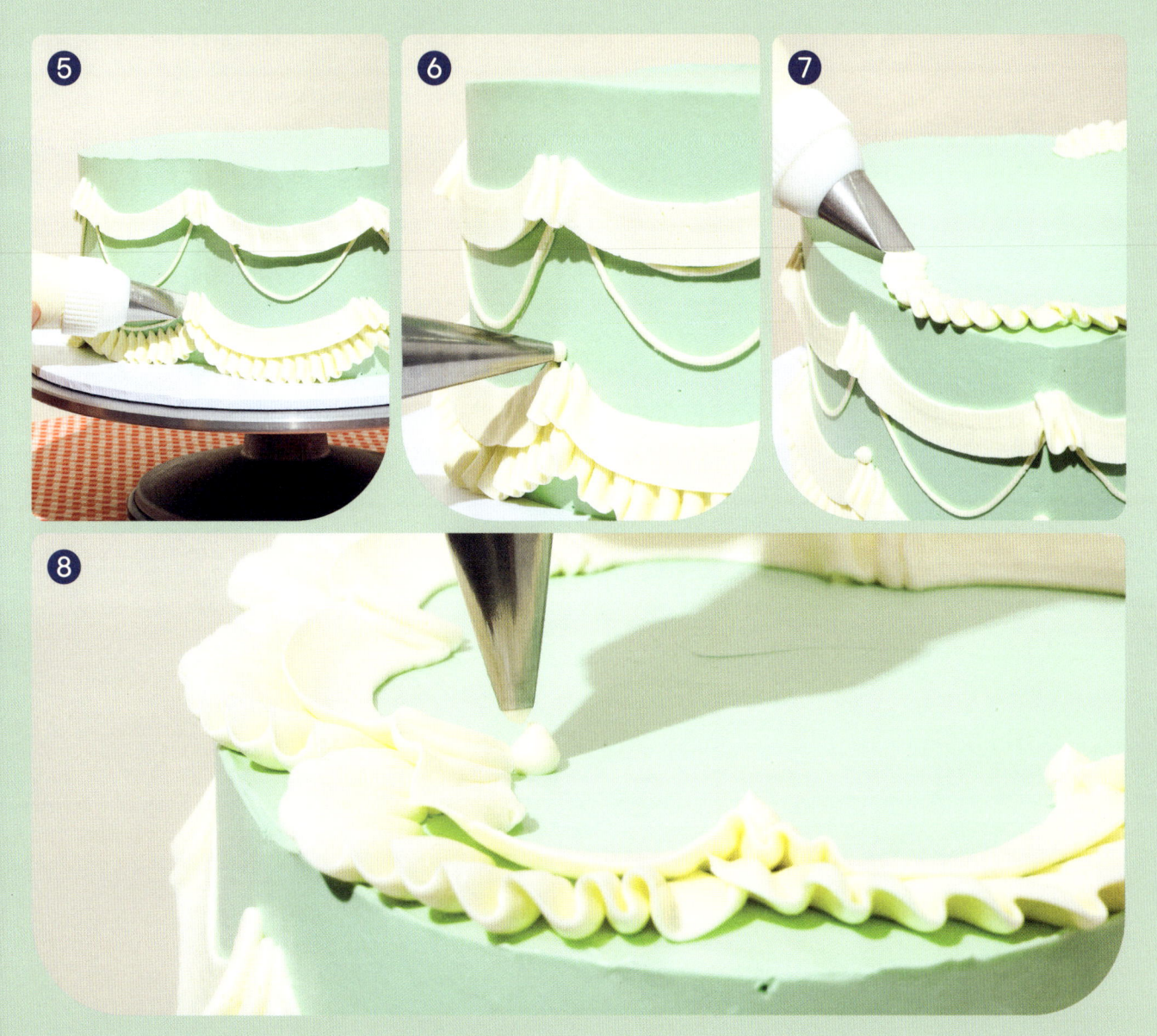

Images continue

DECORATING PROJECTS

257

258

MALI BAKES

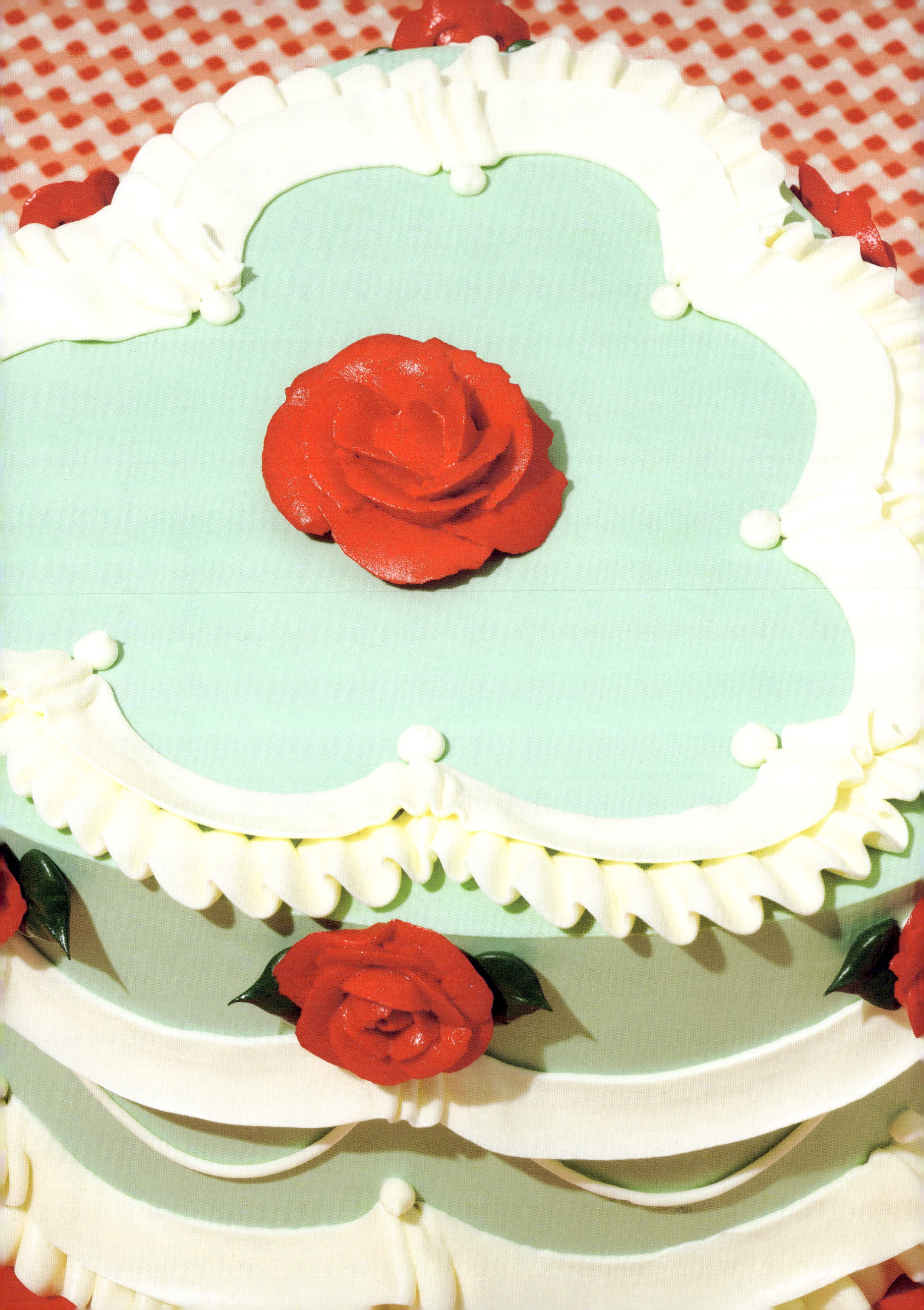

PROJECT 10

Daisy Fields

This cake captures that perfect springtime moment. It's one of the most adored wedding cakes at Mali Bakes, and is surprisingly simple to create – making it a wonderful starting point for your double-tier cake journey. The monochromatic finish not only creates a stunning canvas for fresh flowers but also highlights the piping work beautifully, with gentle shadows adding depth to the design, especially on the raked base. Feel free to get creative with colour and flower choices! You can stick with chamomile as shown here, or mix in other types of flowers to make it your own. Just make sure the flowers are completely chemical-free to keep everything safe to eat.

Project timeline

○ **DAY 1**
Prepare the fillings and bake the cake layers

○ **DAY 2**
Prepare the buttercream and assemble the cake

○ **DAY 3**
Decorate the cake

You'll need

Project basics
Cake: 18 cm (7 in) four-layer round cake, plus a 30 cm (12 in) three-layer round cake, crumb coated and chilled
Cake board: 41 cm (16 in) round board at least 1 cm (½ in) thick, plus an 18 cm (7 in) perforated board, and a temporary board larger than 18 cm (7 in)
Food colouring: Yellow, mustard
Buttercream: 2200 g (77.60 oz) Italian meringue buttercream (pages 43–46), medium consistency, bubbles removed
Decoration: 1 bunch of fresh chamomile flowers

Frosting tools
Angled palette knife
Straight palette knife
Stainless steel cake scraper, at least 15 cm (6 in) tall
Rake scraper, at least 15 cm (6 in) tall
Bench scraper with plastic handle (for smoothing the top of the cake)
Heatproof container or jug, taller than the scraper and palette knives
Turntable and non-slip mat

Tier stacking tools
1 centre dowel, at least 28 cm (11 in) tall
3 supporting dowels, at least 12.5 cm (5 in) tall
Edible marker
Masking tape
Cutting pliers or dowel cutter

Decorating tools
5 piping nozzles:
  Standard round 5;
  Medium petal 126K;
  Medium star S/S5, S/S9 and S/S13
2 large piping bags
1 standard coupler
1 medium coupler
Small pointed palette knife for marking
5 floral wires, 22 gauge
Wire cutter
Waterproof florist tape

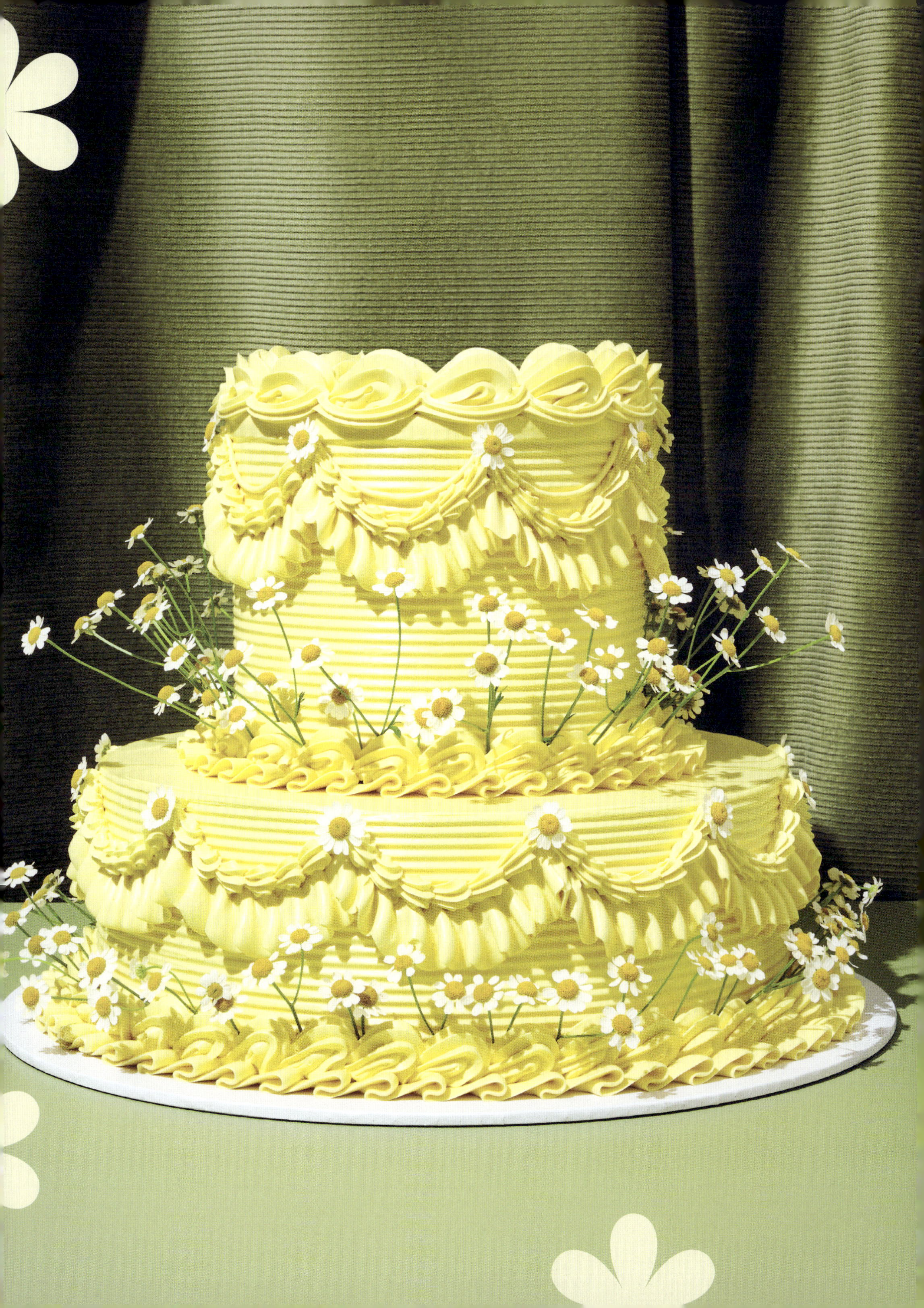

Piping Practice

1

2

3

4

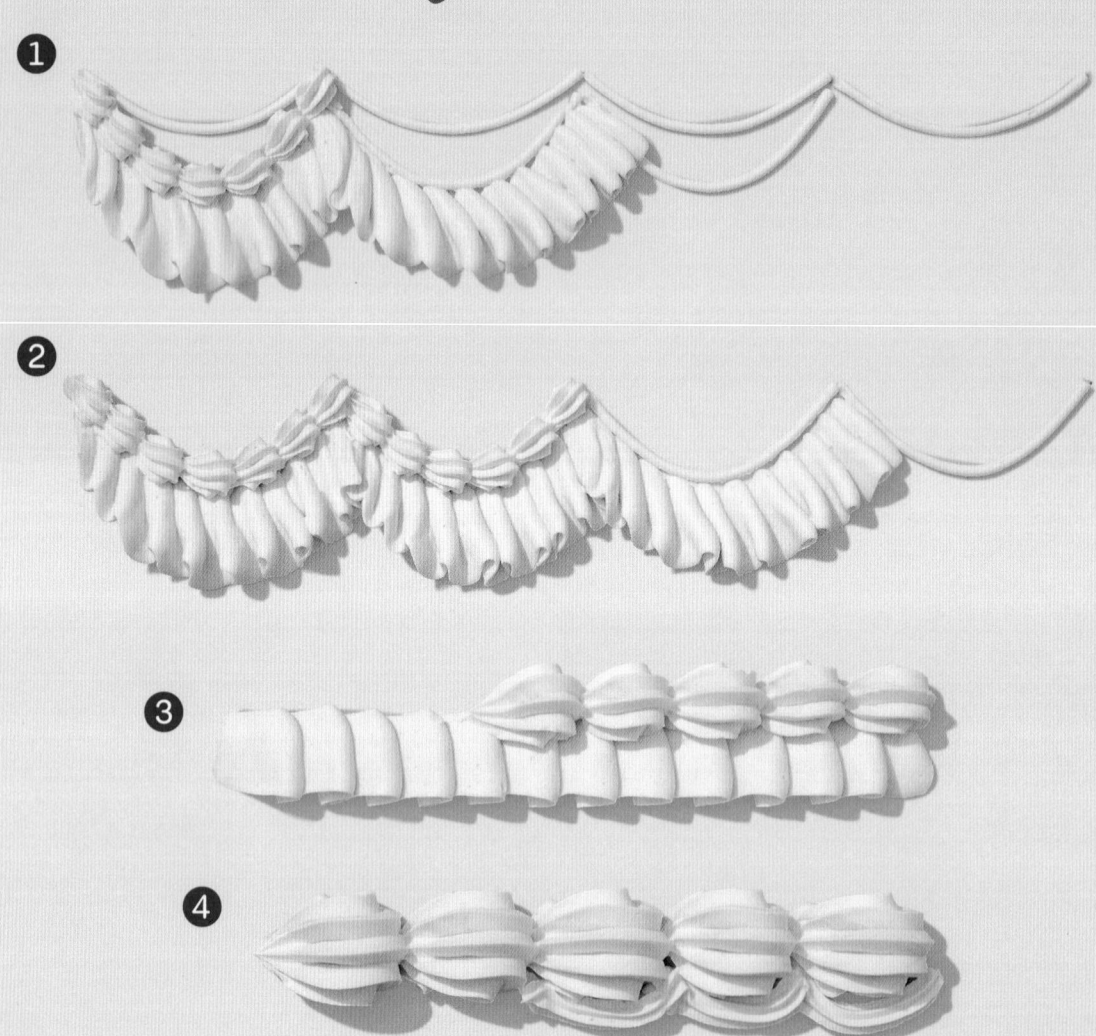

1. **Fluted ruffle garland with drop string & shell trim (top tier)**
   Nozzle (double drop string): Standard round 5 · **Angle:** 90°
   Nozzle (fluted ruffle): Medium petal 126K · **Angle:** 45°
   Nozzle (shells): Medium star S/S5 · **Angle:** 45°
   Pipe double drop strings as an outline (page 162). Pipe a fluted ruffle garland on the bottom row of drop strings (page 164) and finish the top of the ruffle with a ow of continuous shells (page 161).

2. **Fluted ruffle garland with shell trim (bottom tier)**
   Nozzle (drop string): Standard round 5 · **Angle:** 90°
   Nozzle (fluted ruffle garland): Medium petal 126K · **Angle:** 45°
   Nozzle (shells): Medium star S/S5 · **Angle:** 45°
   Start with the drop string as an outline. Then pipe a fluted ruffle garland and finish with a row of continuous shells along the top edge of the ruffle garland.

3. **Folded ruffle with shells**
   Nozzle (folded ruffle): Medium petal 126K · **Angle:** 45°
   Nozzle (shells): Medium star S/S9 · **Angle:** 45°
   Pipe a folded ruffle (page 165) in a straight line. Cover the top edge with a row of medium continuous shells.

4. **Continuous shells with scallop trim**
   Nozzle (shells): Medium star S/S13 **Angle:** 45°
   Nozzle (scallop trim): Medium star S/S5 · **Angle:** 90°
   Follow the instructions on page 206 to add a scallop trim to the continuous shells.

Set up

Make sure you have followed the set-up checklist on page 191 before starting.

Both layer cakes should already be assembled, crumb coated and chilled separately in the fridge: the 30 cm (12 in) cake on the 41 cm (16 in) cake board, and the 18 cm (7 in) cake on the perforated board with the temporary board underneath.

Let's begin!

Tint the buttercream. Tint all the buttercream with small drops of yellow and a touch of mustard food colouring until a pale creamy yellow shade is achieved.

Frost the cakes separately. Adjust 1000 g (35.25 oz) of the tinted buttercream to a thin but spreadable consistency (page 40). Follow the instructions on pages 51–56, to frost and rake both cakes until a neat smooth base is achieved, working with one cake at a time. Allow the frosted cakes to chill in the fridge for at least 15 minutes until the frosting is fully set.

Mark the top tier's side border into eight sections. Working on one cake at a time, start by cutting a round piece of baking paper to match the size of the top cake tier by tracing around an 18 cm (7 in) cake tin. Follow the instructions on page 172 to create a template for marking eight sections from the baking paper.

Gently place the paper on top of the cold frosted cake, aligning the edges. Use a pointed palette knife to gently make small marks about 5 mm (¼ in) below where the folded lines meet the cake's top edge. Gently remove the baking paper. You'll now have eight even sections marked on the side of the cake, ready for the border. Return the cake to the fridge while you move on to the bottom tier.

Mark the bottom tier's side border into 12 sections. Cut another piece of round baking paper to match the size of the bottom cake tier by tracing around a 30 cm (12 in) cake tin. Repeat the above instructions, but this time create a template for marking 12 sections on the side of the cake.

Gently place the paper on top of the cold frosted cake, aligning the edges. Use a pointed palette knife to gently make small marks about 5 mm (¼ in) below where the folded lines meet the cake's top edge. Gently remove the baking paper. You'll now have 12 even sections marked on the side of the cake, ready for the border.

Project continues

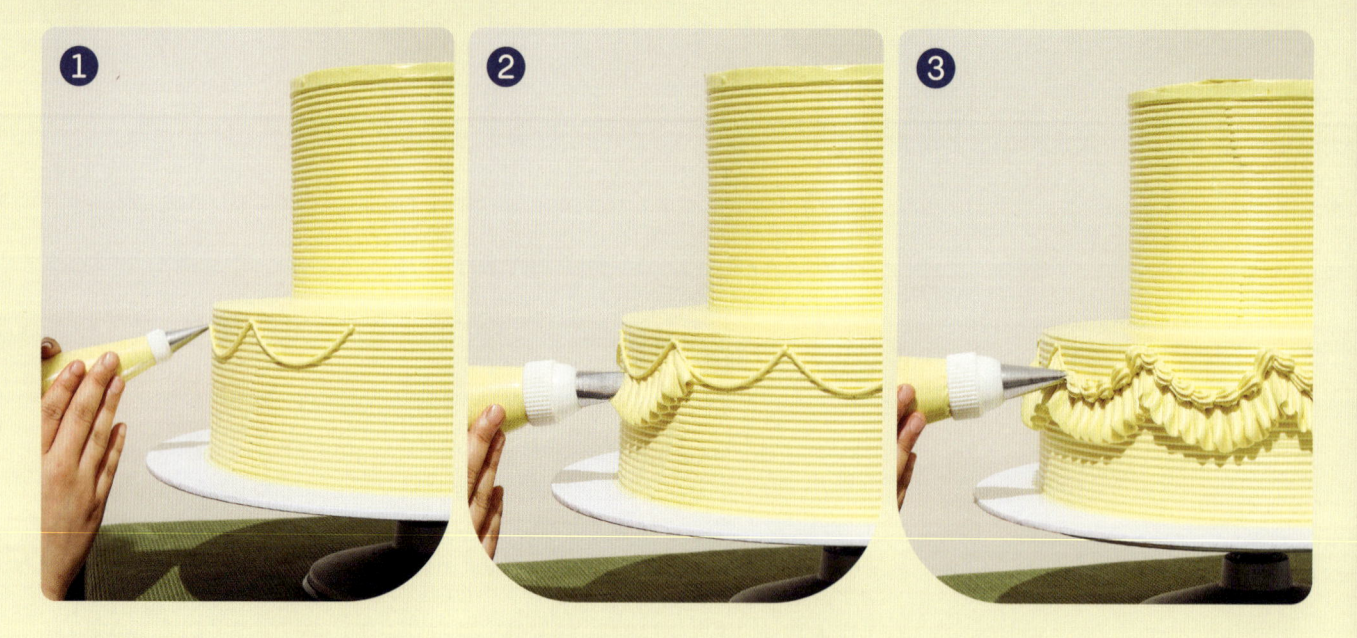

PROJECT 10   **DAISY FIELDS**

Stack the tiers. Follow the instructions on pages 175–177 to carefully stack the tiers, aligning one marking from each tier to establish the front of the cake.

Pipe the bottom tier's side border. Fit the first piping bag with a standard coupler and a round 5 nozzle. Working around the top of the bottom cake, pipe a drop string outline from one marked point to the next, allowing each string to drop about 2.5 cm (1 in) below the marked level (image 1). Next, fit the second piping bag with a medium coupler and a 126K petal nozzle, fill halfway with buttercream and pipe fluted ruffles directly beneath each string (image 2). Using the same piping bag, switch to a star S/S5 nozzle and pipe continuous shells along the top edge of the ruffle (image 3).

Pipe the top tier's side border. Take the piping bag with the round 5 nozzle and pipe double drop strings from one marked point to the next; the top string should drop about 2.5 cm (1 in) and the bottom string about 4 cm (1½ in) from the marked level (image 4). Finish the border with fluted ruffles and shells along the bottom string, just as you did on the bottom tier, but leave the top string visible (images 5 & 6).

Pipe the bottom border around each tier. Take the piping bag with the medium coupler and switch to a 126K petal nozzle. Pipe folded ruffles around the base of both the top and bottom tiers, leaving a 1.25 cm (½ in) gap from the cake to allow space for the shells (image 7). To make piping easier, chill the cake to set the ruffles before adding the shells. Next, switch to a star S/S9 nozzle and pipe a continuous shell border along the edge of each tier (image 8).

Project continues

MALI BAKES

DECORATING PROJECTS

265

PROJECT 10 　　　　　　　　　　　　　　　　　　　　　　　　　　　　　　　　　　DAISY FIELDS

Pipe the border on top of the cake. Take the piping bag with the medium coupler and switch to a star S/S13 nozzle. Pipe a continuous shell on top of the top tier, along the edge (image 9). Once complete, switch to a star S/S5 nozzle and pipe a scalloped trim along the outer edge of the shells to finish the design (image 10).

Chill the cake. Pop your beautifully decorated cake in the fridge for at least 2 hours to set the decoration in place.

Add the flowers. To keep them looking fresh and perky, only add the flowers right before you head out or when you arrive at your destination. Trim the flower stems to a length of 6–8 cm (2½–3¼ in) and cut your florist wire into 3 cm (1¼ in) pieces. Secure each flower stem to a piece of wire and wrap tightly with florist tape to fully conceal the wire (image 11). Gently insert the flowers into the cake, ensuring the wire is fully hidden. Arrange longer stems around the space between the top and bottom tiers of the cake, and use shorter stems to decorate the base of the bottom tier.

For the ruffle garlands, snip the flowers into individual blooms, leaving about 1 cm (½ in) of stem. Use a skewer to gently create small holes at each point where the ruffle garland meets, then carefully insert the flowers into the holes (image 12).

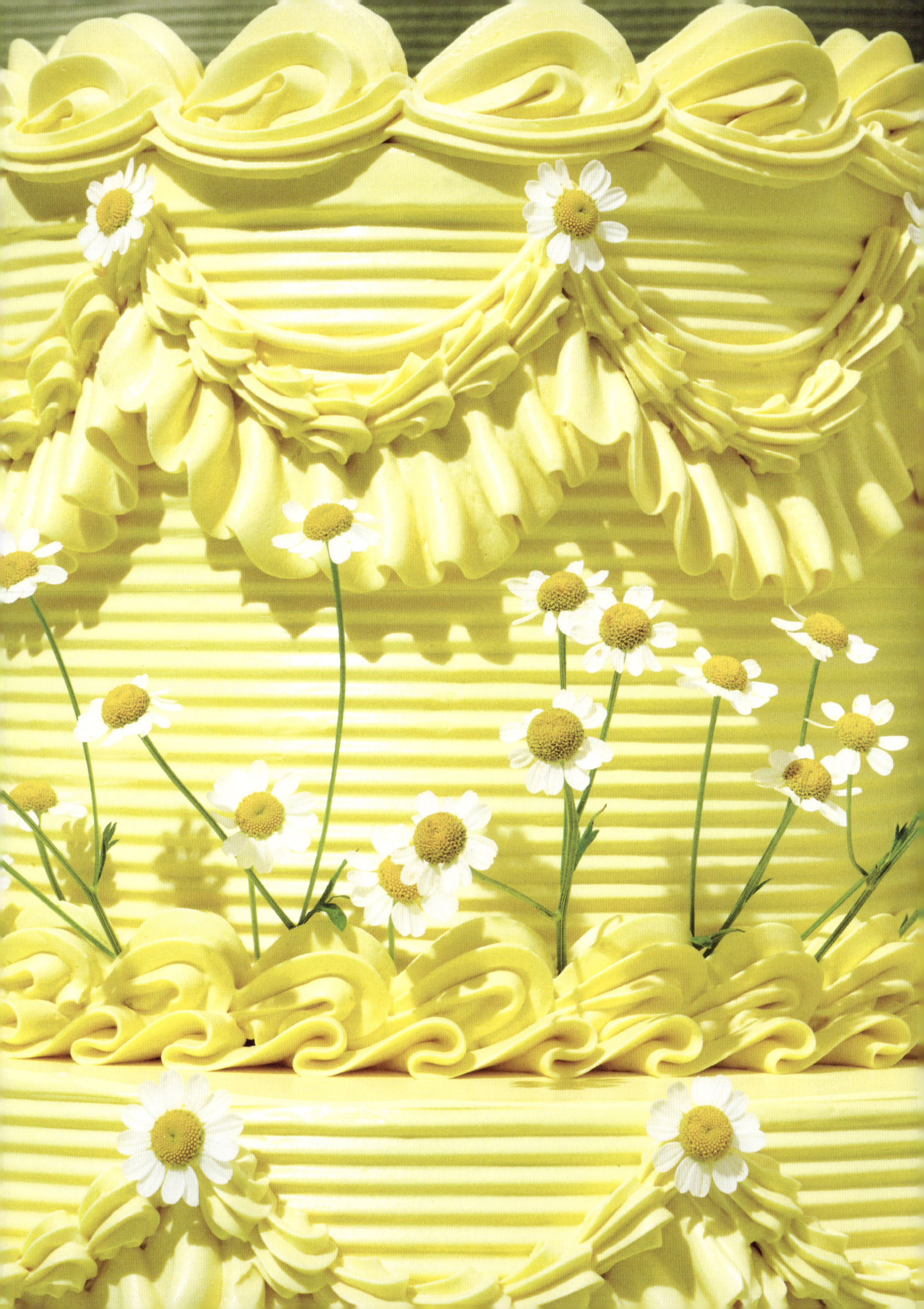

PROJECT 11

Cherry Blossom Bows

If you live by the mantra 'more is more' and can't resist something bursting with fun and flair, this cake is your dream come true! It's a stunning example of how thoughtful colour choices can elevate a design. Despite the abundance of intricate piping – like ruffles, bows and rosettes – it doesn't feel visually cluttered. The design strikes a balance by each tier being frosted in two vibrant, analogous tones, while the piping, instead of competing for attention, remains subtle in an ivory hue. To create flow and movement, the top tier's border takes an unexpected twist. Instead of even garlands all the way around, it flows down gracefully at the front, like a drape. It's a small detail, but it makes the whole design feel much more dynamic.

Project timeline

○ **DAY 1**
Prepare the fillings and bake the cake layers

○ **DAY 2**
Prepare the buttercream and assemble the cake

○ **DAY 3**
Decorate the cake

You'll need

Project basics
Cake: 15 cm (6 in) three-layer round cake, plus a 23 cm (9 in) three-layer round cake, crumb coated and chilled
Cake board: 33 cm (13 in) round board at least 1 cm (½ in) thick, plus a 15 cm (6 in) perforated board, and a temporary board larger than 15 cm (6 in)
Food colouring: Red, hot pink, sky blue, white, purple
Buttercream: 1600 g (56.44 oz) Italian meringue buttercream (pages 43–46), medium consistency, bubbles removed
Topping: 6 maraschino cherries, with stems

Frosting tools
Angled palette knife
Straight palette knife
Stainless steel cake scraper, at least 10 cm (4 in) tall
Bench scraper with plastic handle (for smoothing the top of the cake)
Heatproof container or jug, taller than the scraper and palette knives
Turntable and non-slip mat

Tier stacking tools
1 centre dowel, at least 23 cm (9 in) tall
3 supporting dowels, at least 12.5 cm (5 in) tall
Edible marker
Masking tape
Cutting pliers or dowel cutter

Decorating tools
8 piping nozzles:
  Standard round 4;
  Medium round S/P4;
  Standard round 5;
  Standard petal 104W;
  Medium star S/S7 and S/S11;
  Standard star 18;
  Standard leaf 352
3 large piping bags
2 standard couplers
1 medium coupler
Wing caliper
Small pointed palette knife for marking

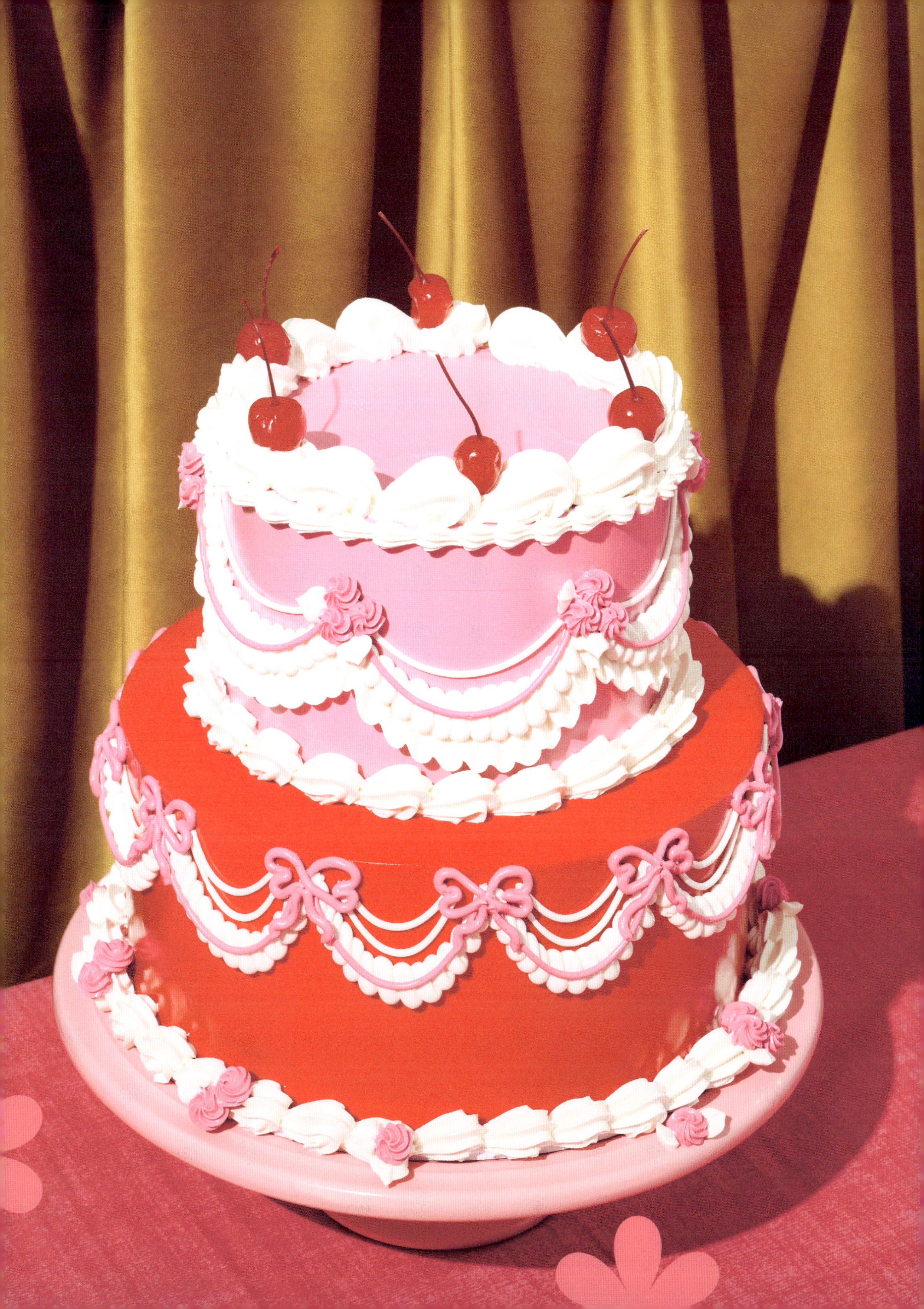

Piping Practice

1

2

3

1. **Loop garland with strings (bottom tier)**
   Nozzle (white & pink drop strings): Standard round 4 · **Angle:** 90°
   Nozzle (loop garland): Medium round S/P4 · **Angle:** 90°
   Pipe a white triple drop string. Start by piping the bottom row of drop strings (page 162), connecting each one. Within each drop string section, pipe a top and middle row of drop strings. Do not run them on continuously. Pipe a loop garland (page 163) on top of the lowest row of strings, to cover them. Finish with a pink drop string on top of the loop garland.

2. **Bows**
   Nozzle: Standard round 5 · **Angle:** 90°
   Pipe two sideways heart shapes, with the points facing each other. Add two tails to finish.

3. **Rosettes & leaves (pages 161 & 165)**
   Nozzle (rosettes): Standard star 18 · **Angle:** 90°
   Nozzle (leaves): Standard leaf 352 · **Angle:** 45°

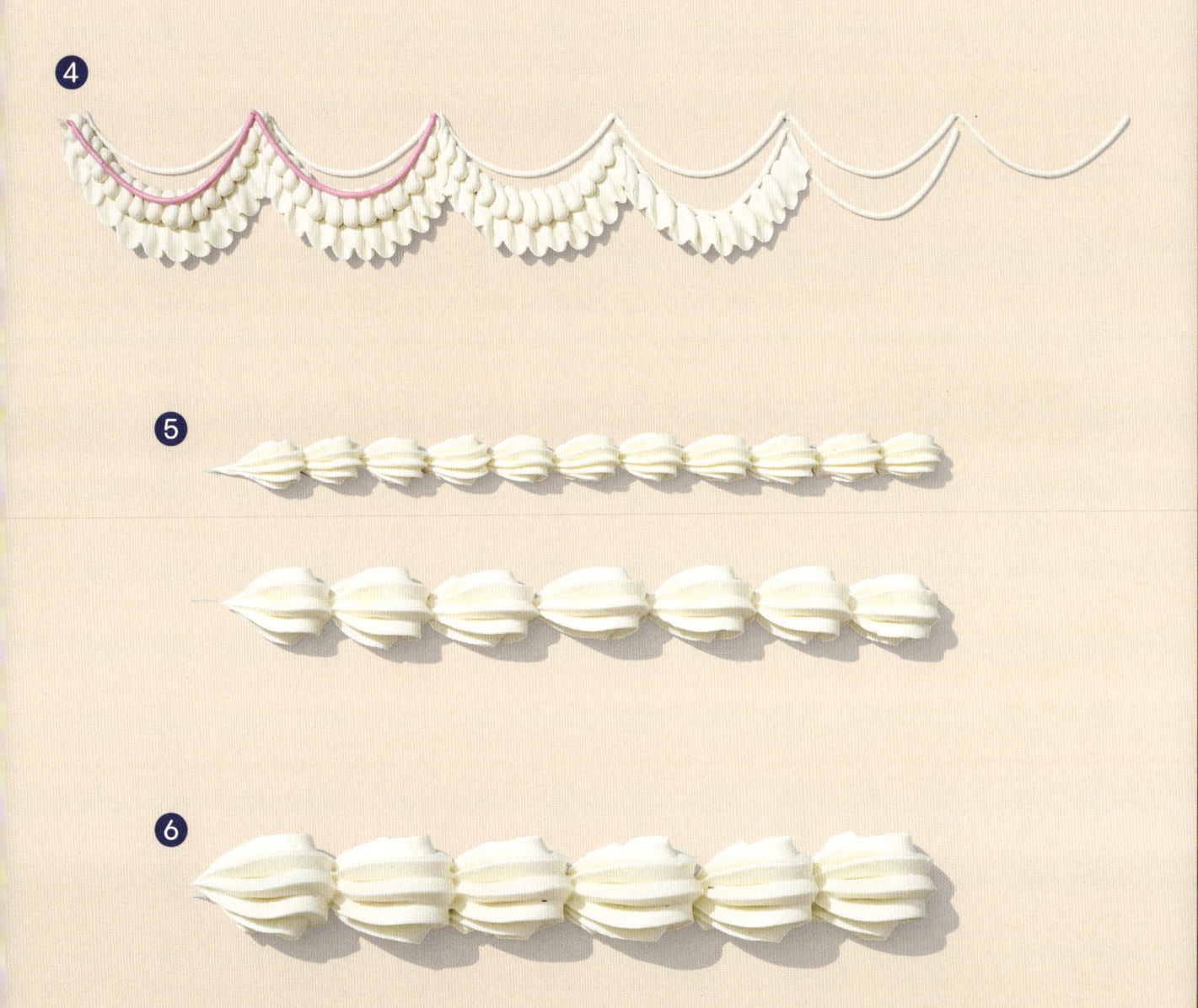

4. Loop garland with strings & fluted ruffles (top tier)
Nozzle (white & pink drop strings): Standard round 4 · **Angle:** 90°
Nozzle (fluted ruffles): Standard petal 104W · **Angle:** 45°
Nozzle (loop garland): Medium round S/P4 · **Angle:** 90°

Pipe white double drop strings, then pipe a fluted ruffle garland (page 164) just beneath the lowest row of strings. Pipe the loop garland on the top edge of the ruffle. Finish with a pink drop string on top of the loop garland.

5. Continuous medium shells (page 161)
Nozzles: Medium star S/S7 & Medium star S/S11 · **Angle:** 45°

6. Continuous large shells
Nozzle: Standard star 18 · **Angle:** 45°

Set up

Make sure you have followed the set-up checklist on page 191 before starting.

Both layer cakes should already be assembled, crumb coated and chilled separately in the fridge: the larger cake on the 33 cm (13 in) cake board, and the smaller cake on the perforated board, with the temporary board underneath.

Let's begin!

Tint the buttercream. Prepare the buttercream in three shades for decorating. Start by tinting 400 g (14 oz) of the buttercream with red food colouring until it reaches a bold red tone. Tint another 400 g (14 oz) with hot pink food colouring and a small touch of sky blue to achieve a cool, medium-pink shade. Create an ivory shade with the remaining buttercream by adding white food colouring and a small drop of purple.

Frost the cakes separately. Adjust 400 g (14 oz) red buttercream and 250 g (8.82 oz) of pink buttercream to a thin but spreadable consistency (page 40). Follow the instructions on pages 51–53 to frost both cakes until a neat smooth base is achieved. Use the red buttercream for the larger cake and the pink buttercream for the smaller cake, working on one cake at a time. Chill the frosted cakes in the refrigerator for at least 15 minutes until the frosting is fully set.

Mark the top tier's side border into six sections. Working on one cake at a time, start by cutting a round piece of baking paper to match the size of the top cake tier by tracing around a 15 cm (6 in) cake tin. Follow the instructions on page 172 to create a template for marking six sections from the baking paper.

Gently place the paper on top of the cold frosted cake, aligning the edges. Use a pointed palette knife to gently make small marks about 5 mm (¼ in) below where the folded lines meet the cake's top edge. Gently remove the baking paper. You'll now have six even sections marked on the side of the cake.

Next, using a wing caliper set to 2.5 cm (1 in), mark the front lower garland on the top cake tier by measuring down from any two adjacent marked spots of the six sections – this will be the front of your cake.

You'll now have six evenly spaced sections marked on the side, with one lower section ready for the border. Return the cake to the fridge while you move on to the bottom tier.

Mark the bottom tier's side border into 12 sections. Cut another piece of round baking paper to match the size of the bottom cake tier by tracing around a 23 cm (9 in) cake tin. Follow the instructions on page 172 to create a template for marking 12 sections from the baking paper.

Gently place the paper on top of the cold frosted cake, aligning the edges. Use a pointed palette knife to gently make small marks about 5 mm (¼ in) below where the folded lines meet the cake's top edge. Gently remove the baking paper. You'll now have 12 even sections marked on the side of the cake, ready for the border.

Stack the tiers. Follow the instructions on pages 175–177 to carefully stack the tiers, aligning the centre of the lower section on the top tier with one of the marked spots on the bottom tier to establish the front of the cake.

Pipe the bottom tier's side border. Fit the first piping bag with a standard coupler and round 4 nozzle, then fill halfway with ivory buttercream. Pipe a drop string from one marked spot to the next around the cake, allowing each string to drop about 3.5 cm (1½ in) from the marked level. Once complete, pipe a series of double drop strings above each lower string (image 1).

Next, fit a second piping bag with the medium coupler and a round S/P4 nozzle, fill halfway with ivory buttercream, then pipe a loop garland on top of each bottom string, using the strings as a guide (image 2).

To finish the border, fit the third piping bag with the other standard coupler and a clean round 4 nozzle, and fill halfway with pink buttercream. Pipe a drop string directly onto each garland, positioning it neatly in the centre of each loop garland (image 3). Then switch to a round 5 nozzle and pipe bow details at the points where each garland meets (image 4).

Project continues

DECORATING PROJECTS

273

PROJECT 11 CHERRY BLOSSOM BOWS

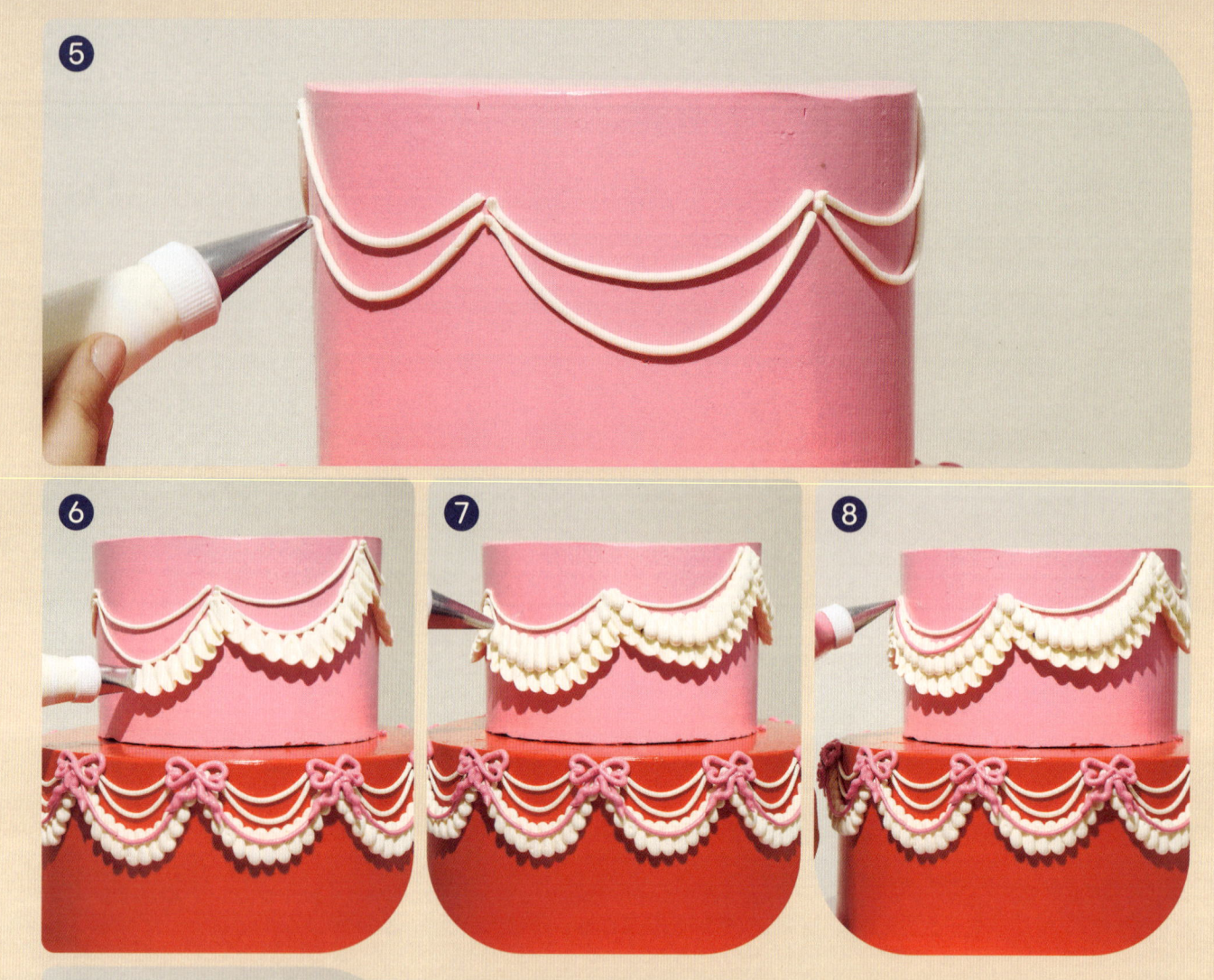

Pipe the top tier's side border. Take the piping bag with the standard coupler and ivory buttercream and switch to a clean round 4 nozzle. Pipe a double drop string from one marked point to the next, allowing the top string to drop about 2.5 cm (1 in) and the bottom string about 4 cm (1½ in) from the marked level (image 5). Using the same piping bag, switch to a petal 104W nozzle, then pipe fluted ruffles just below each bottom string (image 6).

Now use the piping bag fitted with the ivory buttercream and round S/P4 nozzle to pipe a loop garland directly along each bottom string, concealing the strings while still leaving the ruffles visible (image 7).

Next, take the piping bag with a standard coupler and pink buttercream, fit it with a clean round 4 nozzle, and pipe a drop string directly onto each garland, positioning it neatly in the centre of each loop garland (image 8).

Pipe the bottom border around each tier. Switch the nozzle with the medium coupler to a star S/S7 nozzle. Fill the bag halfway with more ivory buttercream and pipe continuous shells around the bottom edge of both the top and bottom tiers (image 9).

274 MALI BAKES

Pipe the border on top of the cake. Using the same piping bag with the medium coupler, switch to a star S/S11 nozzle and pipe a continuous ivory shell on top of the cake, along the edge (image 10).

Now take the piping bag with the ivory buttercream and standard coupler and switch to a star 18 nozzle. Working in the opposite direction to the larger shells, pipe another continuous row of smaller shell along the top edge of the side of the cake (image 11).

Pipe the rosettes. Using the piping bag filled with pink buttercream and fitted with a clean star 18 nozzle, pipe three rosettes at the points where the garlands meet on the top tier (image 12). Then pipe additional rosettes randomly around the base of the bottom tier and the cake board.

Once all the rosettes are complete, switch the nozzle on the ivory buttercream piping bag to a leaf 352 nozzle and pipe a leaf on each side of the rosettes (image 13).

Finish with the cherries. Trim off the knotty part of each cherry stem, leaving the stem as long as possible. Pat the cherries dry with paper towels to remove any excess syrup. Once dry, place each cherry along the top tier shell border, spacing them evenly around the cake (image 14).

Chill the cake. Pop your beautifully decorated cake in the fridge for at least 2 hours before party time. This will help set the decorations in place, keeping everything secure so your cake looks picture-perfect when it's ready to shine!

Images continue

DECORATING PROJECTS

13

14

276

MALI BAKES

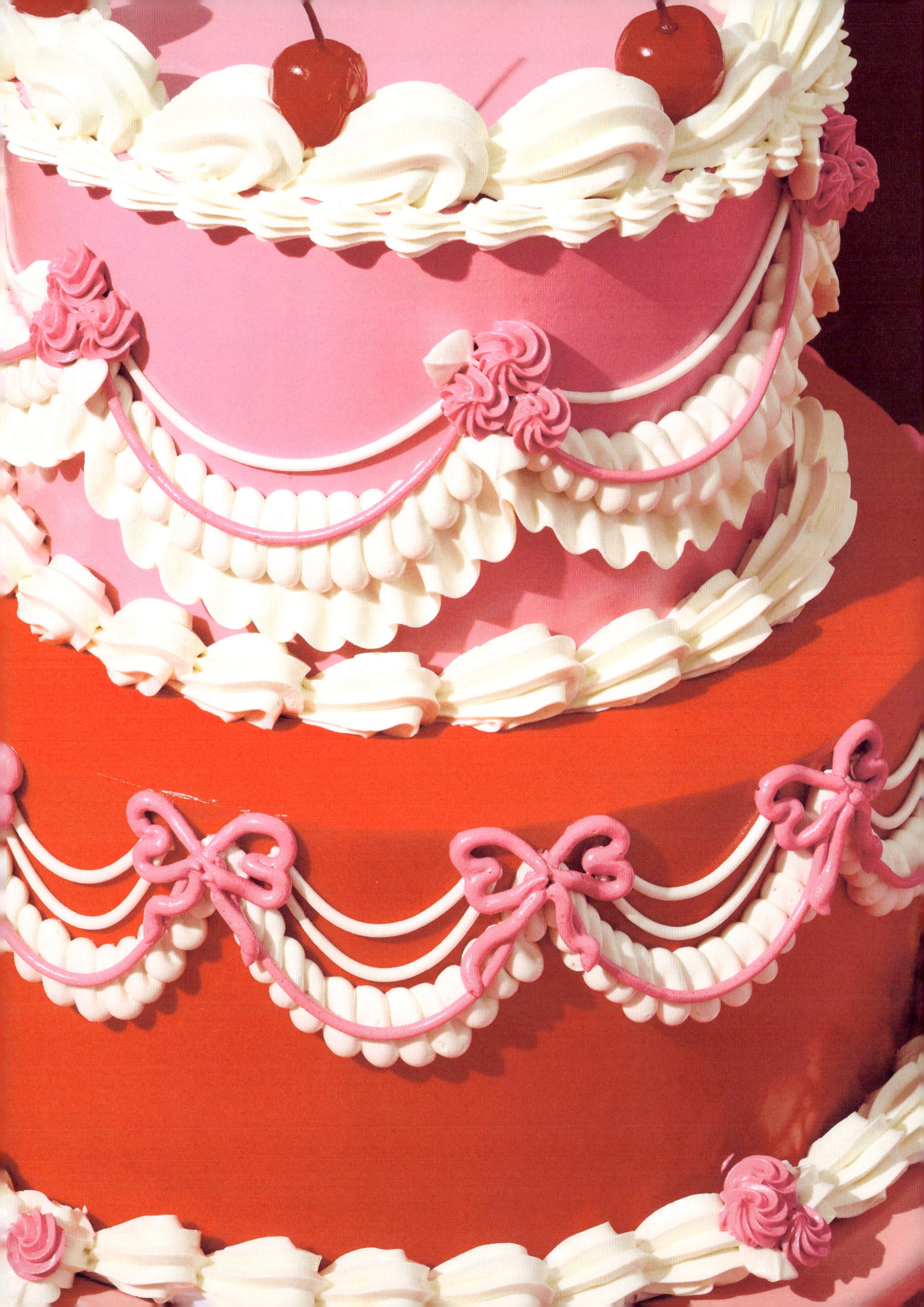

PROJECT 12

The Wedding Cake

A stunning three-tier cake, embellished with intricate piping work reminiscent of delicate lace, makes a perfect centrepiece at a summer garden wedding. Pairing a single colour with ivory or white is a tried-and-true colour scheme, and it works wonderfully on a large-scale highly detailed cake without creating any visual clutter.

When working with soft shades like ivory or pastel blue, remember that the natural yellow tint of buttercream can affect the final colour. To create a true ivory shade, add a small amount of violet or purple to neutralise the yellow.

Project timeline

DAY 1
Prepare the fillings and bake the cake layers

DAY 2
Prepare the buttercream and assemble the cake

DAY 3
Decorate the cake

You'll need

Project basics
Cake: 15 cm (6 in) three-layer round cake, plus a 23 cm (9 in) three-layer round cake, and a 30 cm (12 in) three-layer round cake, crumb coated and chilled
Cake board: 41 cm (16 in) round board at least 1 cm (½ in) thick; 23 cm (9 in) perforated board; 15 cm (6 in) perforated board; and two temporary boards: one larger than 23 cm (9 in), and one larger than 15 cm (6 in)
Food colouring: Sky blue, pink, white, purple
Buttercream: 2600 g (91.71 oz) Italian meringue buttercream (pages 43–46), medium consistency, bubbles removed
Decorations: Cake topper, 36 × 6 mm (½ in) edible sugar pearls

Frosting tools
Angled palette knife
Straight palette knife
Stainless steel cake scraper, at least 10 cm (4 in) tall
Bench scraper with plastic handle (for smoothing the top of the cake)
Heatproof container or jug, taller than the scraper and palette knives
Turntable and non-slip mat

Tier stacking tools
1 centre dowel, at least 32.5 cm (13 in) tall
6 supporting dowels, at least 12.5 cm (5 in) tall
Edible marker
Masking tape
Cutting pliers or dowel cutter

Decorating tools
8 piping nozzles:
    Medium star S/S3;
    Standard round 4,
    Standard star 16;
    Standard petal 104W and 102;
    Medium French star S/F11 and S/F13;
    Standard leaf 352
2 large piping bags
1 standard coupler
1 medium coupler
Wing caliper
Small pointed palette knife for marking

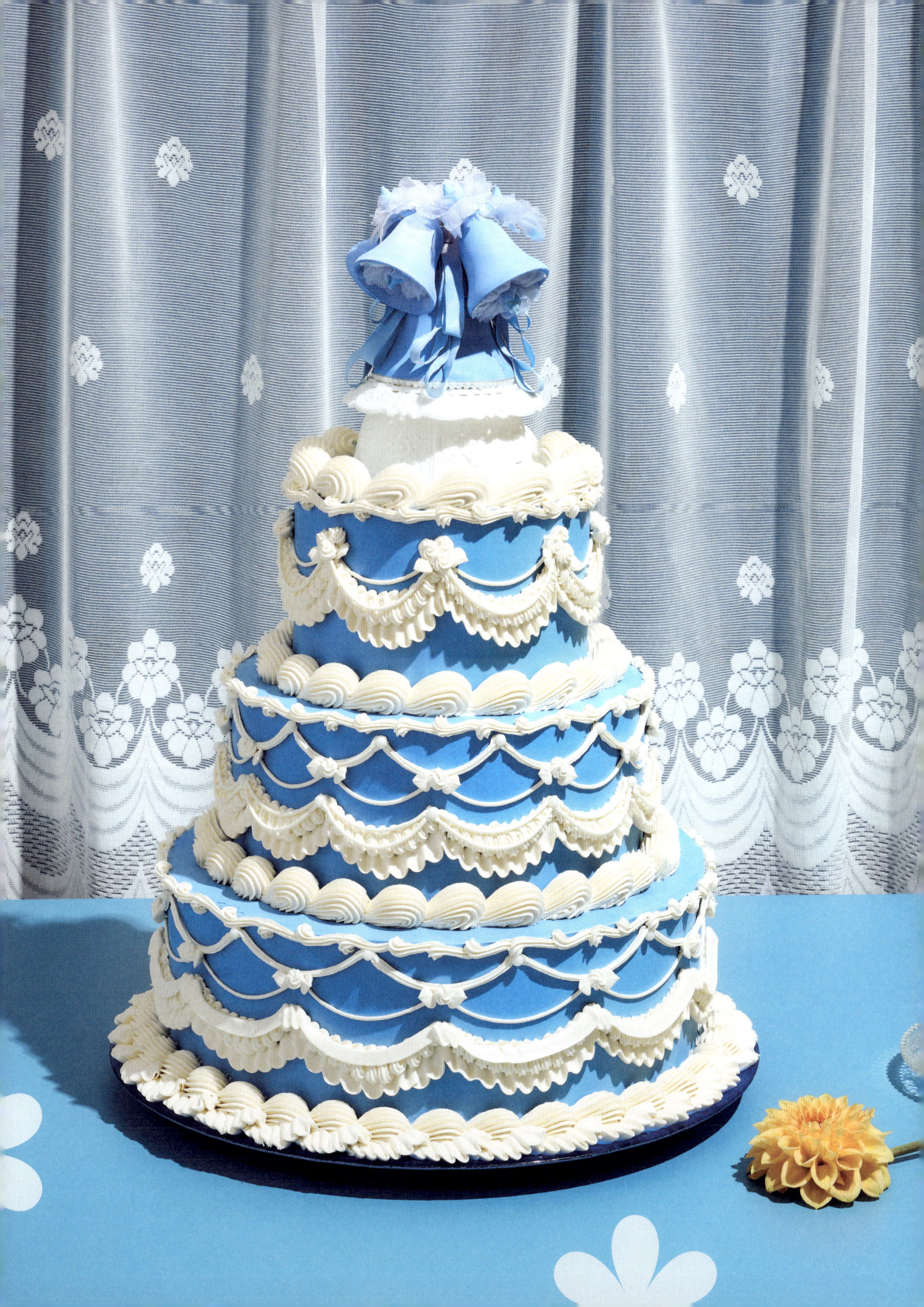

Piping Practice

①

②

③

④

1. **Lattice strings with rosettes**
   Nozzle (star drop string): Medium star S/S3 · **Angle:** 90°
   Nozzle (round drop string): Standard round 4 · **Angle:** 90°
   Nozzle (rosette): Standard star 16 · **Angle:** 90°
   Nozzle (leaves): Standard leaf 352 · **Angle:** 45°

   Pipe the first drop string (page 162) with the star nozzle, then use the round nozzle to pipe another drop string, offsetting the arcs so the drop string connects at the lowest point of the star drop string. Then pipe a rosette (page 161) where the two drop strings connect, and finish with leaves (page 165) on either side of the rosettes.

2. **Ruffle garland with swag (bottom tier)**
   Nozzle (drop string): Standard round 4 · **Angle:** 90°
   Nozzle (fluted ruffle): Standard petal 104W · **Angle:** 45°
   Nozzle (loop garland): Standard star 16 · **Angle:** 90°
   Nozzle (swag): Standard petal 102 · **Angle:** 45°

   Pipe a drop string as an outline, then pipe a fluted ruffle garland (page 164) just below the drop string. Pipe the loop garland (page 163) on the top edge of the fluted ruffle. Finish with a swag (page 164) on the top edge of the loop garland.

⑤

⑥

⑦

3. Ruffle garland with strings (middle tier)
Nozzle (drop string): Standard round 4 · **Angle:** 90°
Nozzle (fluted ruffle): Standard petal 104W · **Angle:** 45°
Nozzle (loop garland): Standard star 16 · **Angle:** 90°

Follow the instructions for the bottom tier ruffle garland with swag, but top the loop garland with a row of double strings.

4. Ruffle garland with strings (top tier)
Nozzle (strings): Standard round 4 · **Angle:** 90°
Nozzle (fluted ruffle): Standard petal 104W · **Angle:** 45°
Nozzle (loop garland): Standard star 16 · **Angle:** 90°

Start with a row of double strings, then pipe a fluted ruffle garland, followed by a loop garland and top with a row of single drop strings.

5. Continuous shells with fluted ruffle (bottom border, bottom tier)
Nozzle (shells): Medium French star S/ F11 · **Angle:** 45°
Nozzle (fluted ruffle): Standard petal 104W · **Angle:** 45°

Pipe continuous shells (page 161), then add a fluted ruffle underneath each shell. Start at the narrowest point of each shell and release at the next narrowest point. Repeat for all shells.

6. Continuous large shells (top border)
Nozzle: Medium French star S/F13 · **Angle:** 45°

7. Reverse small shells (page 162)
Nozzle: Medium star S/S3 · **Angle:** 45°

PROJECT 12　　　　　　　　　　　　　　　　　　　　　　THE WEDDING CAKE

Set up

Make sure you have followed the set-up checklist on page 191 before starting.

All layer cakes should already be assembled, crumb coated and chilled separately in the fridge: the largest cake on the 41 cm (16 in) cake board, and the two smaller cakes on the perforated boards, with the temporary boards underneath.

Let's begin!

Tint the buttercream. Prepare the buttercream in two shades for decorating. For the frosting, tint 1400 g (49.38 oz) of the buttercream with a small amount of sky blue and a hint of pink to achieve a soft light blue shade. Tint the remaining buttercream an ivory shade by adding a little white food colouring with just a touch of purple.

Frost the cakes separately. Adjust all the blue buttercream to a thin but spreadable consistency (page 40). Follow the instructions on pages 51–53 to frost each cake until a neat smooth base is achieved. Chill the frosted cakes in the refrigerator for at least 15 minutes, until the frosting is fully set.

Mark the top tier's side border into eight sections. Working on one cake at a time, start by cutting a round piece of baking paper to match the size of the top cake tier by tracing around a 15 cm (6 in) cake tin. Follow the instructions on page 172 to create a template for marking eight sections from the baking paper.

Gently place the paper on top of the cold frosted cake, aligning the edges. Use a pointed palette knife to gently make small marks along the edge of the cake where the folded lines meet the cake's top edge. Gently remove the baking paper. You'll now have eight even sections marked on the top edge of the cake.

Next, using a wing caliper set to 2.5 cm (1 in) to mark the starting point of the side border by measuring straight down from each mark on the top edge, creating gentle marks around the cake. You will now have eight evenly spaced sections marked on the side of the cake. Return the cake to the fridge while you move on to the middle tier.

Mark the middle tier's side border into 12 sections. Cut another piece of round baking paper to match the size of the middle cake tier by tracing around a 23 cm (9 in) cake tin. Follow the instructions on page 172 to create a template for marking 12 sections from the baking paper.

Gently place the paper on top of the cold frosted cake, aligning the edges. Use a pointed palette knife to gently make small marks about 5 mm (¼ in) below where the folded lines meet the cake top edge. Gently remove the baking paper. You'll now have 12 even sections marked on the side of the cake, ready for the border. Return the cake to the fridge while you move on to the bottom tier.

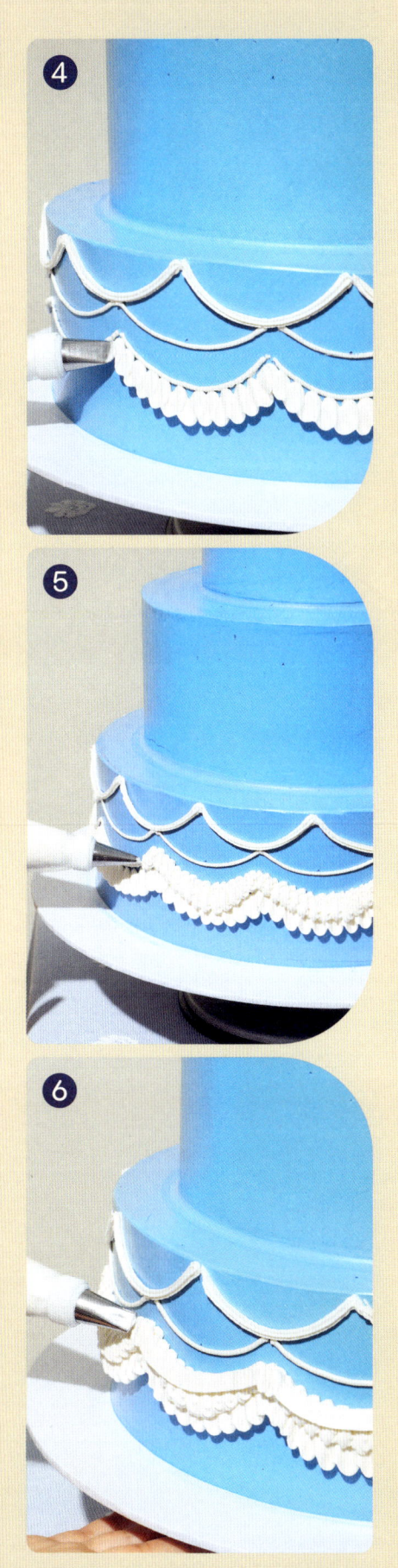

Mark the bottom tier's side border into 12 sections. Cut another piece of round baking paper to match the size of the bottom cake tier by tracing around a 30 cm (12 in) cake tin. Repeat the steps for the middle tier to make a template for marking 12 sections from the baking paper. Follow the same steps to place and align the baking paper with the cake's edge and mark about 5 mm (¼ in) below where the folded lines meet the cake top edge. Gently remove the baking paper. You'll now have 12 even sections marked on the side of the cake, ready for the border.

Stack the tiers. Following the instructions on 175–177, carefully stack the tiers, aligning one marking from each tier to establish the front of the cake.

Pipe the bottom tier's side border. To create the lace design, start by fitting the first piping bag with the medium coupler and a star S/S3 nozzle, then fill halfway with ivory buttercream. Pipe a drop string from one marked point to the next, allowing each string to drop about 1.5 cm (½ in) below the marked level (image 1). Once the first row is complete, gently mark the centre of each drop string to establish starting points for the next row.

Next, fit the second piping bag with the standard coupler and round 4 nozzle and fill halfway with more ivory buttercream. Pipe a second row of drop strings, again letting them drop 1.5 cm (½ in) below the marked level (image 2).

For the lower side border, use a wing caliper set to 1.5 cm (½ in) to measure directly down from the starting point of each bottom-row string. Using the round 4 nozzle, pipe an outline drop string connecting these marked points, allowing each string to drop about 1.5 cm (½ in) below the marked level (image 3). Then, switch to a 104W petal nozzle and pipe fluted ruffles underneath this last group of drop strings, using the strings as a guide (image 4).

Next, using the same piping bag with a standard coupler, switch to a star 16 nozzle and pipe a loop garland overlapping the ruffle (image 5). To finish the border, use a 102 petal nozzle to pipe a swag on top, positioning each one neatly on the top edge of the loop garland (image 6).

Project continues

DECORATING PROJECTS

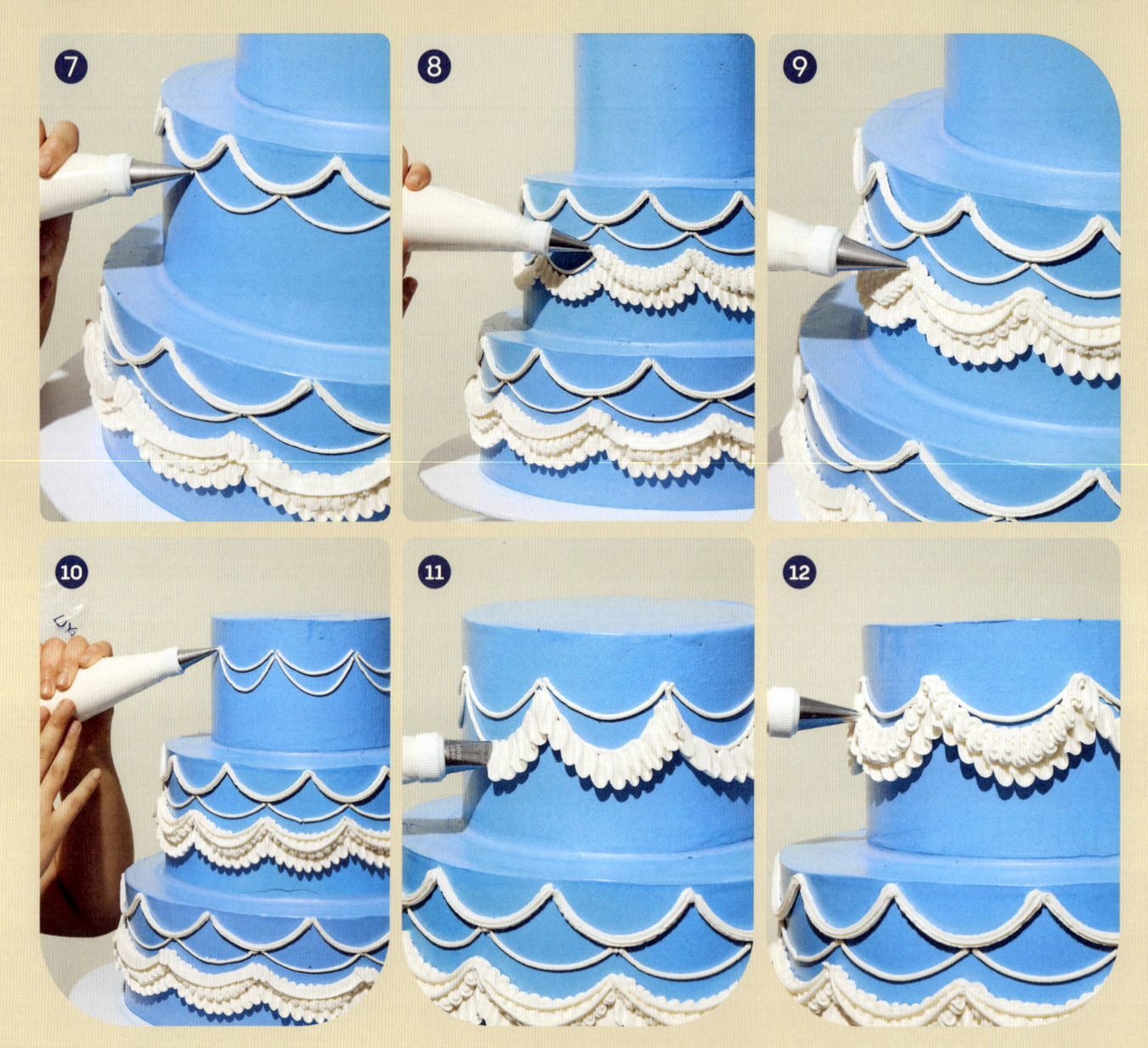

Pipe the middle tier's side border. Repeat the piping instructions for the borders around the bottom tier to complete the upper and lower borders around the middle tier (images 7 & 8). To complete the lower border, use the round 4 nozzle to pipe a double string in place of a swag (image 9). Begin and end both the upper and lower strings at the same points as the loop garlands, allowing the lower string to extend to the bottom edge of the loop garland.

Pipe the top tier's side border. Using the round 4 nozzle, pipe a double drop string from each of the marked points to the next (image 10). Let the upper string drop about 1.5 cm (½ in) and the lower string about 3 cm (1¼ in) below the marked level. Next, switch to the 104W petal nozzle and pipe fluted ruffles just below each bottom string (image 11). Now use the star 16 nozzle to pipe a loop garland along each bottom string, overlapping the ruffle (image 12).

To complete the border, switch back to the round 4 nozzle and pipe a drop string on top of each garland. Start each string at the same points as the top strings, letting them drop down to align with each loop garland (image 13).

Pipe the bottom border around each tier. Take the piping bag fitted with the medium coupler and attach a French star S/F11 nozzle. Pipe a continuous shell along the bottom edge of all three tiers (image 14).

For the bottom tier, add a fluted ruffle trim using the 104W petal nozzle (image 15).

Pipe the border on top of the top tier. Switch the nozzle on the piping bag with the medium coupler to the French star S/F13 nozzle, and pipe a continuous shell border on top of the cake, along the top edge. Using the same piping bag, switch back to the star S/S3 nozzle and pipe reverse shells around the top side edge of the cake to conceal the edge completely (image 16).

Pipe the border on top of the middle tier and bottom tier. Using the same star S/S3 nozzle, pipe reverse shells around the top edge of both tiers.

Project continues

DECORATING PROJECTS

285

PROJECT 12   THE WEDDING CAKE

Add sugar pearls. Place one sugar pearl at each starting point of the lace design on both the bottom and middle tiers. Then, add one sugar pearl at each point where the garlands meet along the lower borders of the middle tier (image 17).

Pipe the rosettes. Take the piping bag with the standard coupler and switch to the star 16 nozzle. Pipe three rosettes at each point where the garlands meet on the top tier. For the two bottom tiers, pipe a single rosette at each connecting point of the lace design (image 18).

Once done, switch to a leaf 352 nozzle and pipe a leaf on both sides of each single rosette and the three rosettes (image 19).

Chill the cake. Pop your beautifully decorated cake in the fridge for at least 2 hours before party time. This will help set the decorations in place, keeping everything secure so your cake looks picture-perfect when it's ready to shine!

Crown the cake. It is best to add the topper once the cake is at the party and positioned in place. Simply place the topper on top of the cake (image 20).

286   MALI BAKES

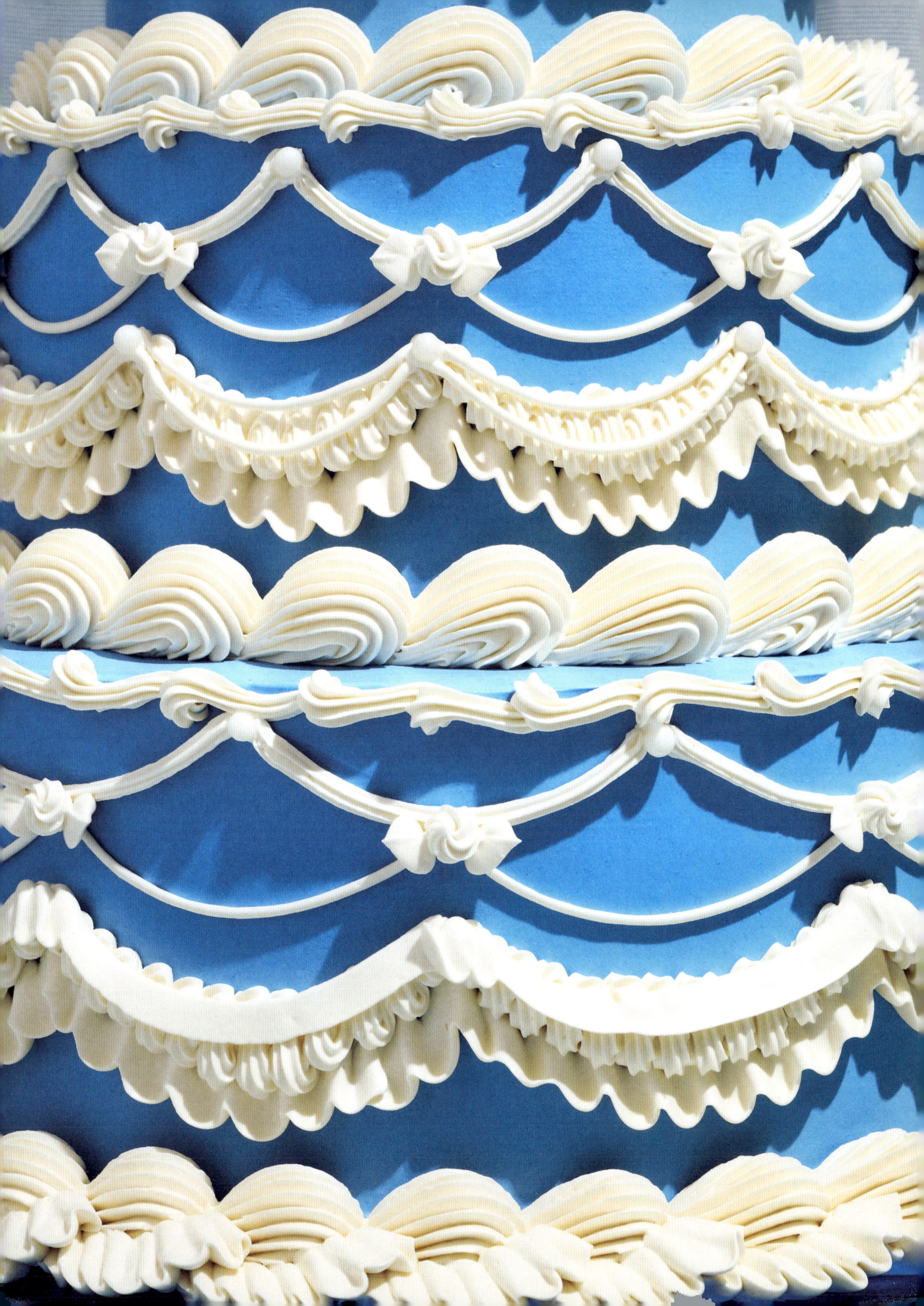

PROJECT 13

Secret Garden

Two years ago, a client requested a cake inspired by the exuberant artwork of Ken Done, the iconic Australian artist and designer. I was captivated by his use of bold vibrant colours, often contrasted against a deep, rich blue. For this book, I decided to revisit that design – a double-tier square cake decorated in two shades of blue, with an abundance of small flowers cascading down the sides. To create a harmony with the warm tones of the flowers, a small amount of mustard food colouring is added to the blues. The drop flowers are made from royal icing and left to dry overnight. Don't be intimidated by the number of flowers – they're surprisingly quick and easy to make! Plus, any leftovers can be saved for your next project, as they are incredibly shelf-stable.

Project timeline

DAY 1
Prepare the fillings and bake the cake layers

DAY 2
Prepare the buttercream, assemble the cake and prepare the drop flowers; the drop flowers need at least 24 hours to dry, or longer in humid locations

DAY 3
Decorate the cake

You'll need

Project basics
Cake: 15 cm (6 in) three-layer square cake, plus a 25 cm (10 in) three-layer square cake, crumb coated and chilled
Cake board: 36 cm (14 in) square board at least 1 cm (½ in) thick, plus a 15 cm (6 in) square perforated board, and a temporary board larger than 15 cm (6 in)
Food colouring for buttercream: Cobalt blue, mustard
Food colouring for royal icing: Orange, red, neon brite pink, egg yellow – all gel type
Buttercream: 1500 g (53 oz) Italian meringue buttercream (pages 43–46), medium consistency, bubbles removed, plus 360 g (12.7 oz) Royal icing (page 168)

Frosting tools
Angled palette knife
Straight palette knife
Stainless steel cake scraper, at least 10 cm (4 in) tall
Bench scraper with plastic handle (for smoothing the top of the cake)
Heatproof container or jug, taller than the scraper and palette knives
Turntable and non-slip mat

Tier stacking tools
1 centre dowel, at least 23 cm (9 in) tall
3 supporting dowels, at least 12.5 cm (5 in) tall
Edible marker
Masking tape
Cutting pliers or dowel cutter

Decorating tools
8 piping nozzles:
  Standard drop flower 232, 129 and 30;
  Standard round 3, 2 and 5;
  Medium French star S/F9;
  Standard star 16
3 large piping bags
3 standard couplers
1 medium coupler
Wing caliper
Round cookie cutter, about 8 cm (3¼ in), for marking

MALI BAKES

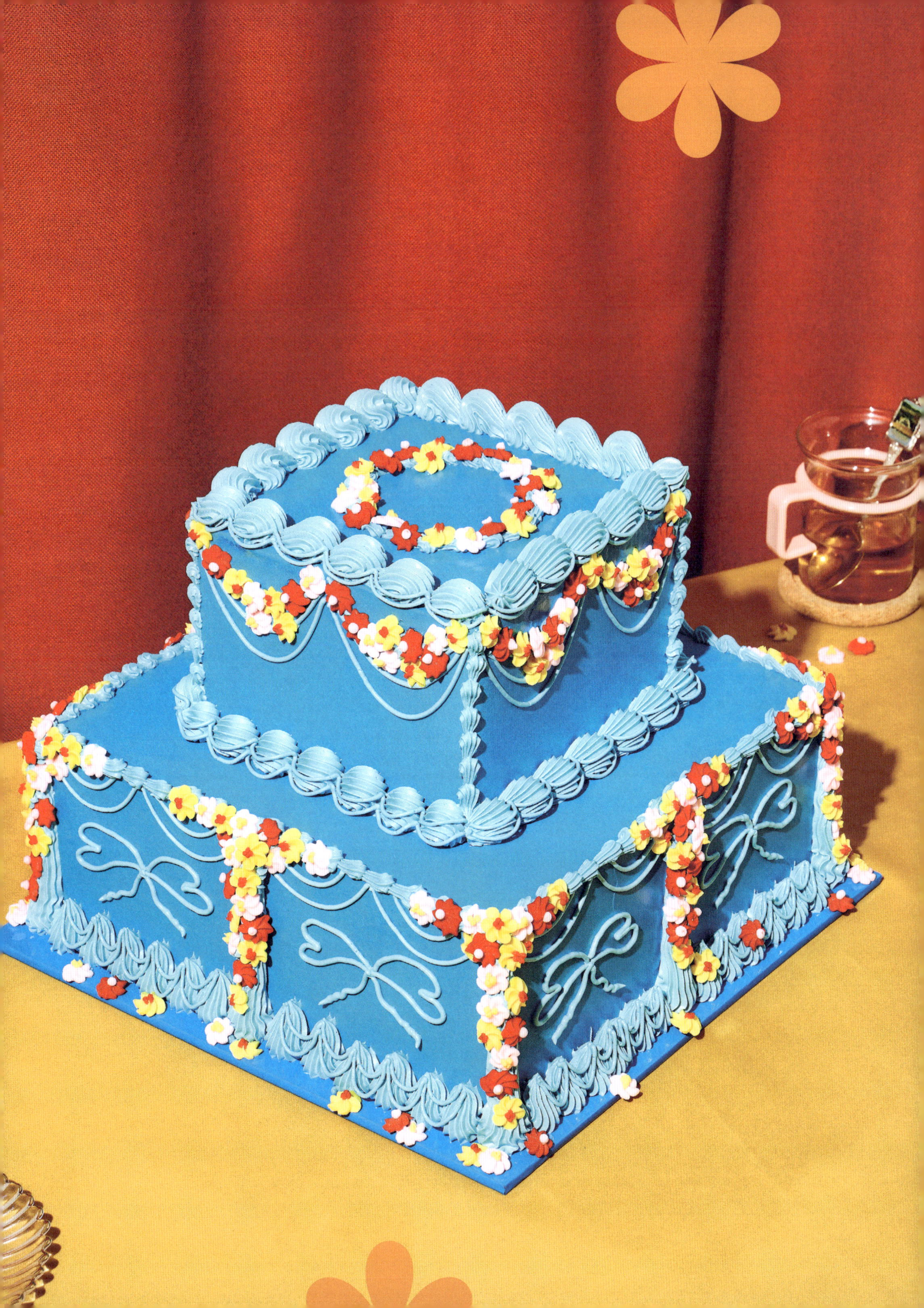

Piping Practice

1

2

3

1. **Drop flowers (page 170)**
   Nozzle (flowers): Standard drop flower 232 (pink), 129 (yellow) and 30 (burnt orange) · **Angle:** 90°
   Nozzle (centres): Standard round 3 (pink flowers), 2 (yellow flowers) and 5 (burnt orange flowers) · **Angle:** 90°

2. **Parallel strings (bottom tier)**
   Nozzle: Standard round 3 · **Angle:** 90°
   Pipe two rows of strings as you would a drop string (page 162), but ensure the two rows run parallel to each other.

3. **Triple strings (top tier)**
   Nozzle: Standard round 3 · **Angle:** 90°
   Pipe the top row of strings first, ensuring they run continuously around the cake. Within each section, pipe the bottom row of strings, and finish with the middle row. Do not run the lowest and middle rows continuously.

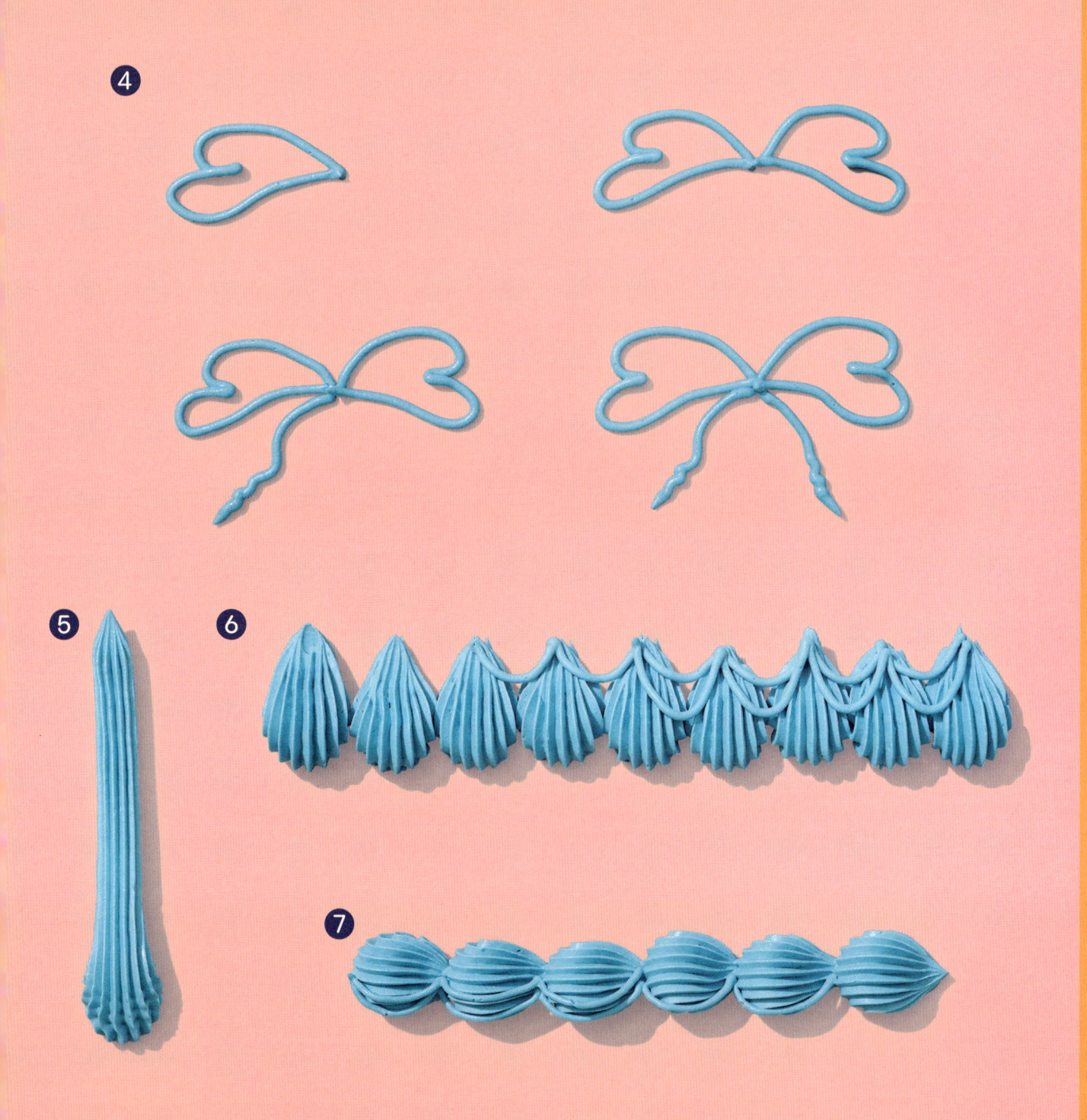

4. Bows (bottom tier)
Nozzle: Standard round 3 · **Angle:** 90°

Follow the method on page 270, but elongate the heart shapes so they are more exaggerated.

5. Vertical pillar (bottom tier)
Nozzle: Medium French star S/F9 · **Angle:** 45°

Start from the bottom as if you are piping a single shell (page 161), then continue piping as if piping a straight line (page 160).

6. Upward shells with strings (bottom tier)
Nozzle: Standard round 3 · **Angle:** 90°

Pipe upward shells, then finish the top edge with a row of double strings.

7. Continuous shells with double scallop trim (top tier)
Nozzle (shells): Medium French star S/F9 · **Angle:** 45°
Nozzle (scallop trim): Standard round 2 · **Angle:** 90°

See instructions on page 206, but add a second scallop trim halfway up the shells.

For the drop flowers

Tint the royal icing. It's important to use only gel food colouring here, as oil-based options can cause the icing to separate, making it difficult for the flowers to dry properly. Divide the royal icing into three equal portions for the drop flowers. For the first batch, mix orange and red food colouring to achieve a vibrant burnt orange shade. For the second, use neon brite pink food colouring to create a soft pink tone. Finally, tint the third batch with egg yellow food colouring to achieve a gentle yellow hue.

Pipe the flowers. Prepare three trays, each measuring at least 20 × 30 cm (8 × 12 in). Thoroughly grease the trays with cooking oil spray and line them with baking paper, making sure the paper is securely adhered so it doesn't lift during piping. (Alternatively, a silicone baking mat can be used if you have one.)

For more guidance on piping drop flowers, see page 170. Fit the first piping bag with a standard coupler and a drop flower 232 nozzle, fill halfway with pink royal icing and pipe about 120 pink flowers. Fit a second piping bag with another standard coupler and a drop flower 129 nozzle, fill halfway with yellow icing and pipe another 120 yellow flowers (image 1). Fit a third piping bag with another standard coupler and a drop flower 30 nozzle, fill halfway with burnt orange royal icing and pipe a final 120 orange flowers. It's always a good idea to make a few extra flowers just in case of any mishaps. Any leftovers can be stored and used for other cakes for up to 3 months.

Finish the flower centres and let dry. To finish the pink flowers, switch the nozzle on the piping bag filled with yellow icing to a round 3 nozzle and pipe three small dots in the centre of each flower. For the yellow flowers, attach a round 2 nozzle to the piping bag filled with burnt orange icing and pipe four small dots on each flower (image 2). For the orange flowers, use a round 5 nozzle with pink icing to pipe one dot in the centre of each flower.

Once all the flowers are completed, leave them to air dry completely at room temperature, uncovered, for at least 24 hours. Keep them away from direct sunlight to prevent colour fading, and do not refrigerate. In humid or colder environments, drying may take longer.

For the cake

Set up. Make sure you have followed the set-up checklist on page 191 before starting.

Both layer cakes should already be assembled, crumb coated and chilled separately in the fridge: the larger cake on the 36 cm (14 in) square cake board, and the smaller cake on the perforated board, with the temporary board underneath.

Tint the buttercream. Prepare the buttercream in two shades for decorating. For frosting, tint 800 g (28.22 oz) of buttercream with cobalt blue food colouring and a touch of mustard to create a deep blue shade. Tint the remaining buttercream a lighter variation of the same colour for piping.

Frost the cakes separately. Adjust the deep blue frosting buttercream to a thin but spreadable consistency (page 40). Follow the instructions on pages 43–46 to frost the cakes until a neat smooth base is achieved, working with one cake at a time. Allow the frosted cakes to chill in the fridge for at least 15 minutes until the frosting on both cakes is fully set.

Mark the top tier's side border. Working on one cake at a time, start by dividing the cake's top edge into two equal sections on each side. Set a wing caliper to 7.5 cm (3 in) and use it to gently make small marks about 5 mm (¼ in) below the cake's top edge. Once complete, return the cake to the fridge to firm up the frosting while you move on to the bottom tier.

Mark the bottom tier's side borders. Reset the wing caliper to 6.5 cm (2.5 in) and divide the cake's top edge into four equal sections on each side. Next, use a warm, dry scraper to create a straight line down the cake from the centre mark on each side to outline the pillars.

Stack the tiers and mark the cake's top surface. Carefully stack the tiers, following the instructions on pages 175–177. Then use the cookie cutter to gently mark a circle on top of the cake, right in the centre.

Pipe the bottom tier's top border. Fit a clean piping bag with a standard coupler and a round 3 nozzle, then fill halfway with the pale blue buttercream. Pipe two parallel strings from one marked point to the next around the cake (image 3). Allow the first string to drop about 1.5 cm (½ in) and the bottom string to drop about 2.5 cm (1 in).

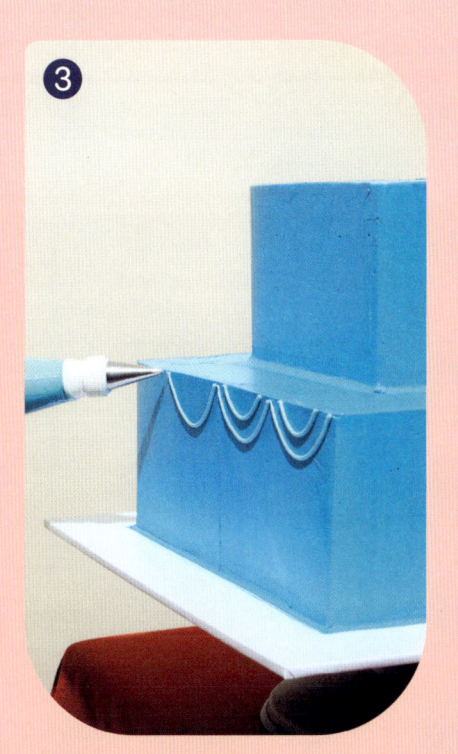

Project continues

DECORATING PROJECTS

PROJECT 13 SECRET GARDEN

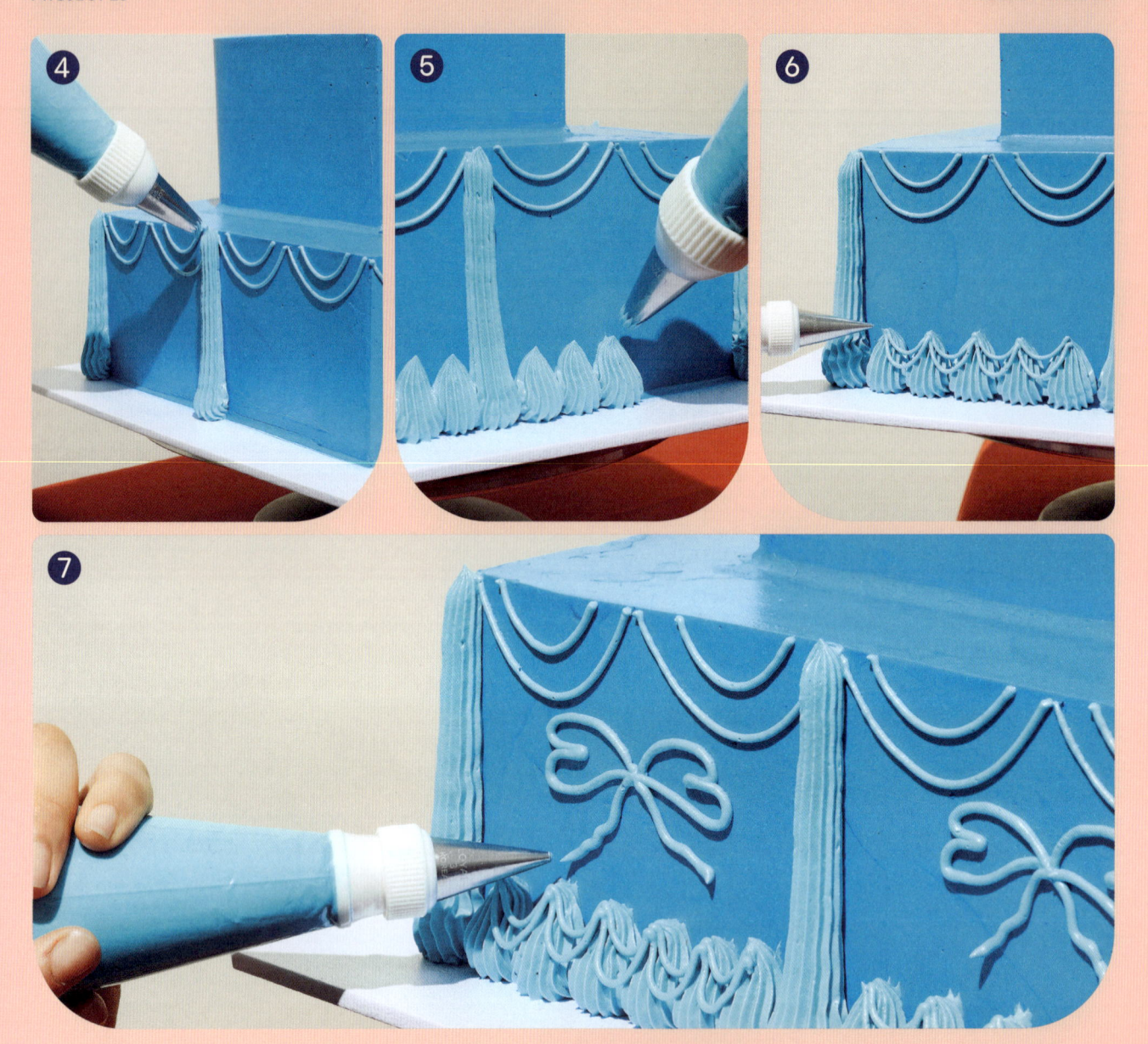

Pipe the bottom tier's bottom border. Fit another clean piping bag with the medium coupler and a French star S/F9 nozzle, then fill halfway with more pale blue buttercream. Starting from the bottom, pipe a vertical column straight up along each corner of the cake to the top edge, then along each vertical mark line in the middle of each side (image 4). Next, pipe upward shells to fill the gaps along the bottom edge (image 5).

To finish the border, use the piping bag with the standard coupler, switch to a round 2 nozzle, and pipe a double drop string connecting the pointed tips of each upward shell along the bottom edge (image 6).

Pipe the bows on the bottom tier. Take the piping bag with the standard coupler and switch back to the round 3 nozzle. Pipe a bow in the centre of each window on the side of the cake (image 7).

Pipe the top tier's side border. Still using the round 3 nozzle, pipe a triple drop string from one marked point to the next around the cake (image 8). Let the first string drop about 2.5 cm (1 in), and the bottom string about 5.5 cm (2¼ in). Next, switch to a star 16 nozzle and pipe continuous shells in a vertical line along each side edge, working your way from the top to the bottom corner of the cake (image 9).

Pipe the top tier's top and bottom borders. Using the piping bag fitted with the star S/F9 nozzle, pipe continuous shells along the bottom and top edges of the top tier, completing one side at a time. Once the shells are in place, switch the nozzle on the piping bag with a standard coupler to the round 2 nozzle. Pipe double scalloped trims just on both borders (image 10).

Finish the top surface. Using the piping bag with the standard coupler, switch to the star 16 nozzle. Pipe continuous shells along the circle outline on top of the cake to complete the design (image 11).

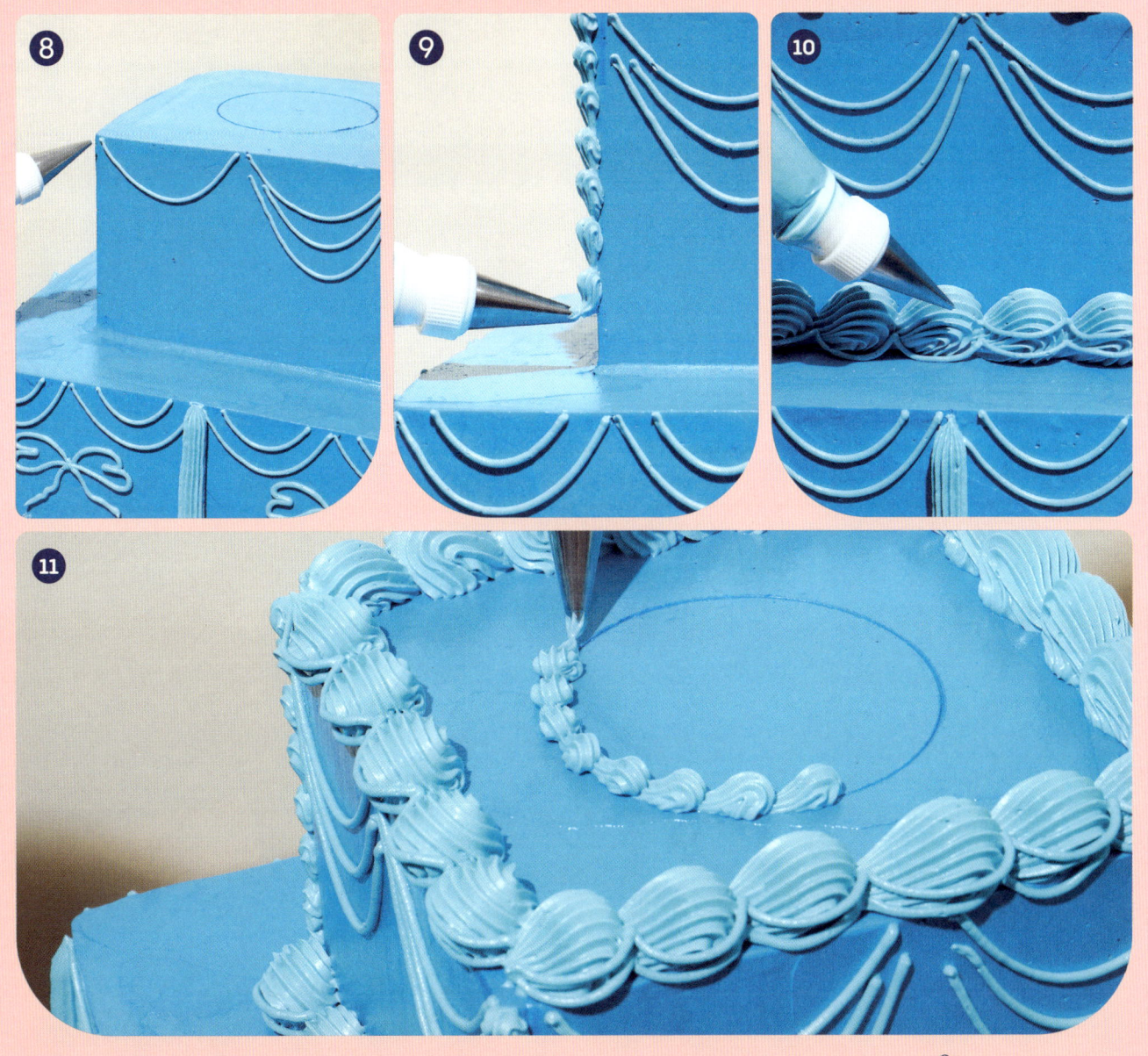

Project continues

DECORATING PROJECTS

295

PROJECT 13   SECRET GARDEN

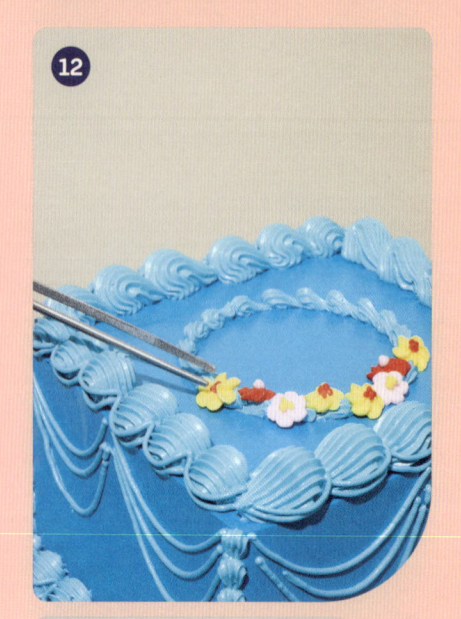

Add the drop flowers. Work while the buttercream is still soft to ensure the flowers stick easily to the cake. Begin with the top tier, arranging the flowers neatly on the shell circle on top of the cake (image 12). To create a floral garland along the upper drop string, place two flowers directly beneath each upper string, centring them carefully (image 13), then add more flowers along the string line to form the garlands.

For the bottom tier, arrange the flowers along the vertical columns, allowing them to extend slightly over the top edge to create a cascading effect. Work from the bottom of the cake upwards and from the outside inwards, so the flowers overlap naturally. If there are areas where the flowers don't sit properly, use a small blob of buttercream piped with a round 3 nozzle to secure them (image 14).

For a final touch, place extra flowers randomly on the cake board, securing them in place with small blobs of buttercream.

Chill the cake. Pop your beautifully decorated cake in the fridge for at least 2 hours before party time. This will help set the decorations in place, keeping everything secure so your cake looks picture-perfect when it's ready to shine!

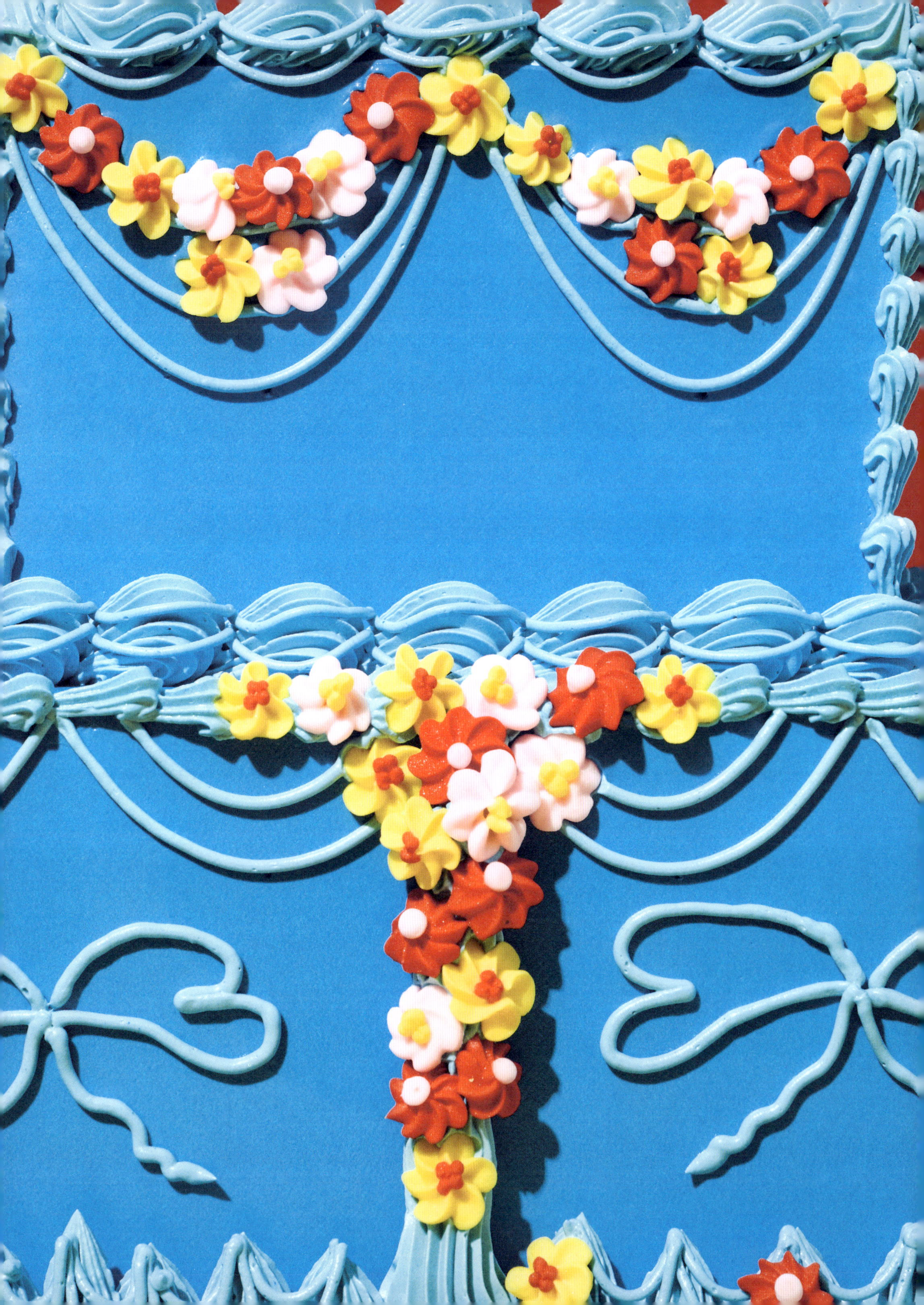

PROJECT 14

Lovers Lace

Designing a tiered cake is all about exploring and experimenting with ideas – combining shapes, textures and themes to create a unique and cohesive design. In this cake, a wide, round base is paired with a heart-shaped top tier, creating the perfect opportunity to highlight the cake's theme. Lattice heart motifs tie the design together, introducing a delicate, fabric-like texture that contrasts beautifully with the smooth finish of the frosting. As the latticework requires a practised and steady hand, this beautiful cake is the perfect project for you to utilise all the skills you've learned from this book.

Project timeline

○ **DAY 1**
Prepare the fillings and bake the cake layers

○ **DAY 2**
Prepare the buttercream and assemble the cake

○ **DAY 3**
Decorate the cake

You'll need

Project basics
Cake: 20 cm (8 in) three-layer heart-shaped cake, plus a 30 cm (12 in) three-layer round cake, crumb coated and chilled
Cake board: 41 cm (16 in) round board at least 1 cm (½ in) thick, plus a 20 cm (8 in) heart-shaped perforated board, and a temporary board larger than 20 cm (8 in)
Food colouring: Red, yellow
Buttercream: 1800 g (63.5 oz) Italian meringue buttercream (pages 43–46), medium consistency, bubbles removed, plus 100 g (3.5 oz) Stabilised buttercream (page 167)

Frosting tools
Angled palette knife
Straight palette knife
Stainless steel cake scraper, at least 10 cm (4 in) tall
Bench scraper with plastic handle (for smoothing the top of the cake)
Heatproof container or jug, taller than the scraper and palette knives
Turntable and non-slip mat

Tier stacking tools
1 centre dowel, at least 23 cm (9 in) tall
3 supporting dowels, at least 12.5 cm (5 in) tall
Edible marker
Masking tape
Cutting pliers or dowel cutter

Decorating tools
8 piping nozzles:
  Standard petal 103 and 101;
  Standard round 2;
  Standard star 16;
  Standard round 3;
  Standard petal 104W;
  Standard leaf 75;
  Medium open star 1M
5 large piping bags
4 standard couplers
1 medium coupler
Wing caliper
Small pointed palette knife for marking
1 medium flower nail, number 13
2 heart-shaped cookie cutters, about 5 cm (2 in) and 11.5 cm (4½ in) for marking

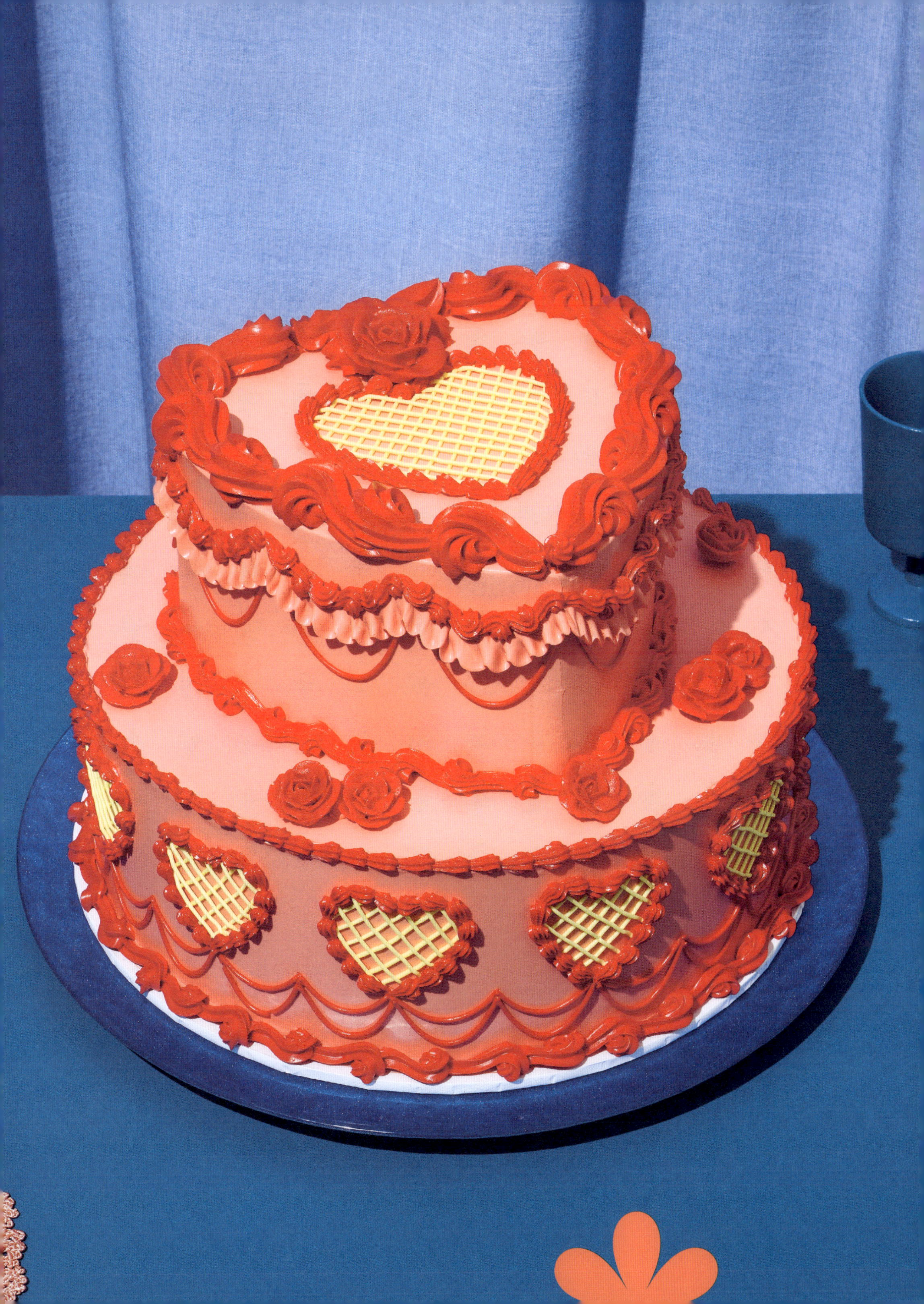

Piping Practice

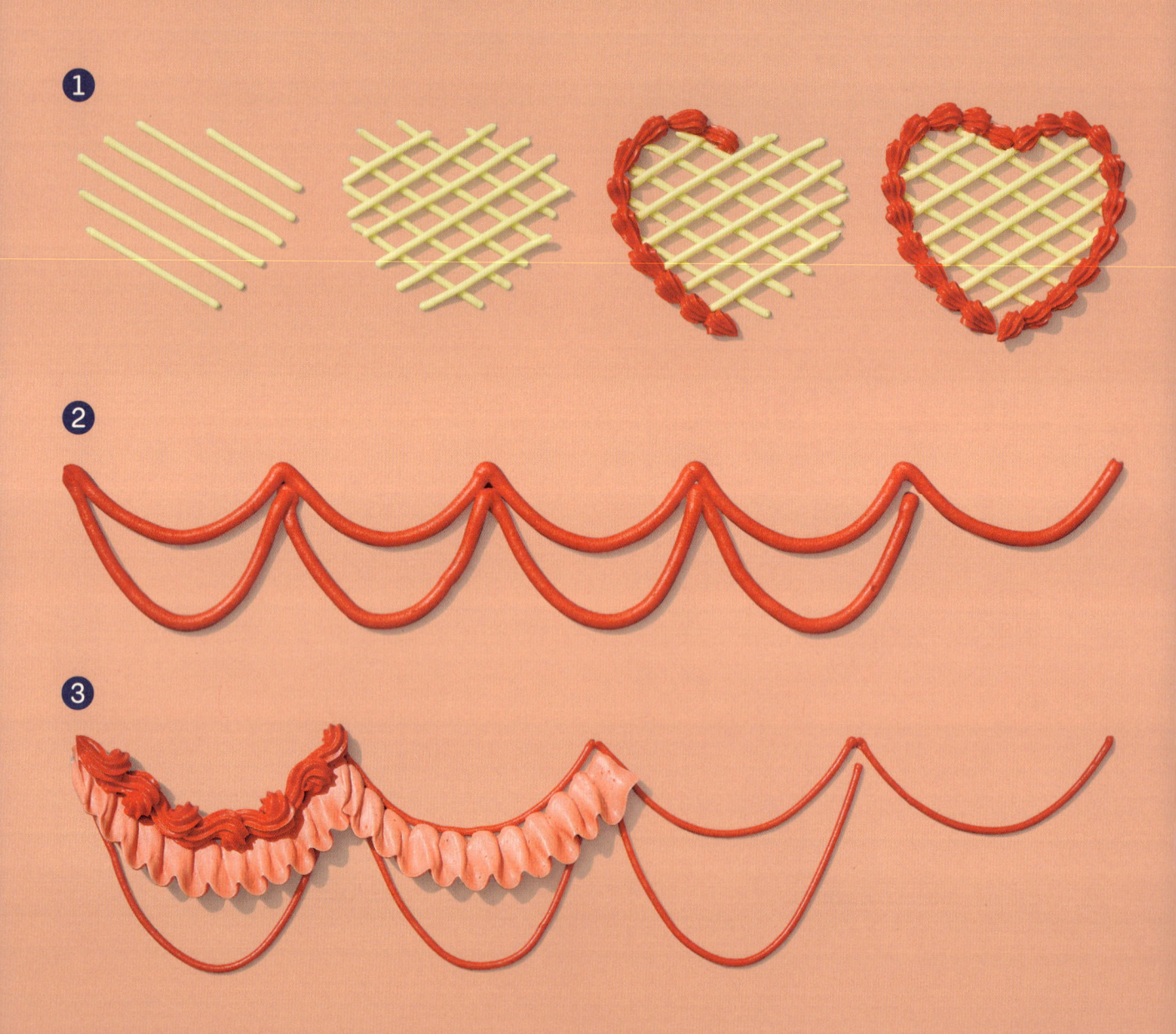

1

2

3

1. **Lattice heart (bottom tier)**

   Nozzle (straight lines): Standard round 2 · **Angle:** 30°

   Nozzle (shells): Standard star 16 · **Angle:** 45°

   See project method, pipe straight diagonal lines (page 160), and finish with a border of continuous shells (page 161).

2. **Double strings (bottom tier; page 162)**

   Nozzle: Standard round 3 · **Angle:** 90°

3. **Reverse shell garland with fluted ruffle & string (top tier)**

   Nozzle (drop strings): Standard round 3 · **Angle:** 90°

   Nozzle (fluted ruffle): Standard petal 104W · **Angle:** 45°

   Nozzle (reverse shells): Standard star 16 · **Angle:** 45°

   Start with the double drop strings, then pipe the fluted ruffle (page 164) over the top row of strings. Finish with a row of reverse shells (page 162) over the top edge of the ruffle.

4. Continuous small shells
Nozzle: Standard star 16 · **Angle:** 45°

5. Reverse small shells
Nozzle: Standard leaf 75 · **Angle:** 45°

6. Reverse large shells
Nozzle: Medium open star 1M · **Angle:** 45°

PROJECT 14　　　　　　　　　　　　　　　　　　　　　　　　　　　　　　　LOVERS LACE

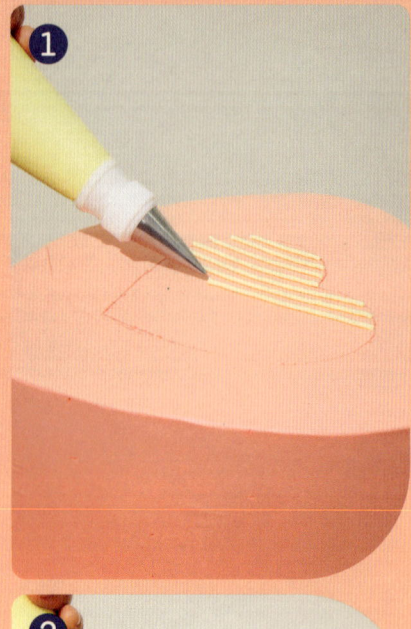

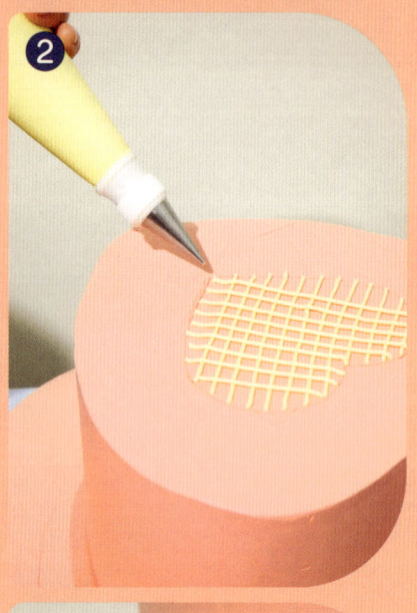

Set up

Make sure you have followed the set-up checklist on page 191 before starting.

Both layer cakes should already be assembled, crumb coated and chilled separately in the fridge: the large round cake on a 41 cm (16 in) cake board, and the heart-shaped cake on the heart-shaped perforated board, with the temporary board underneath.

Let's begin!

Tint the buttercream. Prepare the buttercream in three shades for decorating. For frosting and ruffles, tint 1000 g (35.25 oz) of the buttercream with red food colouring and a touch of yellow to create a medium peachy-pink shade. Next, tint 700 g (24.7 oz) buttercream with red food colouring to create a deep bold red shade. Tint the remaining buttercream with just a touch of yellow food colouring to create a soft yellow shade.

Prepare the buttercream roses. Tint the stabilised buttercream with red food colouring to a bold red shade. Ensure the buttercream has a stiff consistency for the roses to hold their shape, adjusting if needed.

Cut out at least ten 8 cm (3¼ in) squares of baking paper as bases. Fit the first piping bag with a standard coupler and a 103 petal nozzle. Fill the piping bag halfway with the red stabilised buttercream. Dab some of the buttercream onto a flower nail, press a baking paper square onto it and pipe one large rose onto the paper, following the instructions on page 171. Place the paper square on a tray, with the rose still on it. Switch to a 101 petal nozzle and pipe nine smaller roses using the same technique, transferring each rose with its baking paper to the tray. (It's always a good idea to pipe a few extra roses as spares.) Freeze until ready to use, so the roses remain firm and easy to handle; they will keep in the freezer for up to 3 months.

Frost the cakes separately. Adjust 900 g (31.75 oz) of the peach buttercream to a thin but spreadable consistency (page 40). Follow the instructions on page 51–54 to frost both cakes until a neat smooth base is achieved, working with one cake at a time. Allow the frosted cakes to chill in the fridge for at least 15 minutes until the frosting on both cakes is fully set.

Mark the top tier's side border. Mark each side of the heart-shaped cake into five sections using a wing caliper set to 6.5 cm (2½ in). Gently mark along the top edge of the cake, starting at the pointed front, and working towards the curved back on each side. Any slight size differences in the back sections will not be noticeable. Adjust the caliper to 2 cm (¾ in) and measure directly below each marked spot to indicate the starting points for each ruffle garland. Return the cake to the fridge while you move on to the bottom tier.

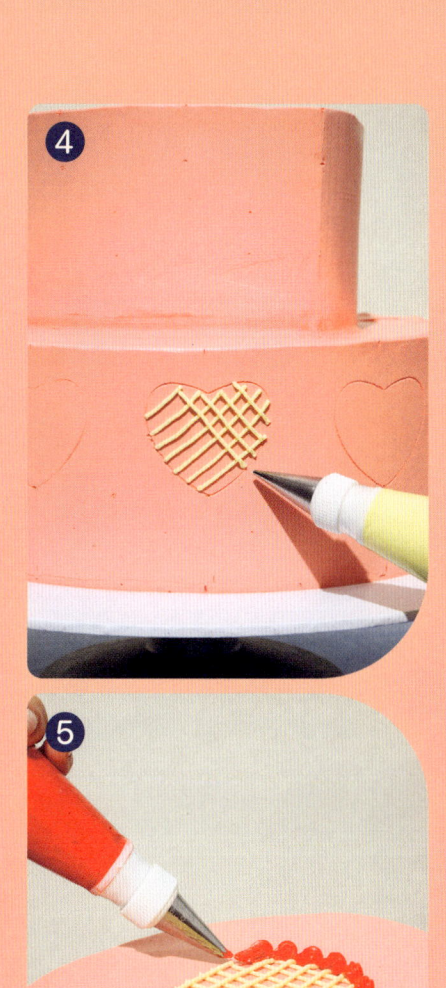

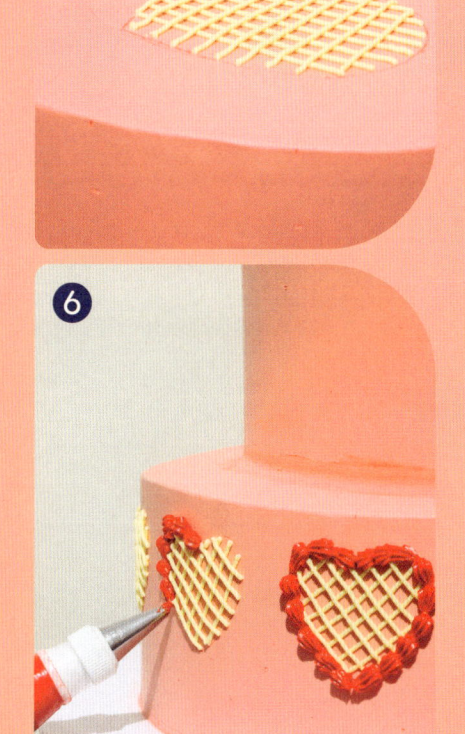

Mark the bottom tier's side border into 12 sections. Cut a piece of round baking paper to match the size of the bottom tier cake by tracing around a 30 cm (12 in) cake tin. Follow the instructions on page 172 to create a template for marking 12 sections from the baking paper.

Gently place the paper on top of the cold frosted cake, aligning the edges. Use a pointed palette knife to gently make small marks along the cake's bottom edge aligning where the folded lines meet the cake's top edge. Gently remove the baking paper. You'll now have 12 even sections marked along the bottom edge of the cake.

Next, set a wing caliper to 4 cm (1½ in) and use it to make marks straight up the side of the cake from each base mark. These marks will serve as the starting points for each lattice heart. Then take the small heart-shaped cookie cutter and lightly press it onto the surface to create the outline of the hearts, making sure to position the pointed bottom of the cutter on each marked point.

Once all 12 hearts are outlined, go back to the bottom edge and mark the centre of the spaces between each heart, dividing the cake further into 24 equal sections. Finally, to mark the starting points for the double drop strings, use the caliper still set to 4 cm (1½ in) and make marks directly up the side of the cake from each of these midpoint marks.

You will now have 12 heart outlines evenly spaced around the cake, with 24 evenly spaced points below them.

Stack the tiers and mark the top of the cake. Following the instructions on pages 175–177, carefully stack the tiers. Align the pointed front of the top tier with the centre of one of the heart outlines on the bottom tier to establish the front of the cake.

For the cake's top surface, gently press the larger heart-shaped cookie cutter into the centre of the top tier to create another heart outline.

Pipe the heart lattices. Fit a second piping bag with another standard coupler and a round 2 nozzle, and fill it halfway with yellow buttercream. Starting on the top of the cake, pipe evenly spaced diagonal lines, about 5 mm (¼ in) apart, across the inside of the heart outline. Then pipe a second set of diagonal lines in the opposite direction to form a neat crisscross lattice pattern (images 1 & 2). Repeat for all the hearts on the side of the bottom tier (images 3 & 4).

Fit a third piping bag with another standard coupler and a star 16 nozzle, filling it halfway with red buttercream. Pipe continuous small shells around each heart, starting at the top centre and working down each side to the pointed bottom (images 5 & 6).

Project continues

DECORATING PROJECTS

PROJECT 14 · LOVERS LACE

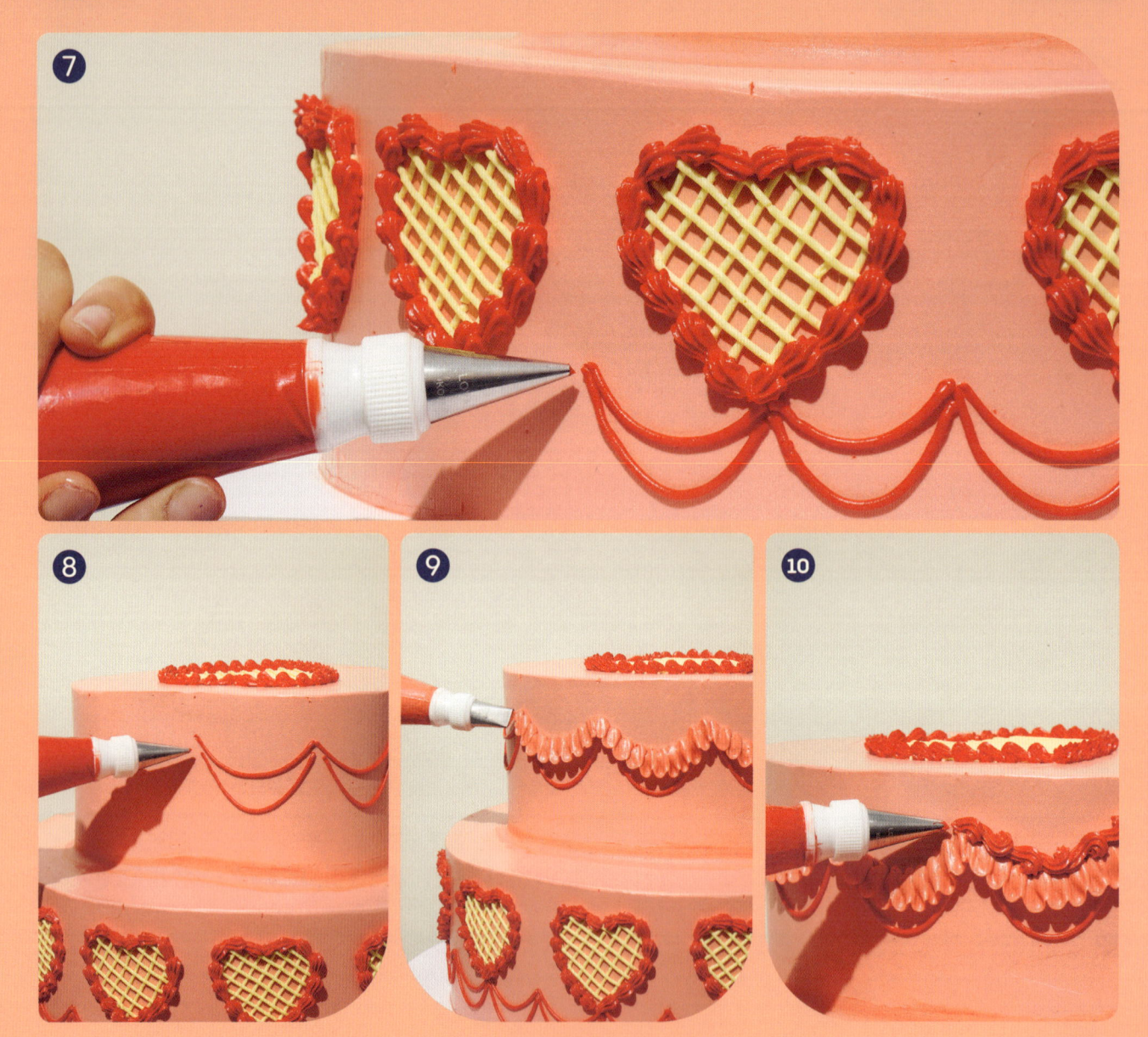

Pipe the bottom tier's double string. Switch the nozzle on the piping bag with red buttercream to a round 3 nozzle. Pipe a double drop string between each marked line, letting the upper string drop about 1 cm (½ in) and the lower string about 2 cm (¾ in) (image 7).

Pipe the top tier's side border. Using the round 3 nozzle and red buttercream, pipe a double drop string connecting each marked point to the next (image 8). Allow the upper string to drop about 2 cm (¾ in) and the lower string about 5 cm (2 in) below the marked level.

Next, fit a new piping bag with another standard coupler and a petal 104W nozzle, filling it halfway with peach buttercream. Pipe a fluted ruffle directly along the upper drop string (image 9). Then, take the piping bag with red buttercream and switch to the star 16 nozzle and pipe reverse shells along the top edge of the fluted ruffles, overlapping the ruffles nicely (image 10).

Pipe the bottom borders. Using the same piping bag filled with red buttercream, switch to a leaf 75 nozzle and pipe reverse shells along the bottom edge of both the bottom and top tiers (images 11 & 12).

Pipe the bottom tier's top edge. Using the same piping bag filled with red buttercream, switch back to the star 16 nozzle and pipe a continuous shell border along the top edge of the bottom cake (image 13).

Pipe the top tier's top edge. Fit the final piping bag with a medium coupler and an open star 1M nozzle, then fill halfway with red buttercream. Pipe reverse shells along the top edge of the cake, starting at the centre of the back curve and working your way towards the pointed front of the heart on each side, ensuring the shells meet neatly at the front (image 14).

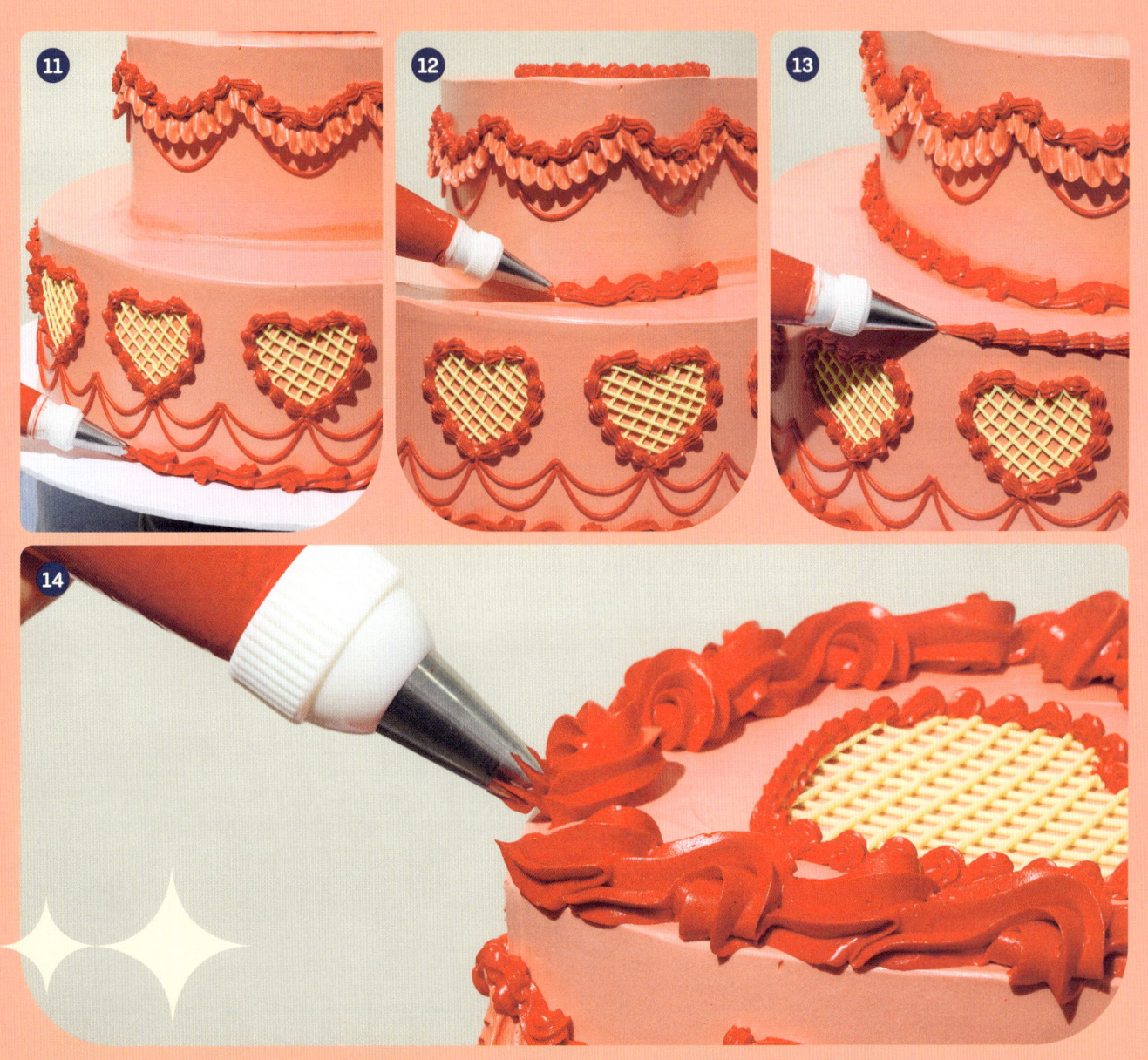

Project continues

DECORATING PROJECTS

305

PROJECT 14 LOVERS LACE

Add the roses. Remove the buttercream roses from the freezer. Switch the piping bag with red buttercream and a standard coupler to a round 3 nozzle. Pipe a small dot of buttercream at the centre of the heart's curve on the top tier to secure the largest rose. Position the rose slightly closer to the centre of the heart to accentuate its shape (image 15).

Randomly arrange the smaller roses on top of the bottom cake (image 16), also adding small buttercream dots beneath each rose with the round 3 nozzle to keep them securely in place. If necessary, return the flowers to the freezer to keep them firm and prevent any damage during placement.

Chill the cake. Pop your beautifully decorated cake in the fridge for at least 2 hours before party time. This will help set the decorations in place, keeping everything secure so your cake looks picture-perfect when it's ready to shine!

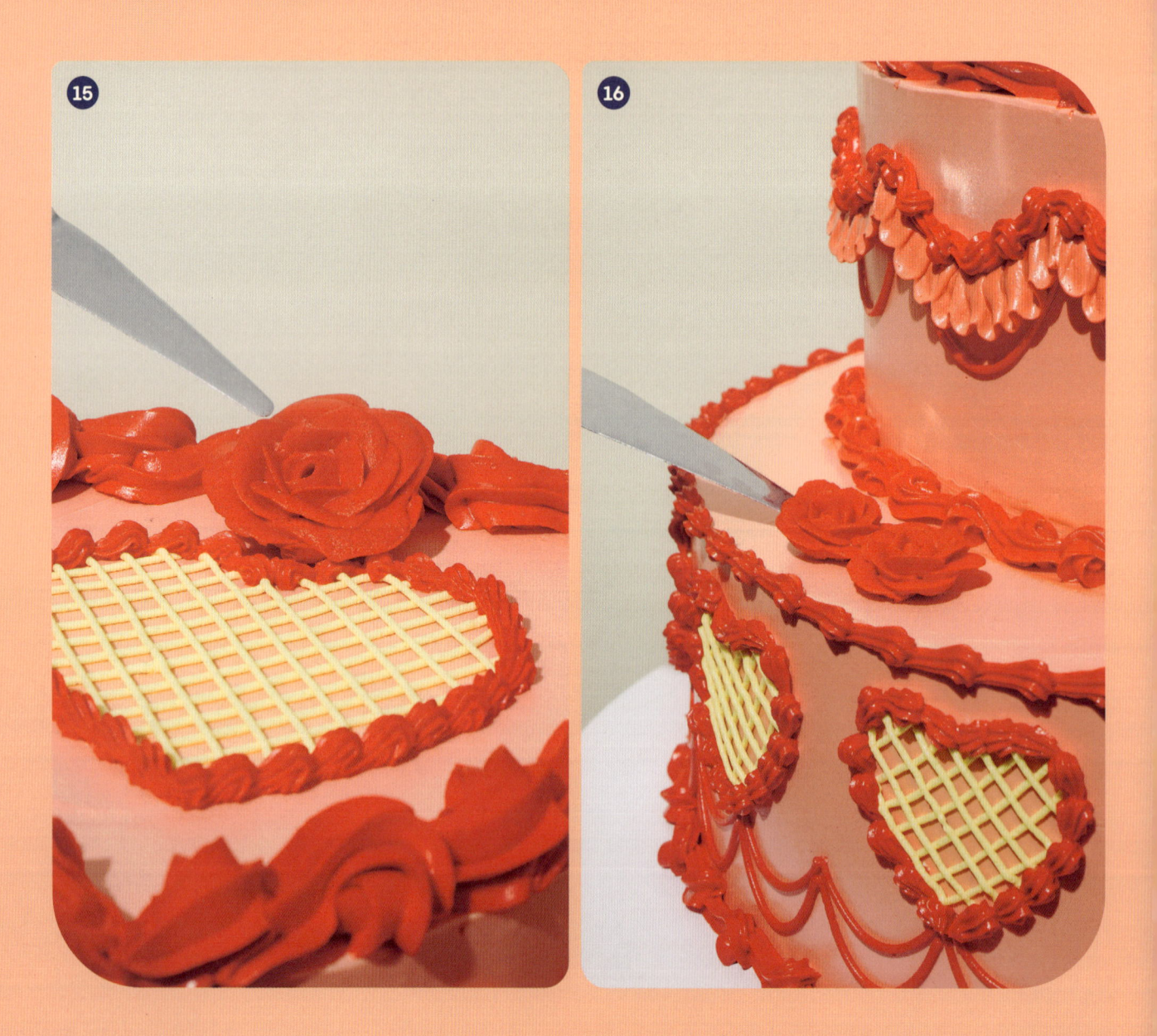

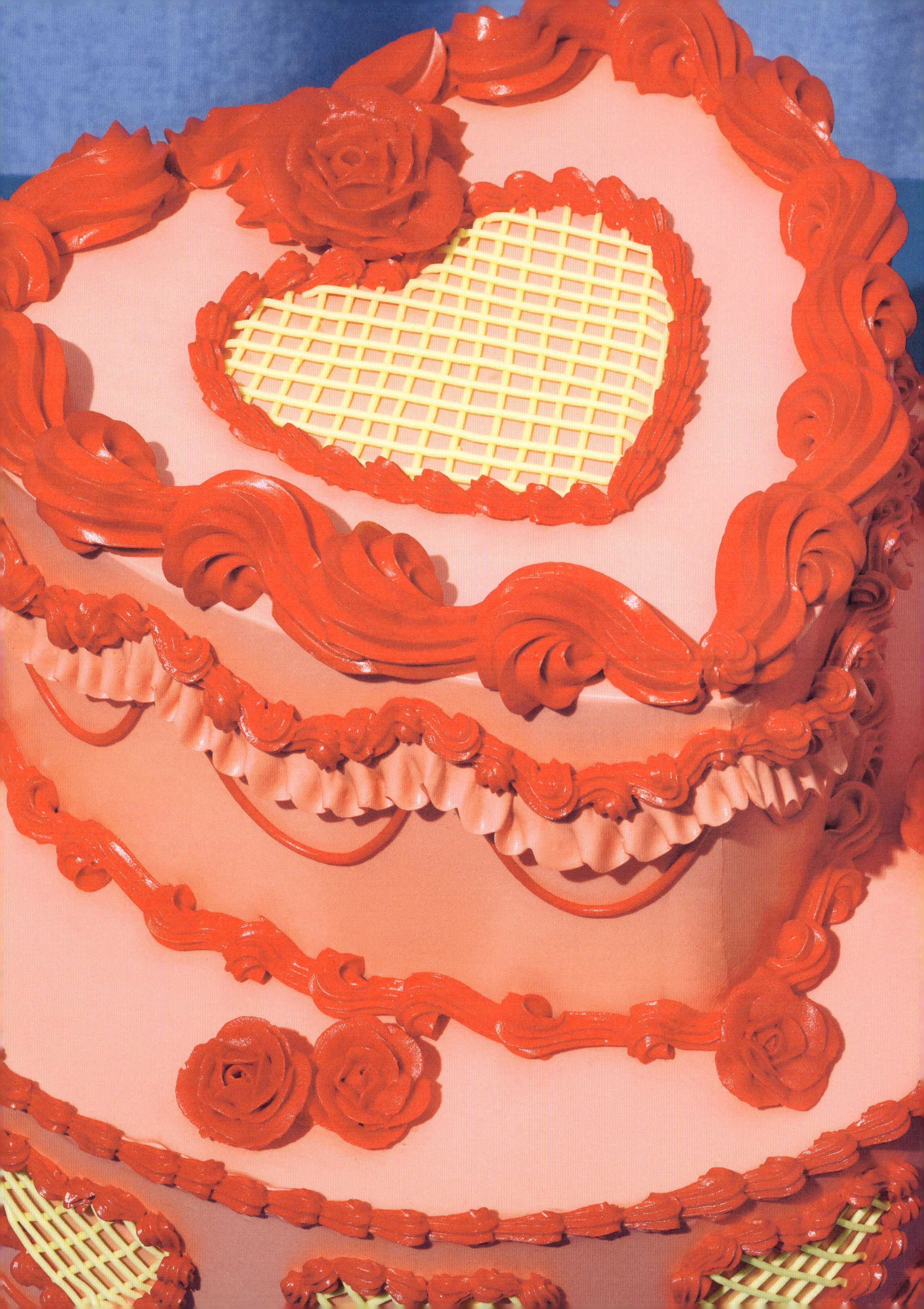

PROJECT 15

Heart of Glass

One of the things I love most about working with wedding couples at Mali Bakes is how they let their personalities shine through in their cake designs. Many choose to break away from traditional white and embrace colourful, playful creations instead.

This retro-inspired cake is a perfect example. It's decorated primarily in chartreuse – a delightful shade that dances between green and yellow. While the borders are fairly simple, the glass-like surface and vibrantly coloured heart candies add a playful and eye-catching touch. The royal icing topper pieces, though requiring finesse and ample drying time, are well worth the effort – just be sure to prepare them in advance for the perfect finishing touch!

Project timeline

- **DAY 1**
  Prepare the heart topper frames; these need at least 72 hours to dry, or longer in humid locations
- **DAY 2**
  Prepare the fillings and bake the cake layers
- **DAY 3**
  Prepare the buttercream and assemble the cake
- **DAY 4**
  Decorate the cake, prepare the heart candies and finish the topper; the topper can be added at the party

You'll need

Project basics
Cake: 15 cm (6 in) three-layer round cake, plus a 25 cm (10 in) three-layer square cake, crumb coated and chilled
Cake board: 36 cm (14 in) square board, plus a 20 cm (8 in) round board – both at least 5 mm (¼ in) thick
Food colouring: Egg yellow, neon brite green, Dijon, neon brite pink (must be gel food colouring)
Buttercream: 1400 g (49.38 oz) Italian meringue buttercream (pages 43–46), medium consistency, bubbles removed, plus 300 g (10.58 oz) Royal icing (page 168)

Heart candies
300 g (10.58 oz) isomalt crystals
50 g (1.75 oz) glucose syrup

Frosting tools
Angled palette knife
Straight palette knife
Stainless steel cake scraper, at least 10 cm (4 in) tall
Bench scraper with plastic handle (for smoothing the top of the cake)
Heatproof container or jug, taller than the scraper and palette knives
Turntable and non-slip mat

Elevated tier tools
1 cake separator set with a 15 cm (6 in) separator plate and 3 plastic dowels that can click into the plate's feet
3 cake pillars, 11.5 cm (4½ in) tall
3 supporting dowels, at least 23 cm (9 in) tall
Cutting pliers or dowel cutter
Double-sided tape

Decorating tools
7 piping nozzles:
  Standard round 3, 5 and 10;
  Standard petal 104W;
  Medium petal 124K;
  Standard star 16 and 32
4 large piping bags
3 standard couplers
1 medium coupler
Small pointed palette knife for marking
Wing caliper
1 transparent silicone baking mat, for tracing
Heart-shaped candy mould with multiple cavities, to make 30 small heart candies (the candy mould I use has 21 cavities)
Heatproof rubber spatula
2 small skewers to secure the topper
1 round cookie cutter, about 4.8 cm (1⅞ in), for marking

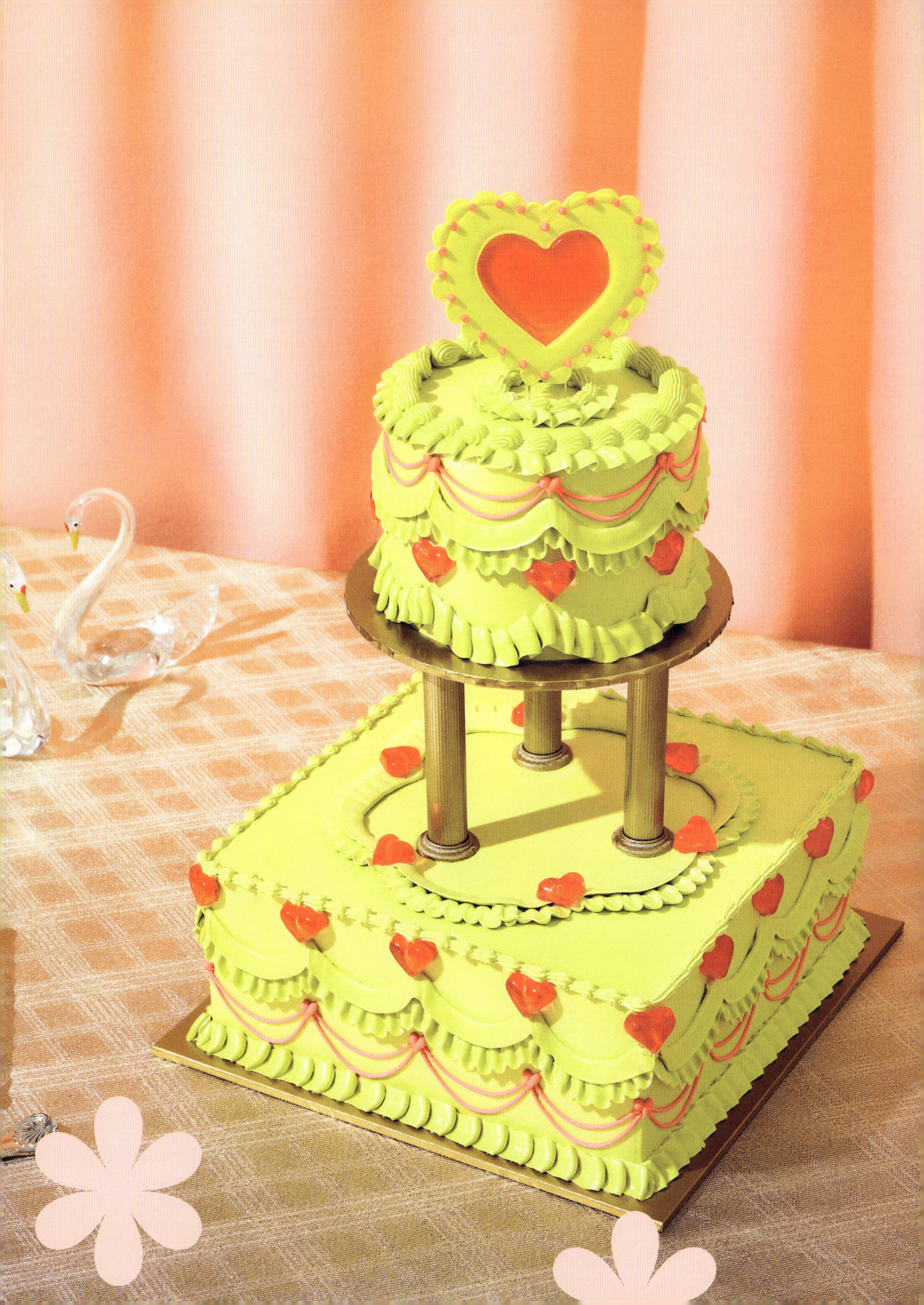

Piping Practice

1

2

3

4

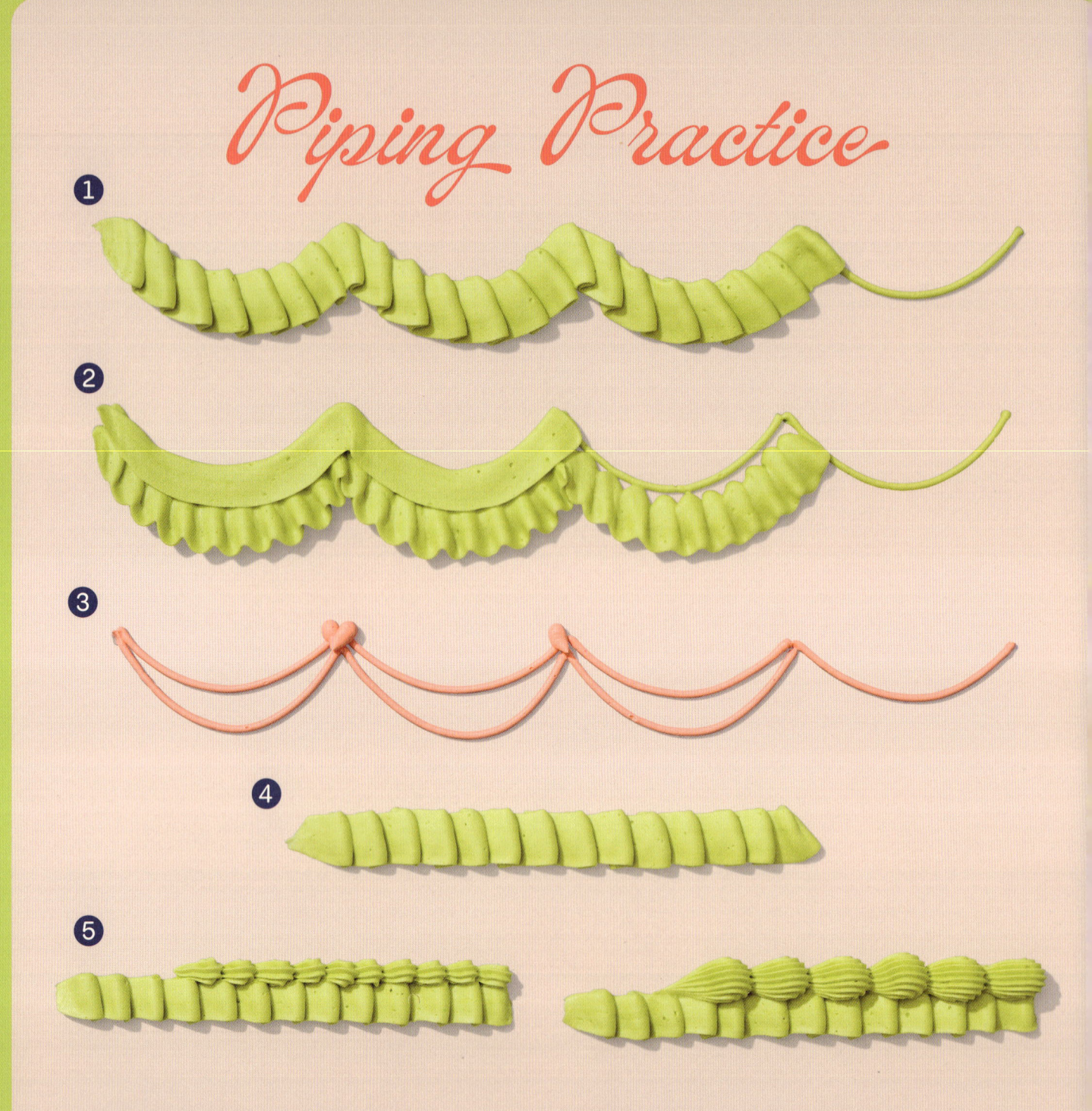

5

1. **Folded ruffle garland**
   Nozzle (drop string): Standard round 3 · **Angle:** 90°
   Nozzle (folded ruffle garland): Medium petal 124K · **Angle:** 45°
   Pipe a drop string (page 162) as an outline, then pipe the folded ruffle garland (page 165) on top to cover.

2. **Fluted ruffle and ribbon garland**
   Nozzle (drop string): Standard round 3 · **Angle:** 90°
   Nozzle (fluted ruffle garland & ribbon): Standard petal 104W · **Angle:** 45°
   Start by piping a drop string as an outline. Then pipe the fluted ruffle garland to cover the drop string. Finish by piping a ribbon (page 163) over the top edge of the ruffle.

3. **Double string with heart**
   Nozzle (double string): Standard round 3 · **Angle:** 90°
   Nozzle (heart): Standard round 5 · **Angle:** 90°
   Pipe double drop strings and finish by piping hearts at the points where the drop strings meet.

4. **Folded ruffle (page 164)**
   Nozzle: Medium petal 124K · **Angle:** 45°

5. **Folded ruffle and shells**
   Nozzle (folded ruffle): Standard petal 104W · **Angle:** 45°
   Nozzle (shells): Standard star 16 & Standard star 32 **Angle:** 45°
   Pipe a folded ruffle in a straight line, and finish by piping a row of continuous shells (page 161) on the top edge of the ruffle.

PROJECT 15   HEART OF GLASS

For the topper pieces

Tint the royal icing. Tint 200 g (7 oz) of the royal icing with equal parts egg yellow, neon brite green and a touch of Dijon gel food colouring to create a medium chartreuse tone. It's important to use only gel food colouring here, as oil-based options can cause the icing to separate, making it difficult to dry properly. Ensure the icing is at a medium consistency, adjusting with water or icing (confectioners') sugar as needed. See page 168 for how to adjust the consistency of royal icing.

Reserve the remaining untinted royal icing to use on the day you decorate the cake. Store at room temperature in an airtight container. Place a wet paper towel or clean cloth directly on the surface to prevent it drying out.

Pipe the borders and let dry slightly. Scan and print the pattern from page 320, alternatively trace it with some paper and a marker. Line a tray with a transparent silicone mat, placing the pattern underneath and ensuring the pattern lines are clearly visible. Fit the first piping bag with a standard coupler and round 3 nozzle and fill halfway with the medium-consistency chartreuse royal icing.

For the front piece, start by tracing the two heart outlines and the scallop trim. For the back piece, simply trace the two heart outlines (image 1). Allow the borders to dry slightly for about 10 minutes, or until they are just firm to the touch, before moving on to the next step.

Fill in the outlines and let dry completely. Empty any remaining royal icing from the piping bag. Adjust the remaining chartreuse royal icing to a 'flooding' consistency by adding a few drops of water at a time. To check the consistency, lift the icing with a spatula and let it drip back into the bowl: the line should disappear and self-level within 8–10 seconds.

Once the royal icing is ready, refill the same piping bag with the round 3 nozzle still attached. Begin flooding the scallop trim areas on the front piece (image 2). Working on one section at a time, hold the nozzle lightly against the mat and gently squeeze to allow the royal icing to flow evenly and fill each section. If any air bubbles appear, pop them immediately with a small skewer before the surface sets, then move on to the next section.

Next, using the same piping bag with chartreuse royal icing, switch to a round 5 nozzle to flood the larger areas. For the front piece, fill only the outer heart section. For the back piece, fill both the outer and inner heart sections. To fill each area, start at one corner, applying gentle pressure to allow the icing to flow smoothly (image 3). Move steadily through the section, letting the icing spread evenly. Use a skewer to touch up any imperfections as needed.

When you're finished, leave the icing to air dry completely at room temperature, uncovered, for at least 72 hours. Keep it away from direct sunlight to prevent colour fading, and do not refrigerate. In humid or colder environments, drying may take longer. This topper can be made up to 2 weeks in advance and should be stored in a cool, dry place.

Project continues

DECORATING PROJECTS

PROJECT 15　　　　　　　　　　　　　　　　　　　　　　　　　　　　　　　　　　　HEART OF GLASS

To finish the topper and prepare the heart candies

Fill the isomalt glass heart on the front of the topper on the day you are decorating the cake, as isomalt can become cloudy and sticky if left out too long or made too far in advance.

Pipe small dots on the front topper. When the front topper piece is fully dried, tint the remaining untinted royal icing with small drops of equal parts neon brite pink, egg yellow and a touch of Dijon gel food colouring to achieve a medium peachy tone. Ensure the icing is of medium consistency.

Fit a clean piping bag with a clean standard coupler and a clean round 5 nozzle, the fill halfway with the peachy royal icing. Pipe small dot details along the scallop trim (images 4 & 5)

Allow the design to dry completely for at least 1 hour before moving on to the next step. Reserve the remaining peach royal icing for decorating the cake.

Prepare the heart candy mould and the front topper piece. Lightly grease each cavity of the candy mould with oil spray, then use your finger to smooth out any bubbles created by the oil spray in each cavity.

Ensure the front topper piece is completely dry on both sides. Place both the candy mould and front topper piece near the stove so the isomalt can be poured quickly, keeping the front topper piece on the silicone mat.

Heat and tint the isomalt. When working with isomalt, take extra precautions. Wear heatproof protective gloves if possible, as isomalt is extremely hot and can cause severe burns and stick to your skin.

In a saucepan, combine the isomalt and glucose, then bring to the boil over medium heat. Avoid stirring; instead, gently swirl the pan to ensure even heating. Once the isomalt is fully dissolved and bubbling or reaches 170°C (340°F), remove it from the heat and pour it into a small heatproof jug to stop the cooking process. Use a heatproof rubber spatula to scrape out any remaining isomalt from the pan. Let the bubbles settle for about 30 seconds, then add 2 drops of neon brite pink food colouring to achieve a medium pink shade (which will appear peachy against the chartreuse cake). Allow the isomalt to cool down slightly for 3–5 minutes or until it reaches 135°C (275°F) before pouring.

Pour and let set. Start by finishing the front heart topper. Slowly pour the isomalt into the centre section, allowing it to flood the area. Stop once the area is just filled (image 6). Avoid over-pouring, as this can cause the design to crack. Make sure to fill the area in one go. Once poured, do not go back to add more isomalt, as the first layer will already have started to set, and it won't dry smoothly.

Next, pour the isomalt into the candy mould cavities, filling each cavity about two-thirds of the way. You will need 30 heart candies in total — so if you only have one candy mould and need to pour the candies in batches, you should cook and tint all the isomalt at once. Any remaining isomalt can be left to set in a heatproof, microwave-safe jug. Once the first batch of candies has hardened, reheat the isomalt in the microwave in 15-second intervals until it fully melts and reaches 135°C (275°F), then pour the next batch. Repeat until you have enough candies.

Allow the isomalt to fully harden before removing it from the moulds. To remove the heart candies, simply tap the mould gently on the bench to release them.

The heart candies can be kept for up to 2 days at room temperature in an airtight container. Do not refrigerate, as this can cause the isomalt to melt.

Assemble the topper. Start by using a very thin knife to carefully peel the entire front and back pieces away from the silicone mat to ensure they can be removed easily. Keep the front piece on the silicone mat and flip the back topper piece so the underside (the side that will not be visible) is facing upwards, then place it back on the silicone mat.

Next, take a second piping bag, fit it with another standard coupler and a round 10 nozzle, then fill with the remaining chartreuse royal icing. Pipe a thick line of icing along the edges of the back piece (image 7).

Place two skewers at the bottom of the heart, pressing them gently into the icing. Make sure half of each skewer sits in the icing while the other half sticks out. These will be used to secure the topper to the cake. Pipe more icing over the skewers to hold them firmly in place. You may need to place something underneath the ends of the skewers to keep them straight as the icing sets (image 8).

Once the skewers are secured, gently place the front topper piece directly on top of the back piece. Press down lightly to adhere the pieces together (image 9).

Allow the topper to dry completely on the silicone mat while you decorate the cake. Once dry, store in an airtight container until ready to add to the cake.

Project continues

DECORATING PROJECTS

313

For the cake

Set up. Make sure you have followed the set-up checklist on page 191 before starting. Both layer cakes should already be assembled, crumb coated and chilled separately in the fridge: the larger cake on the 36 cm (14 in) square cake board, and the smaller cake on the 20 cm (8 in) round board.

Tint the buttercream. Tint all the buttercream with equal parts egg yellow, neon brite green and a touch of Dijon food colouring to create a medium chartreuse tone to match the royal icing. Have your peach royal icing ready for piping.

Frost the cakes separately. Adjust 700 g (24.7 oz) of the tinted buttercream to a thin but spreadable consistency (page 40). Follow the instructions on pages 51–54 to frost both cakes until a neat smooth base is achieved, working with one cake at a time. Allow the frosted cakes to chill in the fridge for at least 15 minutes until the frosting on both cakes is fully set.

Mark the bottom tier's top surface. Starting with the top surface, cut a square piece of baking paper to match the size of the bottom-tier cake by tracing around a 25 cm (10 in) square cake tin. Fold the paper in half across its diameter to create a rectangle, then fold it in half again to make a square. Snip out about 5 mm (¼ in) from the corner where all the folds meet. When you unfold the paper, the cut-out spot will indicate the centre of the square. Gently place the paper on top of the cold, frosted cake, making sure the edges are aligned. Use a pointed palette knife to lightly mark the centre of the cake's top surface.

Next, prepare a guide for the top ruffle border. Cut a round piece of baking paper by tracing around an 18 cm (7 in) cake tin. Follow the instructions on page 172 to create a template for marking six sections from the baking paper. Snip out a small piece, about 5 mm (¼ in), from the tip of the folds. When you unfold the paper, you'll have six even sections, with the cut-out area indicating the centre of the circle.

Place this paper circle on the cold, frosted cake, aligning the centre of the circle with the centre mark on the cake's top surface you previously marked. Make sure one of the folded points aligns with the centre of one of the cake's sides to establish the front of the cake. Gently mark each of the six folded points on the cake's surface – these will be your starting positions for the top ruffle border.

Insert elevated pillars to the bottom tier. Following the instructions on pages 178–180, carefully install the dowels, pillars and separator plate. The separator plate can be removed while you are decorating the cake to ensure it doesn't get in the way. However, make sure to test-assemble the pieces first to check that the plate sits level on the pillars and dowels – otherwise, the top tier won't sit straight. Leave the dowels and pillars in place on the cake while decorating.

After completing the assembly, briefly return the cake to the fridge for about 10 minutes to firm up the frosting before marking the sides.

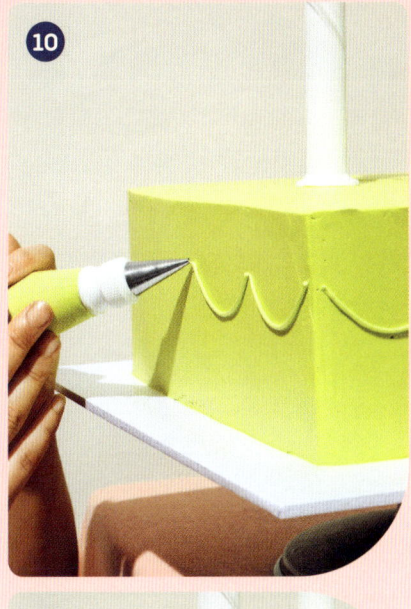

Mark the sides of the bottom tier. Start by dividing the top edge of the cake into four equal sections on each side. Set a wing caliper to 6.25 cm (2½ in) and use it to mark along the top edge of the cake at equal intervals. Next, adjust the wing caliper to 2.5 cm (1 in), or the height of your heart candies, and mark straight down the side of the cake from each spot you just marked on the top edge. These marks will act as starting points for the upper side border (fluted ruffle and ribbon garland).

To mark the lower side border, reset the caliper to 4 cm (1½ in) and measure upwards from the bottom edge of the cake, aligning the new marks with the ones above.

By now, you should have four evenly spaced sections marked on both the upper and lower sides of the cake on each side, ready for the borders. Return the cake to the fridge while you move on to the top tier.

Mark the top tier's top surface. Use the cookie cutter to gently imprint a circle in the centre of the cake's top surface.

Mark the side of the top tier into eight sections. Start by cutting another piece of round baking paper to match the size of the top tier cake by tracing around a 15 cm (6 in) cake tin. Follow the instructions on page 172 to create a template for marking eight sections from the baking paper. Use a pointed palette knife to gently make small marks along the cake's top edge at the folded points, then remove the baking paper.

Next, reset the wing caliper to 1 cm (½ in) and mark straight down the side of the cake from each previously marked spot on the top edge. These marks will act as starting points for the peach double drop strings.

Then, keeping the wing caliper set to 1 cm (½ in), continue marking straight down the side of the cake from each of the marks you just made. These additional marks will act as the starting points for the fluted ruffle and ribbon garlands.

For the bottom border, reset the wing caliper to 2 cm (¾ in) and measure upwards from the bottom edge of the cake, aligning the new marks with those above.

By now, you should have three sets of evenly spaced sections marked: two on the upper side of the cake and one on the lower side, ready for the borders. Once complete, return the cake to the fridge to firm up the frosting while you decorate the bottom tier.

Pipe the bottom tier's side border. Fit a piping bag with a standard coupler and a [round 3 nozzle](#), filling it halfway with chartreuse buttercream. Pipe a drop string outline, connecting each upper marked point around the cake, ensuring each string drops about 2 cm (¾ in) below the marked level (image 10). Next, switch to a [104W petal nozzle](#) and pipe a fluted ruffle garland just beneath each drop string (image 11). Then, use the same [104W petal nozzle](#) to pipe a ribbon on top of each ruffle garland. Position the ribbon above the string to overlap the fluted ruffles nicely (image 12).

Project continues

DECORATING PROJECTS

PROJECT 15   HEART OF GLASS

Once the chartreuse buttercream details are complete, take the piping bag with the peach royal icing and fit it with a clean round 3 nozzle. Pipe a double drop string, connecting the lower marked points around the cake. Allow the first string to drop about 1.5 cm (½ in) and the second string to drop about 2.5 cm (1 in) from the marked level. Once the strings are in place, switch to a clean round 5 nozzle and pipe small hearts at each point where the strings meet (image 13).

Pipe the bottom tier's bottom border. Fit the fourth piping bag with the medium coupler and a 124K petal nozzle, then fill halfway with chartreuse buttercream. Pipe a folded ruffle along the bottom edge around the cake (image 14).

Pipe the top surface of the bottom tier. Switch to the piping bag with chartreuse buttercream and the 104W petal nozzle. Pipe a fluted ruffle garland connecting each marked point on the centre circle on top of the cake, ensuring each ruffle garland curves outwards evenly to form a scalloped design around the pillars. Then, using the same 104W petal nozzle, pipe a ribbon on top of each ruffle garland. Position the ribbon so that each one overlaps the fluted ruffles nicely (image 15).

To finish the bottom tier, use the same piping bag with the chartreuse buttercream and a standard coupler, and switch to a star 16 nozzle. Pipe continuous shells along the top edge of the cake (image 16).

Once the bottom tier is completed, return the bottom tier cake to the fridge to set the frosting while you move on to the top tier.

Pipe the top tier's side border. Starting from the lower marked sections on the upper side of the small tier, repeat the same steps used for the bottom tier to pipe the fluted ruffle and ribbon garlands. Begin by using the round 3 nozzle to pipe a drop string outline, connecting the marked points around the cake. Then, switch to the 104W petal nozzle to pipe fluted ruffle and ribbon garlands around the cake (image 17).

Once the chartreuse buttercream details are completed, move on to the upper marked sections. Take the piping bag with the peach royal icing and fit it with a clean round 3 nozzle. Pipe a double drop string, connecting each marked point to the next. Allow the upper string to drop about 1.5 cm (½ in) and the lower string to drop about 2.5 cm (1 in), ensuring the lower string drapes neatly and aligns with the top edge of the ruffle garland. Once the strings are in place, switch to the clean round 5 nozzle and pipe small hearts at each point where the strings meet (image 18).

Pipe the top tier's bottom border. Switch back to the piping bag with chartreuse buttercream and a standard coupler, and fit with a clean round 3 nozzle. Pipe an outline drop string connecting each lower marked point around the cake, allowing each string to drop about 1 cm (½ in) from the marked level. Next, take the piping bag with chartreuse buttercream and the 124K petal nozzle and pipe a folded ruffle garland along the curve of the outline string, positioning the ruffles so they fully conceal the strings (image 19).

Pipe the top surface of the top tier. Using the piping bag with chartreuse buttercream and the 104W petal nozzle, pipe a folded ruffle along the marked circle line (image 20). Next, switch to the star 16 nozzle and pipe a continuous shell along the inner edge of the ruffle.

Project continues

DECORATING PROJECTS

PROJECT 15 HEART OF GLASS

For the outer edge, using the same piping bag, switch back to the 104W petal nozzle. Pipe a folded ruffle along the outer edge of the cake, ensuring the ruffle extends beyond the cake's edge to fully conceal it. To finish, switch to a star 32 nozzle and pipe continuous shells along the inner edge of the ruffle (image 21).

Once the top tier is finished, place the cake in the fridge for at least 30 minutes to allow the decoration to fully firm up before adding the heart candies and topper.

Reserve the remaining chartreuse buttercream to use as an adhesive for attaching the heart candies to the cake.

Add the heart candies and topper. It is best to add the candies just before assembling and serving, to ensure they stay in perfect condition.

To attach the heart candies, use the piping bag with the chartreuse buttercream and a standard coupler. Fit it with a clean round 5 nozzle. Working with one heart candy at a time, pipe a small dot of buttercream onto the back of the heart candy, then press it firmly onto the cake to adhere. Attach 16 candies along the sides of the bottom tier, placing each one at the highest points of the ruffle garland. On the top surface of the bottom tier, position six candies at the highest points of the inner ruffle, all angled inwards towards the centre of the cake (image 22). Around the top tier, attach eight candies beneath the highest points of the centre ruffle.

Position the heart topper inside the circle on top of the smaller cake and gently push the skewers into the cake to secure the topper firmly in place.

Once completed, store both tiers in the fridge until ready to head out or set up. Transport the cakes separately.

Assemble the tiers. Set the bottom tier in its final position at the party venue. Remove the backing from the double-sided tape on the separator plate, then carefully place the top tier on the plate. Make sure the top tier is centred and align the highest point of one of its garlands with the centre of the bottom tier (image 23).

Now it's time to enjoy the amazing cake you've decorated! Congratulations on completing the most involved project in this book!

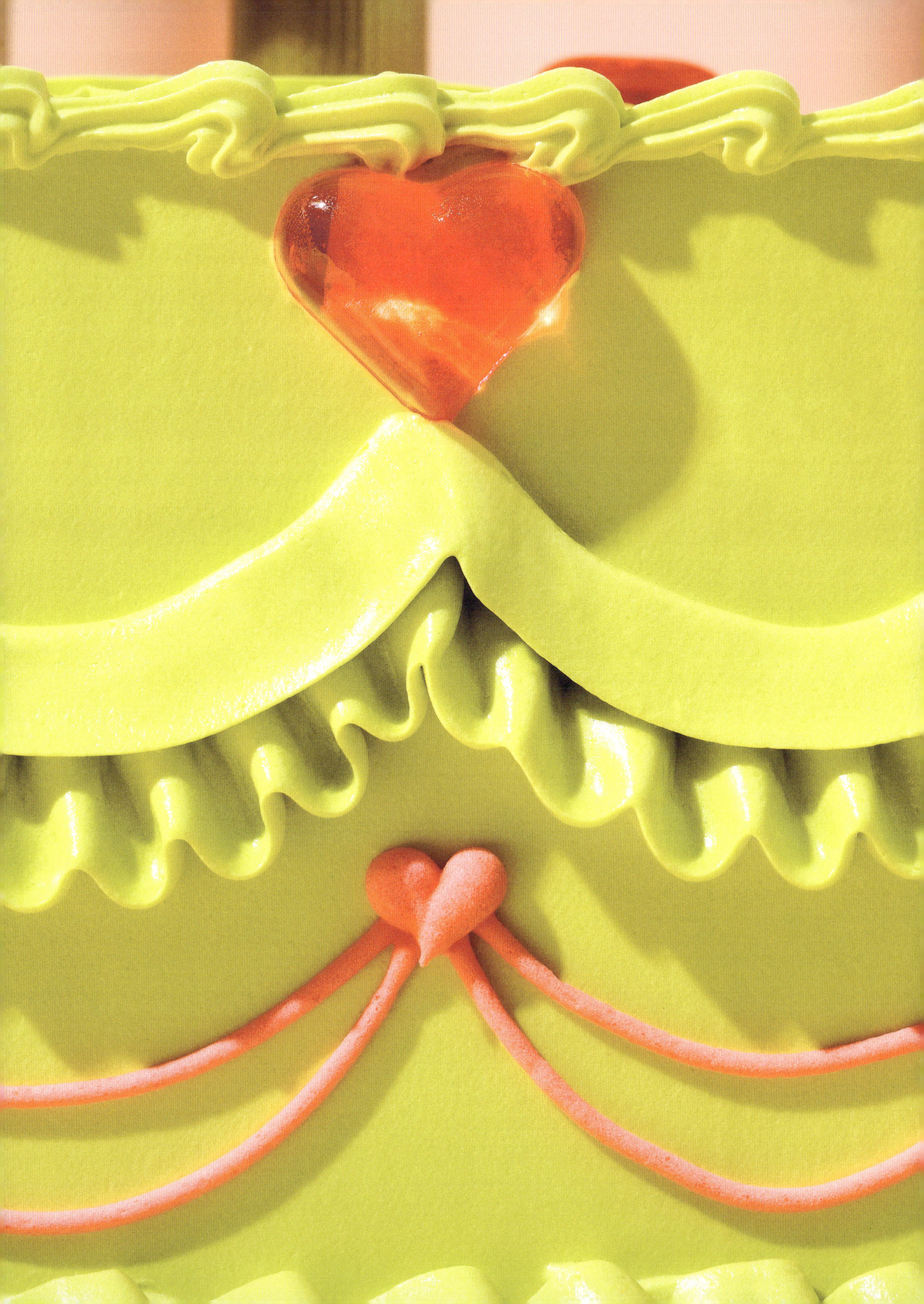

HEART OF GLASS TEMPLATE

Isomalt

Front piece

Back piece

320 MALI BAKES

SCALING UP RECIPES FOR DECORATING PROJECTS

You can use any of the layer cake recipes from Chapter 3 as the base for the decorating projects in Chapter 5, but depending on which decorating project you choose, you might need to prepare a larger quantity of cake, buttercream and filling than the original recipe yields. This section of the book outlines the revised ingredient quantities you will need to use any of the layer cakes in the projects. There will be some maths involved, but it won't be more than a bit of simple addition and multiplication. I suggest taking some time before you start baking to do these calculations.

How to use this section

To scale up the layer cake recipes. Find the page with the cake recipe you want to bake. The first column lists all of the ingredients, and the following columns have the measurements for different sized cake tins. All you need to do is find the cake tin size(s) you need for the project you want to complete (you will find this information in the 'You'll need' section of the project), and adjust the ingredient quantities to match the cake size you need. The final row of each table outlines any adjustments you need to make to cooking times.

Here's an example. If you want to decorate the Pressed Flower cake (page 212), you will need a 20 cm (8 in) three-layer heart-shaped cake. To scale up any cake for this project, simply follow the ingredient quantities from the heart-shaped 20 cm (8 in) three-layer cake column and adjust the cooking time.

For larger projects with multiple tiers. You can either keep all the tiers the same flavour or mix it up and choose a different flavour for each one. If you're using the same flavour for all tiers, it's best to make each tier separately rather than combining everything into one big batch. You want to prevent overmixing the batter, which can happen easily when working with large amounts of batter.

For example, if you're making the Cherry Blossom Bows cake (page 268), you'll need to bake a 15 cm (6 in) three-layer round cake and a 23 cm (9 in) three-layer round cake. If you'd like both tiers to be the same flavour – let's say Sour cream chocolate cake – prepare and bake the cakes tier by tier. Start with the recipe and bake time for the 15 cm size (first column), then move on to the 23 cm size (third column).

If you'd prefer each tier to be a different flavour – for example, the smaller tier as Sour cream chocolate and the larger tier as Buttermilk vanilla – mix and bake the 15 cm chocolate cake first, followed by the 23 cm vanilla cake.

DECORATING PROJECTS

Adjusting the cake baking process when working with larger quantities. If you're planning on decorating a larger project (such as Lovers Lace, page 298, or Heart of Glass, page 308), you will be working with a large quantity of cake batter. This may require you to bake the cakes in batches as some home ovens may not fit three round 23 cm (9 in) cake tins (or larger cake tins) at the same time.

For butter-based cakes such as Buttermilk vanilla (page 108), Chocolate chip (page 114), Peanut butter (page 120), Orange yoghurt (page 126), Coffee (page 132) and Pistachio (page 138), prepare all the batter at once (provided your mixer is large enough). Portion the batter into your prepared cake tins and refrigerate any unbaked portions to slow down the activation of the leavening agents. Bake the remaining portions as soon as the first batch is out of the oven. It is important to let the unbaked batter chill in the cake tin without any further handling, as this can interfere with its rise.

For cakes like Sour cream chocolate (page 104), Olive oil ricotta (page 142), and Brown sugar (page 148), which call for hot liquid to be added at the end, the batter needs to be baked immediately – you don't want to rest the batter, as this can affect how the cake rises.

If your oven can't bake all the layers at once, divide the recipe based on how many tins your oven can handle, and prepare the batter in batches.

Scaling up the buttercream, soaks and filling quantities. Find the relevant tables on pages 332–333. Each row lists a different cake tin size: simply find the cake size you need to bake and multiply every ingredient quantity from the original recipe by the relevant number in the table.

If you're making different flavours for each tier, refer to the first table in each section. If you are making a tiered cake with the same flavour for all tiers you can use the second table for your quantities.

Keep in mind that when working with multiple flavours, you may end up with a little extra filling or buttercream. Some elements don't scale down easily. Check the 'Store' section in each recipe for tips on saving leftovers for future bakes.

SCALING CAKE INGREDIENTS
Sour cream chocolate cake
(page 106)

	Round 15 cm (6 in) three-layer cake	Round 18 cm (7 in) four-layer cake OR Heart-shaped 20 cm (8 in) three-layer cake	Round 23 cm (9 in) three-layer cake	Round 30 cm (12 in) three-layer cake	Square 15 cm (6 in) three-layer cake	Square 25 cm (10 in) three-layer cake
plain (all-purpose) flour	160 g (5.64 oz)	290 g (10.23 oz)	355 g (12.35 oz)	635 g (22.4 oz)	210 g (7.41 oz)	560 g (19.75 oz)
cornflour (corn starch)	25 g (0.88 oz)	50 g (1.75 oz)	60 g (2.17 oz)	100 g (3.5 oz)	35 g (1.23 oz)	90 g (3.17 oz)
Dutch-processed cocoa powder	55 g (1.94 oz)	95 g (3.35 oz)	115 g (4.06 oz)	200 g (7 oz)	70 g (2.47 oz)	180 g (6.35 oz)
bicarbonate of soda (baking soda)	9 g (1½ teaspoons)	12 g (0.42 oz)	18 g (0.63 oz)	30 g (1.06 oz)	9 g (1½ teaspoons)	24 g (0.85 oz)
fine sea salt	6 g (1 teaspoon)	9 g (1½ teaspoons)	10 g (1¾ teaspoons)	18 g (0.63 oz)	6 g (1 teaspoon)	15 g (0.53 oz)
vegetable oil	130 g (4.59 oz)	230 g (8.11 oz)	280 g (9.87 oz)	500 g (17.64 oz)	160 g (5.64 oz)	440 g (15.52 oz)
caster (superfine) sugar	270 g (9.52 oz)	480 g (16.93 oz)	600 g (21.16 oz)	1065 g (37.57 oz)	340 g (12 oz)	940 g (33.16 oz)
full-fat sour cream	180 g (6.35 oz)	320 g (11.29 oz)	400 g (14 oz)	700 g (24.7 oz)	230 g (8.11 oz)	630 g (22.22 oz)
eggs	75 g (2.65 oz) (about 1½ eggs)	150 g (5.3 oz) (about 3 eggs)	175 g (6.17 oz) (about 3½ eggs)	300 g (10.58 oz) (about 6 eggs)	100 g (3.5 oz) (about 2 eggs)	250 g (8.82 oz) (about 5 eggs)
water	150 g (5.3 oz)	270 g (9.52 oz)	330 g (11.64 oz)	600 g (21.16 oz)	200 g (7 oz)	520 g (18.34 oz)
instant coffee granules	3 g (1¼ teaspoons)	5 g (2 teaspoons)	7 g (2¾ teaspoons)	12 g (0.42 oz)	4 g (1½ teaspoons)	10 g (4 teaspoons)
Weight per tin	350 g (12.35 oz)	For round 18 cm (7 in) tins: 470 g (16.58 oz) For heart-shaped 20 cm (8 in) tins: 620 g (21.87 oz)	770 g (27.16 oz)	1380 g (48.68 oz)	450 g (15.88 oz)	1200 g (42.33 oz)
Baking time	35–40 minutes	For round 18 cm (7 in) tins: 40–45 minutes For heart-shaped 20 cm (8 in) tins: 45–50 minutes	45–50 minutes	55–60 minutes	40–45 minutes	55–60 minutes

DECORATING PROJECTS

Buttermilk vanilla cake (page 111)

	Round 15 cm (6 in) three-layer cake	Round 18 cm (7 in) four-layer cake OR Heart-shaped 20 cm (8 in) three-layer cake	Round 23 cm (9 in) three-layer cake	Round 30 cm (12 in) three-layer cake	Square 15 cm (6 in) three-layer cake	Square 25 cm (10 in) three-layer cake
caster (superfine) sugar	255 g (9 oz)	450 g (15.88 oz)	560 g (19.75 oz)	1000 g (35.25 oz)	325 g (11.46 oz)	885 g (31.22 oz)
vanilla bean paste	3 g (¾ teaspoon)	5 g (1¼ teaspoons)	7 g (1¾ teaspoons)	12 g (0.42 oz)	4 g (1 teaspoon)	10 g (2½ teaspoons)
plain (all-purpose) flour	245 g (8.64 oz)	435 g (15.34 oz)	540 g (19.05 oz)	960 g (33.86 oz)	300 g (10.58 oz)	845 g (29.81 oz)
baking powder	4 g (¾ teaspoon)	7 g (1½ teaspoons)	8 g (1¾ teaspoons)	15 g (0.53 oz)	5 g (1 teaspoon)	13 g (0.45 oz)
bicarbonate of soda (baking soda)	3 g (½ teaspoon)	5 g (¾ teaspoon)	7 g (1¼ teaspoons)	12 g (0.42 oz)	4 g (⅔ teaspoon)	9 g (1½ teaspoons)
fine sea salt	3 g (½ teaspoon)	5 g (¾ teaspoon)	7 g (1¼ teaspoons)	12 g (0.42 oz)	4 g (⅔ teaspoon)	9 g (1½ teaspoons)
vegetable oil	30 g (1.06 oz)	55 g (1.94 oz)	65 g (2.3 oz)	120 g (4.23 oz)	40 g (1.41 oz)	100 g (3.5 oz)
buttermilk	200 g (7 oz)	360 g (12.70 oz)	445 g (15.70 oz)	800 g (28.22 oz)	260 g (9.17 oz)	700 g (24.7 oz)
eggs	150 g (5.3 oz) (3 eggs)	270 g (9.52 oz) (about 5½ eggs)	330 g (11.64 oz) (about 6½ eggs)	600 g (21.16 oz) (about 12 eggs)	200 g (7 oz) (about 4 eggs)	520 g (18.34 oz) (about 10½ eggs)
unsalted butter	100 g (3.5 oz)	180 g (6.35 oz)	225 g (7.94 oz)	400 g (14 oz)	130 g (4.59 oz)	350 g (12.35 oz)
Weight per tin	330 g (11.64 oz)	For round 18 cm (7 in) tins: 440 g (15.52 oz) For heart-shaped 20 cm (8 in) tins: 590 g (20.81 oz)	730 g (25.75 oz)	1300 g (45.86 oz)	420 g (14.81 oz)	1140 g (40.21 oz)
Baking time	30–35 minutes	For round 18 cm (7 in) tins: 35–40 minutes For heart-shaped 20 cm (8 in) tins: 40–45 minutes	40–45 minutes	50–55 minutes	35–40 minutes	50–55 minutes

Chocolate chip cake
(page 117)

	Round 15 cm (6 in) three-layer cake	Round 18 cm (7 in) four-layer cake OR Heart-shaped 20 cm (8 in) three-layer cake	Round 23 cm (9 in) three-layer cake	Round 30 cm (12 in) three-layer cake	Square 15 cm (6 in) three-layer cake	Square 25 cm (10 in) three-layer cake
caster (superfine) sugar	255 g (9 oz)	450 g (15.88 oz)	560 g (19.75 oz)	1000 g (35.25 oz)	325 g (11.46 oz)	885 g (31.22 oz)
vanilla bean paste	4 g (1 teaspoon)	4 g (1 teaspoon)	6 g (1½ teaspoons)	12 g (0.42 oz)	4 g (1 teaspoon)	10 g (2½ teaspoons)
plain (all-purpose) flour	245 g (8.64 oz)	435 g (15.34 oz)	535 g (18.87 oz)	960 g (33.86 oz)	300 g (10.58 oz)	845 g (29.81 oz)
bittersweet dark chocolate	75 g (2.65 oz)	135 g (4.76 oz)	165 g (5.82 oz)	295 g (10.41 oz)	95 g (3.35 oz)	260 g (9.17 oz)
baking powder	4 g (¾ teaspoon)	7 g (1½ teaspoons)	8 g (1¾ teaspoons)	15 g (0.53 oz)	5 g (1 teaspoon)	13 g (0.45 oz)
bicarbonate of soda (baking soda)	3 g (½ teaspoon)	5 g (¾ teaspoon)	7 g (1¼ teaspoons)	12 g (0.42 oz)	4 g (⅔ teaspoon)	9 g (1½ teaspoons)
fine sea salt	3 g (½ teaspoon)	5 g (¾ teaspoon)	7 g (1¼ teaspoons)	12 g (0.42)	4 g (⅔ teaspoon)	9 g (1½ teaspoons)
vegetable oil	30 g (1.06 oz)	55 g (1.94 oz)	65 g (2.3 oz)	120 g (4.23 oz)	40 g (1.41 oz)	100 g (3.5 oz)
buttermilk	200 g (7 oz)	350 g (12.35 oz)	430 g (15.17 oz)	770 g (27.16 oz)	250 g (8.82 oz)	675 g (23.81 oz)
eggs	150 g (5.3 oz) (about 3 eggs)	270 g (9.52 oz) (about 5½ eggs)	330 g (11.64 oz) (about 6½ eggs)	600 g (21.16 oz) (about 12 eggs)	200 g (7 oz) (about 4 eggs)	520 g (18.34 oz) (about 10½ eggs)
unsalted butter	100 g (3.5 oz)	175 g (6.17 oz)	215 g (7.58 oz)	385 g (13.58 oz)	125 g (4.41 oz)	340 g (12 oz)
Weight per tin	350 g (12.35 oz)	For round 18 cm (7 in) tins: 470 g (16.58 oz) For heart-shaped 20 cm (8 in) tins: 630 g (22.22 oz)	775 g (27.34 oz)	1390 g (49 oz)	440 g (15.52 oz)	1220 g (43 oz)
Baking time	30–35 minutes	For round 18 cm (7 in) tins: 35–40 minutes For heart-shaped 20 cm (8 in) tins: 40–45 minutes	40–45 minutes	50–55 minutes	35–40 minutes	50–55 minutes

Peanut butter cake (page 123)

	Round 15 cm (6 in) three-layer cake	Round 18 cm (7 in) four-layer cake OR Heart-shaped 20 cm (8 in) three-layer cake	Round 23 cm (9 in) three-layer cake	Round 30 cm (12 in) three-layer cake	Square 15 cm (6 in) three-layer cake	Square 25 cm (10 in) three-layer cake
caster (superfine) sugar	125 g (4.41 oz)	220 g (7.76 oz)	275 g (9.7 oz)	490 g (17.28 oz)	160 g (5.64 oz)	430 g (15.17 oz)
brown sugar	85 g (3 oz)	150 g (5.3 oz)	185 g (6.5 oz)	325 g (11.46 oz)	100 g (3.5 oz)	285 g (10 oz)
plain (all-purpose) flour	175 g (6.17 oz)	300 g (10.58 oz)	380 g (13.4 oz)	680 g (24 oz)	220 g (7.76 oz)	600 g (21.16 oz)
cornflour (corn starch)	20 g (0.7 oz)	40 g (1.41 oz)	45 g (1.59 oz)	80 g (2.82 oz)	25 g (0.88 oz)	70 g (2.47 oz)
baking powder	8 g (1½ teaspoons)	13 g (0.45 oz)	17 g (0.6 oz)	30 g (1.06 oz)	10 g (2 teaspoons)	25 g (0.88 oz)
bicarbonate of soda (baking soda)	5 g (¾ teaspoon)	8 g (1¼ teaspoons)	10 g (1¾ teaspoons)	18 g (0.63 oz)	6 g (1 teaspoon)	16 g (0.56 oz)
fine sea salt	2 g (¼ teaspoon)	4 g (⅔ teaspoon)	6 g (1 teaspoon)	9 g (1½ teaspoons)	3 g (½ teaspoon)	8 g (1¼ teaspoons)
full-cream (whole) milk	190 g (6.7 oz)	335 g (11.81 oz)	415 g (14.64 oz)	740 g (26.10 oz)	240 g (8.47 oz)	650 g (23 oz)
vegetable oil	40 g (1.41 oz)	70 g (2.47 oz)	85 g (3 oz)	150 g (5.3 oz)	50 g (1.75 oz)	130 g (4.59 oz)
eggs	125 g (4.41 oz) (about 2½ eggs)	220 g (7.76 oz) (about 4½ eggs)	275 g (9.7 oz) (about 5½ eggs)	500 g (17.64 oz) (about 10 eggs)	150 g (5.3 oz) (about 3 eggs)	450 g (15.88 oz) (about 9 eggs)
vanilla bean paste	3 g (¾ teaspoon)	5 g (1¼ teaspoons)	7 g (1¾ teaspoons)	12 g (0.42 oz)	4 g (1 teaspoon)	10 g (2½ teaspoons)
unsalted butter	70 g (2.47 oz)	120 g (4.23 oz)	150 g (5.3 oz)	270 g (9.52 oz)	85 g (3 oz)	235 g (8.3 oz)
smooth peanut butter	125 g (4.41 oz)	220 g (7.76 oz)	275 g (9.7 oz)	490 g (17.28 oz)	160 g (5.64 oz)	430 g (15.17 oz)
Weight per tin	320 g (11.29 oz)	For round 18 cm (7 in) tins: 420 g (14.81 oz) For heart-shaped 20 cm (8 in) tins: 560 g (19.75 oz)	700 g (24.7 oz)	1260 g (44.45 oz)	400 g (14 oz)	1100 g (38.8 oz)
Baking time	30–35 minutes	For round 18 cm (7 in) tins: 35–40 minutes For heart-shaped 20 cm (8 in) tins: 40–45 minutes	40–45 minutes	50–55 minutes	35–40 minutes	50–55 minutes

Orange yoghurt cake (page 129)

	Round 15 cm (6 in) three-layer cake	Round 18 cm (7 in) four-layer cake OR Heart-shaped 20 cm (8 in) three-layer cake	Round 23 cm (9 in) three-layer cake	Round 30 cm (12 in) three-layer cake	Square 15 cm (6 in) three-layer cake	Square 25 cm (10 in) three-layer cake
caster (superfine) sugar	240 g (8.47 oz)	435 g (15.34 oz)	535 g (18.87 oz)	960 g (33.86 oz)	300 g (10.58 oz)	845 g (29.81 oz)
orange zest	3 g (1½ teaspoons)	5 g (2½ teaspoons)	7 g (3½ teaspoons)	12 g (0.42 oz)	4 g (2 teaspoons)	10 g (5 teaspoons)
plain (all-purpose) flour	235 g (8.3 oz)	415 g (14.64 oz)	515 g (18.17 oz)	915 g (32.28 oz)	295 g (10.41 oz)	800 g (28.22 oz)
baking powder	5 g (1 teaspoon)	7 g (1½ teaspoons)	8 g (1¾ teaspoons)	15 g (0.53 oz)	5 g (1 teaspoon)	13 g (0.45 oz)
bicarbonate of soda (baking soda)	3 g (½ teaspoon)	5 g (¾ teaspoon)	6 g (1 teaspoon)	12 g (0.42 oz)	4 g (⅔ teaspoon)	10 g (1¾ teaspoons)
fine sea salt	3 g (½ teaspoon)	5 g (¾ teaspoon)	6 g (1 teaspoon)	12 g (0.42 oz)	4 g (¾ teaspoon)	10 g (1¾ teaspoons)
eggs	150 g (5.3 oz) (about 3 eggs)	270 g (9.52 oz) (about 5½ eggs)	330 g (11.64 oz) (about 6½ eggs)	600 g (21.16 oz) (about 12 eggs)	200 g (7 oz) (about 4 eggs)	520 g (18.34 oz) (about 10½ eggs)
buttermilk	75 g (2.65 oz)	135 g (4.76 oz)	165 g (5.82 oz)	295 g (10.41 oz)	95 g (3.35 oz)	260 g (9.17 oz)
vegetable oil	30 g (1.06 oz)	55 g (1.94 oz)	65 g (2.3 oz)	120 g (4.23 oz)	40 g (1.41 oz)	100 g (3.5 oz)
orange juice	30 g (1.06 oz)	55 g (1.94 oz)	65 g (2.3 oz)	120 g (4.23 oz)	40 g (1.41 oz)	100 g (3.5 oz)
unsalted butter	100 g (3.5 oz)	175 g (6.17 oz)	215 g (7.58 oz)	385 g (13.58 oz)	125 g (4.41 oz)	340 g (12 oz)
full-fat yoghurt	100 g (3.5 oz)	175 g (6.17 oz)	215 g (7.58 oz)	385 g (13.58 oz)	125 g (4.41 oz)	340 g (12 oz)
Weight per tin	320 g (11.29 oz)	For round 18 cm (7 in) tins: 430 g (15.17 oz) For heart-shaped 20 cm (8 in) tins: 575 g (20.3 oz)	700 g (24.7 oz)	1270 g (44.8 oz)	400 g (14 oz)	1100 g (38.8 oz)
Baking time	30–35 minutes	For round 18 cm (7 in) tins: 35–40 minutes For heart-shaped 20 cm (8 in) tins: 40–45 minutes	40–45 minutes	50–55 minutes	35–40 minutes	50–55 minutes

DECORATING PROJECTS

Coffee cake
(page 135)

	Round 15 cm (6 in) three-layer cake	Round 18 cm (7 in) four-layer cake OR Heart-shaped 20 cm (8 in) three-layer cake	Round 23 cm (9 in) three-layer cake	Round 30 cm (12 in) three-layer cake	Square 15 cm (6 in) three-layer cake	Square 25 cm (10 in) three-layer cake
brown sugar	110 g (3.88 oz)	200 g (7 oz)	250 g (8.82 oz)	440 g (15.52 oz)	140 g (4.94 oz)	390 g (13.76 oz)
caster (superfine) sugar	110 g (3.88 oz)	200 g (7 oz)	250 g (8.82 oz)	440 g (15.52 oz)	140 g (4.94 oz)	390 g (13.76 oz)
plain (all-purpose) flour	220 g (7.76 oz)	400 g (14 oz)	500 g (17.64 oz)	885 g (31.22 oz)	285 g (10 oz)	780 g (27.5 oz)
cornflour (corn starch)	30 g (1.06 oz)	55 g (1.94 oz)	70 g (2.47 oz)	120 g (4.23 oz)	40 g (1.41 oz)	100 g (3.5 oz)
baking powder	5 g (1 teaspoon)	8 g (1¾ teaspoons)	10 g (2 teaspoons)	18 g (0.63 oz)	6 g (1¼ teaspoons)	16 g (0.56 oz)
bicarbonate of soda (baking soda)	2 g (¼ teaspoon)	4 g (⅔ teaspoon)	6 g (1 teaspoon)	9 g (1½ teaspoons)	3 g (½ teaspoon)	8 g (1¼ teaspoons)
fine sea salt	2 g (¼ teaspoon)	4 g (⅔ teaspoon)	6 g (1 teaspoon)	9 g (1½ teaspoons)	3 g (½ teaspoon)	8 g (1¼ teaspoons)
vegetable oil	75 g (2.65 oz)	140 g (4.94 oz)	165 g (5.82 oz)	300 g (10.58 oz)	95 g (3.35 oz)	260 g (9.17 oz)
buttermilk	260 g (9.17 oz)	470 g (16.58 oz)	580 g (20.5 oz)	1030 g (36.33 oz)	330 g (11.64 oz)	900 g (31.75 oz)
instant coffee granules	10 g (4 teaspoons)	20 g (0.7 oz)	25 g (0.88 oz)	45 g (1.59 oz)	15 g (0.53 oz)	40 g (1.41 oz)
eggs	100 g (3.5 oz) (about 2 eggs)	200 g (7 oz) (about 4 eggs)	250 g (8.82 oz) (about 5 eggs)	450 g (15.88 oz) (about 9 eggs)	150 g (5.3 oz) (about 3 eggs)	400 g (14 oz) (about 8 eggs)
vanilla bean paste	3 g (¾ teaspoon)	6 g (1½ teaspoons)	7 g (1¾ teaspoons)	12 g (0.42 oz)	4 g (1 teaspoon)	10 g (2½ teaspoons)
unsalted butter	75 g (2.65 oz)	135 g (4.76 oz)	165 g (5.82 oz)	295 g (10.41 oz)	95 g (3.35 oz)	260 g (9.17 oz)
Weight per tin	330 g (11.64 oz)	For round 18 cm (7 in) tins: 450 g (15.88 oz) For heart-shaped 20 cm (8 in) tins: 600 g (21.16 oz)	750 g (26.46 oz)	1340 g (47.27 oz)	430 g (15.17 oz)	1180 g (41.62 oz)
Baking time	30–35 minutes	For round 18 cm (7 in) tins: 35–40 minutes For heart-shaped 20 cm (8 in) tins: 40–45 minutes	40–45 minutes	50–55 minutes	35–40 minutes	50–55 minutes

Pistachio cake (page 140)

	Round 15 cm (6 in) three-layer cake	Round 18 cm (7 in) four-layer cake OR Heart-shaped 20 cm (8 in) three-layer cake	Round 23 cm (9 in) three-layer cake	Round 30 cm (12 in) three-layer cake	Square 15 cm (6 in) three-layer cake	Square 25 cm (10 in) three-layer cake
raw shelled pistachios	110 g (3.88 oz)	195 g (6.88 oz)	240 g (8.47 oz)	430 g (15.17 oz)	140 g (4.94 oz)	375 g (13.23 oz)
caster (superfine) sugar	200 g (7 oz)	360 g (12.70 oz)	445 g (15.70 oz)	800 g (28.22 oz)	260 g (9.17 oz)	700 g (24.7 oz)
plain (all-purpose) flour	170 g (6 oz)	300 g (10.58 oz)	370 g (13 oz)	665 g (23.46 oz)	215 g (7.58 oz)	585 g (20.64 oz)
cornflour (corn starch)	15 g (0.53 oz)	30 g (1.06 oz)	35 g (1.23 oz)	60 g (2.17 oz)	20 g (0.7 oz)	50 g (1.75 oz)
baking powder	4 g (¾ teaspoon)	7 g (1½ teaspoons)	8 g (1¾ teaspoons)	15 g (3 teaspoons)	5 g (1 teaspoon)	13 g (2¾ teaspoons)
bicarbonate of soda (baking soda)	2 g (¼ teaspoon)	4 g (⅔ teaspoon)	6 g (1 teaspoon)	9 g (1½ teaspoons)	3 g (½ teaspoon)	8 g (1¼ teaspoons)
fine sea salt	2 g (¼ teaspoon)	4 g (⅔ teaspoon)	6 g (1 teaspoon)	9 g (1½ teaspoons)	3 g (½ teaspoon)	8 g (1¼ teaspoons)
buttermilk	200 g (7 oz)	360 g (12.70 oz)	445 g (15.70 oz)	800 g (28.22 oz)	260 g (9.17 oz)	700 g (24.7 oz)
vegetable oil	40 g (1.41 oz)	70 g (2.47 oz)	85 g (3 oz)	150 g (5.3 oz)	50 g (1.75 oz)	130 g (4.59 oz)
eggs	125 g (4.41 oz) (about 2½ eggs)	200 g (7 oz) (about 4 eggs)	250 g (8.82 oz) (about 5 eggs)	450 g (15.88 oz) (about 9 eggs)	150 g (5.3 oz) (about 3 eggs)	400 g (14 oz) (about 8 eggs)
almond extract	5 g (1¼ teaspoons)	8 g (2 teaspoons)	10 g (2½ teaspoons)	18 g (0.63 oz)	6 g (1½ teaspoons)	16 g (0.56 oz)
green food colouring	5 drops	8 drops	10 drops	18 g (0.63 oz)	6 drops	16 g (0.56 oz)
unsalted butter	120 g (4.23 oz)	215 g (7.58 oz)	265 g (9.35 oz)	475 g (16.76 oz)	150 g (5.3 oz)	415 g (14.64 oz)
Weight per tin	320 g (11.29 oz)	For round 18 cm (7 in) tins: 430 g (15.17 oz) For heart-shaped 20 cm (8 in) tins: 580 g (20.5 oz)	720 g (25.4 oz)	1290 g (45.5 oz)	410 g (14.46 oz)	1130 g (39.86 oz)
Baking time	30–35 minutes	For round 18 cm (7 in) tins: 35–40 minutes For heart-shaped 20 cm (8 in) tins: 40–45 minutes	40–45 minutes	50–55 minutes	35–40 minutes	50–55 minutes

DECORATING PROJECTS

Olive oil ricotta cake (page 145)

	Round 15 cm (6 in) three-layer cake	Round 18 cm (7 in) four-layer cake OR Heart-shaped 20 cm (8 in) three-layer cake	Round 23 cm (9 in) three-layer cake	Round 30 cm (12 in) three-layer cake	Square 15 cm (6 in) three-layer cake	Square 25 cm (10 in) three-layer cake
plain (all-purpose) flour	165 g (5.82 oz)	300 g (10.58 oz)	365 g (12.9 oz)	650 g (23 oz)	200 g (7 oz)	575 g (20.3 oz)
baking powder	8 g (1¾ teaspoons)	13 g (0.45 oz)	17 g (0.6 oz)	30 g (1.06 oz)	10 g (2 teaspoons)	25 g (0.88 oz)
fine sea salt	2 g (¼ teaspoon)	4 g (⅔ teaspoon)	6 g (1 teaspoon)	9 g (1½ teaspoons)	3 g (½ teaspoon)	9 g (1½ teaspoons)
eggs	130 g (20.3 oz) (about 2½ eggs)	230 g (8.11 oz) (about 4½ eggs)	280 g (9.87 oz) (about 5½ eggs)	500 g (17.64 oz) (about 10 eggs)	150 g (5.3 oz) (about 3 eggs)	450 g (15.88 oz) (about 9 eggs)
caster (superfine) sugar	200 g (7 oz)	350 g (12.35 oz)	430 g (15.17 oz)	760 g (26.8 oz)	250 g (8.82 oz)	675 g (23.81 oz)
full-cream (whole) milk	60 g (2.17 oz)	100 g (3.5 oz)	125 g (4.41 oz)	220 g (7.76 oz)	70 g (2.47 oz)	195 g (6.88 oz)
smooth, unstrained ricotta	165 g (5.82 oz)	300 g (10.58 oz)	360 g (12.70 oz)	650 g (23 oz)	200 g (7 oz)	575 g (20.3 oz)
extra virgin olive oil	100 g (3.5 oz)	175 g (6.17 oz)	215 g (7.58 oz)	385 g (13.58 oz)	125 g (4.41 oz)	340 g (12 oz)
Weight per tin	270 g (9.52 oz)	For round 18 cm (7 in) tins: 350 g (12.35 oz) For heart-shaped 20 cm (8 in) tins: 480 g (16.93 oz)	580 g (20.5 oz)	1050 g (37 oz)	330 g (11.64 oz)	940 g (33.16 oz)
Baking time	25–30 minutes	For round 18 cm (7 in) tins: 30–35 minutes For heart-shaped 20 cm (8 in) tins: 35–40 minutes	35–40 minutes	45–50 minutes	30–35 minutes	45–50 minutes

Brown sugar cake (page 151)

	Round 15 cm (6 in) three-layer cake	Round 18 cm (7 in) four-layer cake OR Heart-shaped 20 cm (8 in) three-layer cake	Round 23 cm (9 in) three-layer cake	Round 30 cm (12 in) three-layer cake	Square 15 cm (6 in) three-layer cake	Square 25 cm (10 in) three-layer cake
plain (all-purpose) flour	190 g (6.7 oz)	330 g (11.64 oz)	420 g (14.81 oz)	740 g (26.10 oz)	240 g (8.47 oz)	650 g (23 oz)
baking powder	10 g (2 teaspoons)	15 g (0.53 oz)	20 g (0.7 oz)	35 g (1.23 oz)	10 g (2 teaspoons)	30 g (1.06 oz)
fine sea salt	2 g (¼ teaspoon)	4 g (⅔ teaspoon)	6 g (1 teaspoon)	9 g (1½ teaspoons)	3 g (½ teaspoon)	8 g (1¼ teaspoons)
eggs	150 g (5.3 oz) (about 3 eggs)	270 g (9.52 oz) (about 5½ eggs)	330 g (11.64 oz) (about 6½ eggs)	600 g (21.16 oz) (about 12 eggs)	200 g (7 oz) (about 4 eggs)	520 g (18.34 oz) (about 10½ eggs)
brown sugar	200 g (7 oz)	360 g (12.70 oz)	450 g (15.88 oz)	800 g (28.22 oz)	260 g (9.17 oz)	700 g (24.7 oz)
buttermilk	135 g (4.76 oz)	240 g (8.47 oz)	300 g (10.58 oz)	530 g (18.7 oz)	170 g (6 oz)	470 g (16.58 oz)
unsalted butter	75 g (2.65 oz)	135 g (4.76 oz)	165 g (5.82 oz)	295 g (10.41 oz)	95 g (3.35 oz)	260 g (9.17 oz)
vegetable oil	15 g (0.53 oz)	30 g (1.06 oz)	35 g (1.23 oz)	60 g (2.17 oz)	20 g (0.7 oz)	50 g (1.75 oz)
vanilla bean paste	3 g (¾ teaspoon)	5 g (1¼ teaspoons)	7 g (1¾ teaspoons)	12 g (0.42 oz)	4 g (1 teaspoon)	10 g (2½ teaspoons)
full-fat sour cream	100 g (3.5 oz)	190 g (6.7 oz)	230 g (8.11 oz)	420 g (14.81 oz)	135 g (4.76 oz)	370 g (13 oz)
Weight per tin	290 g (10.23 oz)	For round 18 cm (7 in) tins: 390 g (13.76 oz) For heart-shaped 20 cm (8 in) tins: 520 g (18.34 oz)	650 g (23 oz)	1160 g (40.92 oz)	370 g (13 oz)	1020 g (36 oz)
Baking time	25–30 minutes	For round 18 cm (7 in) tins: 30–35 minutes For heart-shaped 20 cm (8 in) tins: 35–40 minutes	35–40 minutes	45–50 minutes	30–35 minutes	45–50 minutes

DECORATING PROJECTS

Scaling fillings

These measurements apply to all of the fruit fillings, curds, gels and crumbs – except for the whipped mascarpone (see note below).

Whipped mascarpone note: The original recipe makes a generous amount – making a smaller batch can be tricky, so you might have a little extra on your hands. Don't worry, it won't go to waste! Spread it on toast, dollop it on fruit, or sneak a spoonful straight from the bowl (we won't tell). One full recipe is enough to fill any of the cake sizes listed here, including the tiered cakes.

For single-tiered projects and tiered projects (if making each tier a different flavour)

To fill	Multiply ingredient quantities by
Round 15 cm (6 in) three-layer cake	0.5
Round 18 cm (7 in) four-layer cake	use original quantities
Heart-shaped 20 cm (8 in) three-layer cake	use original quantities
Round 23 cm (9 in) three-layer cake	use original quantities
Round 30 cm (12 in) three-layer cake	1.5
Square 15 cm (6 in) three-layer cake	use original quantities
Square 25 cm (10 in) three-layer cake	1.5

For tiered projects (with the same cake flavour used for all tiers)

To fill	Multiply ingredient quantities by
Daisy Fields	2.5
Cherry Blossom Bows	1.5
The Wedding Cake	3
Secret Garden	2
Lovers Lace	2
Heart of Glass	2

Scaling soaks

For single-tiered projects and tiered projects (if making each tier a different flavour)

To soak	Multiply ingredient quantities by
Round 15 cm (6 in) three-layer cake	0.5
Round 18 cm (7 in) four-layer cake	use original quantities
Heart-shaped 20 cm (8 in) three-layer cake	use original quantities
Round 23 cm (9 in) three-layer cake	use original quantities
Round 30 cm (12 in) three-layer cake	use original quantities
Square 15 cm (6 in) three-layer cake	use original quantities
Square 25 cm (10 in) three-layer cake	use original quantities

For tiered projects (with the same cake flavour used for all tiers)

To soak	Multiply ingredient quantities by
Daisy Fields	1.5
Cherry Blossom Bows	use original quantities
The Wedding Cake	2
Secret Garden	1.5
Lovers Lace	1.5
Heart of Glass	1.5

Scaling flavoured buttercream for filling and crumb coating

Buttercream can be a little tricky to scale down – halving the recipe doesn't work well, as the egg white amount becomes too small to whip properly. Most stand mixers can comfortably handle up to 2 batches. If you need a larger amount, like 3½ batches (which yields around 2.5 kg/88 oz) and that's too much for your mixer, it's best to make it in two rounds: start with a 2-batch, then follow with a 1½-batch.

For single tiered projects and tiered projects (if making each tier a different flavour)

To fill and crumb coat	Multiply ingredient quantities by
Round 15 cm (6 in) three-layer cake	use original quantities
Round 18 cm (7 in) four-layer cake	use original quantities
Heart-shaped 20 cm (8 in) three-layer cake	use original quantities
Round 23 cm (9 in) three-layer cake	1.5
Round 30 cm (12 in) three-layer cake	1.5
Square 15 cm (6 in) three-layer cake	use original quantities
Square 25 cm (10 in) three-layer cake	1.5

For tiered projects (with the same cake flavour used for all tiers)

To fill and crumb coat	Multiply ingredient quantities by
Daisy Fields	2.5
Cherry Blossom Bows	2
The Wedding Cake	3.5
Secret Garden	2
Lovers Lace	2.5
Heart of Glass	2

DECORATING PROJECTS

CUTTING CAKES INTO PARTY PORTIONS

There's nothing quite like sinking your fork into a large, triangular slice of cake; however, at larger gatherings, this style of cutting isn't the most practical choice, so instead I suggest using a grid pattern to cut your celebration cake. A grid pattern ensures even portions, making it easier to serve everyone fairly, while also allowing for smaller, more manageable pieces. The diagrams that follow illustrate the optimal portions for every cake size in this book, offering guidance for both dessert portions and coffee portions.

Begin by filling a container with warm-to-hot water to keep your knife clean and warm during the cutting process. Keeping the blade warm not only ensures a clean slice, but also makes cutting through the cake smoother and more precise. Place a tea towel nearby to wipe the knife clean as you work. Identify the size of the cake you are cutting and refer to the diagram as a guide.

Start by slicing the cake into columns as shown in the diagrams opposite. Hold a cutting board vertically against the column, and gently lay the column on the cutting board. Slice this column into the number of portions and sizes indicated in the diagram for that specific column. The slices from the edges are usually cut larger, as they have more buttercream – perfect pieces for the buttercream lovers. Once cut, transfer the slices to serving plates. Repeat until done.

Heart-shaped 20 cm (8 in) three-layer cake

Dessert portions
Portion size: 2.5 × 5 cm (1 × 2 in)
Serves: 23

Coffee portions
Portion size: 2.5 × 2.5 cm (1 × 1 in)
Serves: 44

Round 15 cm (6 in) three-layer cake

Dessert portions
Portion size: 2.5 × 5 cm (1 × 2 in)
Serves: 14

Coffee portions
Portion size: 2.5 × 2.5 cm (1 × 1 in)
Serves: 24

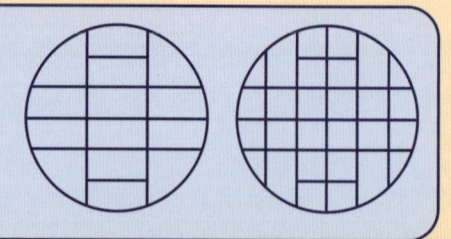

Round 18 cm (7 in) three-layer cake

Dessert portions
Portion size: 2.5 × 5 cm (1 × 2 in)
Serves: 17

Coffee portions
Portion size: 2.5 × 2.5 cm (1 × 1 in)
Serves: 64

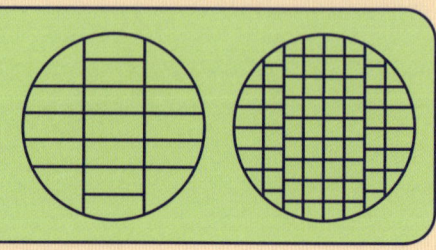

Round 18 cm (7 in) four-layer cake

With this taller four-layer cake, in addition to slicing the columns and portions as shown in the diagrams, once the portions are cut from the column you're working on, slice each portion in half parallel with the layers.

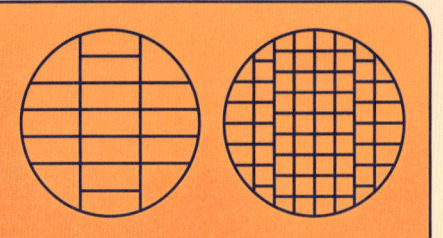

Dessert portions
Portion size: 2.5 × 5 cm (1 × 2 in)
Serves: 34

Coffee portions
Portion size: 2.5 × 2.5 cm (1 × 1 in)
Serves: 128

Round 23 cm (9 in) three-layer cake

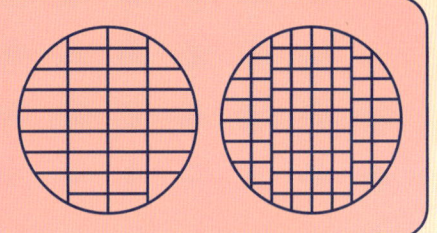

Dessert portions
Portion size: 2.5 × 5 cm (1 × 2 in)
Serves: 32

Coffee portions
Portion size: 2.5 × 2.5 cm (1 × 1 in)
Serves: 64

Round 30 cm (12 in) three-layer cake

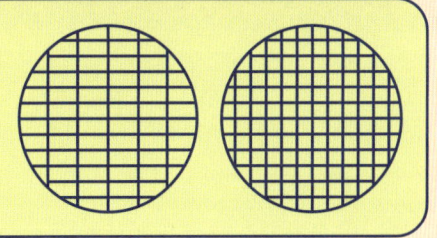

Dessert portions
Portion size: 2.5 × 5 cm (1 × 2 in)
Serves: 56

Coffee portions
Portion size: 2.5 × 2.5 cm (1 × 1 in)
Serves: 112

Square 15 cm (6 in) three-layer cake

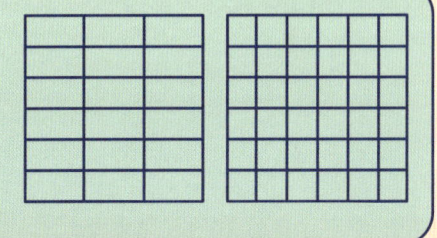

Dessert portions
Portion size: 2.5 × 5 cm (1 × 2 in)
Serves: 18

Coffee portions
Portion size: 2.5 × 2.5 cm (1 × 1 in)
Serves: 36

Square 25 cm (10 in) three-layer cake

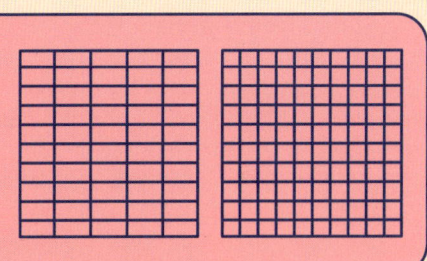

Dessert portions
Portion size: 2.5 × 5 cm (1 × 2 in)
Serves: 50

Coffee portions
Portion size: 2.5 × 2.5 cm (1 × 1 in)
Serves: 100

DECORATING PROJECTS

INDEX

Entries in italics denote piping or decorating techniques

A

air bubbles (in buttercream) 40, 42, 45, 167
Almond cake 60
aluminium foil 13
analogous palettes 185
angled (offset) palette knife 17
apples, Stewed apples 150

B

back seam, starting from 190
bakeware 15–16
baking consumables 13
baking ingredients 23–6
baking paper 13
baking powder 26
baking tools 13–16
balloon whisk 14
basketweave 230
batter, ways with 33–4
beads 230, 246, 254
bench scraper 17
bicarbonate of soda 26
Birthday Confetti (project) 192–7
   piping practice 194
Black sesame swirl 62
Blackberry fennel jam 144
bleached flour 24
blender 14
blobs 194, 222
blueberries, Spiced blueberry jam 132
bowls 14
bows 270, 291
Brown butter crumb 111
Brown butter custard 110
brown sugar 25
Brown sugar cake 151–2
   scaling recipe 331
   with stewed apple, sesame crumb & miso caramel buttercream 148–53

brushes 20
bundt cakes, tin preparation 35
butter 23
butter-based cakes, tin preparation 34
buttercream 38–47
   air bubbles in 40, 42, 45
   Coconut sugar buttercream 136
   consistency 39, 40–1, 158
   Hojicha buttercream 98
   Honey sea salt buttercream 146
   Italian meringue buttercream (IMBC) 38, 39–46
   loading into piping bag 157
   Miso caramel buttercream 153
   Peanut butter cream cheese buttercream 125
   piping techniques 158–65
   practice buttercream 169
   scaling for filling and crumb coating 333
   stabilised 176
   Vanilla bean cream cheese buttercream 112–13
   white chocolate buttercream 107
   Yuzu poppy seed buttercream 131
buttercream roses 171
Buttermilk vanilla cake 111–12
   scaling ingredients 324
   with brown butter custard & vanilla bean cream cheese buttercream 110–13

C

cake board 20
cake flour 25
cake leveller 14
cake pillars 20
cake separator set 20
cake tester 15
cake tins 15–16
   preparing 34–5
caramel 86
   Ginger caramel 70
   Miso caramel 151
Cardamon soak 140
Cardamon-roasted rhubarb 140
carrots
   Carrot cake 70
   Roasted carrot puree 68
   Upside-down pineapple & roasted carrot cake 68–70
caster sugar 25
checkerboard cake, Hojicha & honey checkerboard cake 95–9
checking your cake is ready 35–6
cheesecakes, Mandarin cotton cheesecake 78–81
cheesecloth (muslin) 13
cherries
   Cherry chip poppyseed & toasted rye crumble cake 65–7
   Cherry jam 67
   Roasted sake cherries 90, 93
Cherry Blossom Blows (project) 268–77
   piping practice 270–1
chiffon cakes
   Matcha chiffon sponge 92–3
   Pandan chiffon cake 74–6
   Thai-tea chiffon cake 71–3
   tin preparation 34
chiffon rolls
   rolling 36, 93

Sake cherry & matcha chiffon roll 90–4
chocolate 26
   Choc chip poppyseed cake 67
   Chocolate crumb 117
Chocolate chip cake 117–18
   scaling ingredients 325
   with passionfruit curd, dark chocolate crumb & vanilla bean cream cheese buttercream 114–19
Cinnamon myrtle soak 106
circles 222
cocoa powder 26
coconut
   Coconut dream cake 60
   Coconut sugar buttercream 136
   Coconut topping 60
   Toasted coconut cream 74, 77
coconut sugar 25
coffee
   Coffee soak 134
   Vietnamese coffee flan cake 86–9
Coffee cake 134
   scaling recipe 328
   with spiced blueberry jam, whipped mascarpone & coconut sugar buttercream 132–7
colour mixing 181, 183, 187
colour ratio 186
colour schemes 185–6
colour temperature 184
colour wheel 181, 182
colours
   choosing for your cake 181–4
   lightening and darkening 184
   see also food colourings
complementary palettes 186
confetti (decoration) 222
consistency
   buttercream 39, 40–1, 158
   royal icing 168
continuous shells 161, 194, 206, 238, 262, 281, 291, 301
cookie cutters 18
cooking tools 15
cooling racks 15
Cotton cheesecake 78–80
couplers 18, 156
cream 23
cream of tartar 26
cultured butter 23

curds
   Passionfruit curd 116
   Yuzu curd 128
curvy leaf 165
custard, Brown butter custard 110
cutting cakes into party portions 334–5

D

dairy products 23
daisy (decoration) 206
Daisy Dreams (project) 204–11
   piping practice 206
Daisy Fields (project) 260–7
   piping practice 262
darkening colours 184
decorating ingredients 27
decorating materials 166–8
   see also buttercream
decorating tools 17–21
digital kitchen scales 13
digital thermometer 15
digital timer 15
dots 160, 222
double strings 238, 300, 310
dowels and dowel cutter 20
drop flowers 170, 290
drop strings 162, 238, 254, 262, 270, 271, 281

E

edible marker 18
egg whites 24
   whisking 42
eggs 24
elevated tier, stacking using pillars 178–80

F

fennel, Blackberry fennel jam 144
flat leaf 165
florist tape 21
flour 24–5
flower nail 21
flower wire 21
flowers (decoration) 222
fluted ruffles 164, 238, 254, 262, 280, 281, 300
folded ruffle garlands 194, 246, 310
folded ruffles 165, 214, 271, 310
folding in meringue 34
food colourings 27, 187
food grade plastic wrap 13
food processor 14
fresh and frozen fruits 25
frosting, Thai-tea cream frosting 71
frosting a layer cake 51–2
   heart-shaped cake 54–5
   round cake 52–3
   square or rectangular cake 54
frosting tools 17

G

Garden Strawberry (project) 244–51
   piping practice 246
gel food colouring 27, 187
gelatine
   Sake cherry jelly 90
   Whipped mascarpone cream 123
ginger
   Ginger & black sesame swirl cake 62–4
   Ginger cake 62–4
   Ginger caramel 70
   Ginger glaze 64

H

Heart of Glass (project) 308–20
   piping practice 310
heart-shaped cakes
   cutting into portions 334
   frosting 54–5
   marking your decorations 173
Hojicha & honey checkerboard cake 95–9
Hojicha buttercream 98
honey
   Honey cake 95–7
   Honey sea salt buttercream 146
   Honey soak 144

I

icing sugar 25
immersion (stick) blender 14
ingredient temperature 32
ingredients 23–6
isomalt 27
Italian meringue buttercream (IMBC) 38, 39–46
   adding flavours (for layer cakes) 45
   adding vanilla and removing air bubbles (decorating projects) 45
   adjusting consistency 40–1
   air bubbles and their removal 40, 45
   before you start 40–1
   re-whipping made-ahead buttercream 40
   recipe 43–5
   storing 46
   troubleshooting 46
   uses of different consistencies 39
   whisking and egg white stages 42

J

Jammy strawberry gel 120
jams
   Blackberry fennel jam 144
   Cherry jam 67
   Spiced blueberry jam 132
   Strawberry jam 82

K

knives 14

L

lattice heart 300
lattice strings 280
layer cakes 100–53
   assembly 48–50
   cutting into portions 334–5
   finishing touches 56
   frosting and creating a smooth finish 51–5
   raked finish 56
   tools 20
leavening agents 26
leaves 165, 214, 230, 254, 270
lightening colours 184
loop garlands 163, 238, 270, 271, 280, 281
love cherubs (decoration) 200
Love Cherubs (project) 198–203
   piping practice 200
Lovers Lace (project) 298–307
   piping practice 300–1

M

mandarin
   Mandarin cotton cheesecake 78–81
   Mandarin reduction 78
mangoes, Pandan & mango sandwich cake 77
marking your decorations 18, 172–3
mascarpone, Whipped mascarpone cream 121
Matcha chiffon sponge 92–3
measuring spoons 13
measuring tools 13
measuring your ingredients by weight 30–1
medium consistency (buttercream) 39
meringue, folding in 34
meringue powder 27
Minted Rose (project) 252–9
   piping practice 254
Miso caramel 151
Miso caramel buttercream 153
mistakes, fixing 190
mix and combine 33
mixing and slicing tools 14
monochromatic palettes 185

N

nature-based palettes 186
non-slip mat 20

O

oil 26
oil-based cakes,
  tin preparation 34
oil-based food colouring 27, 187
olive oil 26
Olive oil ricotta cake 145–6
  scaling recipe 330
  with blackberry fennel jam &
    honey sea salt buttercream
    142–7
Olive oil sponge 82, 84–5
one colour plus white
  palettes 185
Orange yoghurt cake 129
  scaling recipe 327
  with yuzu curd, fresh orange
    segments & yuzu poppy
    seed buttercream 126–31
oranges
  Orange segments 131
  Orange soak 128
oven temperature 31
ovens
  bake cake in centre 35
  baking multiple cakes at once
    over two oven racks 35
  checking your cake is
    ready 35
  hot and cool spots 31

P

palette knives 17
Pandan & mango sandwich
  cake 74–7
Pandan chiffon cake 74–6
parallel strings 290
Passionfruit curd 116
Peanut butter cake 121–2
  scaling recipes 326
  with roasted strawberries,
    whipped mascarpone &
    peanut butter cream cheese
    buttercream 120–5
Peanut butter cream cheese
  buttercream 125
pecans, Toasted ground pecans
  68, 70

perforated cake board 20
pestle and mortar 14
pillars, stacking an elevated tier
  using 178–80
pineapple
  Roasted pineapple 68
  Upside-down pineapple &
    roasted carrot cake 68–70
piping 156–7
  knack of 158–9
  techniques 160–5
piping bag 18, 156
  angle and elevation 159
  consistency of
    buttercream 158
  holding 157
  loading buttercream into 157
  pressure control 159
piping nozzles 18, 156
piping practice
  Basic piping techniques 160–5
  Birthday Confetti 194
  Cherry Blossom Bows 270–1
  Daisy Dreams 206
  Daisy Fields 262
  Garden Strawberry 246
  Heart of Glass 310
  Love Cherubs 200
  Lovers Lace 300–1
  Minted Rose 254
  Pressed Flowers 214
  Retro Love 238
  Rosy Plaid 230
  Scribbly Bloom 222
  Secret Garden 290–1
  The Wedding Cake 280–1
piping tools 18, 156
Pistachio cake 140–1
  scaling recipe 329
  with cardamon-roasted
    rhubarb, whipped
    mascarpone & coconut
    sugar buttercream 138–41
plain edge scraper 17
plain flour 24
planning, organising and
  learning from mistakes 30
pointed palette knife 17
poppyseeds
  Choc chip poppyseed cake 67
  Yuzu poppy seed
    buttercream 131
practice buttercream 169
Pressed Flowers (project) 212–19
  piping practice 214

primary colours 183
projects 192–320
  set yourself up for success 191
  tips 190

R

rake scraper/comb 17
raked finish 56
raspberries, Roasted
  raspberries 104
re-whipping made-ahead
  buttercream 40, 167
rectangular cake, frosting 54
resting and cooling 36
Retro Love (project) 236–43
  piping practice 238
reverse creaming 33
reverse shell garland 300
reverse shells 162, 214, 301
rhubarb, Cardamon-roasted
  rhubarb 140
ribbon garland 310
ribbons 163, 230
ricotta
  Olive oil ricotta cake 145
  Whipped ricotta cream 82, 85
Roasted carrot puree 68
Roasted pineapple 68
Roasted raspberries 104
Roasted sake cherries 90
Roasted strawberries 120
roasting trays 15
rosettes 161, 200, 214, 230, 238,
  270, 280
Rosy Plaid (project) 228–35
  piping practice 230
round cakes
  cutting into portions 334, 335
  frosting 52–3
  marking your decorations 172
royal icing 168
ruffle garland 280, 281
ruler 18

S

Sake cherry & matcha chiffon roll 90–4
Sake cherry jelly 90, 93
salt 26
sandwich cakes, Pandan & mango sandwich cake 74–7
saucepans 15
scaling buttercream for filling and crumb coating 333
scaling cake ingredients 323–31
scaling fillings 332
scaling soaks 332
scaling up recipes for decorating projects 321–33
scallop trim 238, 262, 291
scrapers 17
Scribbly Bloom (project) 220–7
   piping practice 222
sea salt, Honey sea salt buttercream 146
secondary colours 183
Secret Garden (project) 288–97
   piping practice 290–1
self-raising flour 25
separating yolks and whites 24
sesame seeds
   Black sesame swirl 62
   Sesame crumb 150
shells 161, 194, 200, 206, 222, 238, 262, 271, 281, 310
sieves 14
silicone baking mats 15
simple finish cakes 58–99
skewer 15
soaks
   Cardamon soak 140
   Cinnamon myrtle soak 16
   Coffee soak 134
   Honey soak 144
   Orange soak 128
   scaling 332
   Vanilla milk soak 112
Sour cream chocolate cake 106
   scaling ingredients 323
   with cinnamon myrtle, raspberry & toasted white chocolate cream cheese buttercream 104–7
spatulas 14
spice grinder 14
Spiced blueberry jam 132

sponge cakes
   Olive oil sponge 82, 84–5
   tin preparation 34
   Vanilla sponge 88
sponge rolls
   rolling 36
   Sake cherry & matcha chiffon roll 90–4
   Strawberry & cream olive oil sponge roll 82–5
sprinkles (decoration) 222
square cakes
   cutting into portions 115
   frosting 54
   marking your decorations 173
squeeze bottle 20
stabilised buttercream 176
stand mixer 14
stars 160
Stewed apples 150
stiff consistency (buttercream) 39
storing
   cakes 37
   Italian meringue buttercream 46
   royal icing 168
straight line 160, 230
straight palette knife 17
strawberries
   Jammy strawberry gel 120
   Roasted strawberries 120
   Strawberry & cream olive oil sponge roll 82–5
   Strawberry jam 82
strawberry leaf (decoration) 246
sugar 25
swag 164, 254, 280

T

teardrop-shaped seeds (decoration) 246
temperature
   colour 184
   ingredients 32
   oven 31
   of your kitchen 190
tertiary colours 183
text (decoration) 222
Thai-tea chiffon cake 71–3
Thai-tea cream frosting 71, 73
thin consistency (buttercream) 39
tiered cakes 174–80
   stacking 175–7
   stacking an elevated tier using pillars 178–80
   tools 20
Toasted coconut cream 74, 77
Toasted ground pecans 68, 70
Toasted rye crumble topping 65
Toasted white chocolate cream cheese buttercream 107
toppings
   Coconut topping 60
   Toasted rye crumble topping 65
triple strings 290
turntable 48, 51, 53, 190

U

unmoulding 36
Upside-down pineapple & roasted carrot cake 68–70
upward shells 238, 291

V

vanilla 26
Vanilla bean cream cheese buttercream 112–13
Vanilla milk soak 112
Vanilla sponge 88
vegetable shortening 27
vertical continuous shells 206
vertical folded ruffles 214
vertical pillar (decoration) 291
Vietnamese coffee flan cake 86–9

W

Wedding Cake (project) 278–87
    piping practice 280–1
weighing ingredients 30–1
Whipped mascarpone cream 121
Whipped ricotta cream 82, 85
whipping with control 33
whisking egg whites 42
white chocolate
    Toasted white chocolate cream cheese buttercream 107
    Whipped mascarpone cream 121
whole egg foam 34
wing calipers 18
wire cutters 21
work surfaces 190

Y

Yoghurt cream 90, 93, 94
yuzu
    Yuzu curd 128
    Yuzu poppy seed buttercream 131

ACKNOWLEDGEMENTS

This book began the way many things in my life do — quietly, with a nudge of curiosity and a little chaos. I never imagined it would become something so full, so me. And yet, here it is — real, in my hands. I'm still catching up to that.

It only happened because of the people who showed up and gave me so much along the way.

I'm forever grateful to Lucy Heaver, Paul McNally and the incredible team at Smith Street Books for seeing something in me and giving me the opportunity to create something that feels truly true to who I am — as a pastry chef and cake decorator.

To Luke Whitten, my love — this book wouldn't exist without you. From the first seed of the concept design, you built the foundation this whole thing stands on. Your eye for design, your deep knowledge of colour and your quiet support behind the scenes have shaped this project in ways most people will never see. Thank you for being in it with me — all of it.

To Elena Callcott — our incredible editor — thank you for holding this book together and making what felt impossible come together so beautifully. Your calm, your patience and your perfectly timed humour made the hardest parts feel lighter. And to Katri Hilden, our wonderful copy editor — thank you for working so patiently with me, page by page. You saw it through with so much care and knowledge.

To the dream team behind the shoot — thank you for making those two chaotic summer weeks some of the most rewarding of my life. Vikky Valsamis, your styling made every cake feel alive. It was exactly what I'd pictured in my head, only better. Daniel Herrmann-Zoll, thank you for your artistic eye, endless patience and ability to find the perfect angle. Thousands of photos of me piping shells and drop strings, and somehow, every shot was captured in the most stunning way.

To Andy Warren, our designer and illustrator — thank you for bringing so much life, colour and joy to this book. From the very beginning, you just got it. You took our vision, ran with it, and turned it into something even bigger and better than we could've hoped for. I feel so incredibly lucky to have worked with you.

To Emma Osborne — my amazing team member at Mali Bakes. I honestly don't have the words to capture how much you've given to this. I'm so grateful to have you by my side, not just through this book, but through all the years of early mornings, full ovens and cake chaos. Your knowledge, your calm, your joy in the kitchen — it's infectious. Thank you for testing the recipes, piping beautiful cakes and sharing this whole experience with me. I've learned so much from you and I feel so lucky to work with someone who brings so much heart to everything they do.

To all the past and present team members at Mali Bakes — Callum, Elliane, Kiara — you've each contributed your own little piece to what Mali Bakes is today. Thank you for being part of this journey.

To Ryan Scott – graphic designer and dear friend. From day one, you've shaped the visual world of Mali Bakes with so much charm, life and character. The identity you created is woven into everything we do – and that spirit lives in the pages of this book, too. I'm so grateful for the mark you've made on it all.

To my family – my grandparents and my dad – thank you for supporting my dreams and for letting me move to another continent to chase them. To Lois and Trevor Whitten for your constant support and love.

To the mentors I've learned from and the chefs I've had the opportunity to work alongside – thank you for shaping my path and showing me what it means to grow in this industry with skill, humility and care. You've influenced how I work, how I lead, and how I think about food. Sean Henley, Brook James, Leon Kennedy, Tinee and Yuan Suntivtana, Gough Amontha, and Tivadee – thank you for your time, your guidance and your generosity. It's all stayed with me.

To all the wonderful businesses that contributed their own beautiful element to this book: Phil and Jessie from Multisonic, thank you for lending us so many beautiful vintage pieces to prop the shoot. Thanisa from Wattle Gully Farm, thank you for the stunning fresh blooms.

To all the great cakers, bakers and writers who built the knowledge that made this book. Each of these people taught me something – about technique, creativity, or simply the joy of baking – and I'm so grateful for the inspiration and knowledge.

The Wilton Way of Cake Decorating edited by Eugene T and Marilynn C Sullivan, with Norman Wilton
The Cake Bible by Rose Levy Beranbaum
Beatrix Bakes by Natalie Paull
The Art and Science of Food Pairing by Bernard Lahousse, Johan Langenbick and Peter Coucquyt
More Than Cake by Natasha Pickowicz
The Last Bite by Anna Higham
The Sqirl Jam Book by Jessica Koslow

And lastly, to every customer who's ever ordered from Mali Bakes – from the early days in my share-house kitchen to those of you holding this book now – thank you. I never imagined that the quirky, colourful cakes I made would be met with so much love. From a single slice to birthday cakes, from just-because treats to wedding centrepieces – thank you for letting my cakes be a part of your life. Truly, from the bottom of my heart, it's been the greatest pleasure to bake for you – and now, somehow, to write for you too.

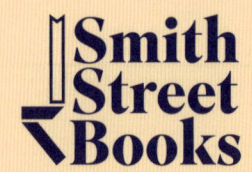

Published in 2025 by Smith Street Books
Naarm (Melbourne) | Australia
smithstreetbooks.com

Distributed outside of ANZ, North & Latin America by
Thames & Hudson Ltd., 6–24 Britannia Street, London, WC1X 9JD
thamesandhudson.com

EU Authorised Representative: Interart S.A.R.L.
19 rue Charles Auray, 93500 Pantin, Paris, France
productsafety@thameshudson.co.uk; www.interart.fr

ISBN: 978-1-9232-3920-3

All rights reserved. No part of this book may be reproduced or transmitted by any person or entity, in any form or by any means, electronic or mechanical, including photocopying, recording, scanning or by any storage and retrieval system, without the prior written permission of the publishers and copyright holders.

Smith Street Books respectfully acknowledges the Wurundjeri People of the Kulin Nation, who are the Traditional Owners of the land on which we work, and we pay our respects to their Elders past and present.

Copyright text © Patti Chimkire
Copyright design © Smith Street Books
Copyright photography © Daniel Herrmann-Zoll

The moral right of the author has been asserted.

Publisher: Paul McNally
Managing editor & proofreader: Lucy Heaver
Project editor: Elena Callcott
Editor: Katri Hilden
Design & layout: Andy Warren
Design & creative consultant: Luke Whitten
Photographer: Daniel Herrmann-Zoll
Stylist: Vicki Valsamis
Photo chefs: Emma Osbourne & Patti Chimkire
Indexer: Max McMaster
Production manager: Aisling Coughlan

Colour reproduction by Splitting Image Colour Studio
Printed & bound in China by C&C Offset Printing Co., Ltd.

Book 412
10 9 8 7 6 5 4 3 2 1